ZODIAC

A GRAPHIC MEMOIR

Ai Weiwei

with Elettra Stamboulis

illustrated by Gianluca Costantini

TEN SPEED GRAPHIC
An imprint of TEN SPEED PRESS
California | New York

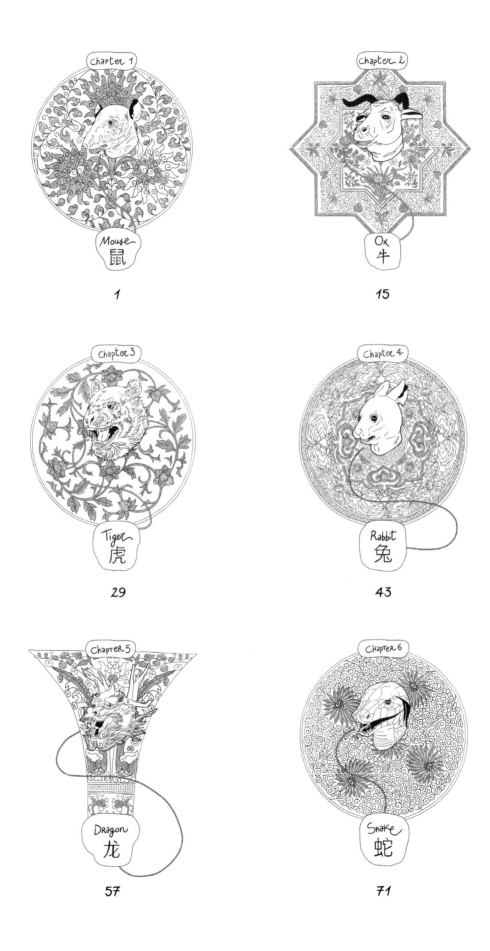

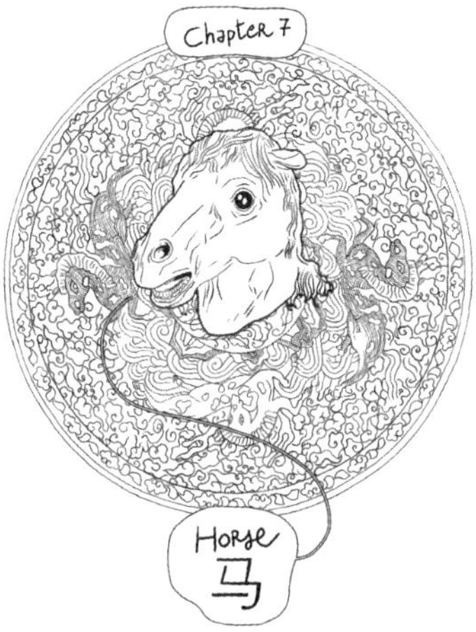
Chapter 7
Horse
马

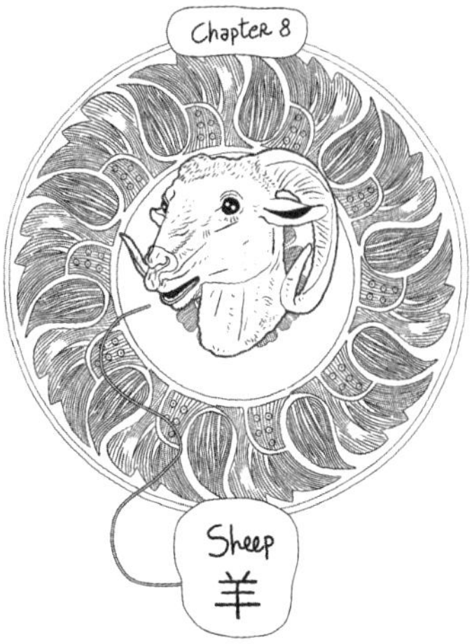
Chapter 8
Sheep
羊

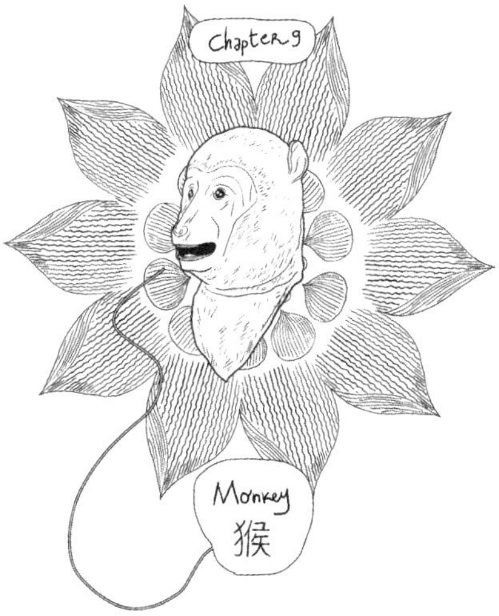
Chapter 9
Monkey
猴

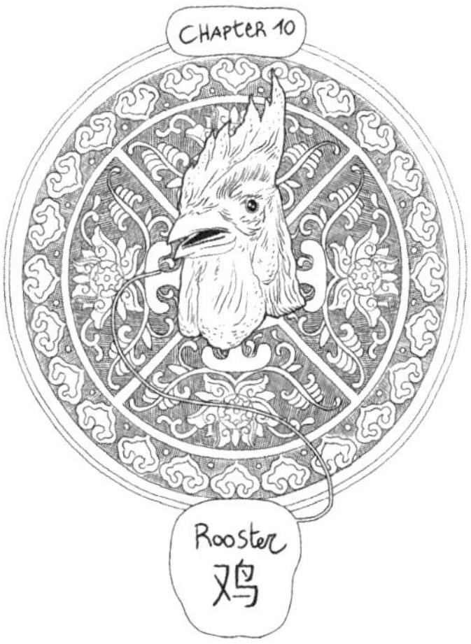
CHAPTER 10
Rooster
鸡

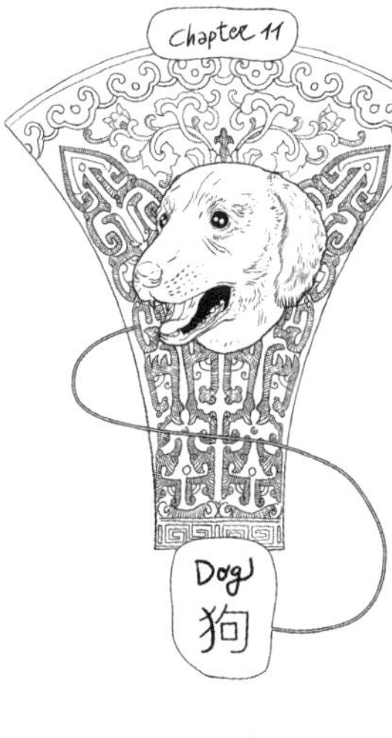
Chapter 11
Dog
狗

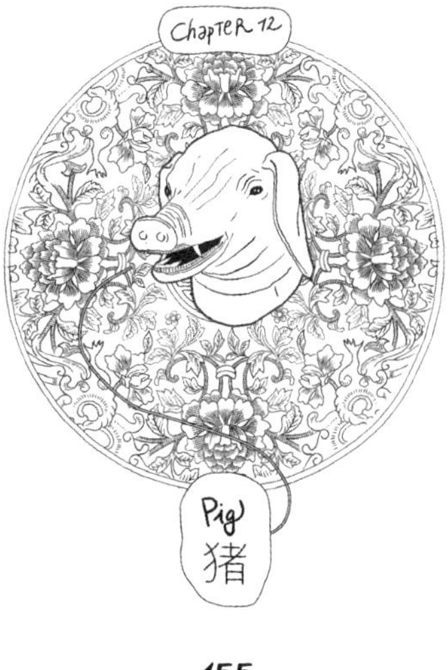
Chapter 12
Pig
猪

Chapter 1

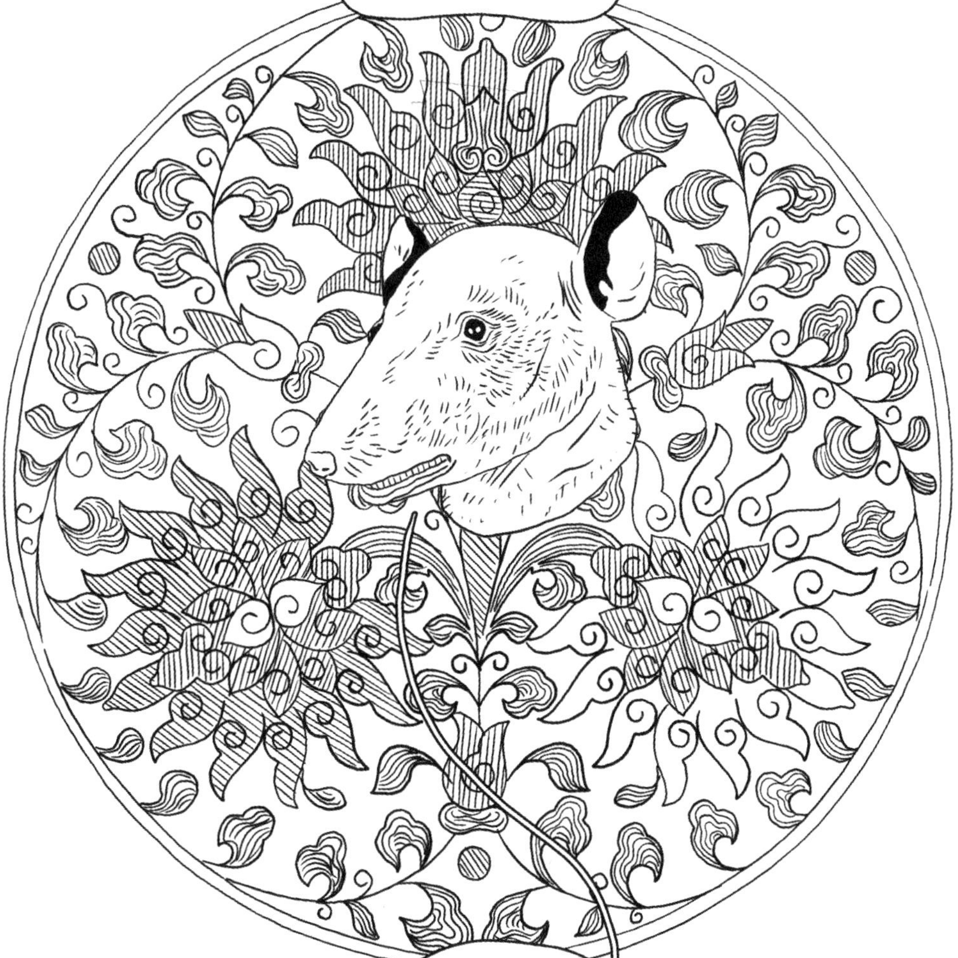

Mouse 鼠

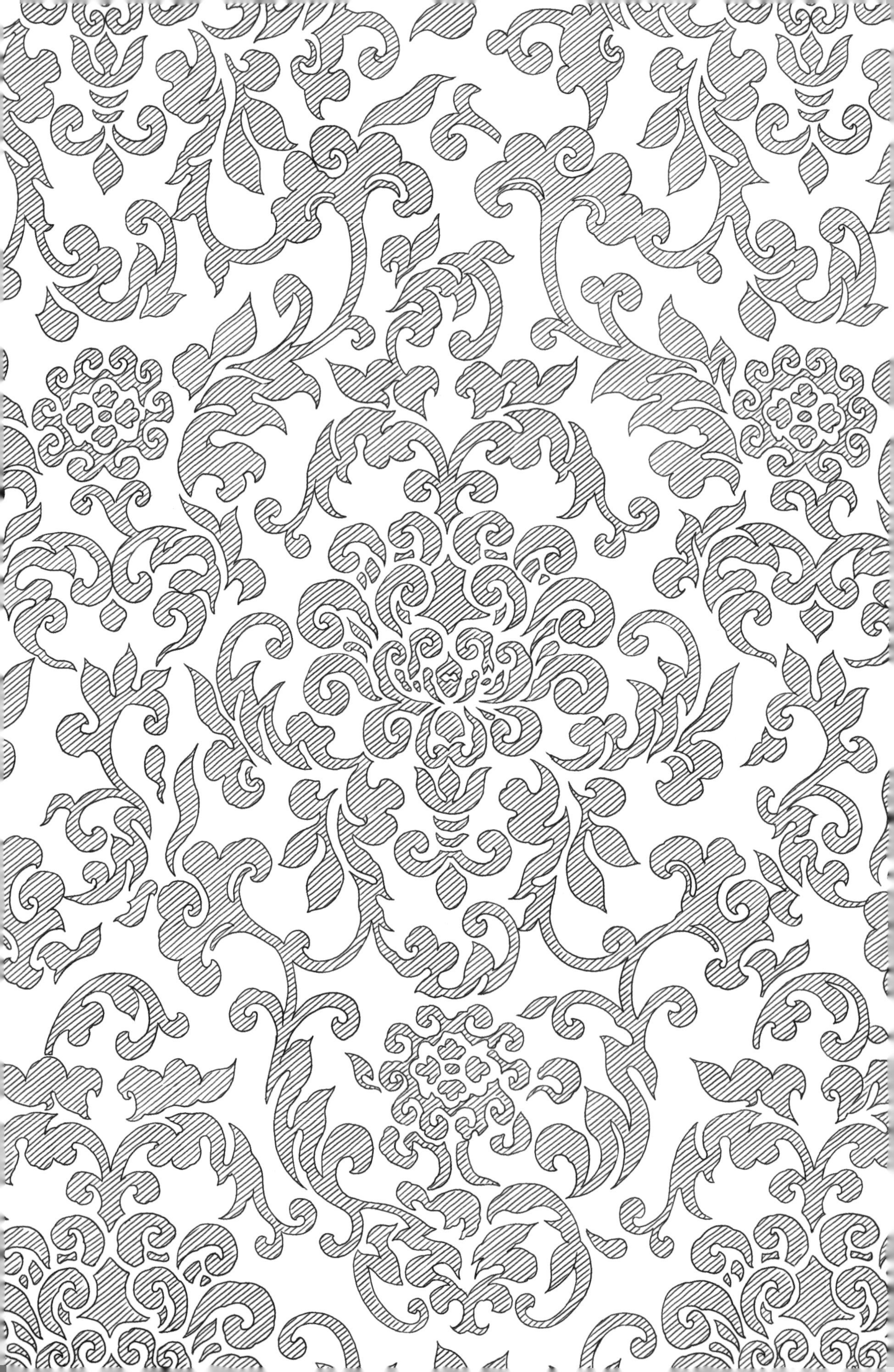

Xinjiang Province, 1967. Near the Gobi Desert.

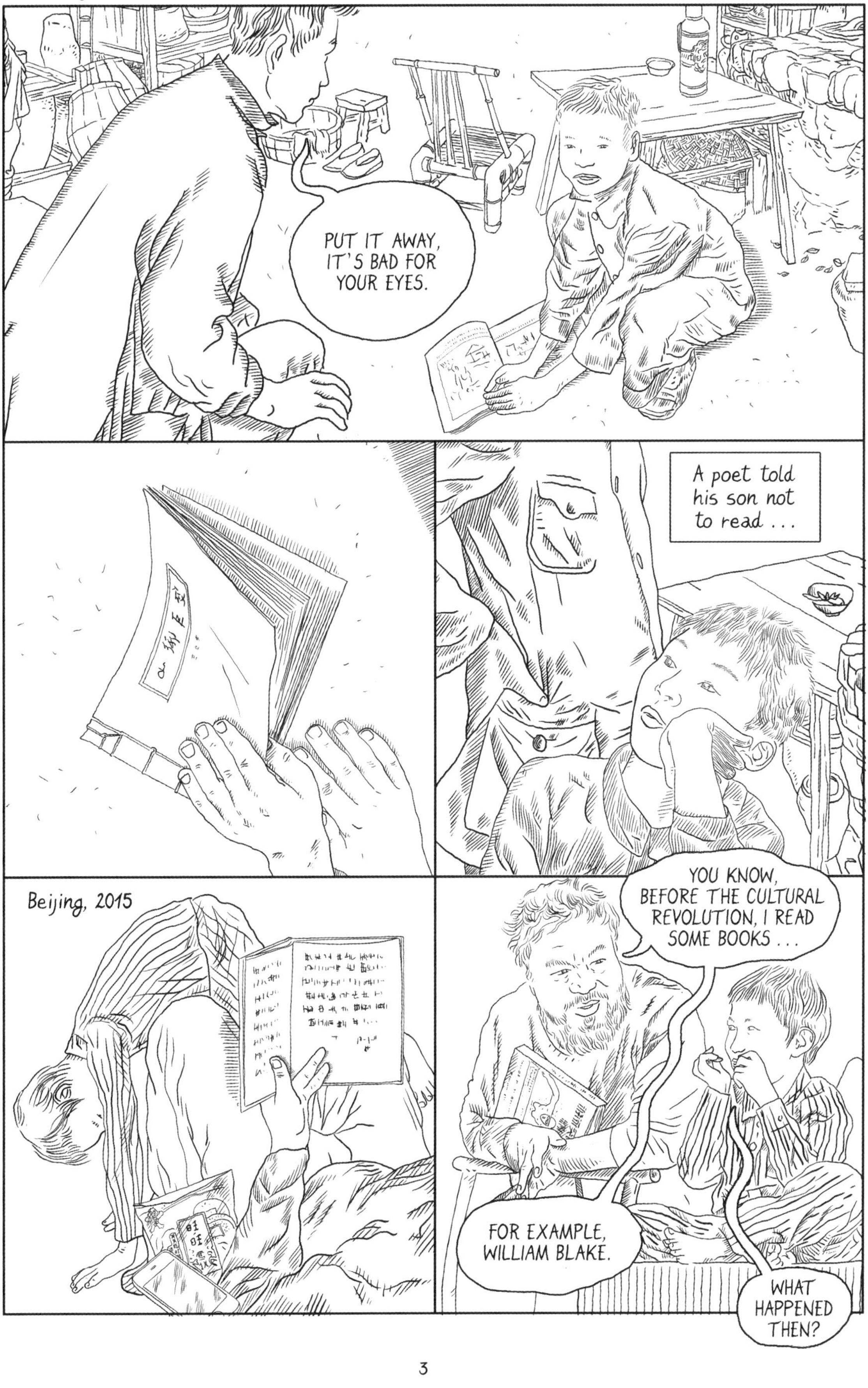
PUT IT AWAY, IT'S BAD FOR YOUR EYES.
A poet told his son not to read . . .
Beijing, 2015
YOU KNOW, BEFORE THE CULTURAL REVOLUTION, I READ SOME BOOKS . . .
FOR EXAMPLE, WILLIAM BLAKE.
WHAT HAPPENED THEN?

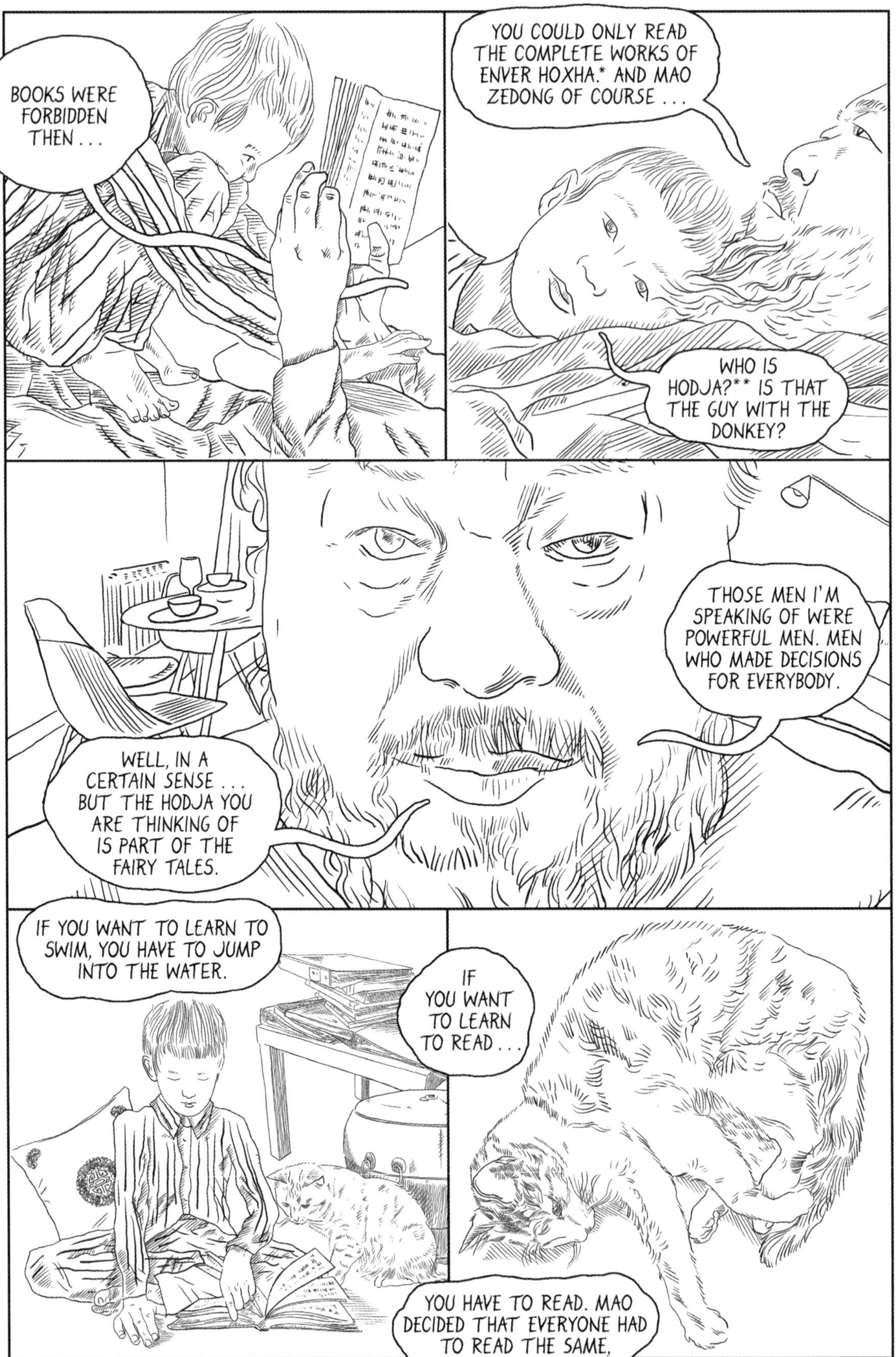
BOOKS WERE FORBIDDEN THEN . . .
YOU COULD ONLY READ THE COMPLETE WORKS OF ENVER HOXHA.* AND MAO ZEDONG OF COURSE . . .
WHO IS HODJA?** IS THAT THE GUY WITH THE DONKEY?
THOSE MEN I'M SPEAKING OF WERE POWERFUL MEN. MEN WHO MADE DECISIONS FOR EVERYBODY.
WELL, IN A CERTAIN SENSE . . . BUT THE HODJA YOU ARE THINKING OF IS PART OF THE FAIRY TALES.
IF YOU WANT TO LEARN TO SWIM, YOU HAVE TO JUMP INTO THE WATER.
IF YOU WANT TO LEARN TO READ . . .
YOU HAVE TO READ. MAO DECIDED THAT EVERYONE HAD TO READ THE SAME, VERY FEW BOOKS.

* Enver Hoxha was the Secretary of the Party of Labour of Albania from 1941 until 1985.

** Nasreddin Hodja was a satirist and philosopher who lived in 8th century in the Ottoman Empire.

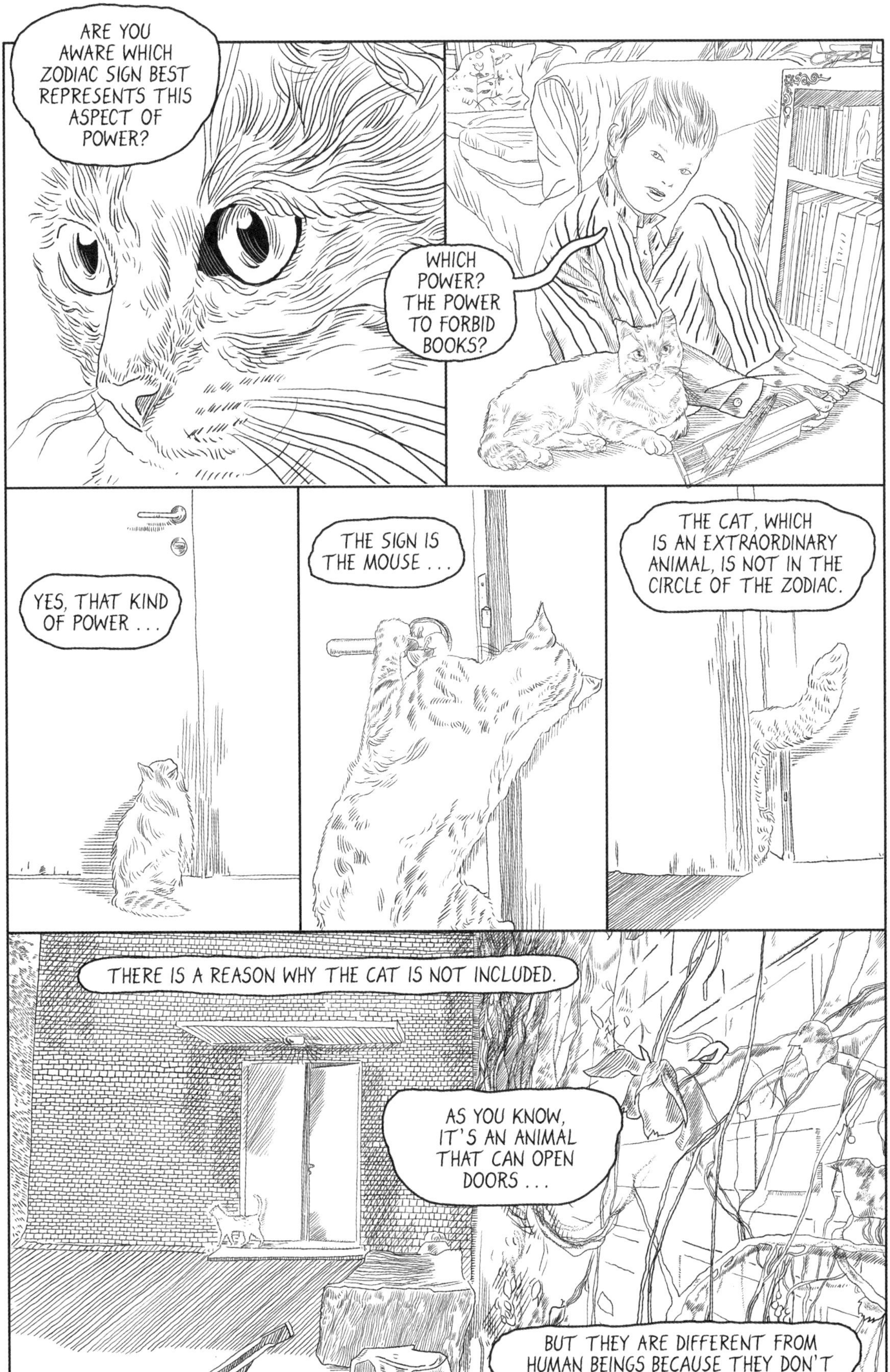
ARE YOU AWARE WHICH ZODIAC SIGN BEST REPRESENTS THIS ASPECT OF POWER?
WHICH POWER? THE POWER TO FORBID BOOKS?
YES, THAT KIND OF POWER . . .
THE SIGN IS THE MOUSE . . .
THE CAT, WHICH IS AN EXTRAORDINARY ANIMAL, IS NOT IN THE CIRCLE OF THE ZODIAC.
THERE IS A REASON WHY THE CAT IS NOT INCLUDED.
AS YOU KNOW, IT'S AN ANIMAL THAT CAN OPEN DOORS . . .
BUT THEY ARE DIFFERENT FROM HUMAN BEINGS BECAUSE THEY DON'T CLOSE THE DOORS BEHIND THEM.

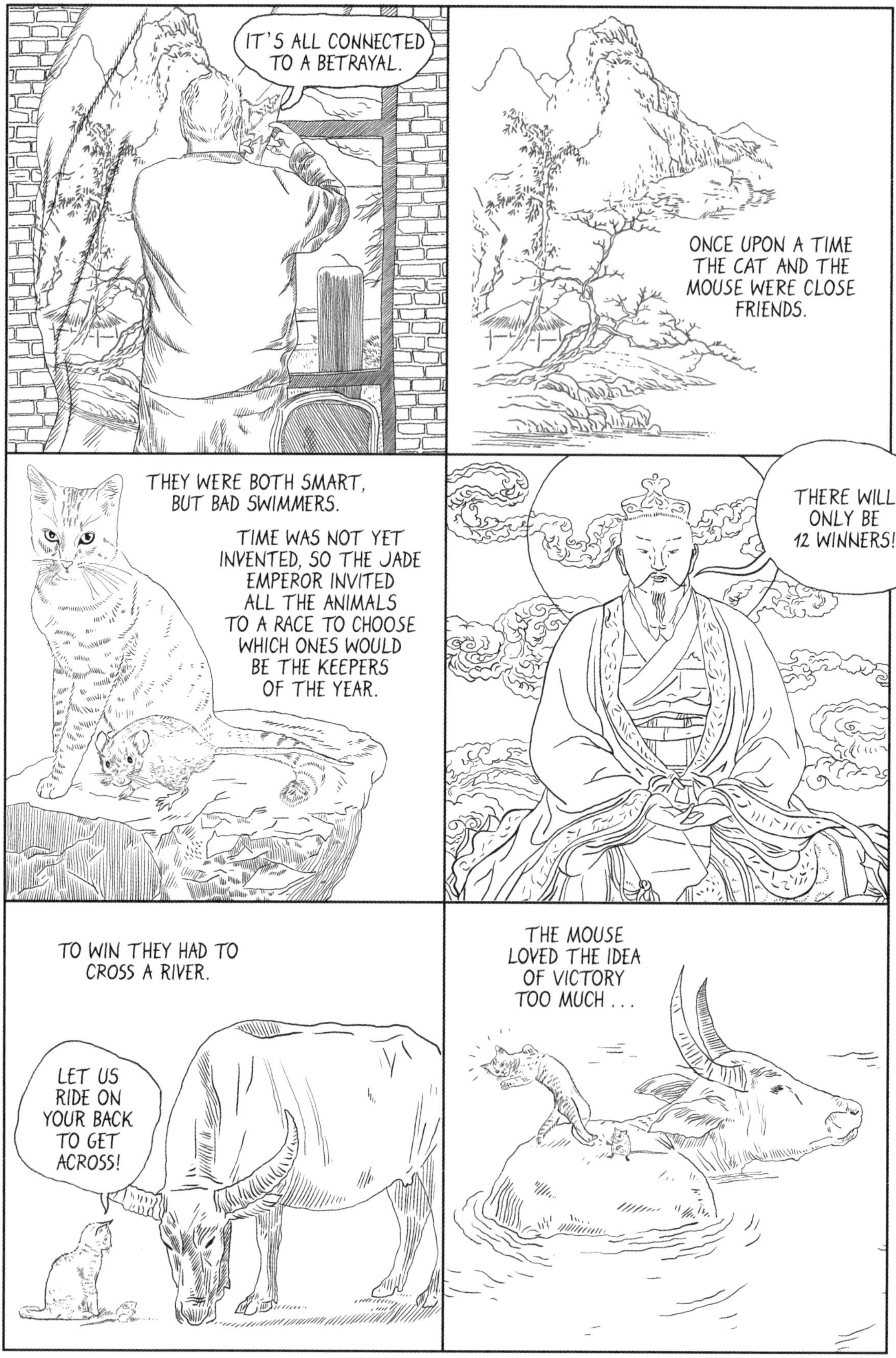
IT'S ALL CONNECTED TO A BETRAYAL.
ONCE UPON A TIME THE CAT AND THE MOUSE WERE CLOSE FRIENDS.
THEY WERE BOTH SMART, BUT BAD SWIMMERS.
TIME WAS NOT YET INVENTED, SO THE JADE EMPEROR INVITED ALL THE ANIMALS TO A RACE TO CHOOSE WHICH ONES WOULD BE THE KEEPERS OF THE YEAR.
THERE WILL ONLY BE 12 WINNERS!
TO WIN THEY HAD TO CROSS A RIVER.
LET US RIDE ON YOUR BACK TO GET ACROSS!
THE MOUSE LOVED THE IDEA OF VICTORY TOO MUCH . . .

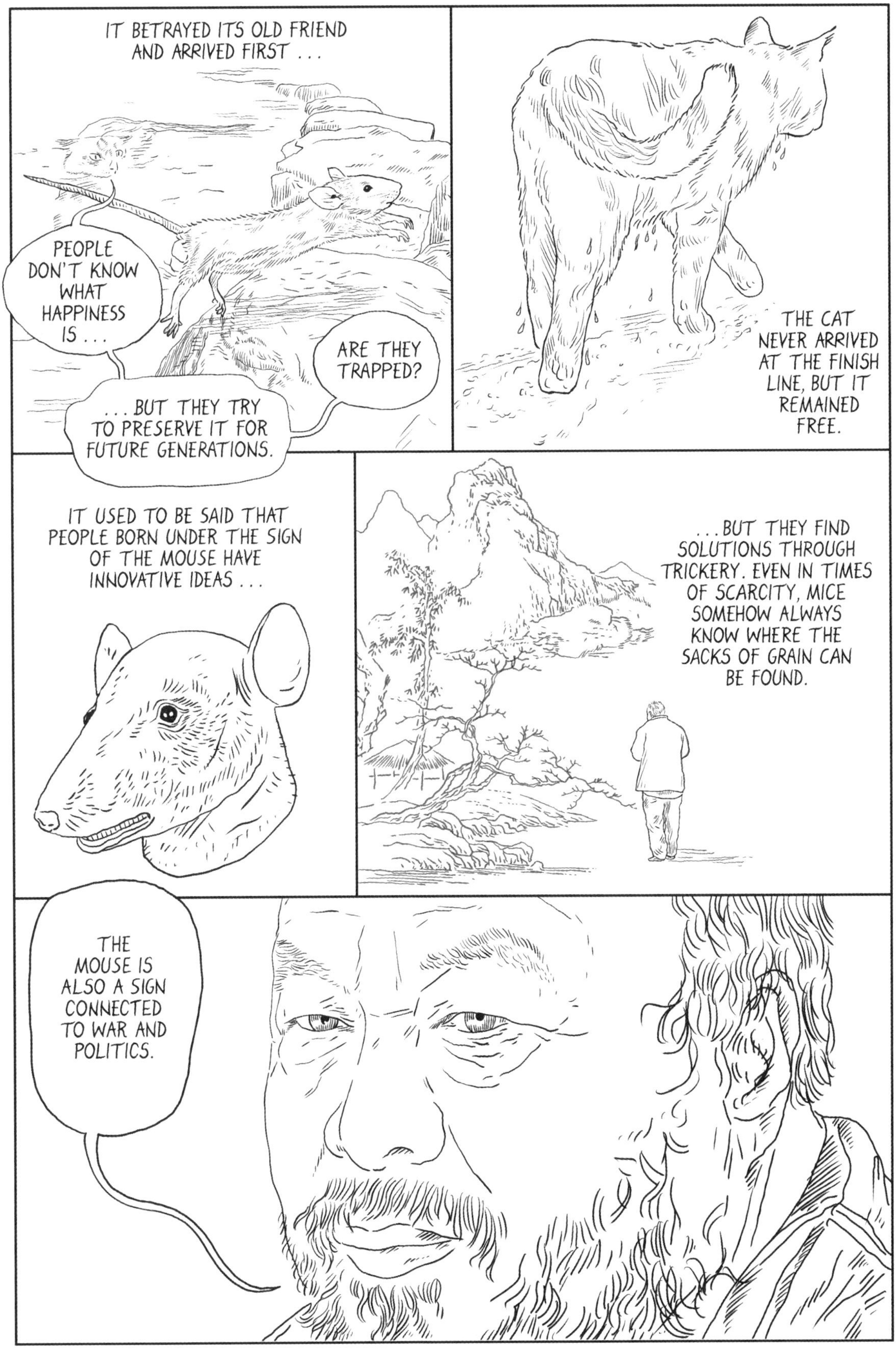
IT BETRAYED ITS OLD FRIEND AND ARRIVED FIRST . . .
PEOPLE DON'T KNOW WHAT HAPPINESS IS . . .
. . . BUT THEY TRY TO PRESERVE IT FOR FUTURE GENERATIONS.
ARE THEY TRAPPED?
THE CAT NEVER ARRIVED AT THE FINISH LINE, BUT IT REMAINED FREE.
IT USED TO BE SAID THAT PEOPLE BORN UNDER THE SIGN OF THE MOUSE HAVE INNOVATIVE IDEAS . . .
. . . BUT THEY FIND SOLUTIONS THROUGH TRICKERY. EVEN IN TIMES OF SCARCITY, MICE SOMEHOW ALWAYS KNOW WHERE THE SACKS OF GRAIN CAN BE FOUND.
THE MOUSE IS ALSO A SIGN CONNECTED TO WAR AND POLITICS.

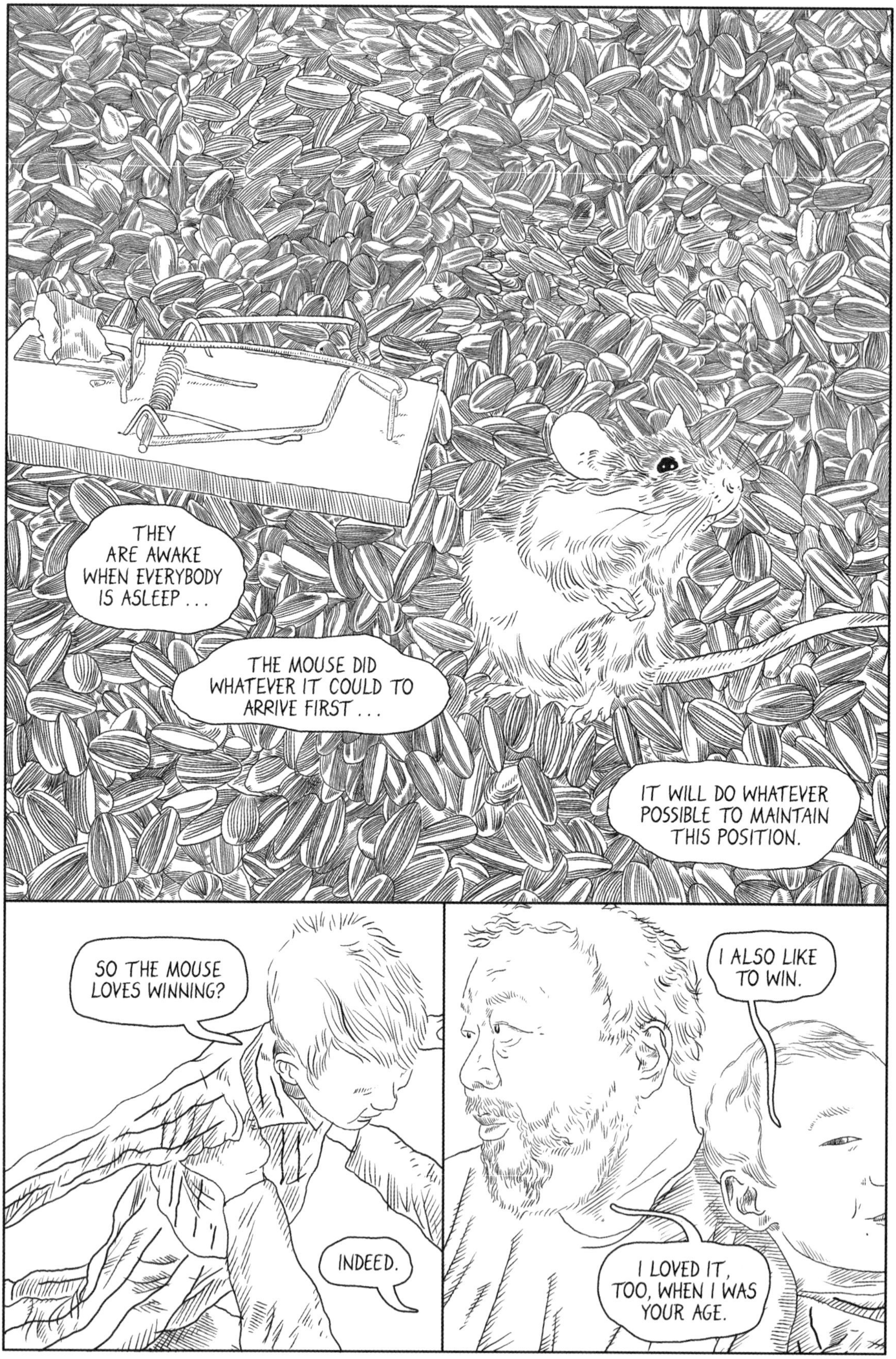
THEY ARE AWAKE WHEN EVERYBODY IS ASLEEP . . .
THE MOUSE DID WHATEVER IT COULD TO ARRIVE FIRST . . .
IT WILL DO WHATEVER POSSIBLE TO MAINTAIN THIS POSITION.
SO THE MOUSE LOVES WINNING?
INDEED.
I ALSO LIKE TO WIN.
I LOVED IT, TOO, WHEN I WAS YOUR AGE.

Xinjiang Province, 1967. Near the Gobi Desert.

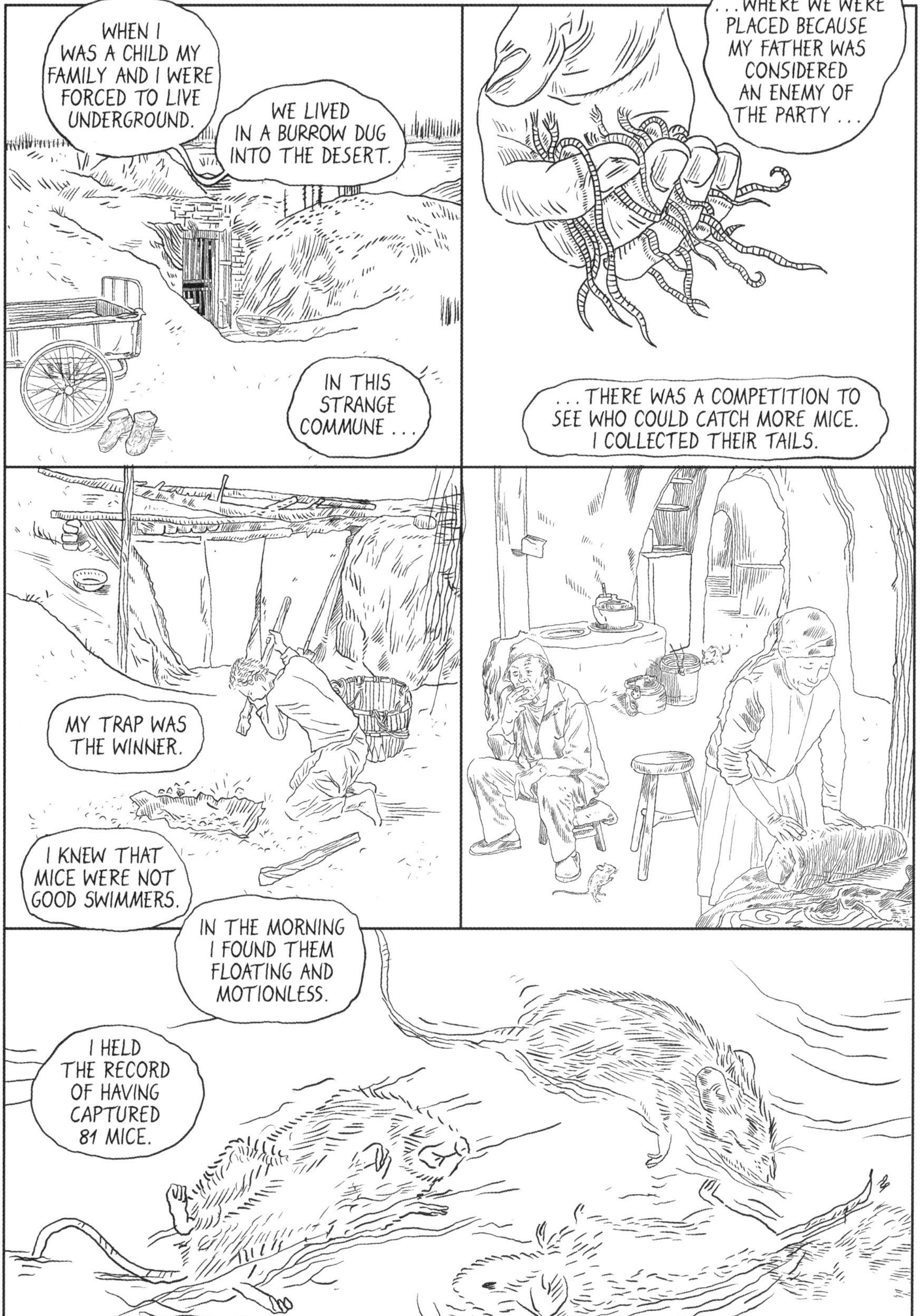
WHEN I WAS A CHILD MY FAMILY AND I WERE FORCED TO LIVE UNDERGROUND.
WE LIVED IN A BURROW DUG INTO THE DESERT.
IN THIS STRANGE COMMUNE . . .
. . . WHERE WE WERE PLACED BECAUSE MY FATHER WAS CONSIDERED AN ENEMY OF THE PARTY . . .
. . . THERE WAS A COMPETITION TO SEE WHO COULD CATCH MORE MICE. I COLLECTED THEIR TAILS.
MY TRAP WAS THE WINNER.
I KNEW THAT MICE WERE NOT GOOD SWIMMERS.
IN THE MORNING I FOUND THEM FLOATING AND MOTIONLESS.
I HELD THE RECORD OF HAVING CAPTURED 81 MICE.

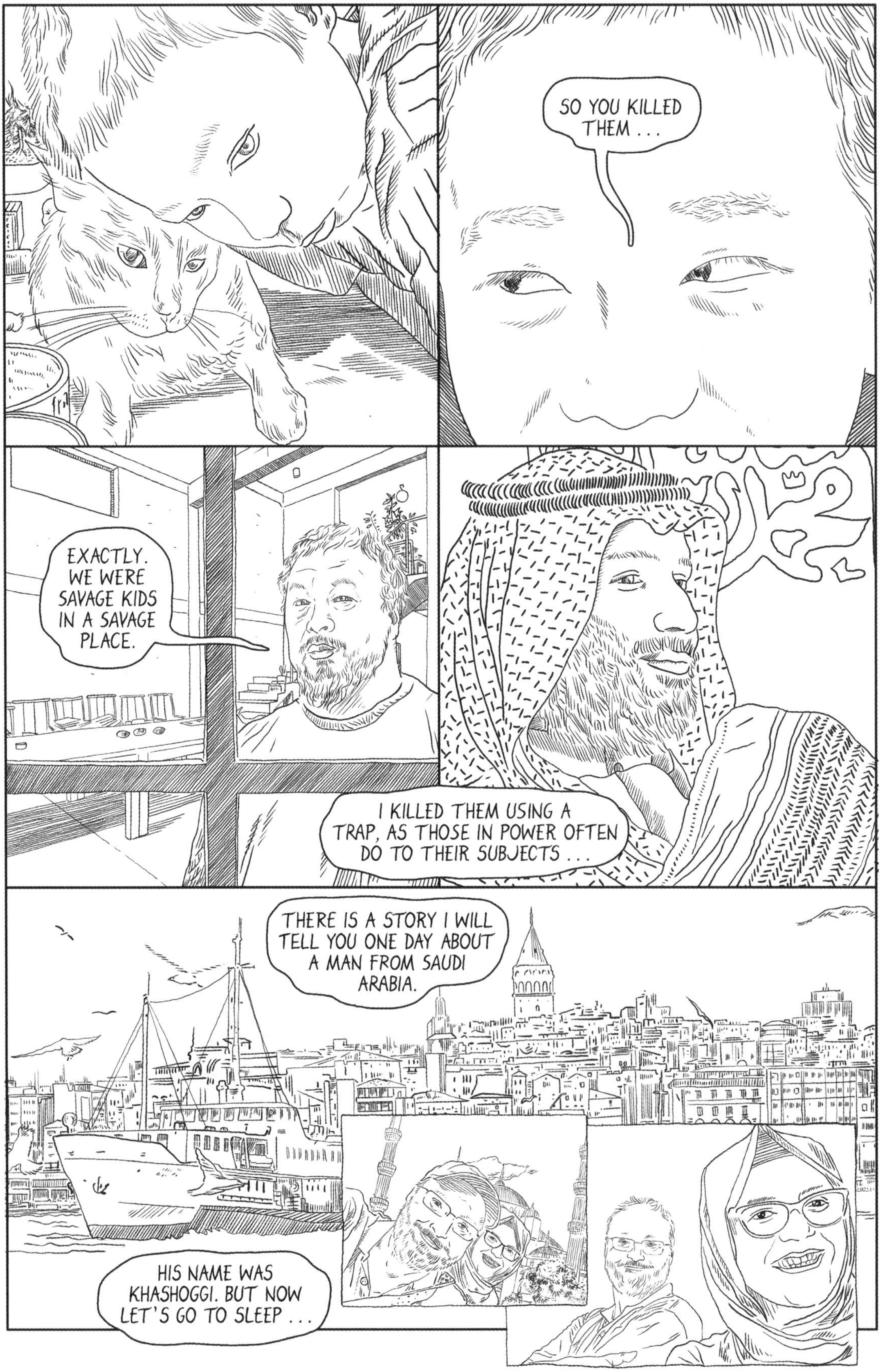
SO YOU KILLED THEM . . .
EXACTLY. WE WERE SAVAGE KIDS IN A SAVAGE PLACE.
I KILLED THEM USING A TRAP, AS THOSE IN POWER OFTEN DO TO THEIR SUBJECTS . . .
THERE IS A STORY I WILL TELL YOU ONE DAY ABOUT A MAN FROM SAUDI ARABIA.
HIS NAME WAS KHASHOGGI. BUT NOW LET'S GO TO SLEEP . . .

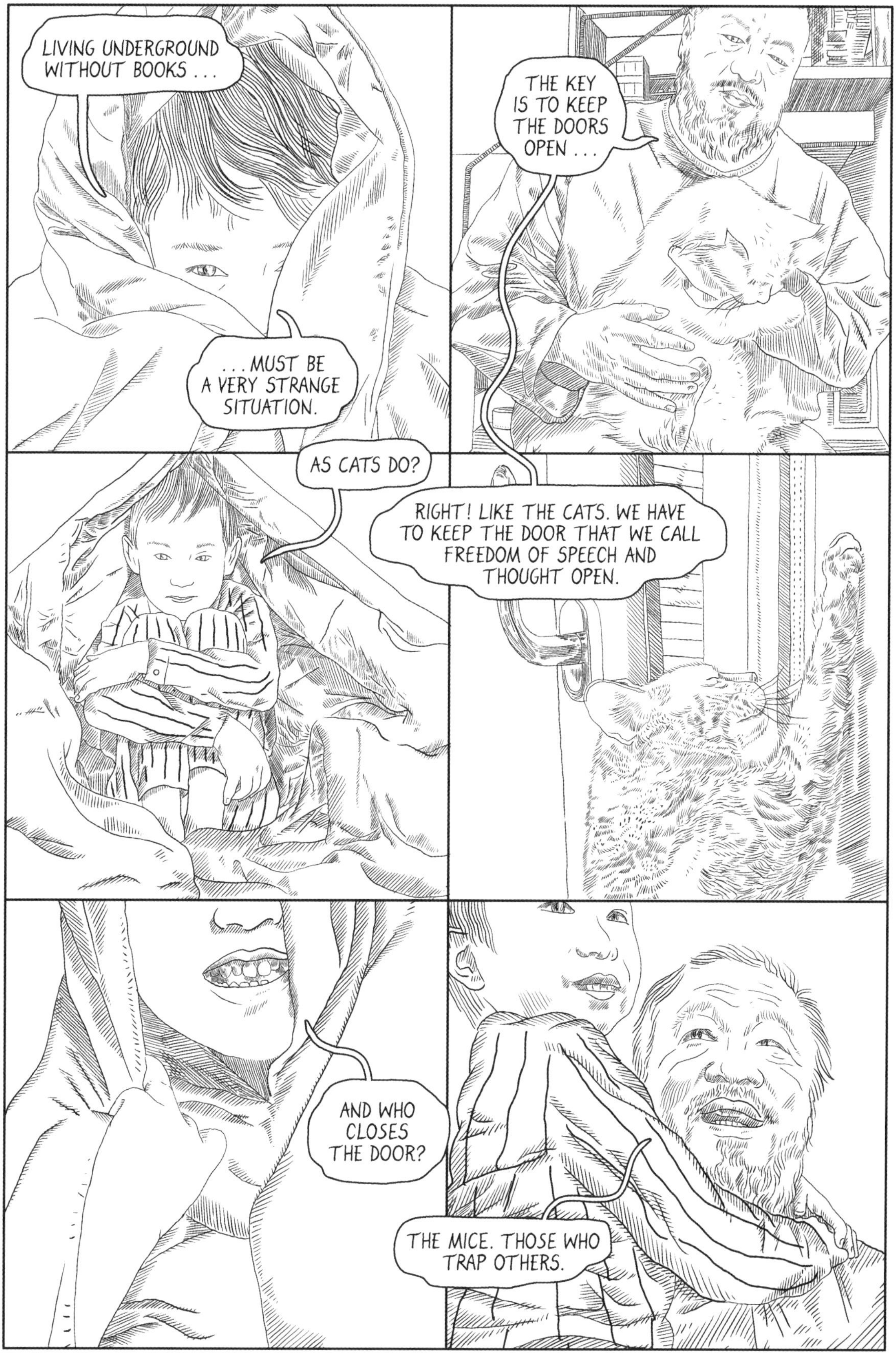
LIVING UNDERGROUND WITHOUT BOOKS . . .
. . . MUST BE A VERY STRANGE SITUATION.
THE KEY IS TO KEEP THE DOORS OPEN . . .
AS CATS DO?
RIGHT! LIKE THE CATS. WE HAVE TO KEEP THE DOOR THAT WE CALL FREEDOM OF SPEECH AND THOUGHT OPEN.
AND WHO CLOSES THE DOOR?
THE MICE. THOSE WHO TRAP OTHERS.

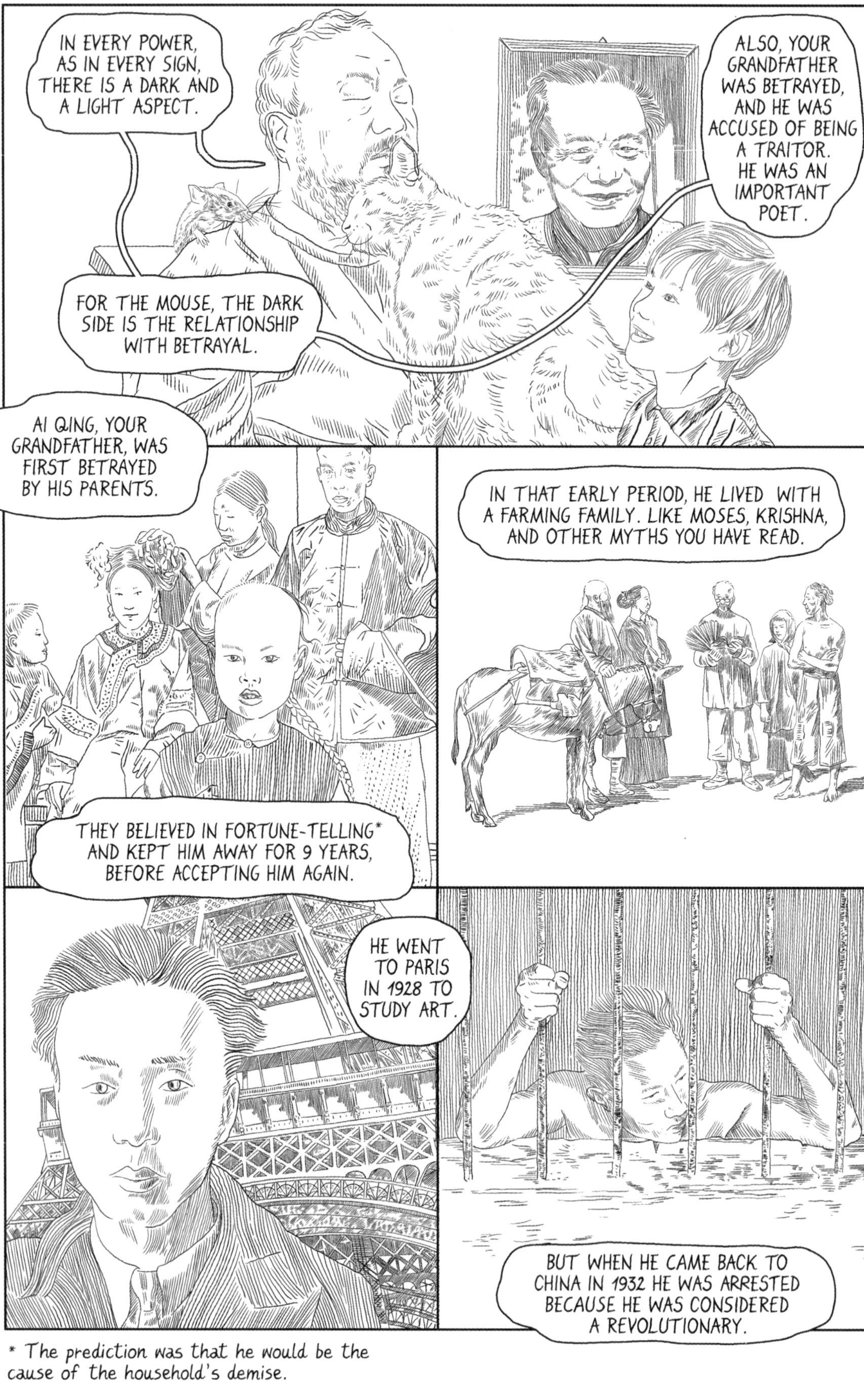
IN EVERY POWER, AS IN EVERY SIGN, THERE IS A DARK AND A LIGHT ASPECT.
FOR THE MOUSE, THE DARK SIDE IS THE RELATIONSHIP WITH BETRAYAL.
ALSO, YOUR GRANDFATHER WAS BETRAYED, AND HE WAS ACCUSED OF BEING A TRAITOR. HE WAS AN IMPORTANT POET.
AI QING, YOUR GRANDFATHER, WAS FIRST BETRAYED BY HIS PARENTS.
THEY BELIEVED IN FORTUNE-TELLING* AND KEPT HIM AWAY FOR 9 YEARS, BEFORE ACCEPTING HIM AGAIN.
IN THAT EARLY PERIOD, HE LIVED WITH A FARMING FAMILY. LIKE MOSES, KRISHNA, AND OTHER MYTHS YOU HAVE READ.
HE WENT TO PARIS IN 1928 TO STUDY ART.
BUT WHEN HE CAME BACK TO CHINA IN 1932 HE WAS ARRESTED BECAUSE HE WAS CONSIDERED A REVOLUTIONARY.

* The prediction was that he would be the cause of the household's demise.

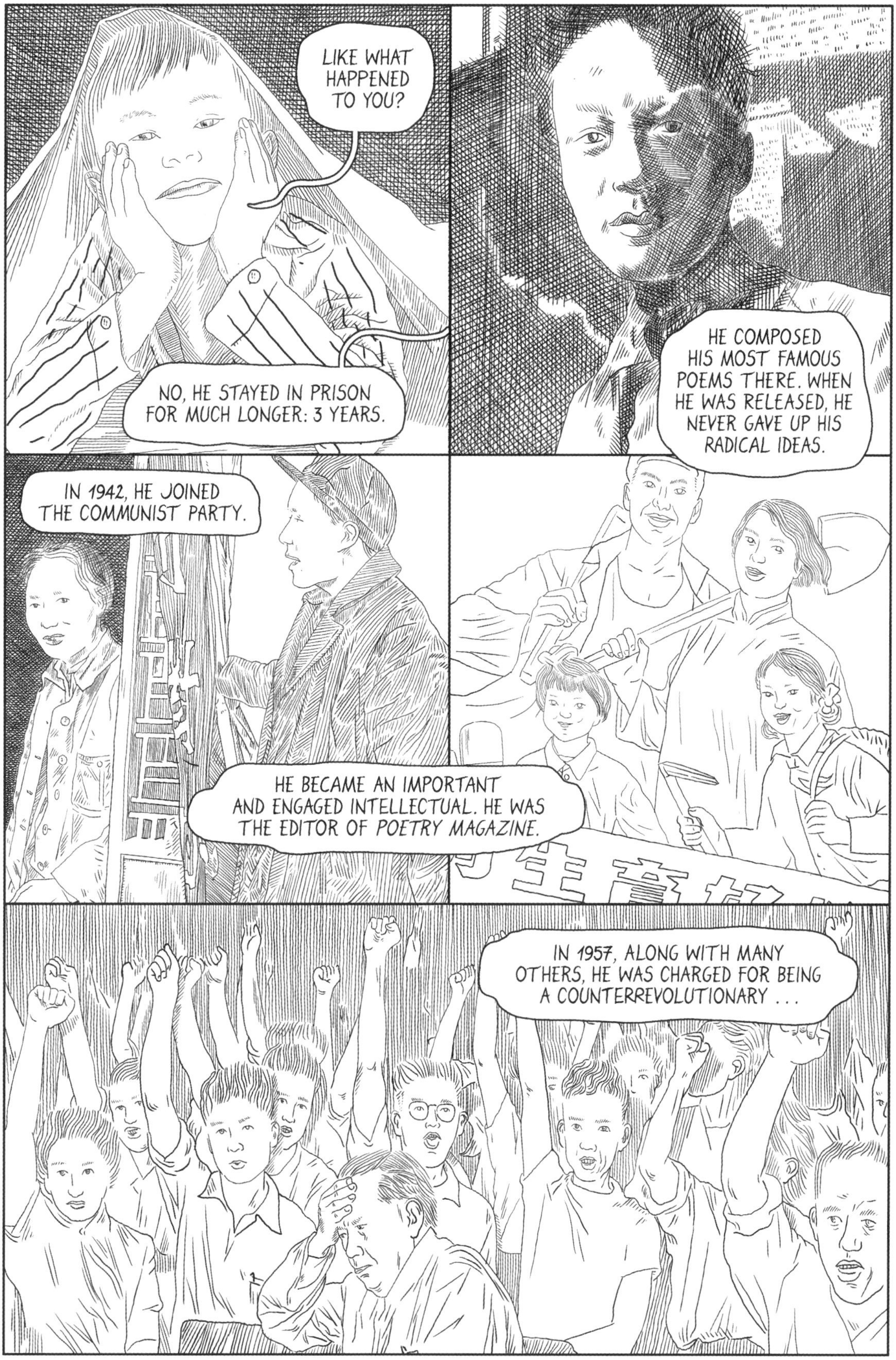
LIKE WHAT HAPPENED TO YOU?
NO, HE STAYED IN PRISON FOR MUCH LONGER: 3 YEARS.
HE COMPOSED HIS MOST FAMOUS POEMS THERE. WHEN HE WAS RELEASED, HE NEVER GAVE UP HIS RADICAL IDEAS.
IN 1942, HE JOINED THE COMMUNIST PARTY.
HE BECAME AN IMPORTANT AND ENGAGED INTELLECTUAL. HE WAS THE EDITOR OF *POETRY MAGAZINE*.
IN 1957, ALONG WITH MANY OTHERS, HE WAS CHARGED FOR BEING A COUNTERREVOLUTIONARY . . .

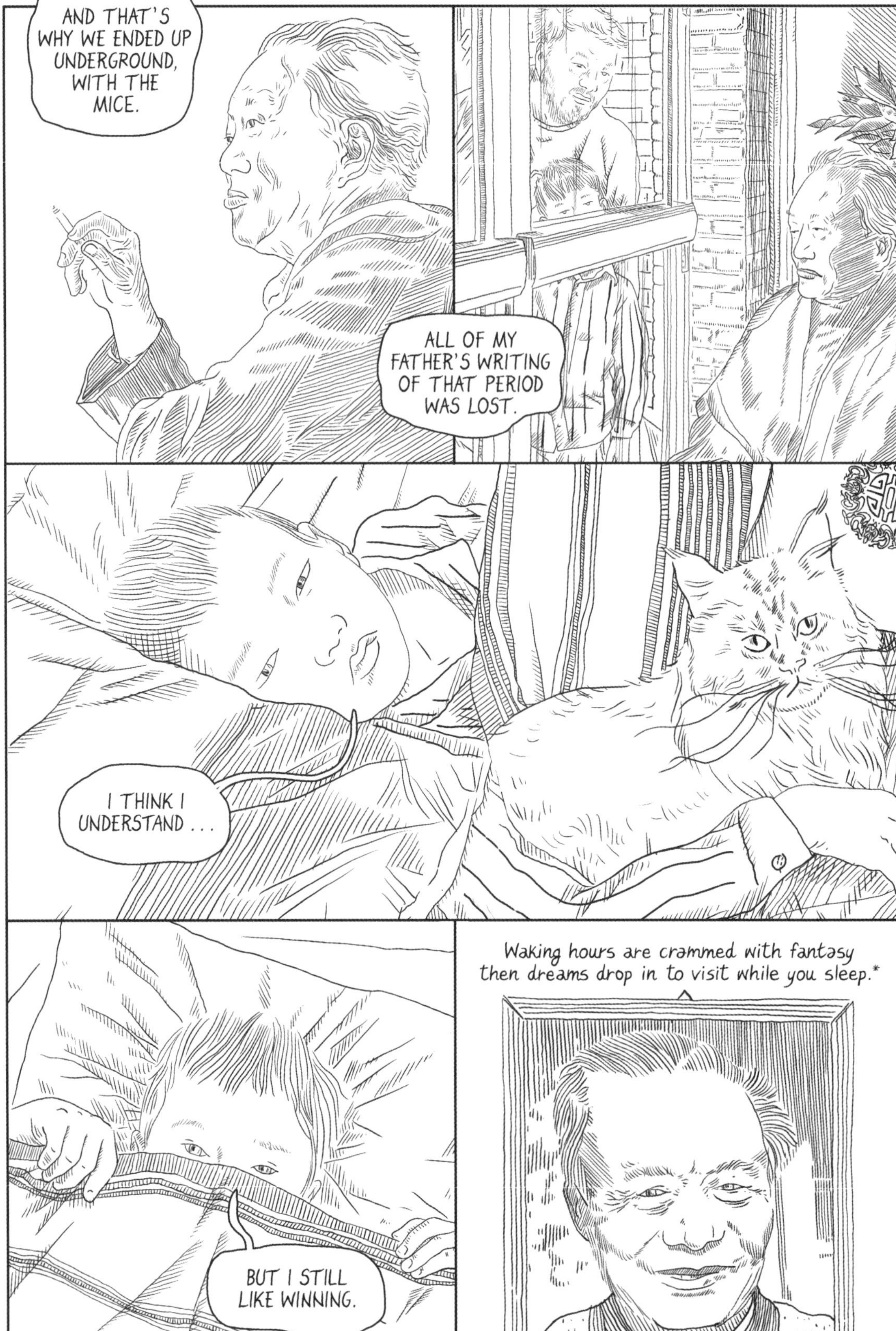
AND THAT'S WHY WE ENDED UP UNDERGROUND, WITH THE MICE.
ALL OF MY FATHER'S WRITING OF THAT PERIOD WAS LOST.
I THINK I UNDERSTAND . . .
BUT I STILL LIKE WINNING.
Waking hours are crammed with fantasy
then dreams drop in to visit while you sleep.*

* Verses from Ai Qing's poem "Dreams" in *The Red Azalea: Chinese Poetry Since the Cultural Revolution*. Edward Morin, ed., trans. by Fang Dai, Dennis Ding, and Edward Morin. Honolulu: University of Hawai'i Press, November 1990.

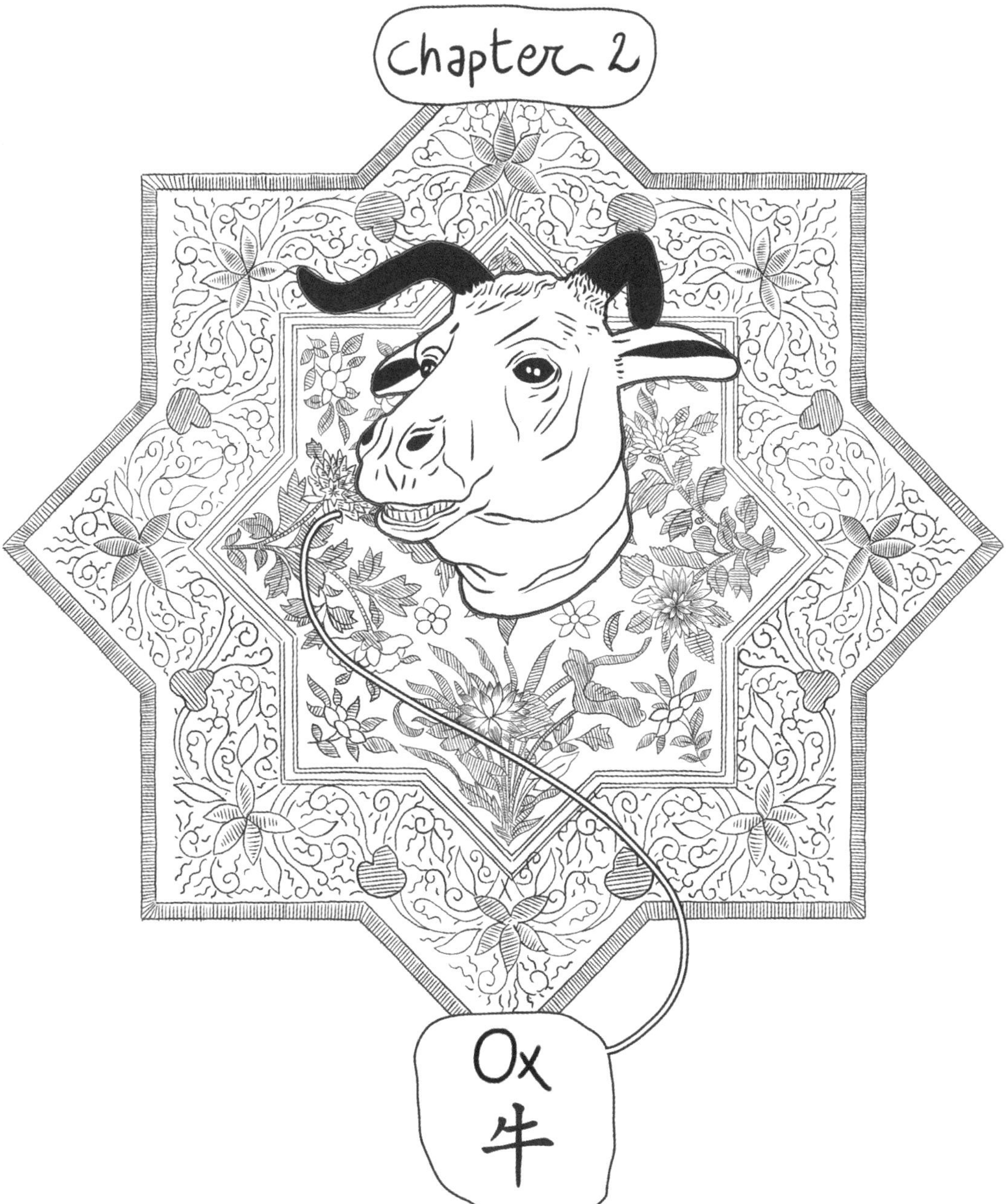
Chapter 2
Ox
牛

Beijing, 2015

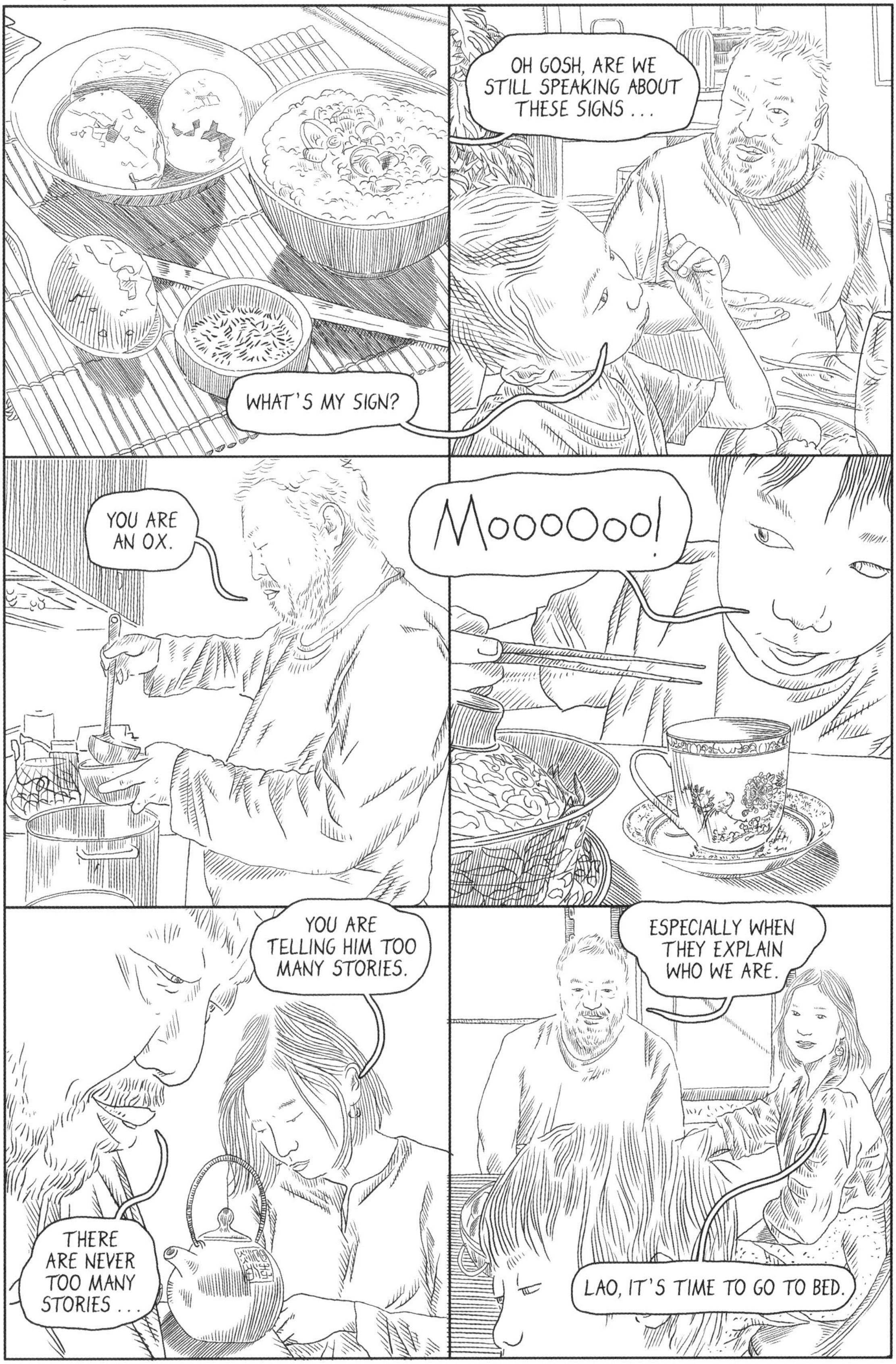
WHAT'S MY SIGN?
OH GOSH, ARE WE STILL SPEAKING ABOUT THESE SIGNS . . .
YOU ARE AN OX.
MoooOoo!
YOU ARE TELLING HIM TOO MANY STORIES.
THERE ARE NEVER TOO MANY STORIES . . .
ESPECIALLY WHEN THEY EXPLAIN WHO WE ARE.
LAO, IT'S TIME TO GO TO BED.

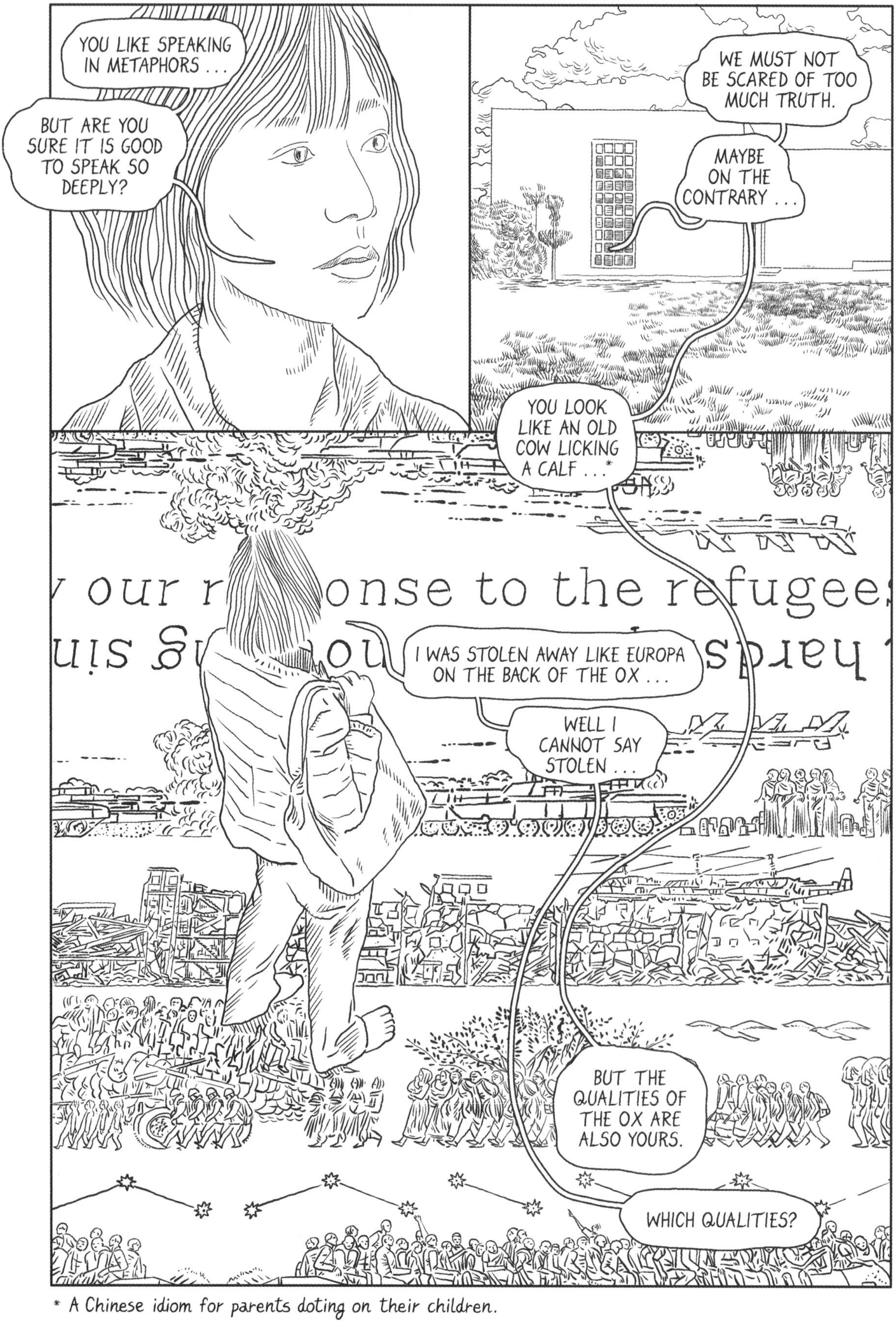
YOU LIKE SPEAKING IN METAPHORS . . .
BUT ARE YOU SURE IT IS GOOD TO SPEAK SO DEEPLY?
WE MUST NOT BE SCARED OF TOO MUCH TRUTH.
MAYBE ON THE CONTRARY . . .
YOU LOOK LIKE AN OLD COW LICKING A CALF . . .*
I WAS STOLEN AWAY LIKE EUROPA ON THE BACK OF THE OX . . .
WELL I CANNOT SAY STOLEN . . .
BUT THE QUALITIES OF THE OX ARE ALSO YOURS.
WHICH QUALITIES?

* A Chinese idiom for parents doting on their children.

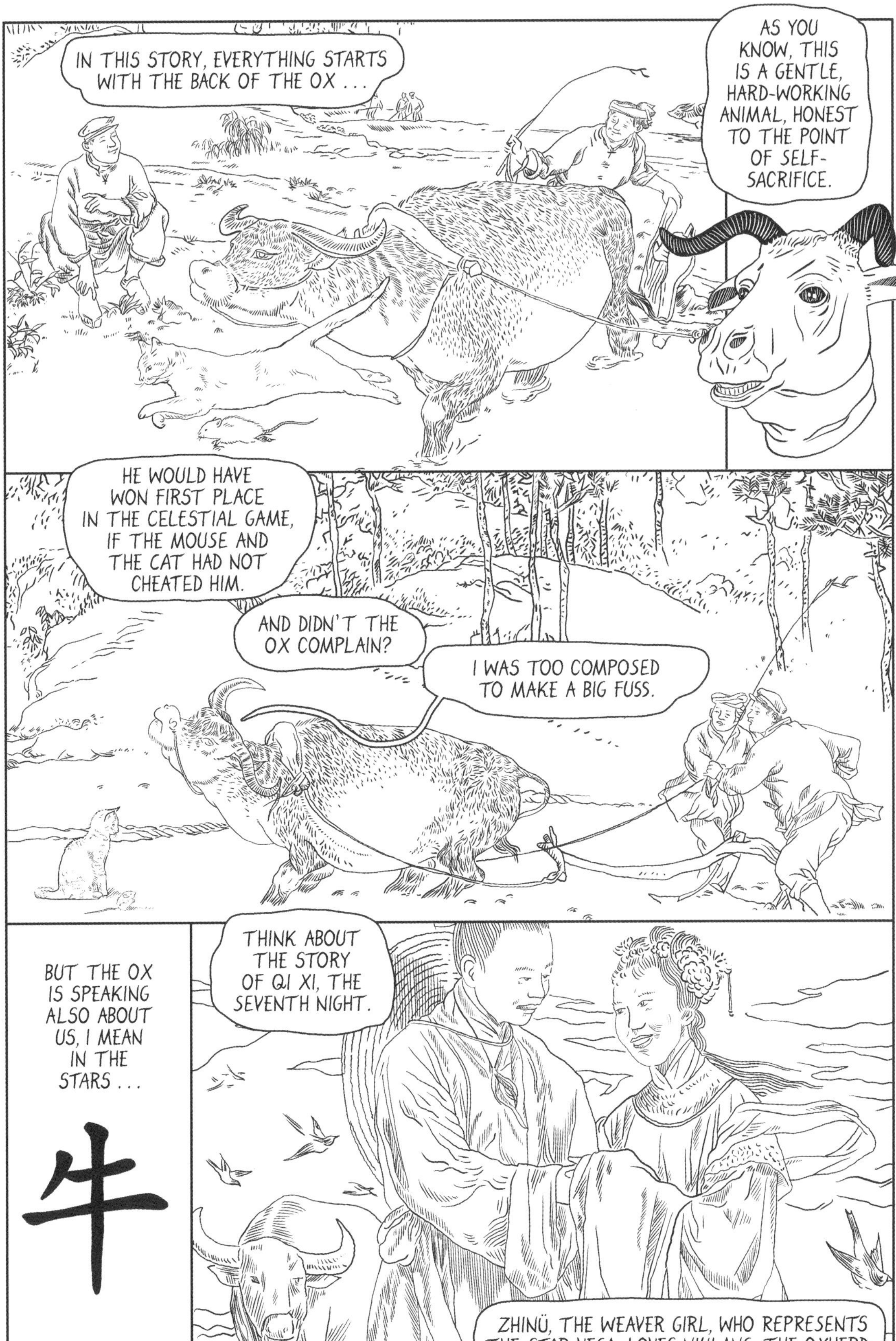
IN THIS STORY, EVERYTHING STARTS WITH THE BACK OF THE OX . . .
AS YOU KNOW, THIS IS A GENTLE, HARD-WORKING ANIMAL, HONEST TO THE POINT OF SELF-SACRIFICE.
HE WOULD HAVE WON FIRST PLACE IN THE CELESTIAL GAME, IF THE MOUSE AND THE CAT HAD NOT CHEATED HIM.
AND DIDN'T THE OX COMPLAIN?
I WAS TOO COMPOSED TO MAKE A BIG FUSS.
BUT THE OX IS SPEAKING ALSO ABOUT US, I MEAN IN THE STARS . . .
牛
THINK ABOUT THE STORY OF QI XI, THE SEVENTH NIGHT.
ZHINÜ, THE WEAVER GIRL, WHO REPRESENTS THE STAR VEGA, LOVES NIULANG, THE OXHERD, WHO REPRESENTS ALTAIR.

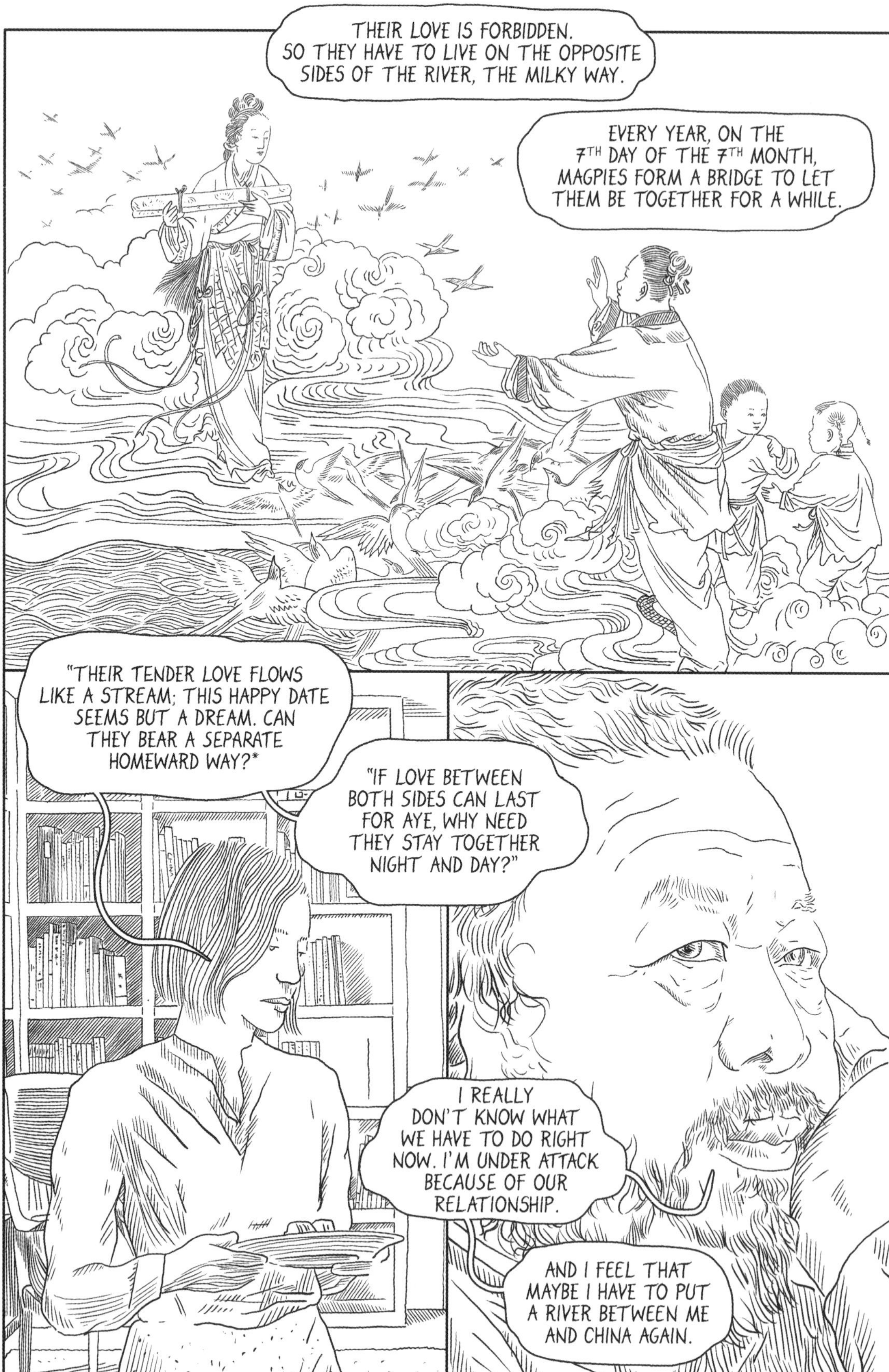
THEIR LOVE IS FORBIDDEN. SO THEY HAVE TO LIVE ON THE OPPOSITE SIDES OF THE RIVER, THE MILKY WAY.
EVERY YEAR, ON THE 7TH DAY OF THE 7TH MONTH, MAGPIES FORM A BRIDGE TO LET THEM BE TOGETHER FOR A WHILE.
"THEIR TENDER LOVE FLOWS LIKE A STREAM; THIS HAPPY DATE SEEMS BUT A DREAM. CAN THEY BEAR A SEPARATE HOMEWARD WAY?*
"IF LOVE BETWEEN BOTH SIDES CAN LAST FOR AYE, WHY NEED THEY STAY TOGETHER NIGHT AND DAY?"
I REALLY DON'T KNOW WHAT WE HAVE TO DO RIGHT NOW. I'M UNDER ATTACK BECAUSE OF OUR RELATIONSHIP.
AND I FEEL THAT MAYBE I HAVE TO PUT A RIVER BETWEEN ME AND CHINA AGAIN.

* From "Immortal at the Magpie Bridge" by Song Dynasty poet Qin Guan, translated by Xu Yuanchong.

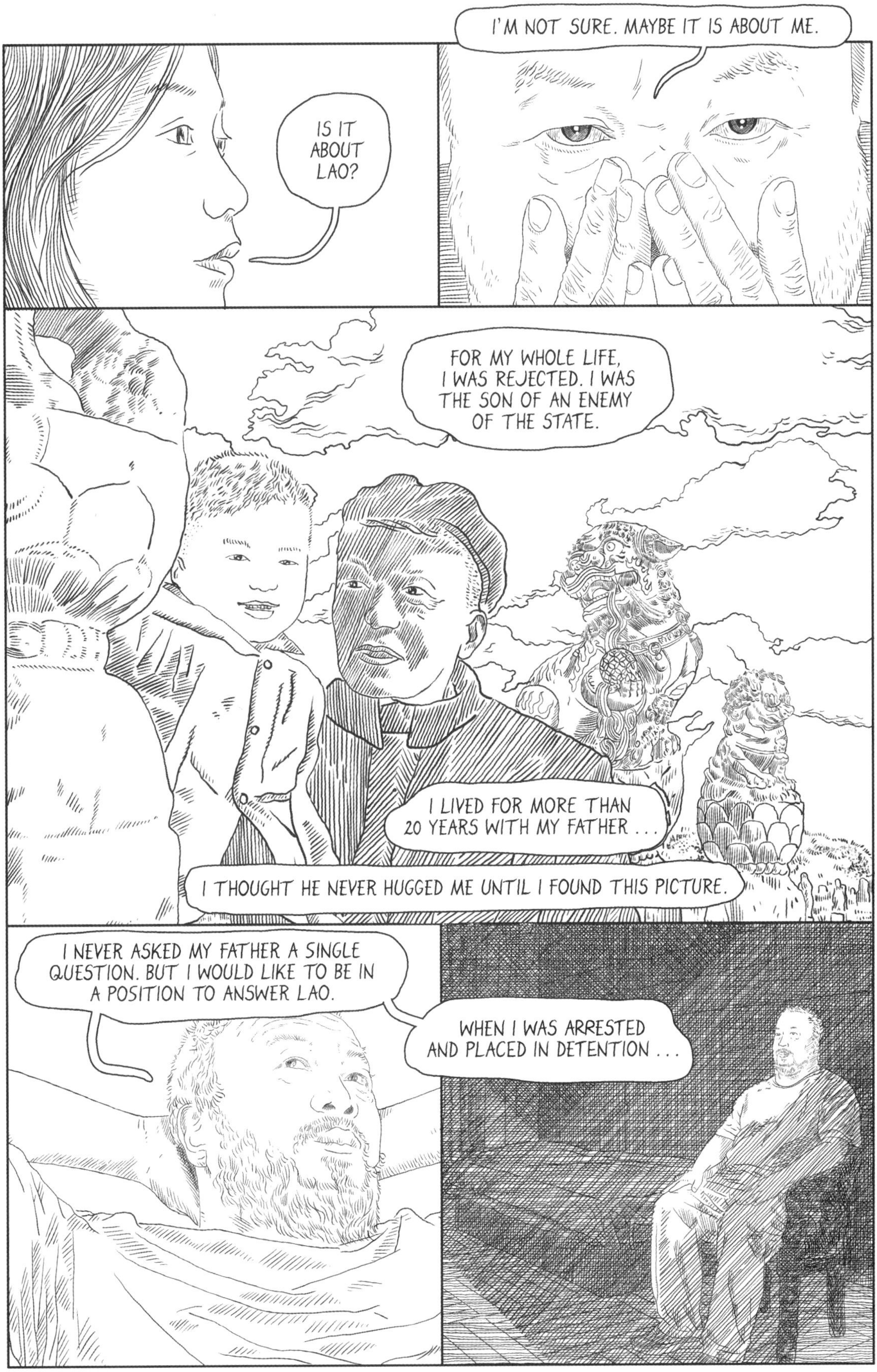
IS IT ABOUT LAO?
I'M NOT SURE. MAYBE IT IS ABOUT ME.
FOR MY WHOLE LIFE, I WAS REJECTED. I WAS THE SON OF AN ENEMY OF THE STATE.
I LIVED FOR MORE THAN 20 YEARS WITH MY FATHER . . .
I THOUGHT HE NEVER HUGGED ME UNTIL I FOUND THIS PICTURE.
I NEVER ASKED MY FATHER A SINGLE QUESTION. BUT I WOULD LIKE TO BE IN A POSITION TO ANSWER LAO.
WHEN I WAS ARRESTED AND PLACED IN DETENTION . . .

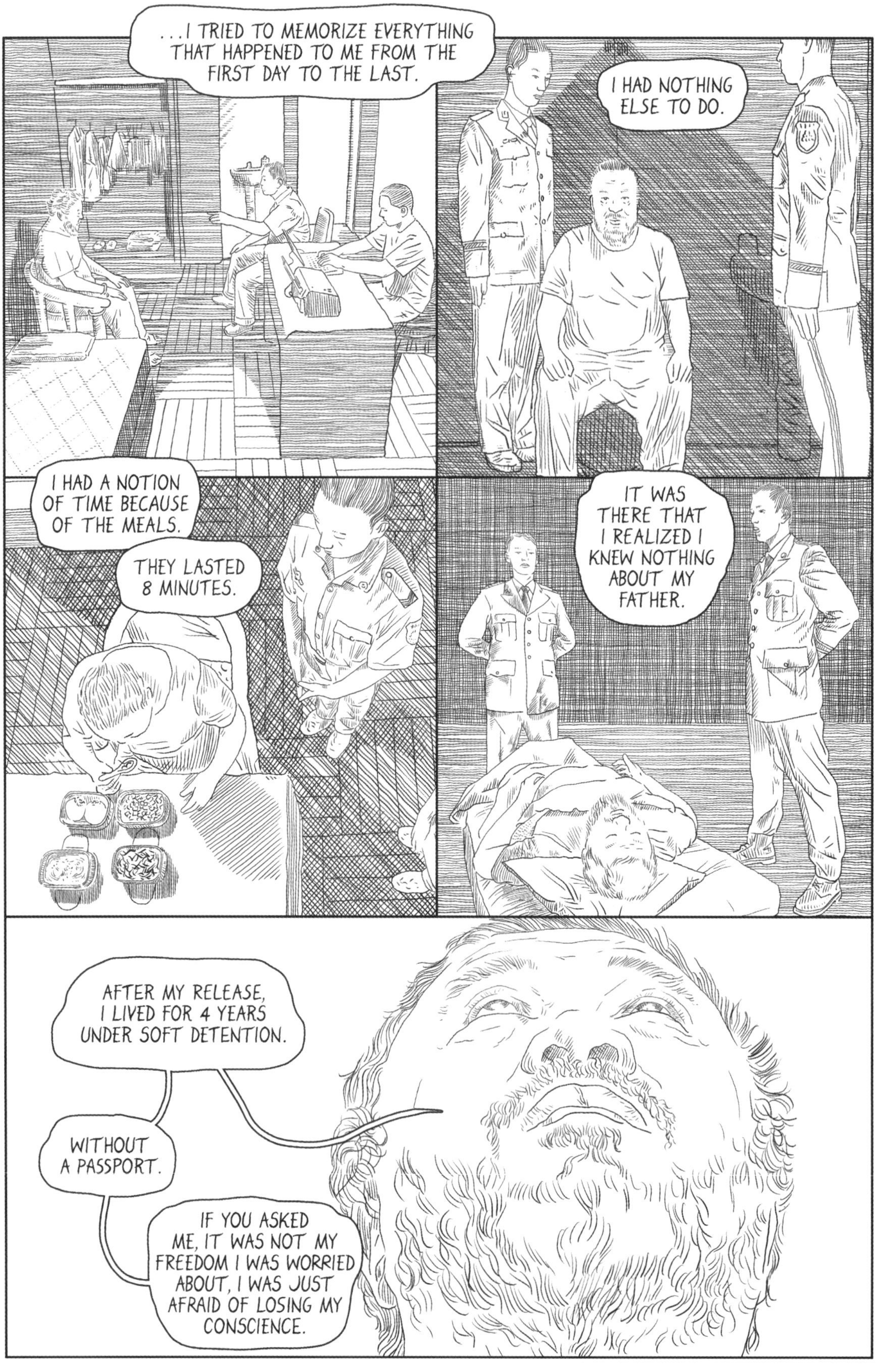
...I TRIED TO MEMORIZE EVERYTHING THAT HAPPENED TO ME FROM THE FIRST DAY TO THE LAST.
I HAD NOTHING ELSE TO DO.
I HAD A NOTION OF TIME BECAUSE OF THE MEALS.
THEY LASTED 8 MINUTES.
IT WAS THERE THAT I REALIZED I KNEW NOTHING ABOUT MY FATHER.
AFTER MY RELEASE, I LIVED FOR 4 YEARS UNDER SOFT DETENTION.
WITHOUT A PASSPORT.
IF YOU ASKED ME, IT WAS NOT MY FREEDOM I WAS WORRIED ABOUT, I WAS JUST AFRAID OF LOSING MY CONSCIENCE.

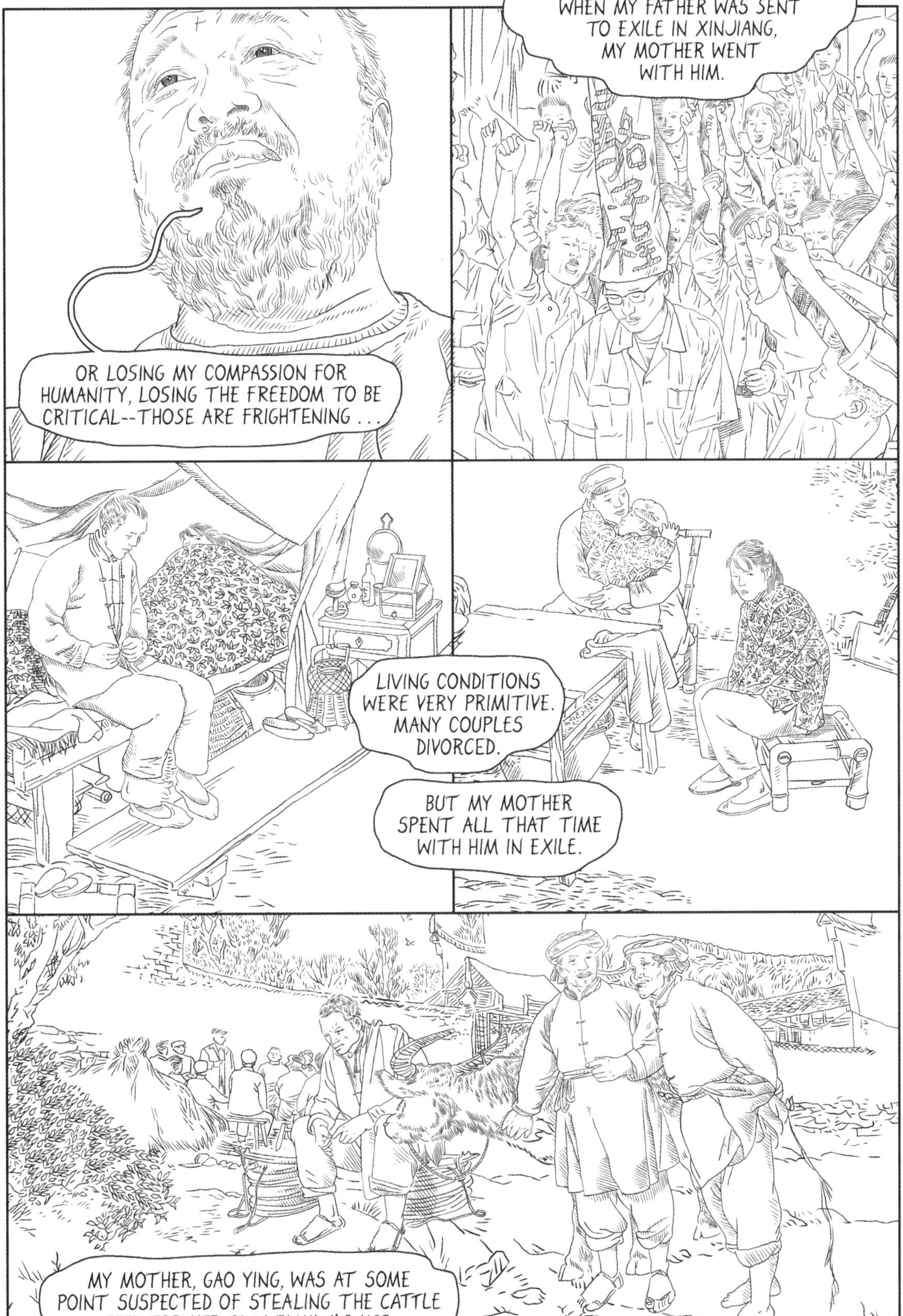

OR LOSING MY COMPASSION FOR HUMANITY, LOSING THE FREEDOM TO BE CRITICAL--THOSE ARE FRIGHTENING . . .
WHEN MY FATHER WAS SENT TO EXILE IN XINJIANG, MY MOTHER WENT WITH HIM.
LIVING CONDITIONS WERE VERY PRIMITIVE. MANY COUPLES DIVORCED.
BUT MY MOTHER SPENT ALL THAT TIME WITH HIM IN EXILE.
MY MOTHER, GAO YING, WAS AT SOME POINT SUSPECTED OF STEALING THE CATTLE FEED FOR HER OWN FAMILY'S USE.

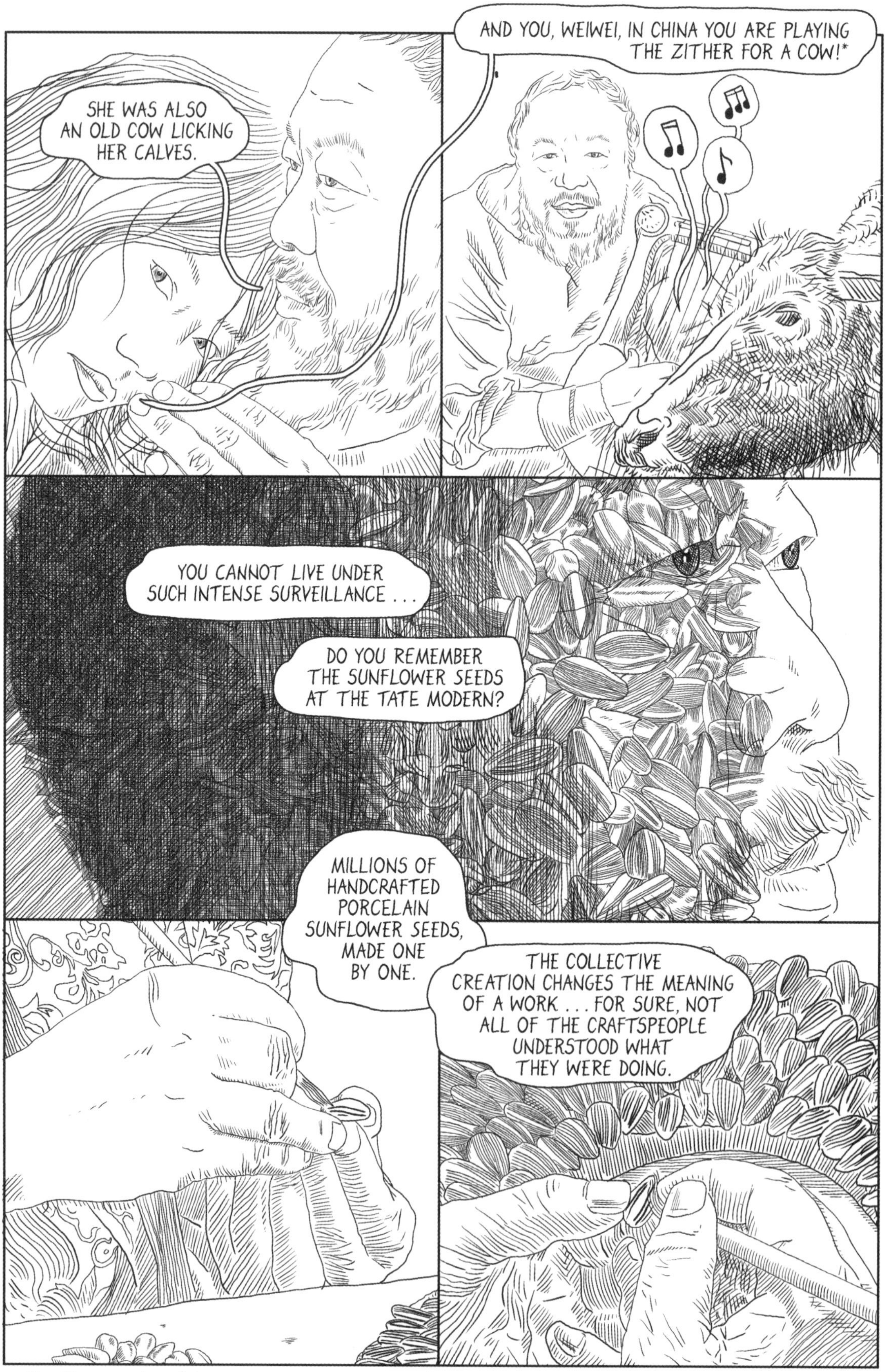
SHE WAS ALSO AN OLD COW LICKING HER CALVES.
AND YOU, WEIWEI, IN CHINA YOU ARE PLAYING THE ZITHER FOR A COW!*
YOU CANNOT LIVE UNDER SUCH INTENSE SURVEILLANCE . . .
DO YOU REMEMBER THE SUNFLOWER SEEDS AT THE TATE MODERN?
MILLIONS OF HANDCRAFTED PORCELAIN SUNFLOWER SEEDS, MADE ONE BY ONE.
THE COLLECTIVE CREATION CHANGES THE MEANING OF A WORK . . . FOR SURE, NOT ALL OF THE CRAFTSPEOPLE UNDERSTOOD WHAT THEY WERE DOING.

* The Chinese idiom "playing the zither for a cow" describes the wasted effort of talking to someone who cannot understand.

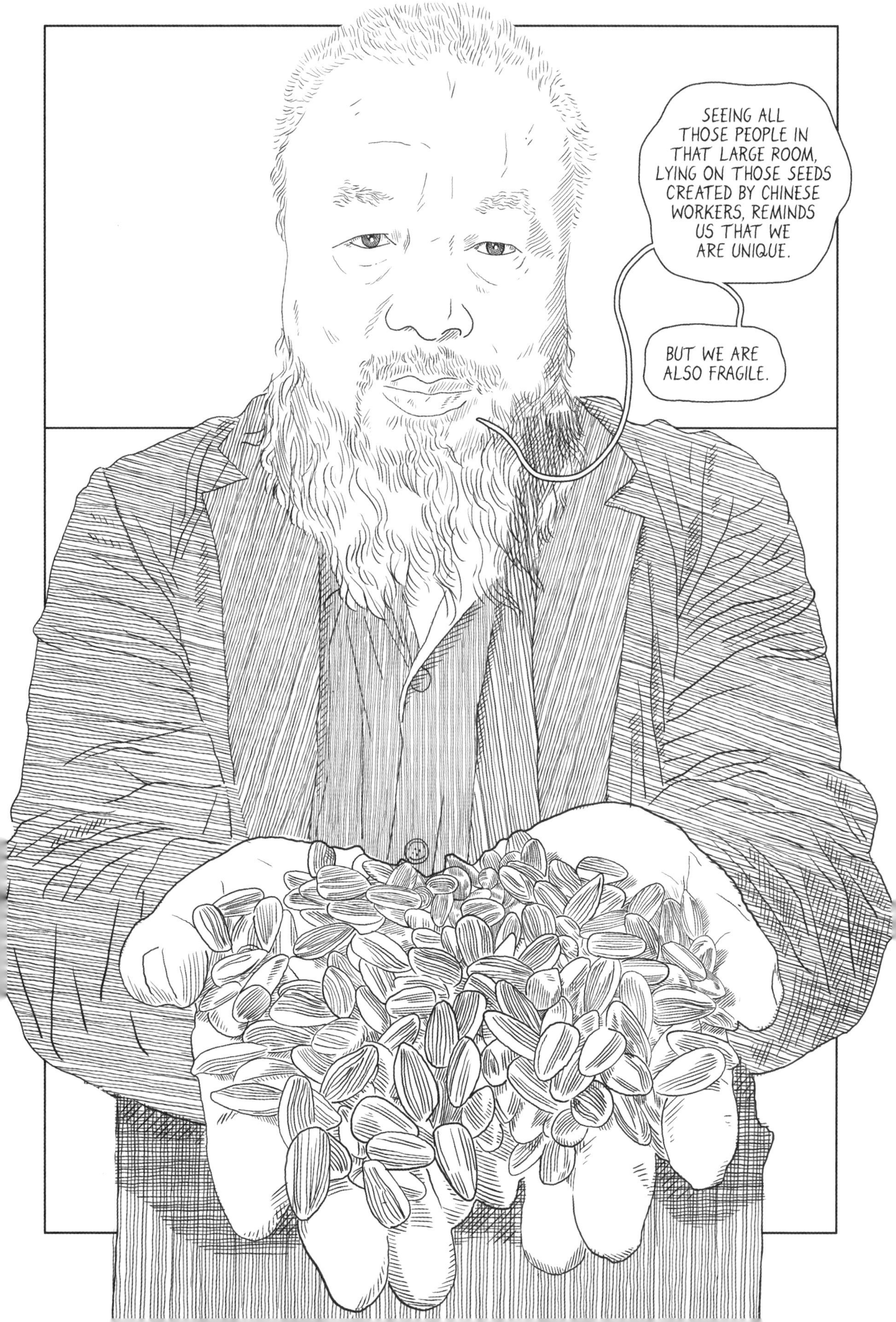
SEEING ALL THOSE PEOPLE IN THAT LARGE ROOM, LYING ON THOSE SEEDS CREATED BY CHINESE WORKERS, REMINDS US THAT WE ARE UNIQUE.
BUT WE ARE ALSO FRAGILE.

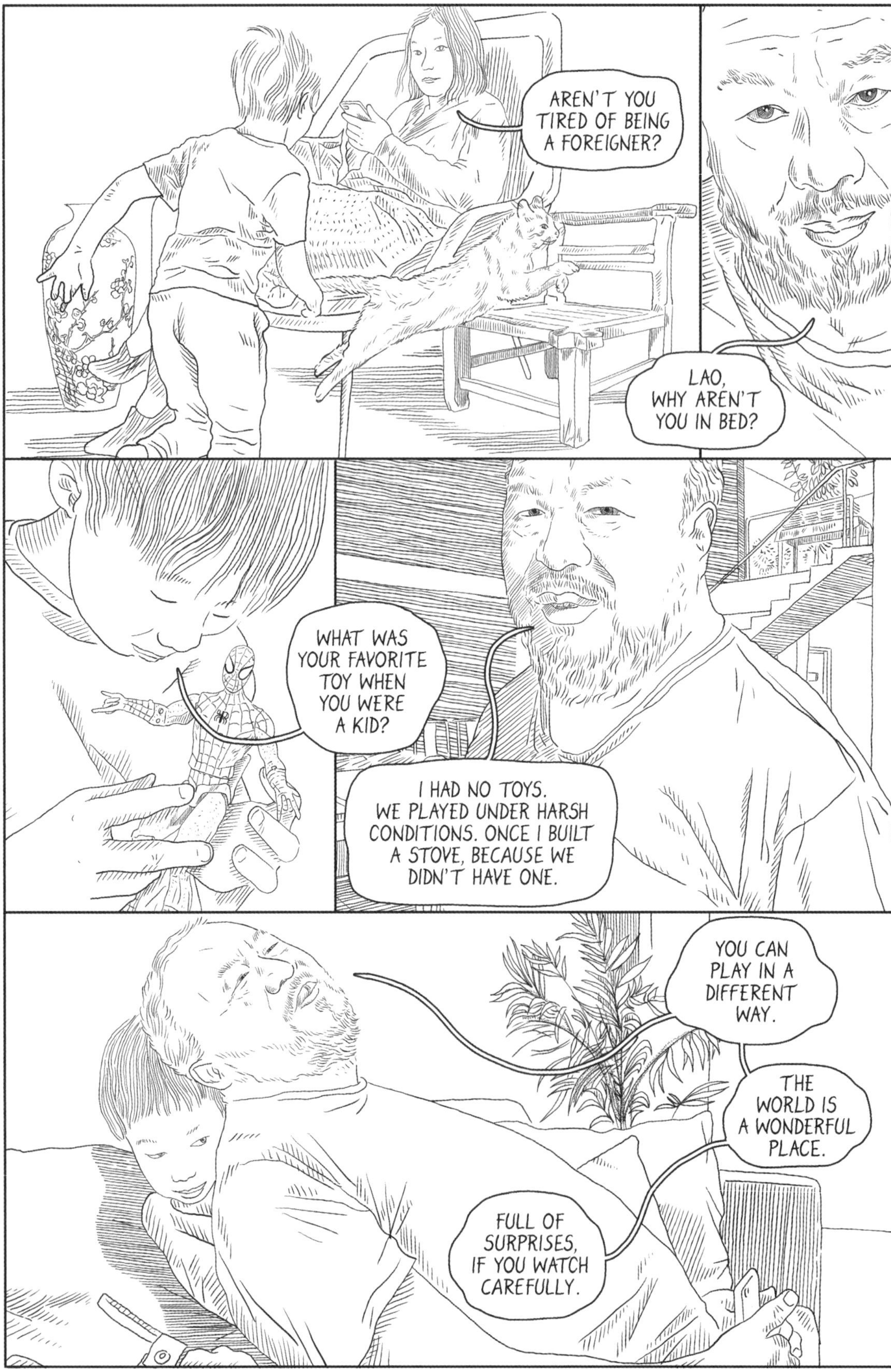

AREN'T YOU TIRED OF BEING A FOREIGNER?
LAO, WHY AREN'T YOU IN BED?
WHAT WAS YOUR FAVORITE TOY WHEN YOU WERE A KID?
I HAD NO TOYS. WE PLAYED UNDER HARSH CONDITIONS. ONCE I BUILT A STOVE, BECAUSE WE DIDN'T HAVE ONE.
YOU CAN PLAY IN A DIFFERENT WAY.
THE WORLD IS A WONDERFUL PLACE.
FULL OF SURPRISES, IF YOU WATCH CAREFULLY.

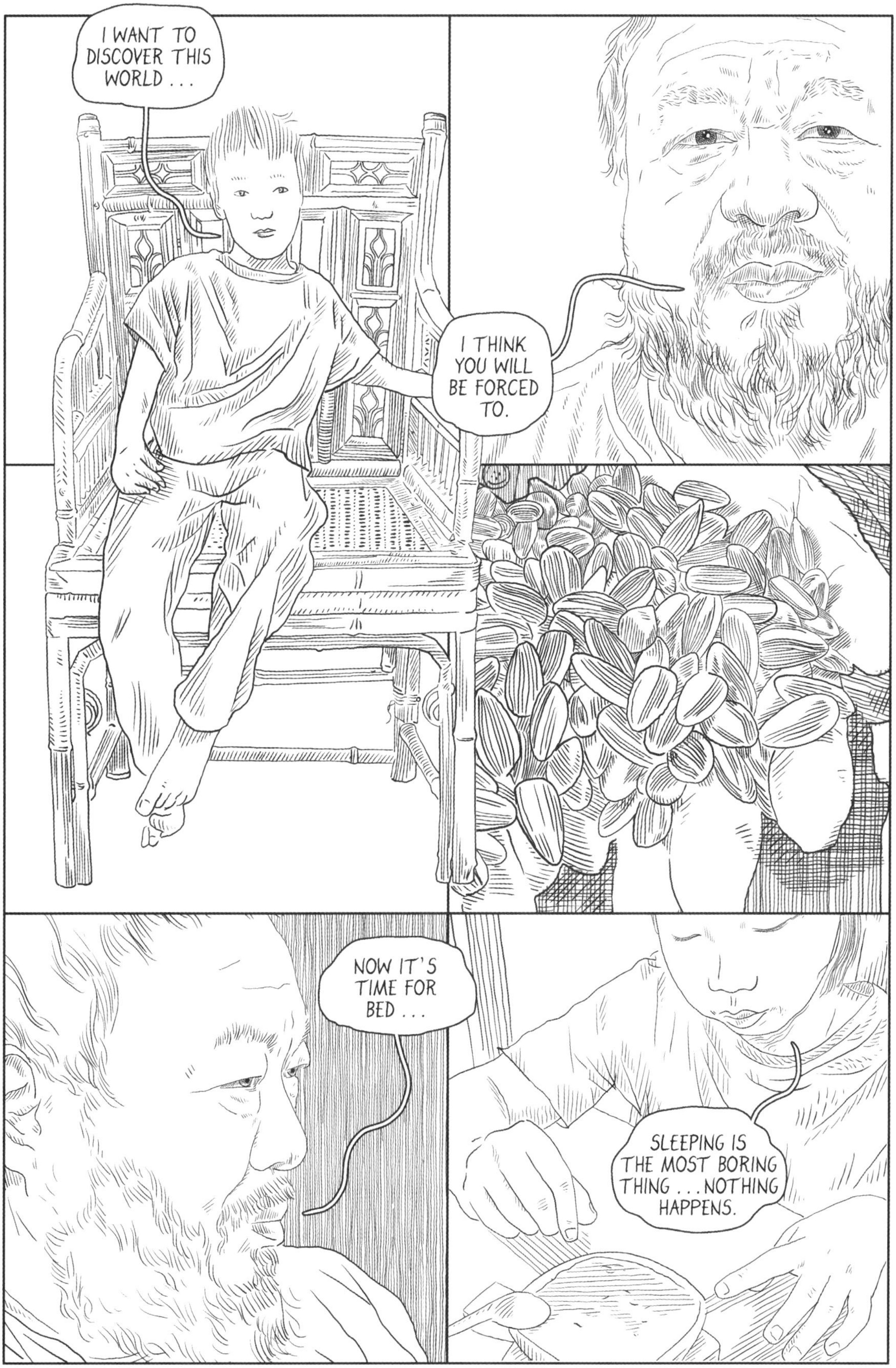
I WANT TO DISCOVER THIS WORLD . . .
I THINK YOU WILL BE FORCED TO.
NOW IT'S TIME FOR BED . . .
SLEEPING IS THE MOST BORING THING . . . NOTHING HAPPENS.

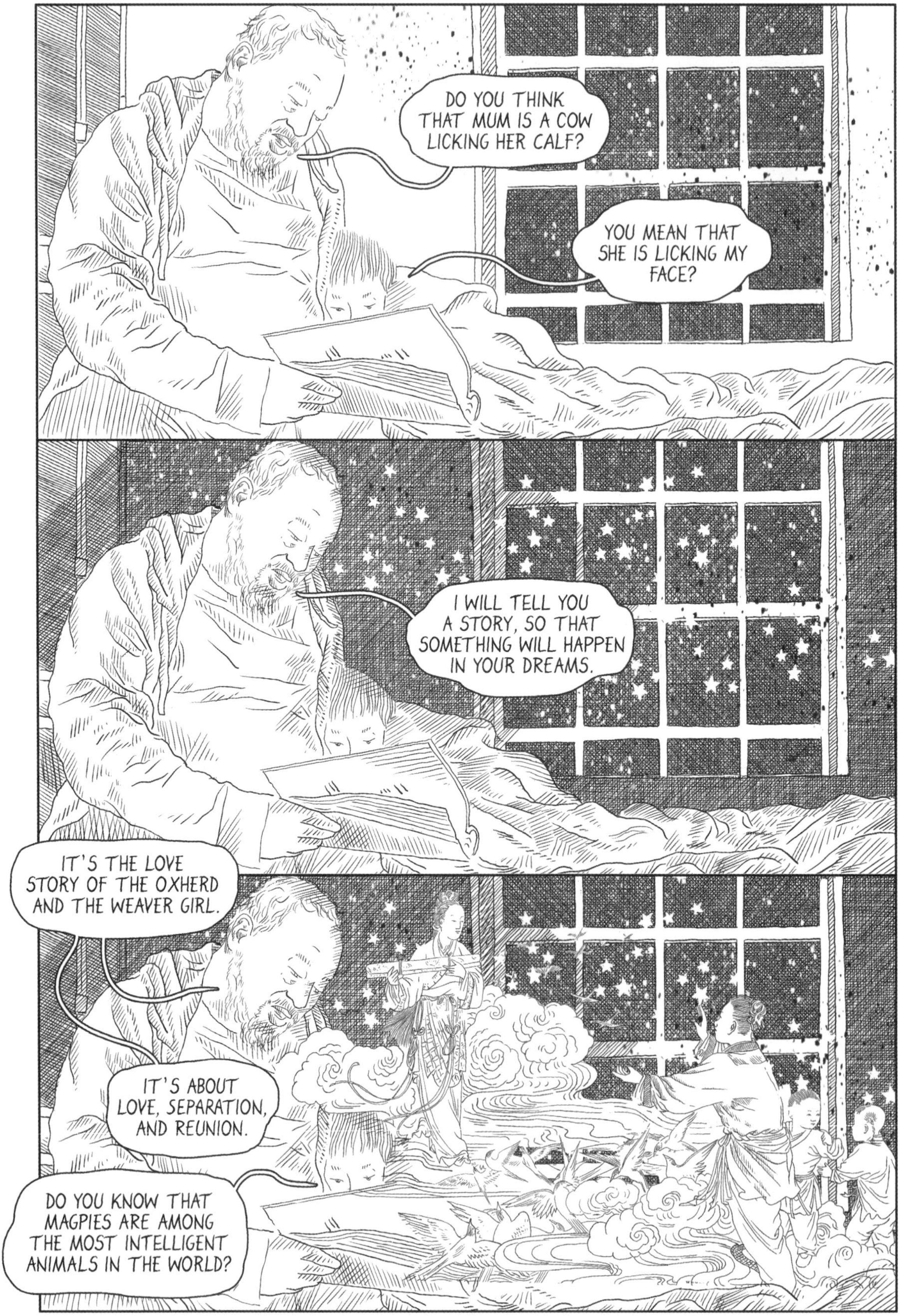
DO YOU THINK THAT MUM IS A COW LICKING HER CALF?
YOU MEAN THAT SHE IS LICKING MY FACE?
I WILL TELL YOU A STORY, SO THAT SOMETHING WILL HAPPEN IN YOUR DREAMS.
IT'S THE LOVE STORY OF THE OXHERD AND THE WEAVER GIRL.
IT'S ABOUT LOVE, SEPARATION, AND REUNION.
DO YOU KNOW THAT MAGPIES ARE AMONG THE MOST INTELLIGENT ANIMALS IN THE WORLD?

Chapter 3

Tiger
虎

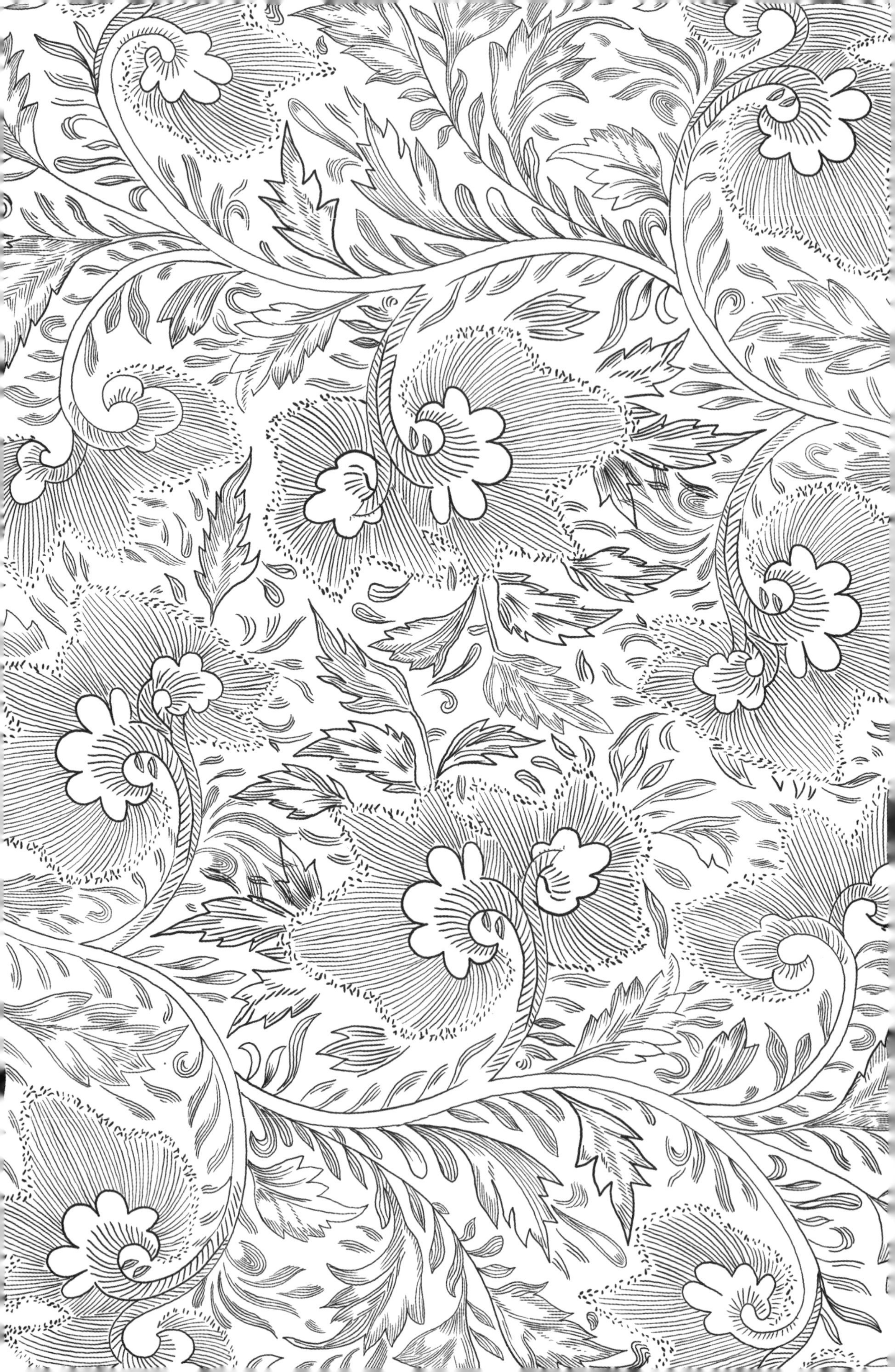

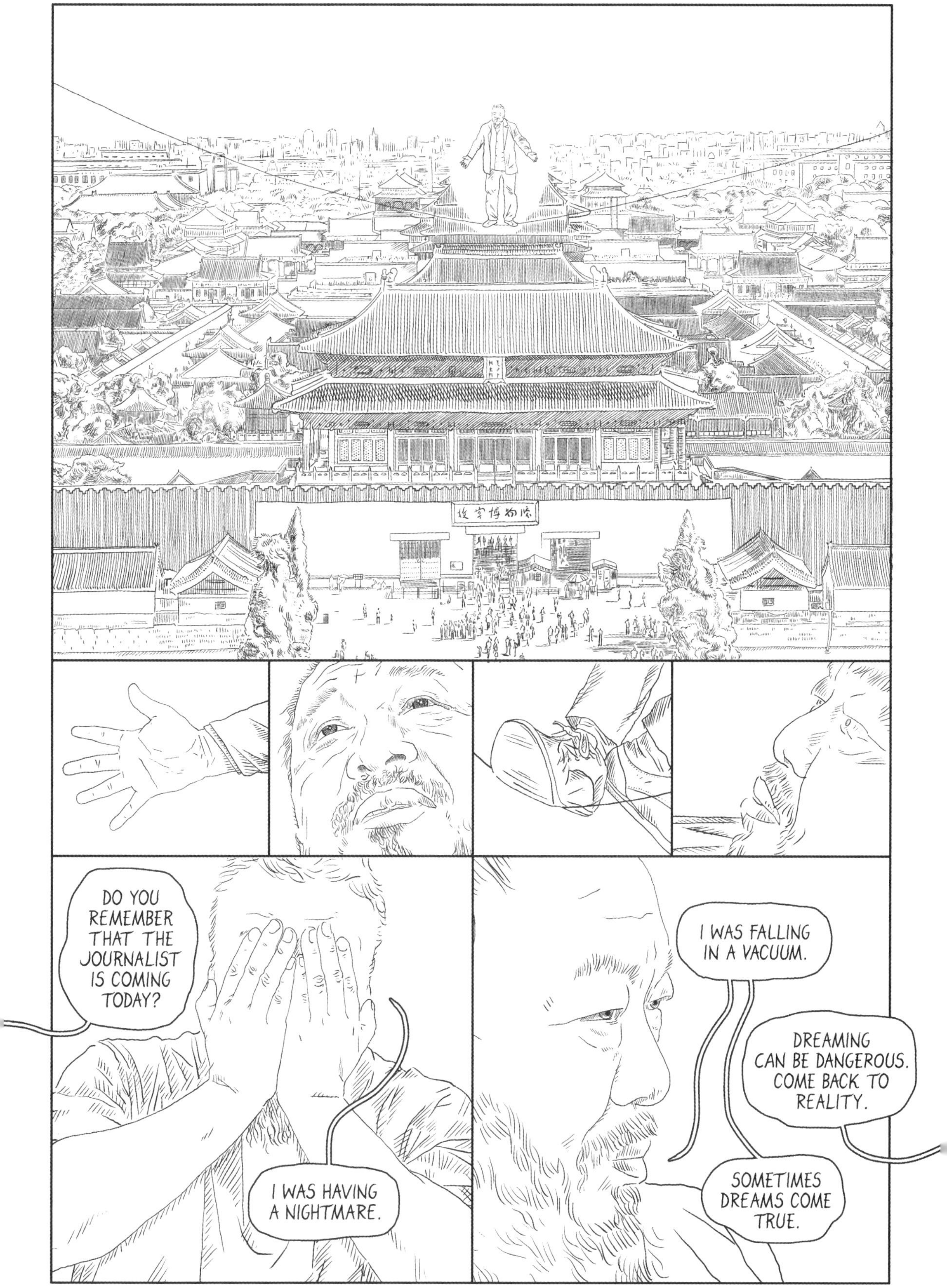
DO YOU REMEMBER THAT THE JOURNALIST IS COMING TODAY?
I WAS HAVING A NIGHTMARE.
I WAS FALLING IN A VACUUM.
DREAMING CAN BE DANGEROUS. COME BACK TO REALITY.
SOMETIMES DREAMS COME TRUE.

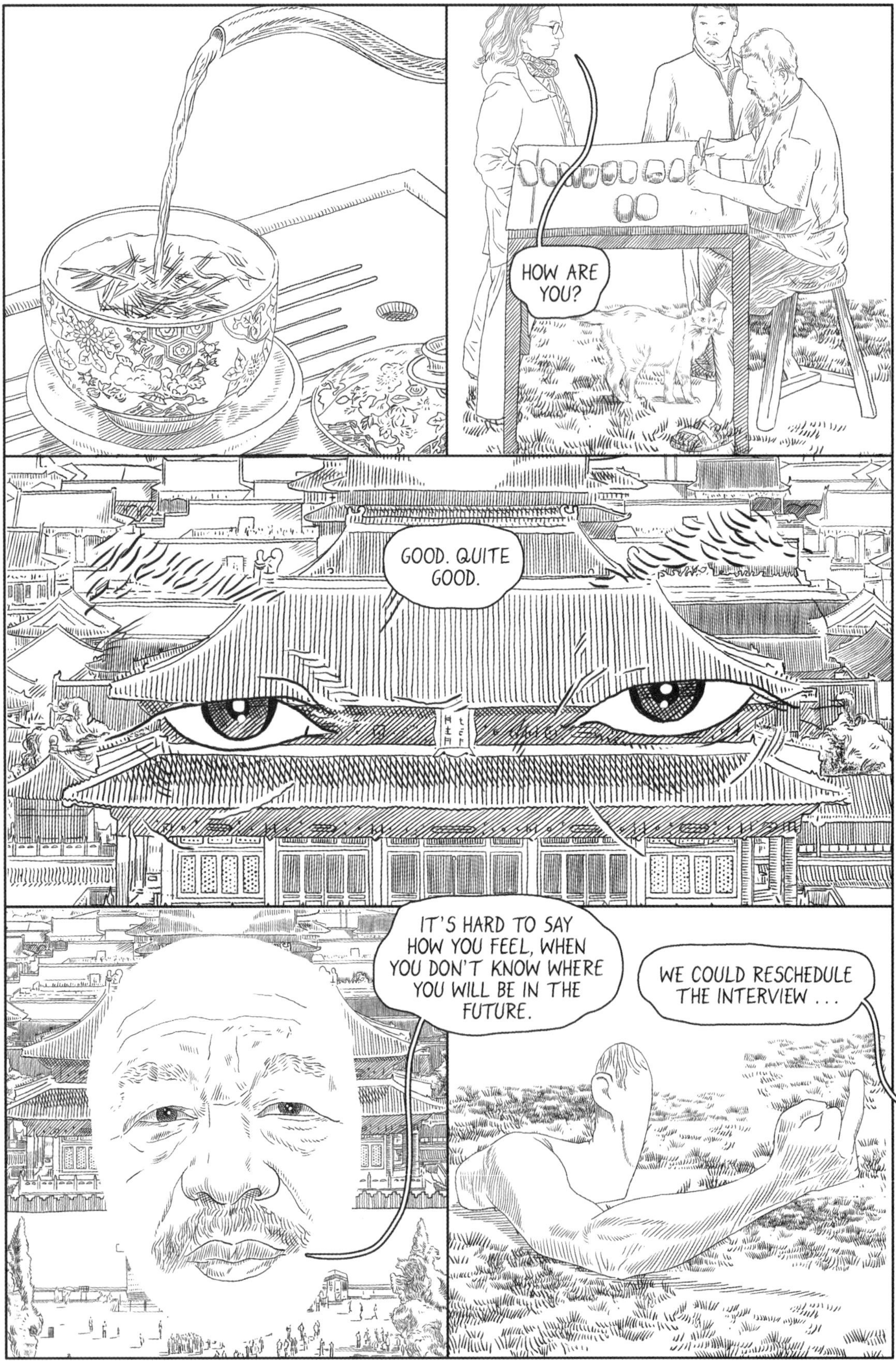
HOW ARE YOU?
GOOD. QUITE GOOD.
IT'S HARD TO SAY HOW YOU FEEL, WHEN YOU DON'T KNOW WHERE YOU WILL BE IN THE FUTURE.
WE COULD RESCHEDULE THE INTERVIEW . . .

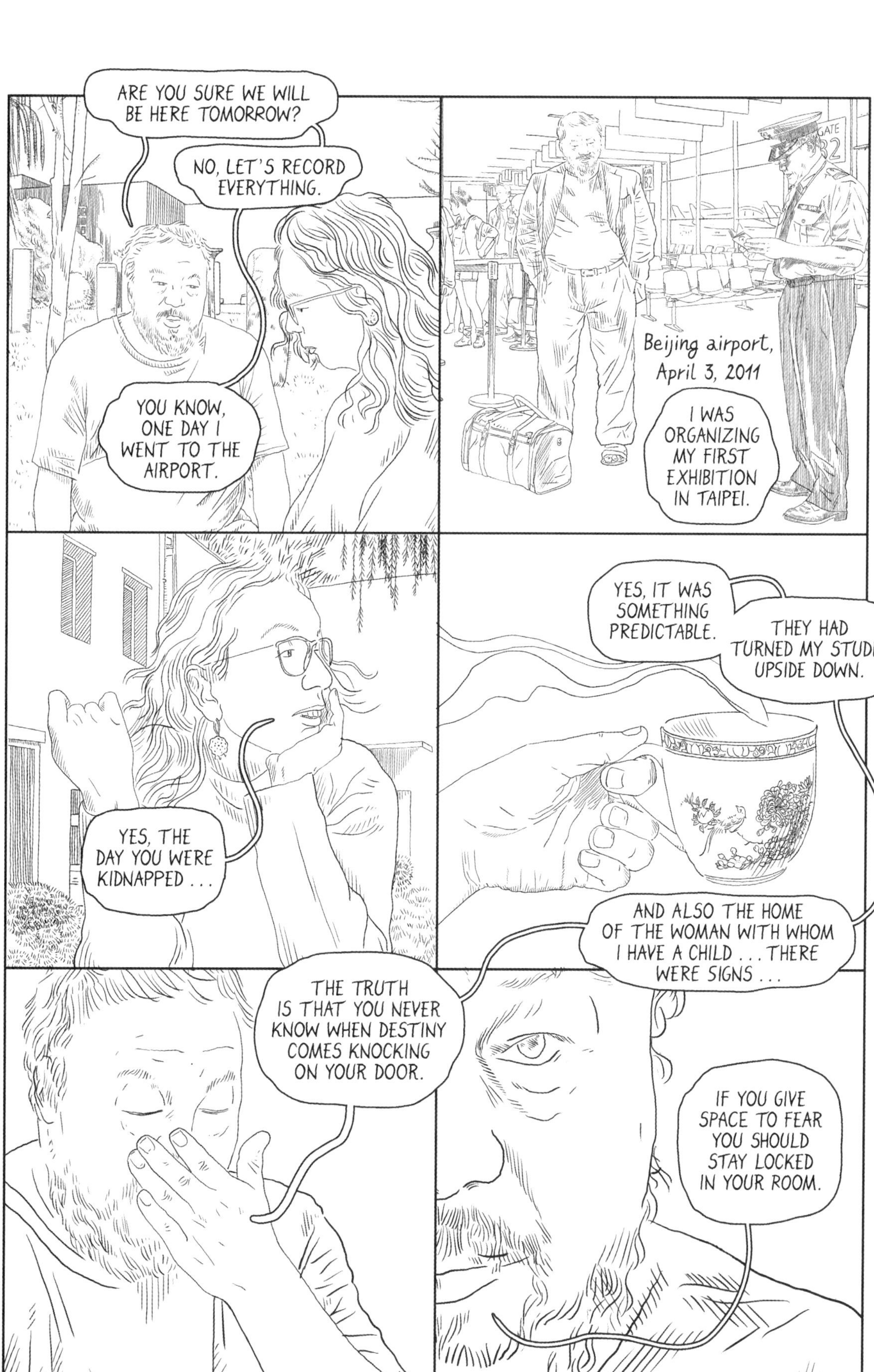
ARE YOU SURE WE WILL BE HERE TOMORROW?
NO, LET'S RECORD EVERYTHING.
YOU KNOW, ONE DAY I WENT TO THE AIRPORT.
Beijing airport, April 3, 2011
I WAS ORGANIZING MY FIRST EXHIBITION IN TAIPEI.
YES, THE DAY YOU WERE KIDNAPPED . . .
YES, IT WAS SOMETHING PREDICTABLE.
THEY HAD TURNED MY STUDIO UPSIDE DOWN.
AND ALSO THE HOME OF THE WOMAN WITH WHOM I HAVE A CHILD . . . THERE WERE SIGNS . . .
THE TRUTH IS THAT YOU NEVER KNOW WHEN DESTINY COMES KNOCKING ON YOUR DOOR.
IF YOU GIVE SPACE TO FEAR YOU SHOULD STAY LOCKED IN YOUR ROOM.

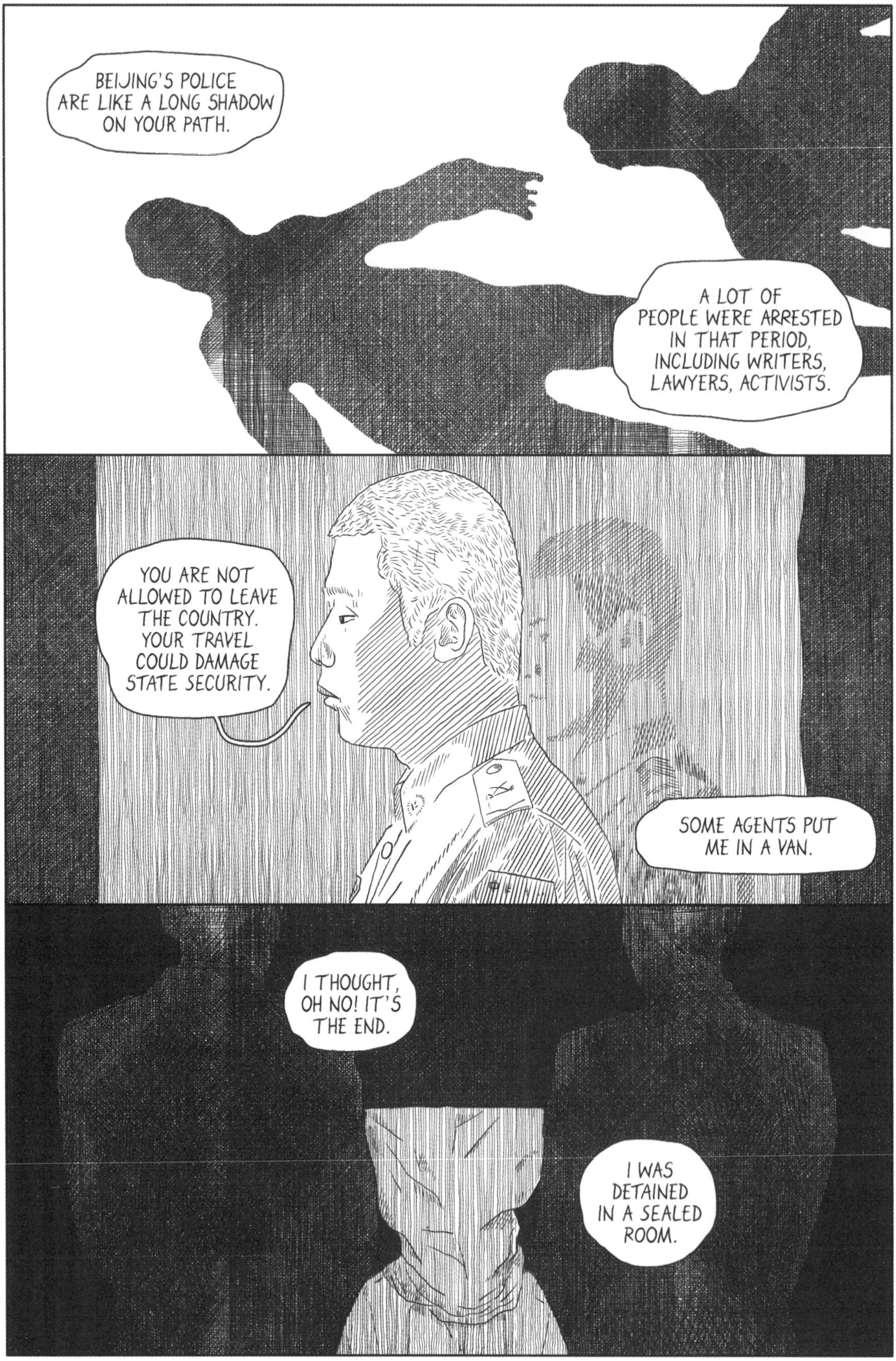
BEIJING'S POLICE ARE LIKE A LONG SHADOW ON YOUR PATH.
A LOT OF PEOPLE WERE ARRESTED IN THAT PERIOD, INCLUDING WRITERS, LAWYERS, ACTIVISTS.
YOU ARE NOT ALLOWED TO LEAVE THE COUNTRY. YOUR TRAVEL COULD DAMAGE STATE SECURITY.
SOME AGENTS PUT ME IN A VAN.
I THOUGHT, OH NO! IT'S THE END.
I WAS DETAINED IN A SEALED ROOM.

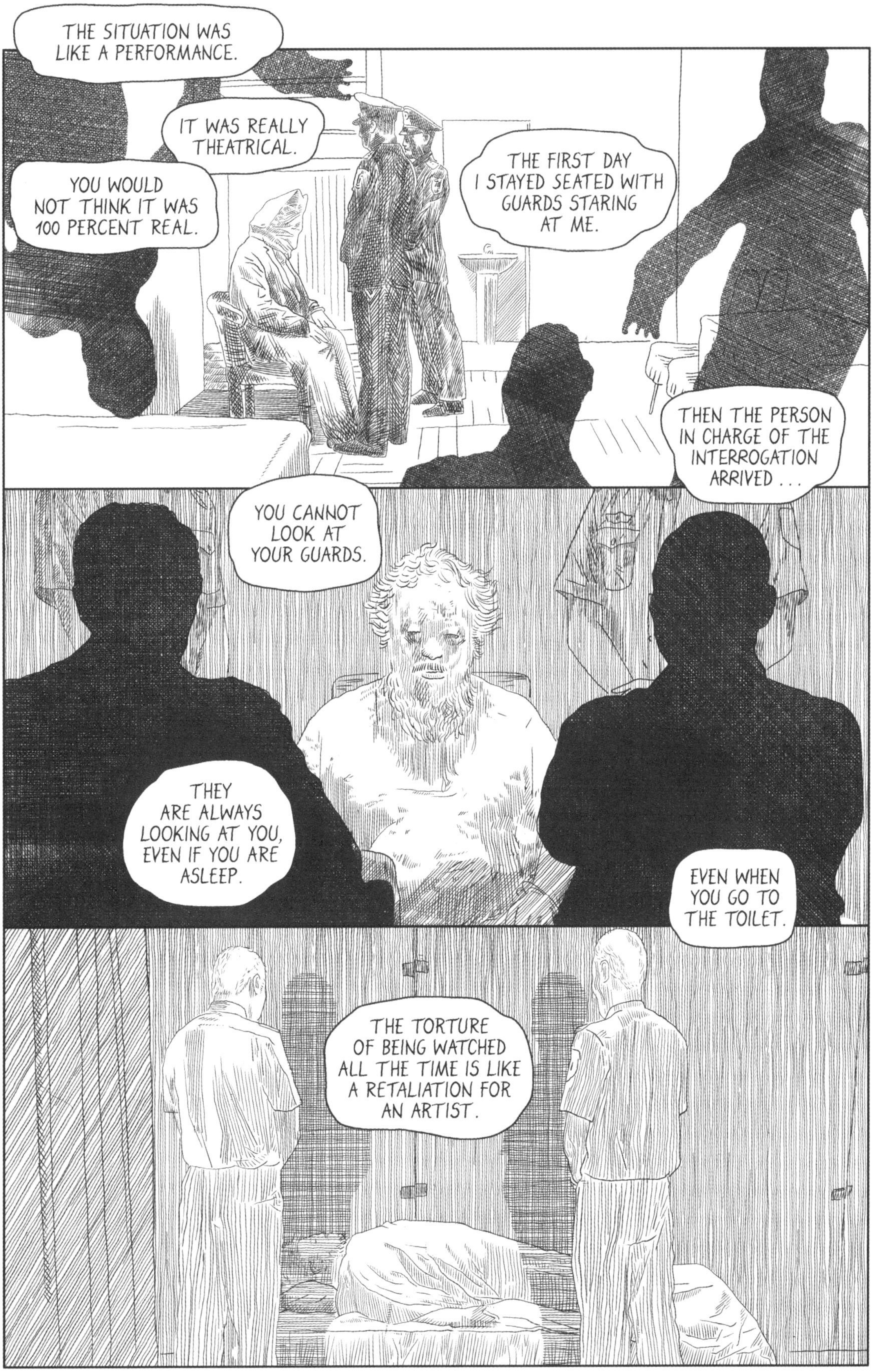
THE SITUATION WAS LIKE A PERFORMANCE.
IT WAS REALLY THEATRICAL.
YOU WOULD NOT THINK IT WAS 100 PERCENT REAL.
THE FIRST DAY I STAYED SEATED WITH GUARDS STARING AT ME.
THEN THE PERSON IN CHARGE OF THE INTERROGATION ARRIVED . . .
YOU CANNOT LOOK AT YOUR GUARDS.
THEY ARE ALWAYS LOOKING AT YOU, EVEN IF YOU ARE ASLEEP.
EVEN WHEN YOU GO TO THE TOILET.
THE TORTURE OF BEING WATCHED ALL THE TIME IS LIKE A RETALIATION FOR AN ARTIST.

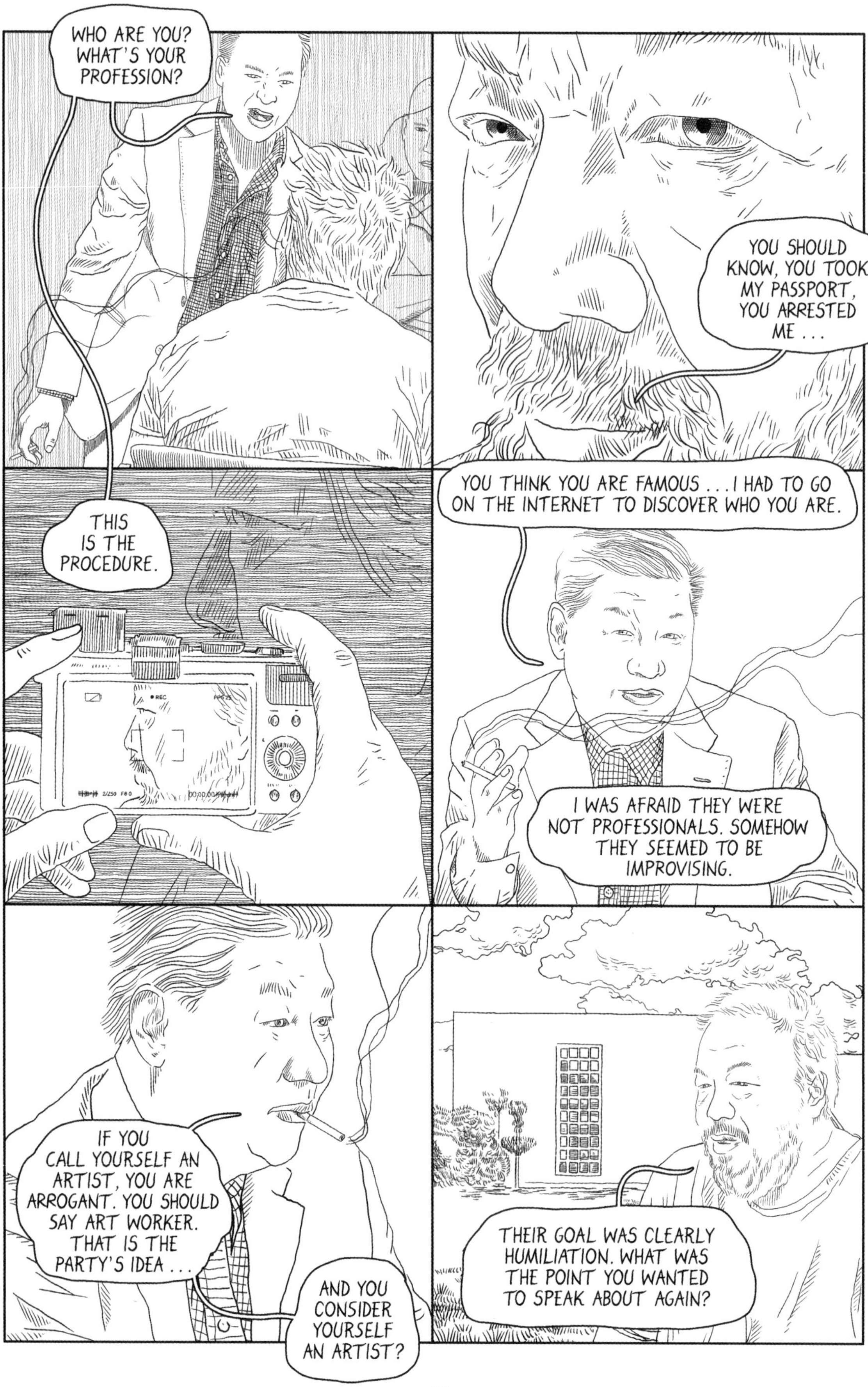
WHO ARE YOU? WHAT'S YOUR PROFESSION?
THIS IS THE PROCEDURE.
YOU SHOULD KNOW, YOU TOOK MY PASSPORT, YOU ARRESTED ME . . .
YOU THINK YOU ARE FAMOUS . . . I HAD TO GO ON THE INTERNET TO DISCOVER WHO YOU ARE.
I WAS AFRAID THEY WERE NOT PROFESSIONALS. SOMEHOW THEY SEEMED TO BE IMPROVISING.
IF YOU CALL YOURSELF AN ARTIST, YOU ARE ARROGANT. YOU SHOULD SAY ART WORKER. THAT IS THE PARTY'S IDEA . . .
AND YOU CONSIDER YOURSELF AN ARTIST?
THEIR GOAL WAS CLEARLY HUMILIATION. WHAT WAS THE POINT YOU WANTED TO SPEAK ABOUT AGAIN?

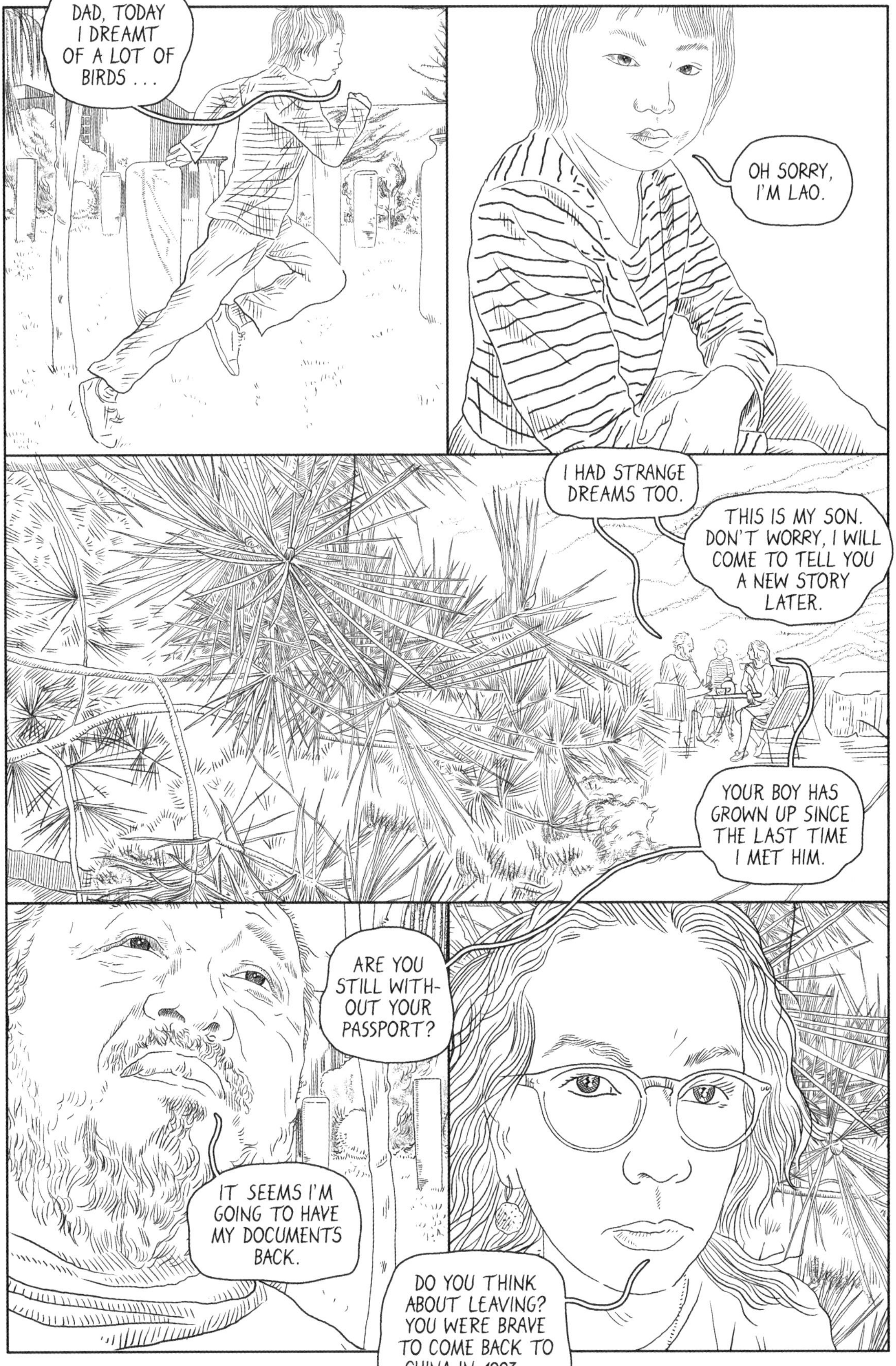
DAD, TODAY I DREAMT OF A LOT OF BIRDS . . .
OH SORRY, I'M LAO.
I HAD STRANGE DREAMS TOO.
THIS IS MY SON. DON'T WORRY, I WILL COME TO TELL YOU A NEW STORY LATER.
YOUR BOY HAS GROWN UP SINCE THE LAST TIME I MET HIM.
ARE YOU STILL WITH-OUT YOUR PASSPORT?
IT SEEMS I'M GOING TO HAVE MY DOCUMENTS BACK.
DO YOU THINK ABOUT LEAVING? YOU WERE BRAVE TO COME BACK TO CHINA IN 1993 . . .

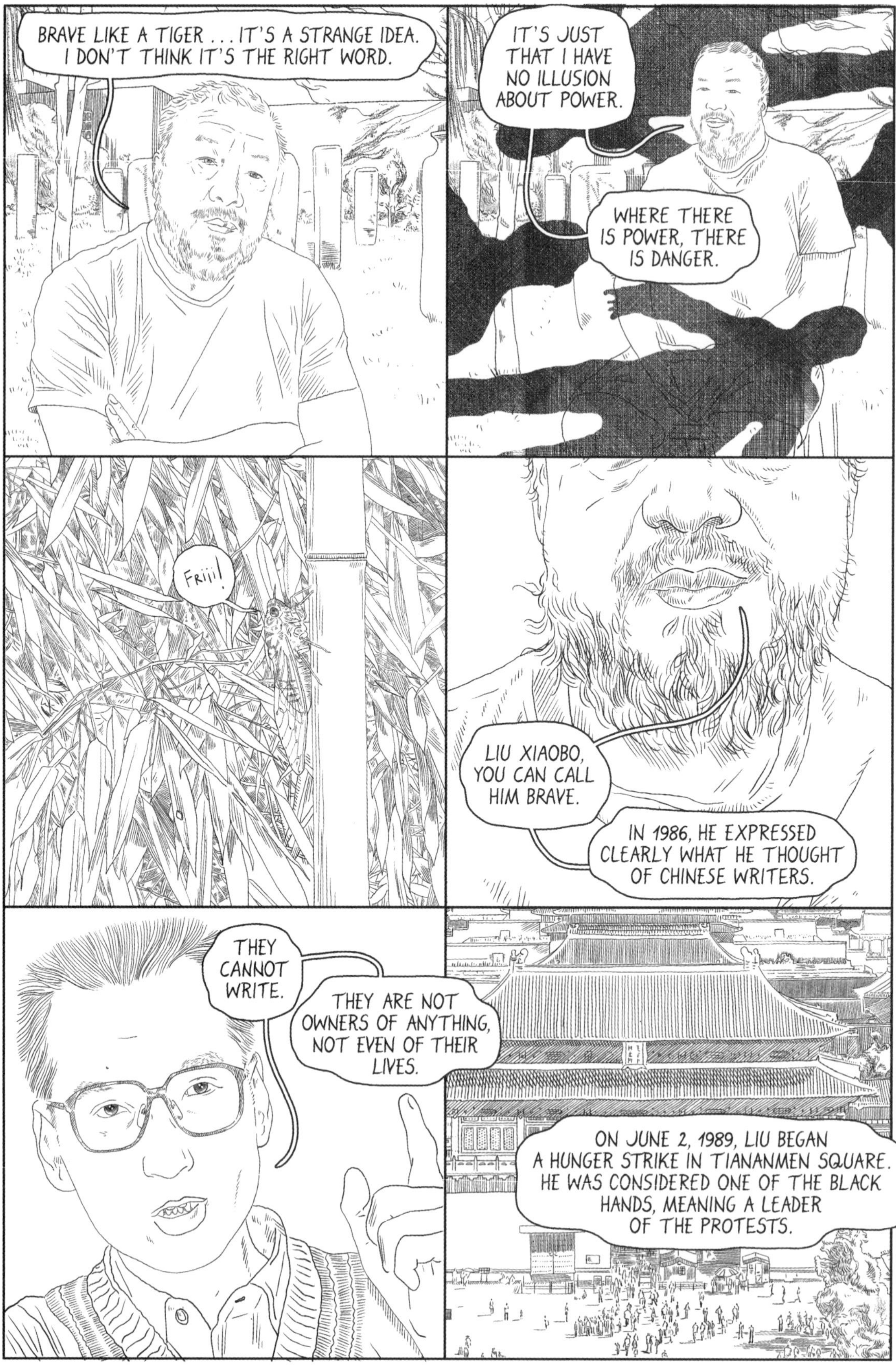
BRAVE LIKE A TIGER . . . IT'S A STRANGE IDEA. I DON'T THINK IT'S THE RIGHT WORD.
IT'S JUST THAT I HAVE NO ILLUSION ABOUT POWER.
WHERE THERE IS POWER, THERE IS DANGER.
Friiii!
LIU XIAOBO, YOU CAN CALL HIM BRAVE.
IN 1986, HE EXPRESSED CLEARLY WHAT HE THOUGHT OF CHINESE WRITERS.
THEY CANNOT WRITE.
THEY ARE NOT OWNERS OF ANYTHING, NOT EVEN OF THEIR LIVES.
ON JUNE 2, 1989, LIU BEGAN A HUNGER STRIKE IN TIANANMEN SQUARE. HE WAS CONSIDERED ONE OF THE BLACK HANDS, MEANING A LEADER OF THE PROTESTS.

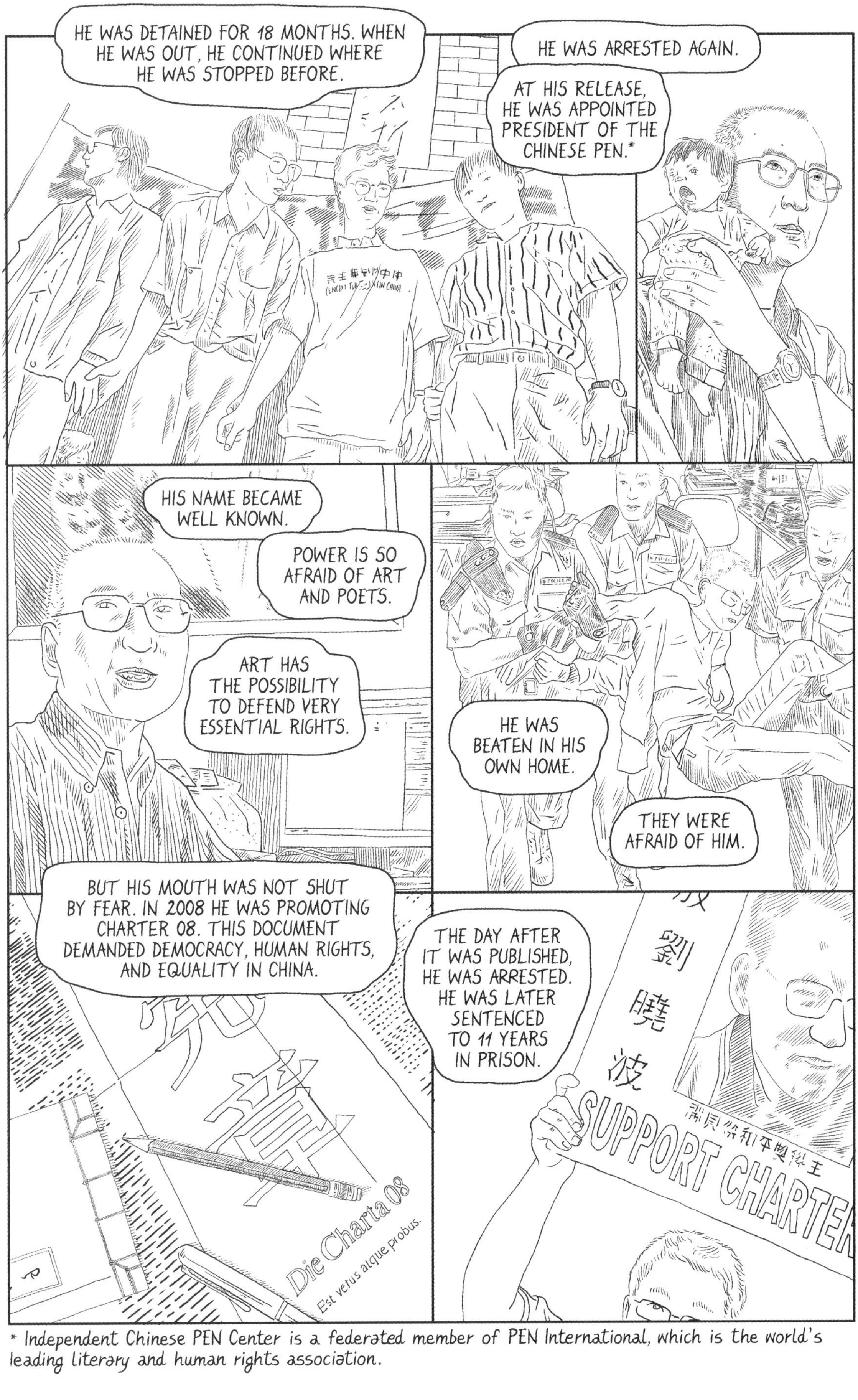
HE WAS DETAINED FOR 18 MONTHS. WHEN HE WAS OUT, HE CONTINUED WHERE HE WAS STOPPED BEFORE.
HE WAS ARRESTED AGAIN.
AT HIS RELEASE, HE WAS APPOINTED PRESIDENT OF THE CHINESE PEN.*
HIS NAME BECAME WELL KNOWN.
POWER IS SO AFRAID OF ART AND POETS.
ART HAS THE POSSIBILITY TO DEFEND VERY ESSENTIAL RIGHTS.
HE WAS BEATEN IN HIS OWN HOME.
THEY WERE AFRAID OF HIM.
BUT HIS MOUTH WAS NOT SHUT BY FEAR. IN 2008 HE WAS PROMOTING CHARTER 08. THIS DOCUMENT DEMANDED DEMOCRACY, HUMAN RIGHTS, AND EQUALITY IN CHINA.
Die Charta 08
Est verus atque probus.
THE DAY AFTER IT WAS PUBLISHED, HE WAS ARRESTED. HE WAS LATER SENTENCED TO 11 YEARS IN PRISON.
劉
曉
波
SUPPORT CHARTER

* Independent Chinese PEN Center is a federated member of PEN International, which is the world's leading literary and human rights association.

Stockholm, 2010

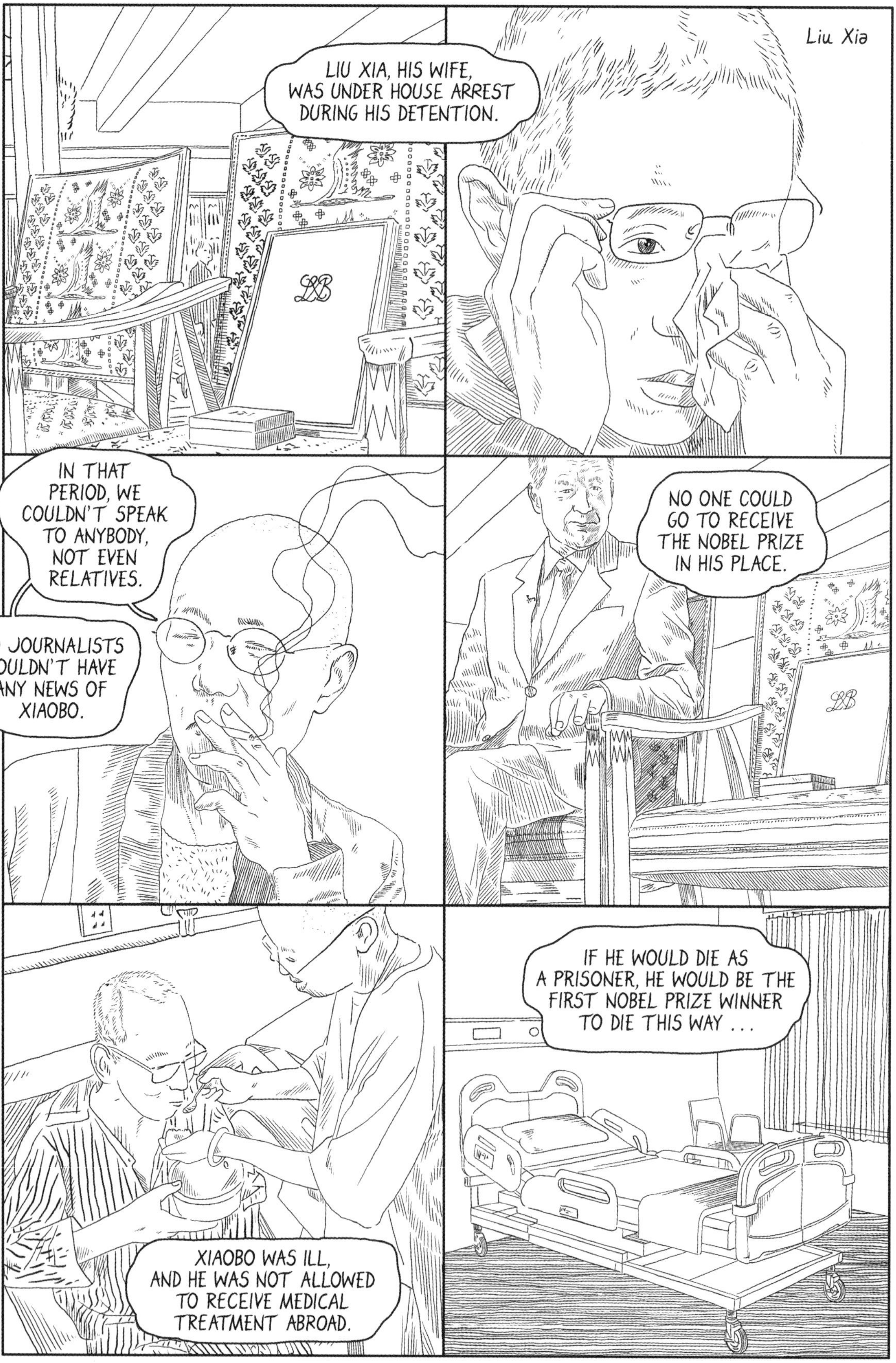
LIU XIA, HIS WIFE, WAS UNDER HOUSE ARREST DURING HIS DETENTION.
Liu Xia
IN THAT PERIOD, WE COULDN'T SPEAK TO ANYBODY, NOT EVEN RELATIVES.
SO JOURNALISTS COULDN'T HAVE ANY NEWS OF XIAOBO.
NO ONE COULD GO TO RECEIVE THE NOBEL PRIZE IN HIS PLACE.
XIAOBO WAS ILL, AND HE WAS NOT ALLOWED TO RECEIVE MEDICAL TREATMENT ABROAD.
IF HE WOULD DIE AS A PRISONER, HE WOULD BE THE FIRST NOBEL PRIZE WINNER TO DIE THIS WAY . . .

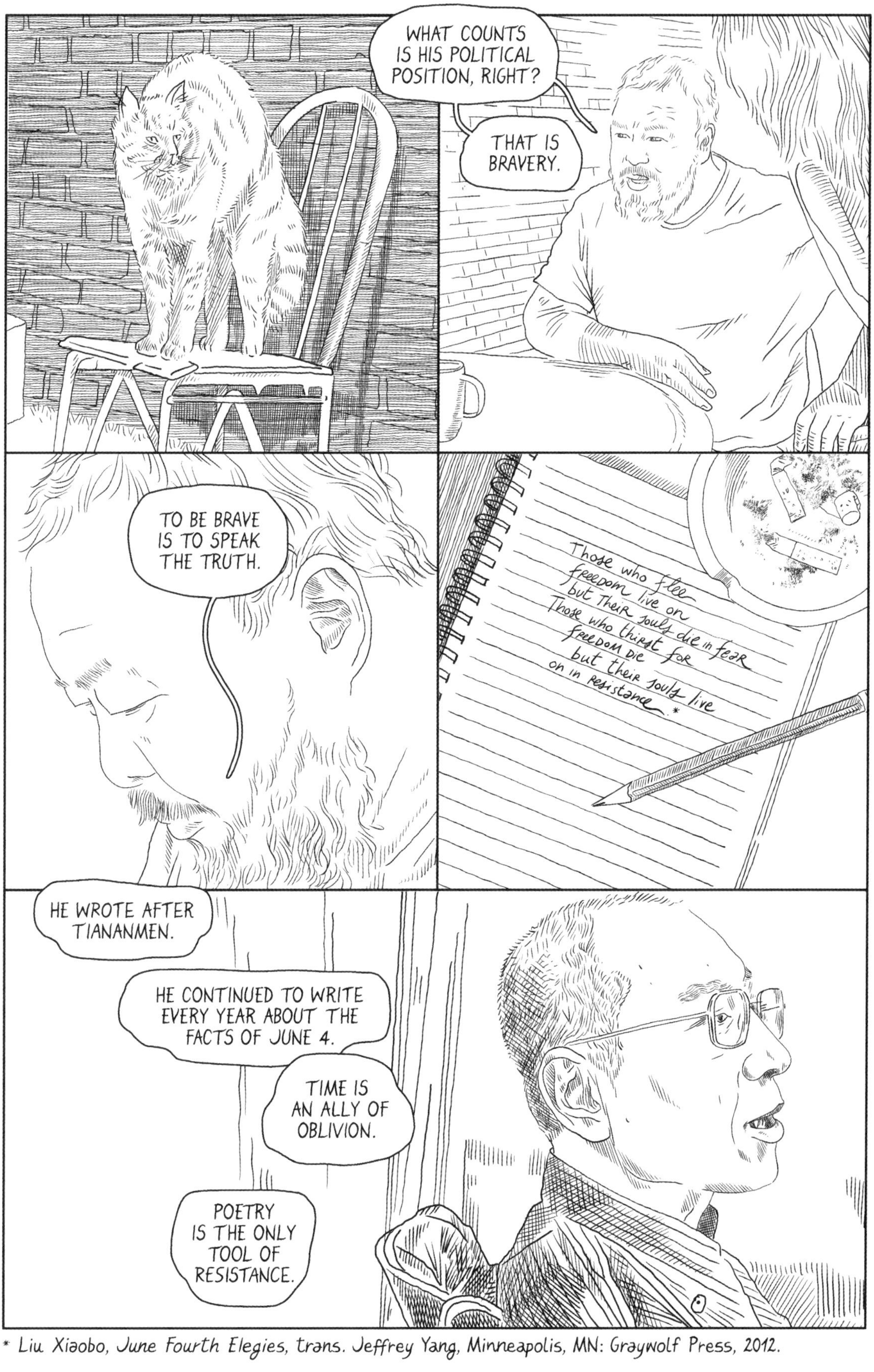
WHAT COUNTS IS HIS POLITICAL POSITION, RIGHT?
THAT IS BRAVERY.
TO BE BRAVE IS TO SPEAK THE TRUTH.
Those who flee freedom live on but their souls die in fear
Those who thirst for freedom die but their souls live on in resistance *
HE WROTE AFTER TIANANMEN.
HE CONTINUED TO WRITE EVERY YEAR ABOUT THE FACTS OF JUNE 4.
TIME IS AN ALLY OF OBLIVION.
POETRY IS THE ONLY TOOL OF RESISTANCE.

* Liu Xiaobo, *June Fourth Elegies*, trans. Jeffrey Yang, Minneapolis, MN: Graywolf Press, 2012.

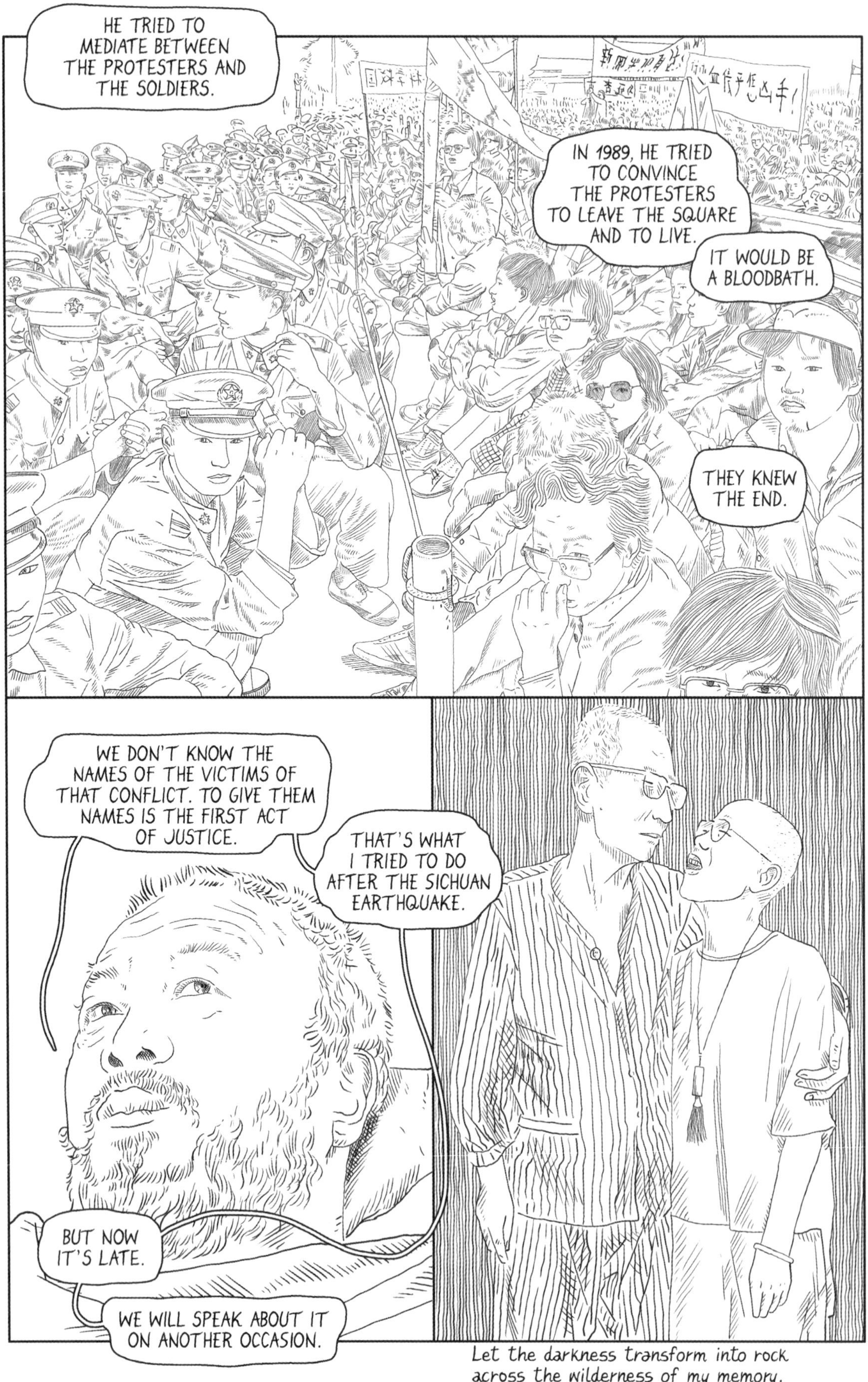
HE TRIED TO MEDIATE BETWEEN THE PROTESTERS AND THE SOLDIERS.
IN 1989, HE TRIED TO CONVINCE THE PROTESTERS TO LEAVE THE SQUARE AND TO LIVE.
IT WOULD BE A BLOODBATH.
THEY KNEW THE END.
WE DON'T KNOW THE NAMES OF THE VICTIMS OF THAT CONFLICT. TO GIVE THEM NAMES IS THE FIRST ACT OF JUSTICE.
THAT'S WHAT I TRIED TO DO AFTER THE SICHUAN EARTHQUAKE.
BUT NOW IT'S LATE.
WE WILL SPEAK ABOUT IT ON ANOTHER OCCASION.

Let the darkness transform into rock
across the wilderness of my memory.
(Liu Xiaobo, "Fifteen Years of Darkness," from June Fourth Elegies)

Chapter 4

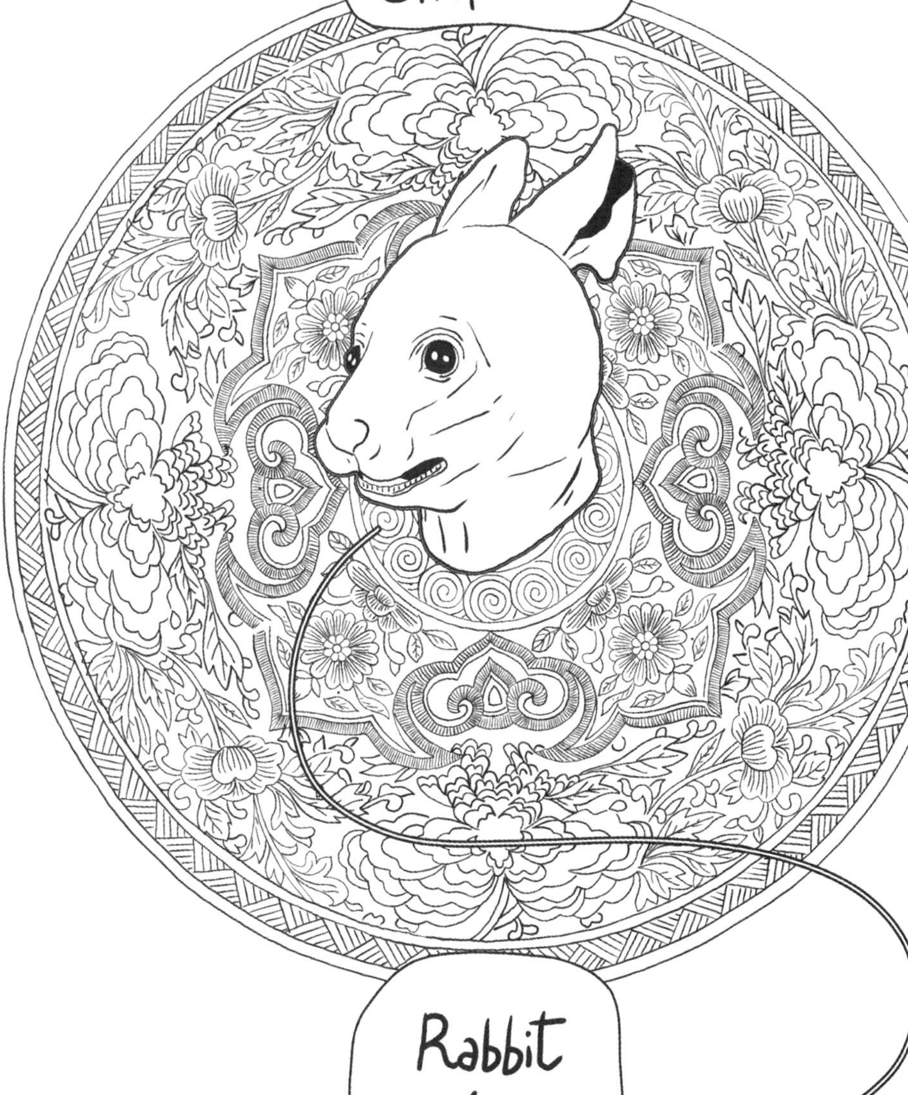

Rabbit 兔

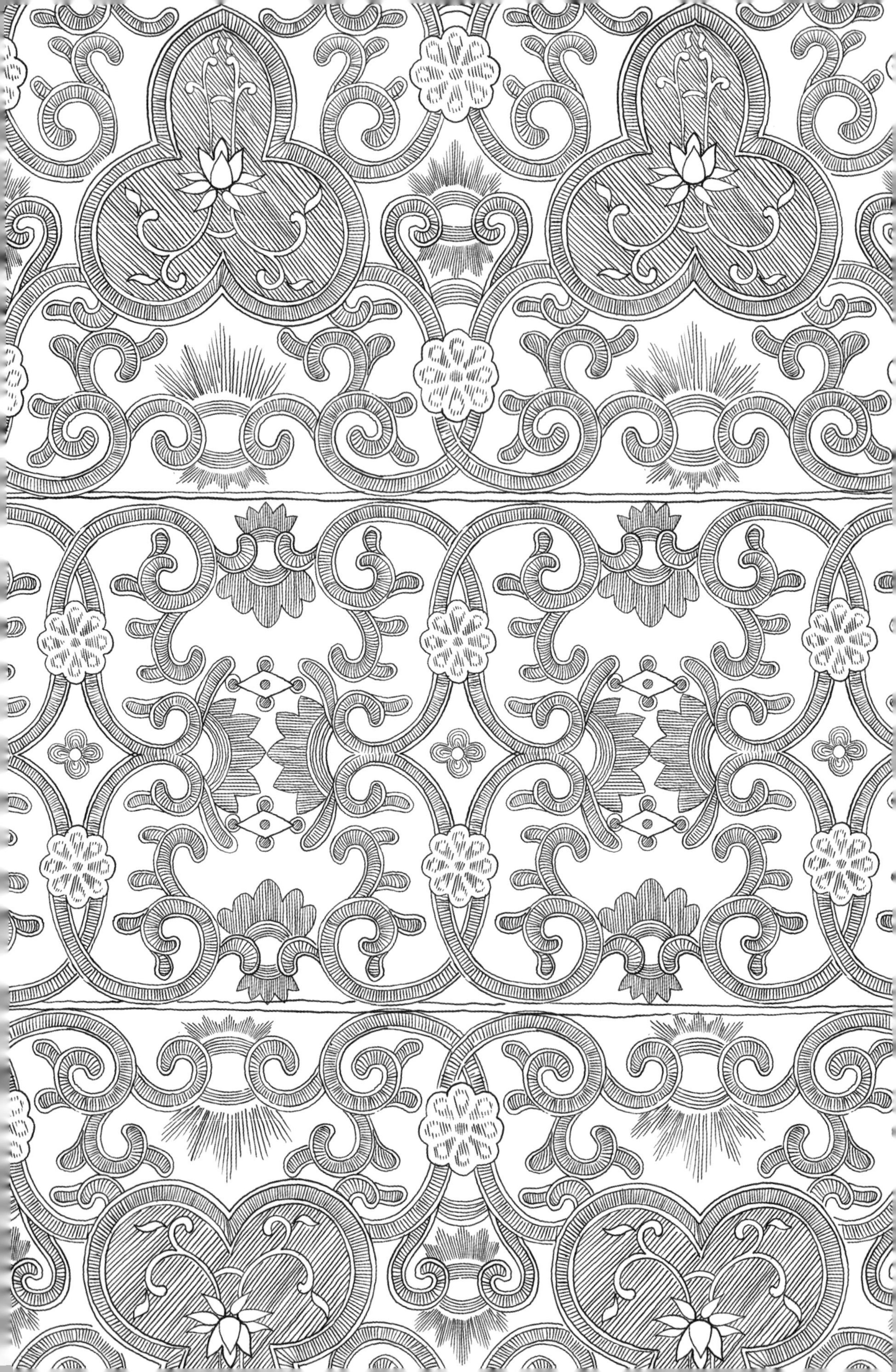

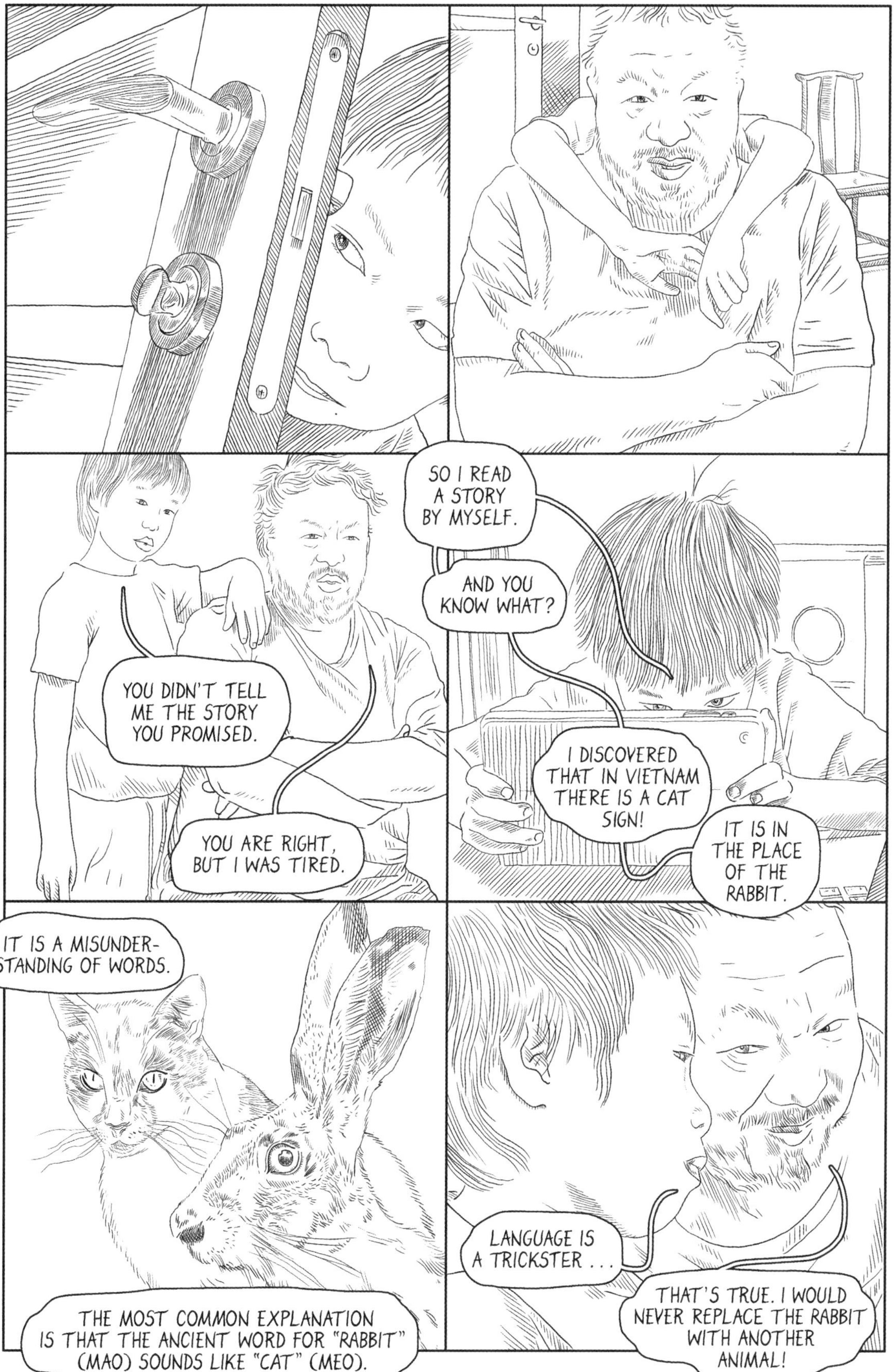

SO I READ A STORY BY MYSELF.
AND YOU KNOW WHAT?
YOU DIDN'T TELL ME THE STORY YOU PROMISED.
YOU ARE RIGHT, BUT I WAS TIRED.
I DISCOVERED THAT IN VIETNAM THERE IS A CAT SIGN!
IT IS IN THE PLACE OF THE RABBIT.
IT IS A MISUNDER-STANDING OF WORDS.
THE MOST COMMON EXPLANATION IS THAT THE ANCIENT WORD FOR "RABBIT" (MAO) SOUNDS LIKE "CAT" (MEO).
LANGUAGE IS A TRICKSTER . . .
THAT'S TRUE. I WOULD NEVER REPLACE THE RABBIT WITH ANOTHER ANIMAL!

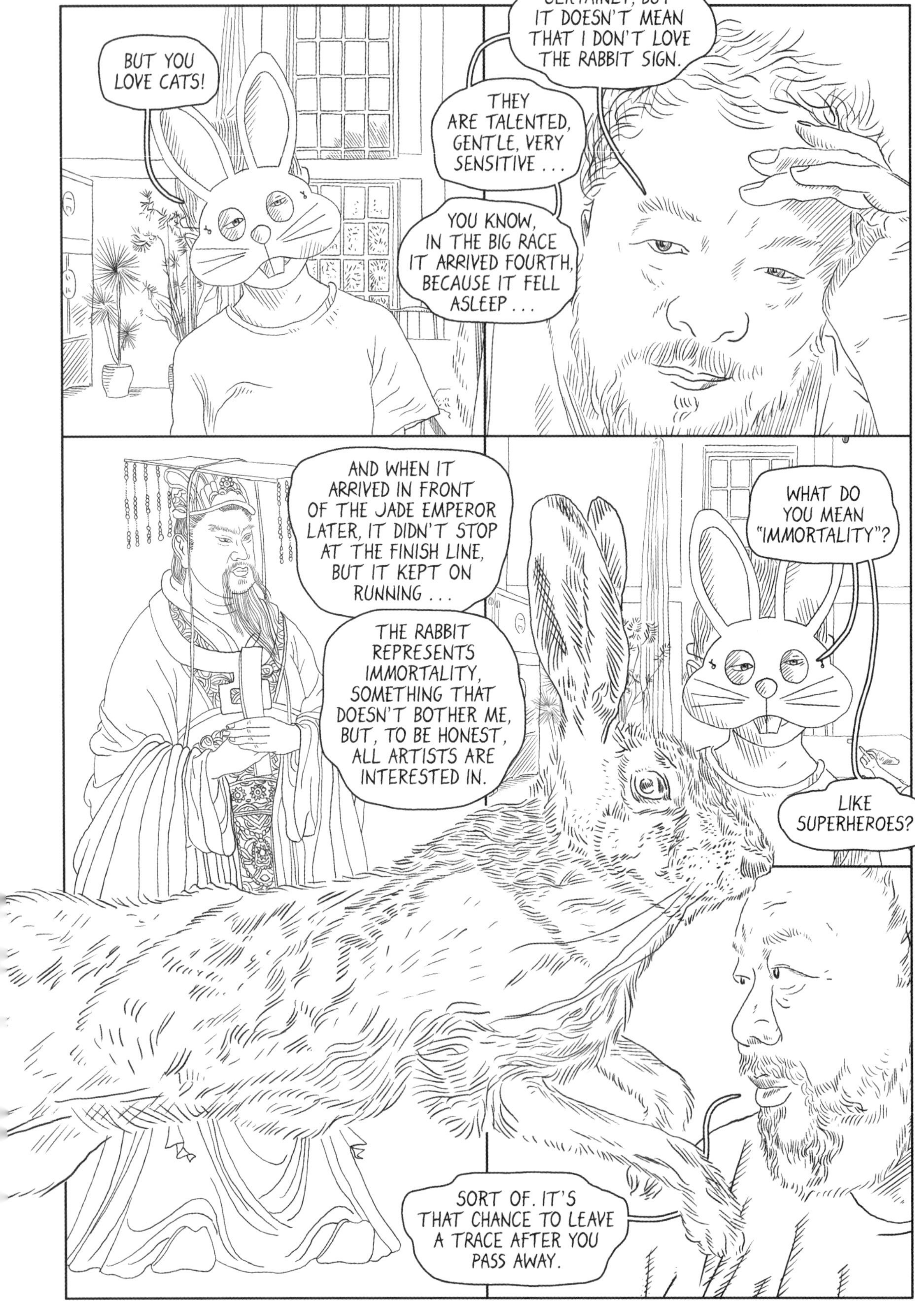
BUT YOU LOVE CATS!
CERTAINLY, BUT IT DOESN'T MEAN THAT I DON'T LOVE THE RABBIT SIGN.
THEY ARE TALENTED, GENTLE, VERY SENSITIVE . . .
YOU KNOW, IN THE BIG RACE IT ARRIVED FOURTH, BECAUSE IT FELL ASLEEP . . .
AND WHEN IT ARRIVED IN FRONT OF THE JADE EMPEROR LATER, IT DIDN'T STOP AT THE FINISH LINE, BUT IT KEPT ON RUNNING . . .
THE RABBIT REPRESENTS IMMORTALITY, SOMETHING THAT DOESN'T BOTHER ME, BUT, TO BE HONEST, ALL ARTISTS ARE INTERESTED IN.
WHAT DO YOU MEAN "IMMORTALITY"?
LIKE SUPERHEROES?
SORT OF. IT'S THAT CHANCE TO LEAVE A TRACE AFTER YOU PASS AWAY.

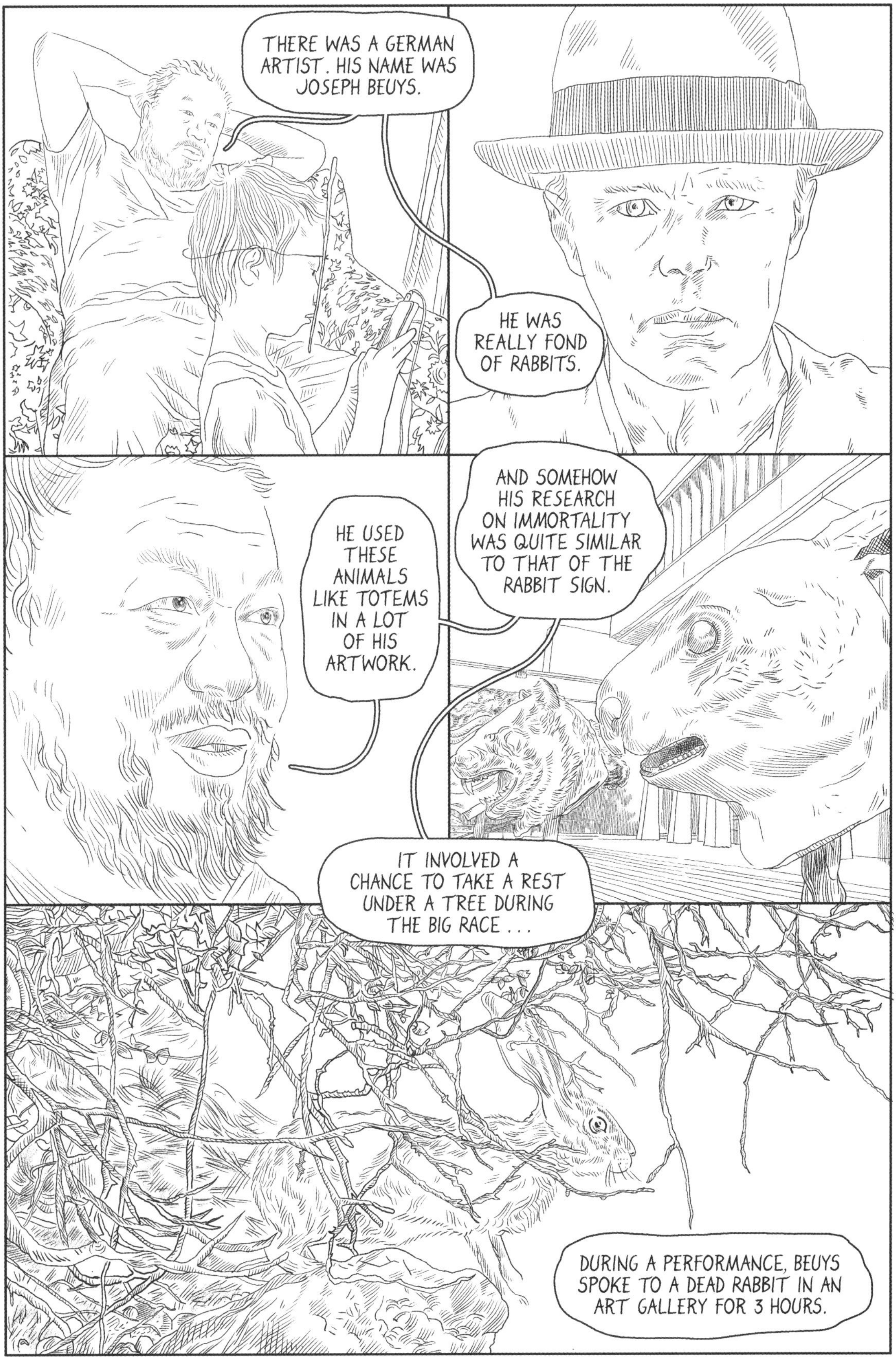
THERE WAS A GERMAN ARTIST. HIS NAME WAS JOSEPH BEUYS.
HE WAS REALLY FOND OF RABBITS.
HE USED THESE ANIMALS LIKE TOTEMS IN A LOT OF HIS ARTWORK.
AND SOMEHOW HIS RESEARCH ON IMMORTALITY WAS QUITE SIMILAR TO THAT OF THE RABBIT SIGN.
IT INVOLVED A CHANCE TO TAKE A REST UNDER A TREE DURING THE BIG RACE . . .
DURING A PERFORMANCE, BEUYS SPOKE TO A DEAD RABBIT IN AN ART GALLERY FOR 3 HOURS.

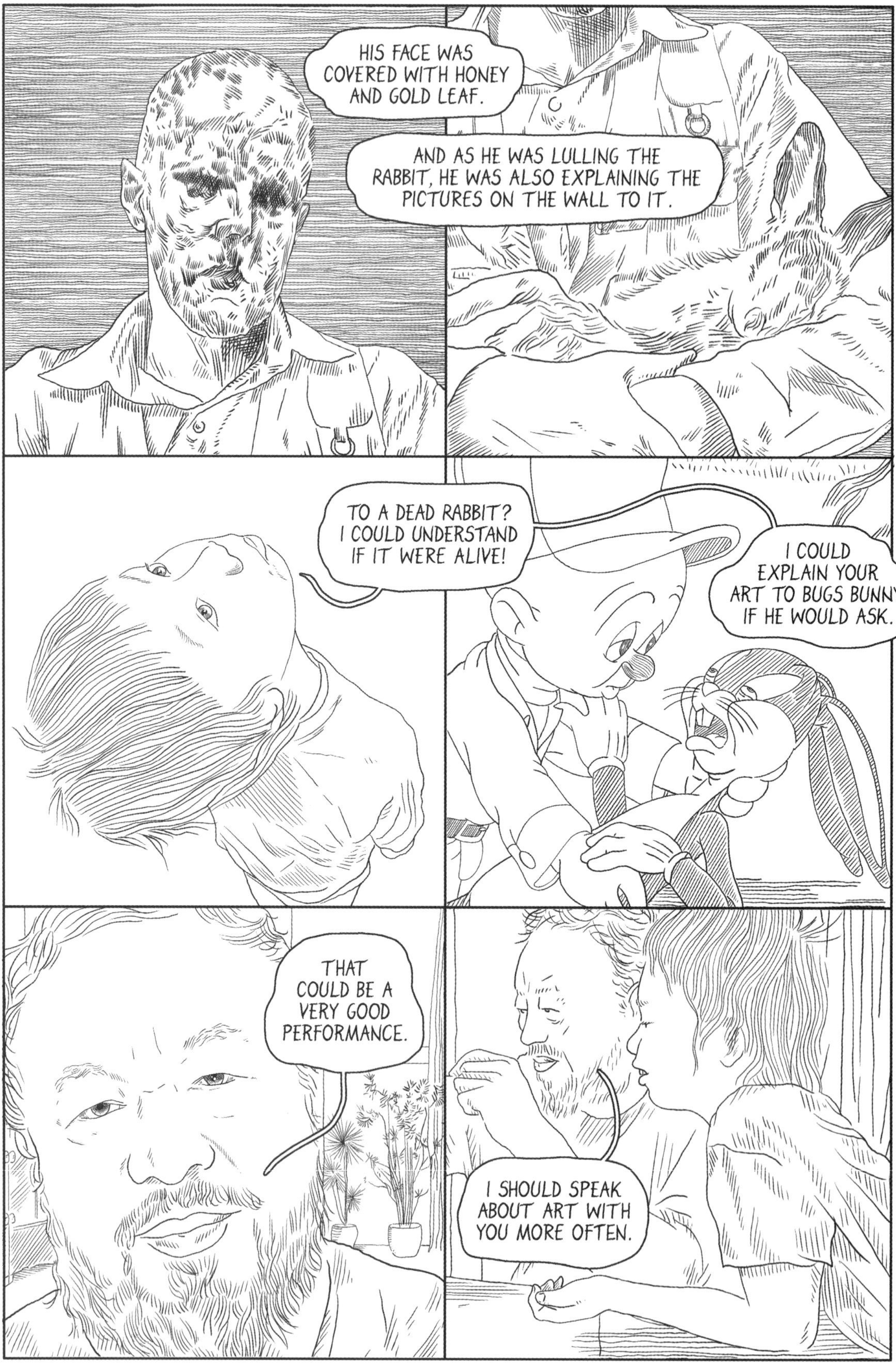
HIS FACE WAS COVERED WITH HONEY AND GOLD LEAF.
AND AS HE WAS LULLING THE RABBIT, HE WAS ALSO EXPLAINING THE PICTURES ON THE WALL TO IT.
TO A DEAD RABBIT? I COULD UNDERSTAND IF IT WERE ALIVE!
I COULD EXPLAIN YOUR ART TO BUGS BUNNY, IF HE WOULD ASK.
THAT COULD BE A VERY GOOD PERFORMANCE.
I SHOULD SPEAK ABOUT ART WITH YOU MORE OFTEN.

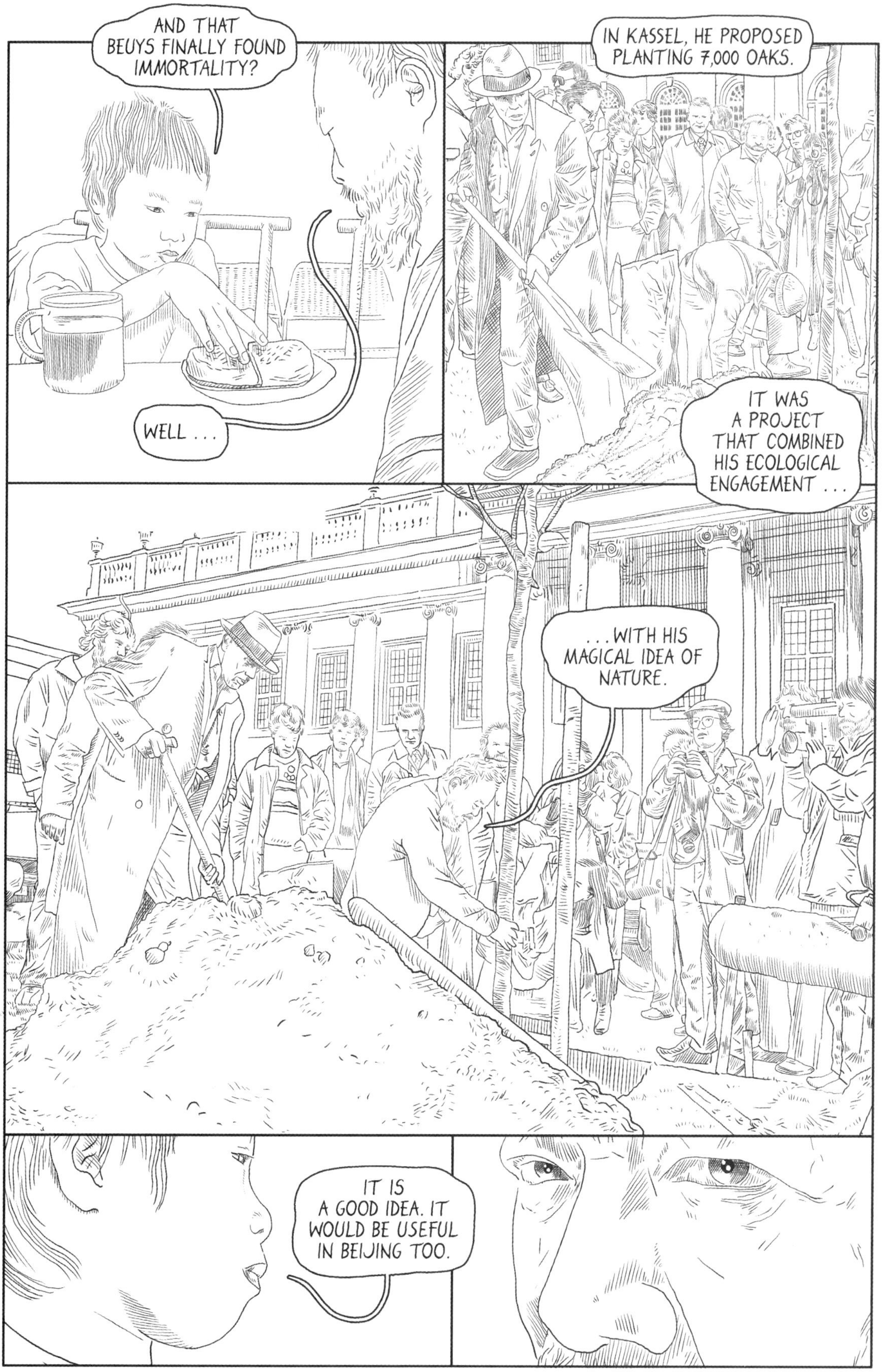
AND THAT BEUYS FINALLY FOUND IMMORTALITY?
WELL . . .
IN KASSEL, HE PROPOSED PLANTING 7,000 OAKS.
IT WAS A PROJECT THAT COMBINED HIS ECOLOGICAL ENGAGEMENT . . .
. . . WITH HIS MAGICAL IDEA OF NATURE.
IT IS A GOOD IDEA. IT WOULD BE USEFUL IN BEIJING TOO.

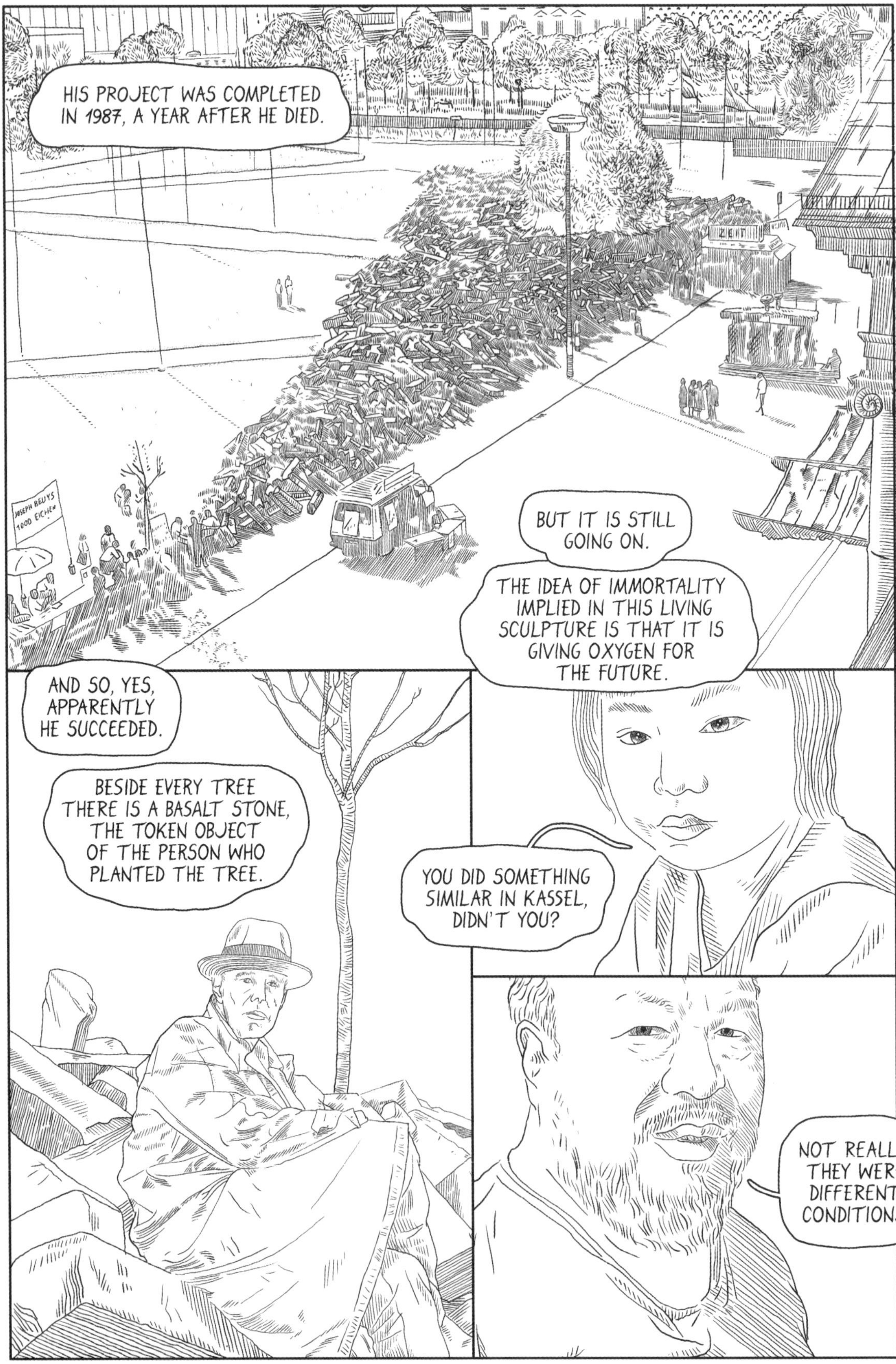
HIS PROJECT WAS COMPLETED IN 1987, A YEAR AFTER HE DIED.
JOSEPH BEUYS 7000 EICHEN
ZEIT
BUT IT IS STILL GOING ON.
THE IDEA OF IMMORTALITY IMPLIED IN THIS LIVING SCULPTURE IS THAT IT IS GIVING OXYGEN FOR THE FUTURE.
AND SO, YES, APPARENTLY HE SUCCEEDED.
BESIDE EVERY TREE THERE IS A BASALT STONE, THE TOKEN OBJECT OF THE PERSON WHO PLANTED THE TREE.
YOU DID SOMETHING SIMILAR IN KASSEL, DIDN'T YOU?
NOT REALLY. THEY WERE DIFFERENT CONDITIONS.

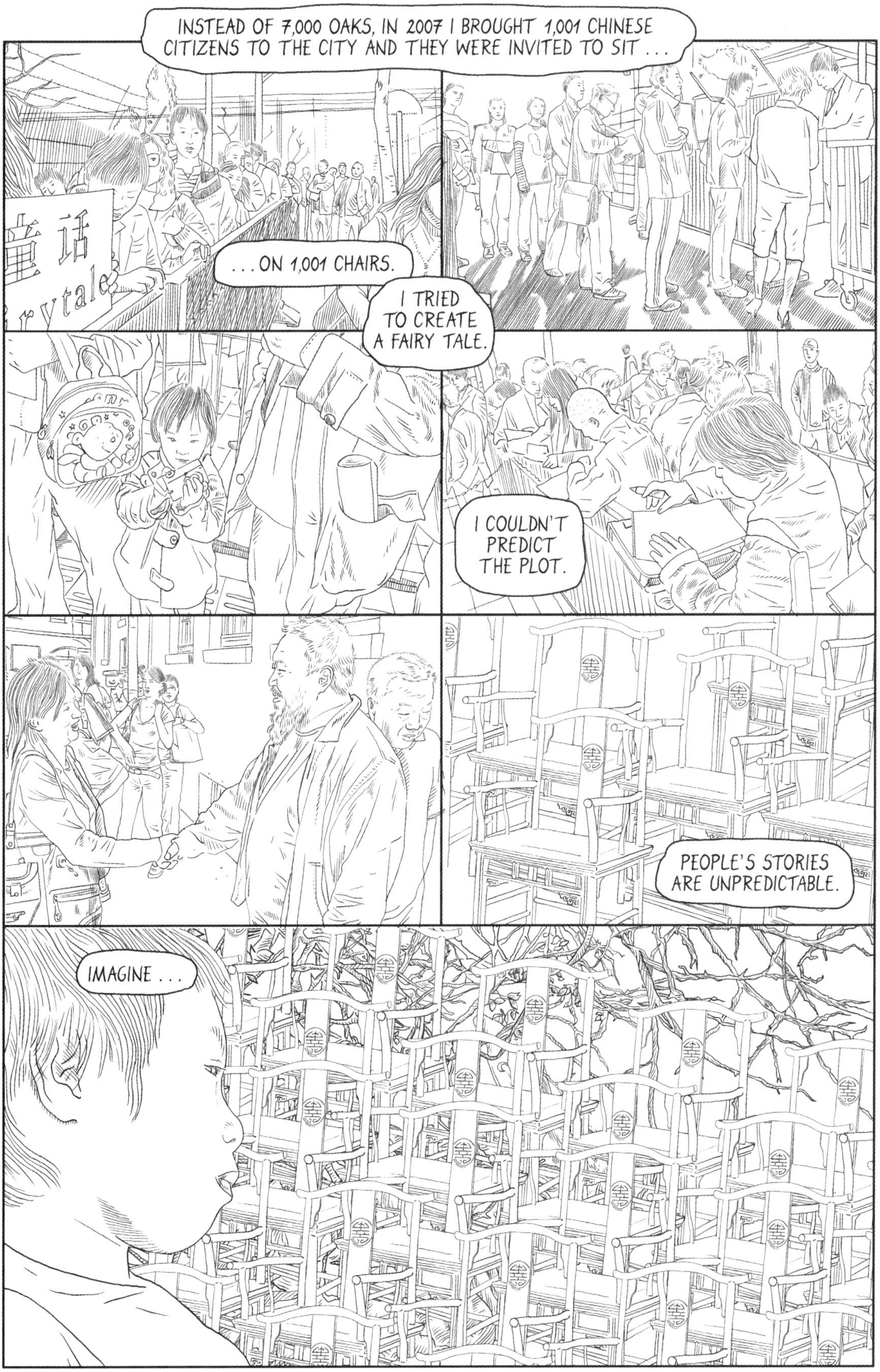
INSTEAD OF 7,000 OAKS, IN 2007 I BROUGHT 1,001 CHINESE CITIZENS TO THE CITY AND THEY WERE INVITED TO SIT . . .
. . . ON 1,001 CHAIRS.
I TRIED TO CREATE A FAIRY TALE.
I COULDN'T PREDICT THE PLOT.
PEOPLE'S STORIES ARE UNPREDICTABLE.
IMAGINE . . .

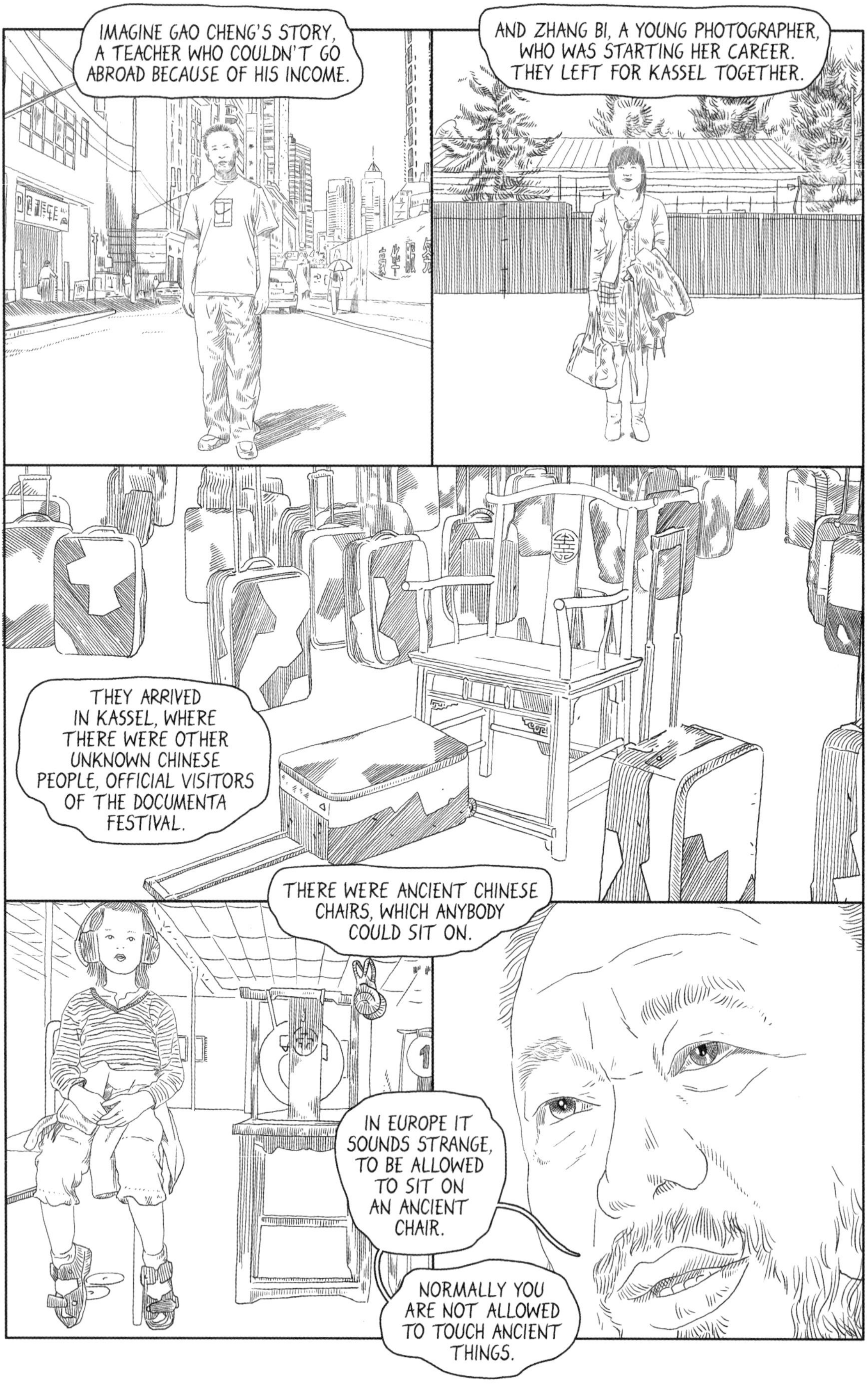
IMAGINE GAO CHENG'S STORY, A TEACHER WHO COULDN'T GO ABROAD BECAUSE OF HIS INCOME.
AND ZHANG BI, A YOUNG PHOTOGRAPHER, WHO WAS STARTING HER CAREER. THEY LEFT FOR KASSEL TOGETHER.
THEY ARRIVED IN KASSEL, WHERE THERE WERE OTHER UNKNOWN CHINESE PEOPLE, OFFICIAL VISITORS OF THE DOCUMENTA FESTIVAL.
THERE WERE ANCIENT CHINESE CHAIRS, WHICH ANYBODY COULD SIT ON.
IN EUROPE IT SOUNDS STRANGE, TO BE ALLOWED TO SIT ON AN ANCIENT CHAIR.
NORMALLY YOU ARE NOT ALLOWED TO TOUCH ANCIENT THINGS.

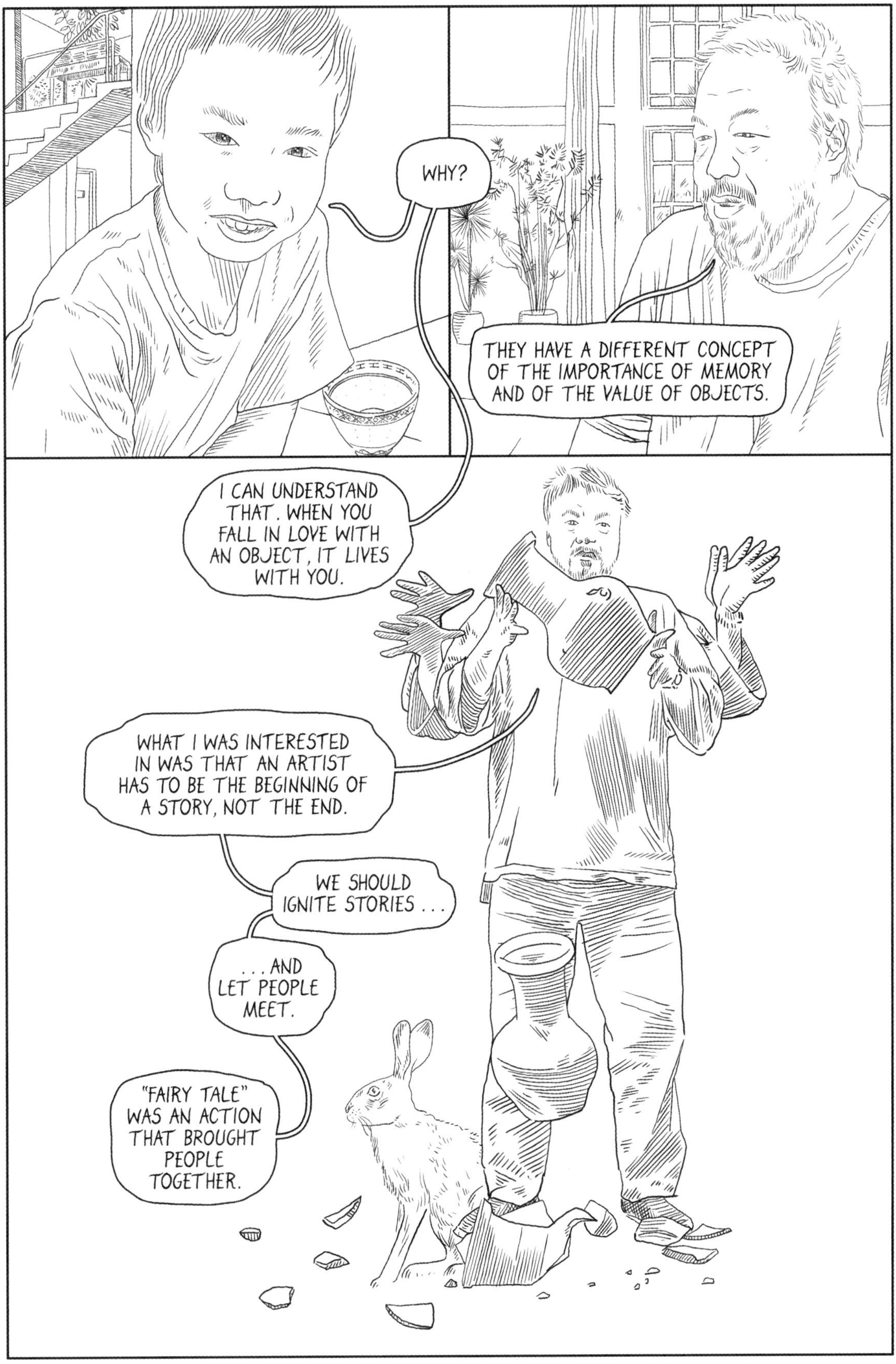
WHY?
THEY HAVE A DIFFERENT CONCEPT OF THE IMPORTANCE OF MEMORY AND OF THE VALUE OF OBJECTS.
I CAN UNDERSTAND THAT. WHEN YOU FALL IN LOVE WITH AN OBJECT, IT LIVES WITH YOU.
WHAT I WAS INTERESTED IN WAS THAT AN ARTIST HAS TO BE THE BEGINNING OF A STORY, NOT THE END.
WE SHOULD IGNITE STORIES . . .
. . . AND LET PEOPLE MEET.
"FAIRY TALE" WAS AN ACTION THAT BROUGHT PEOPLE TOGETHER.

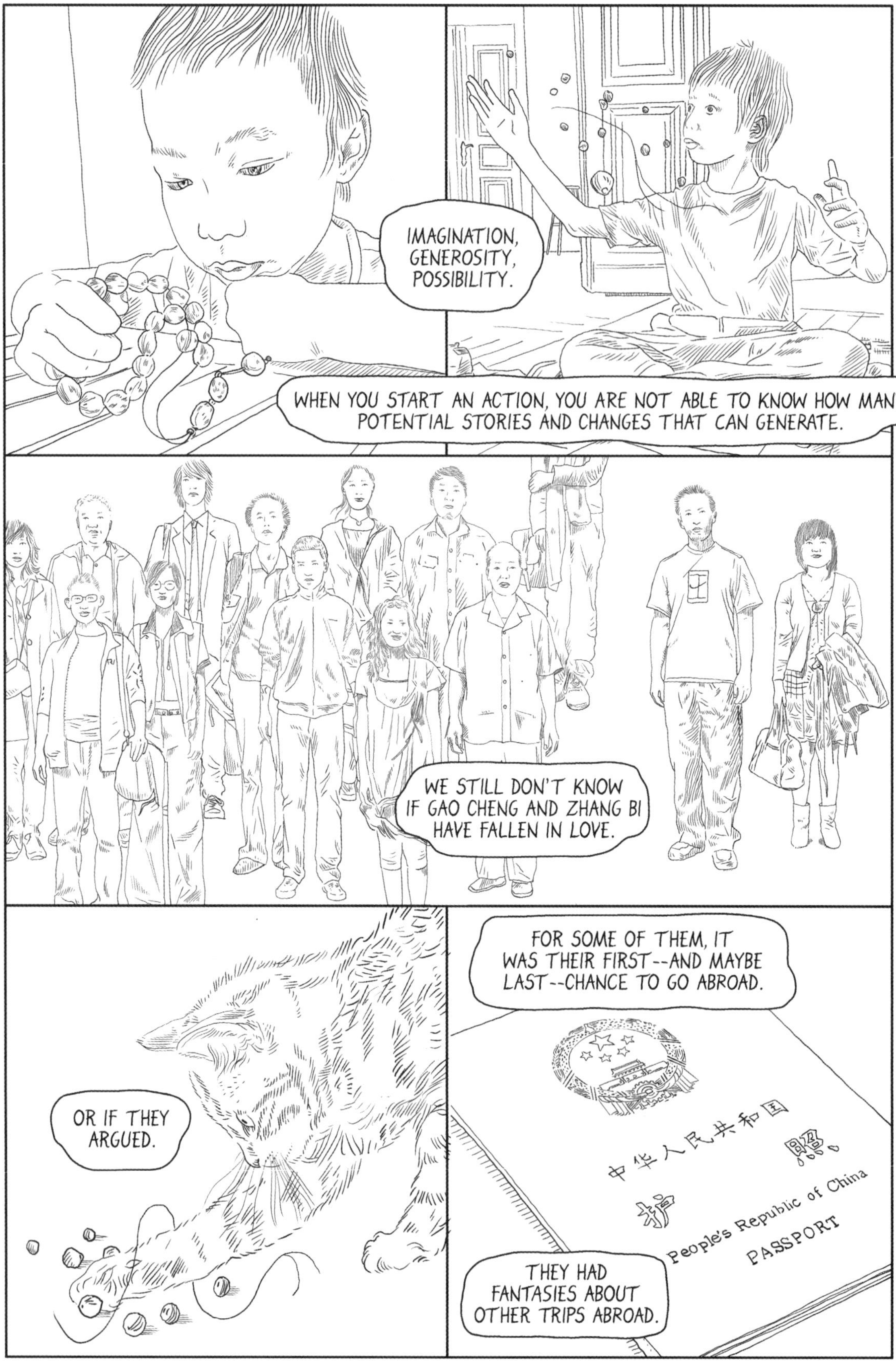
IMAGINATION, GENEROSITY, POSSIBILITY.
WHEN YOU START AN ACTION, YOU ARE NOT ABLE TO KNOW HOW MANY POTENTIAL STORIES AND CHANGES THAT CAN GENERATE.
WE STILL DON'T KNOW IF GAO CHENG AND ZHANG BI HAVE FALLEN IN LOVE.
OR IF THEY ARGUED.
FOR SOME OF THEM, IT WAS THEIR FIRST--AND MAYBE LAST--CHANCE TO GO ABROAD.
中华人民共和国
护 照
People's Republic of China
PASSPORT
THEY HAD FANTASIES ABOUT OTHER TRIPS ABROAD.

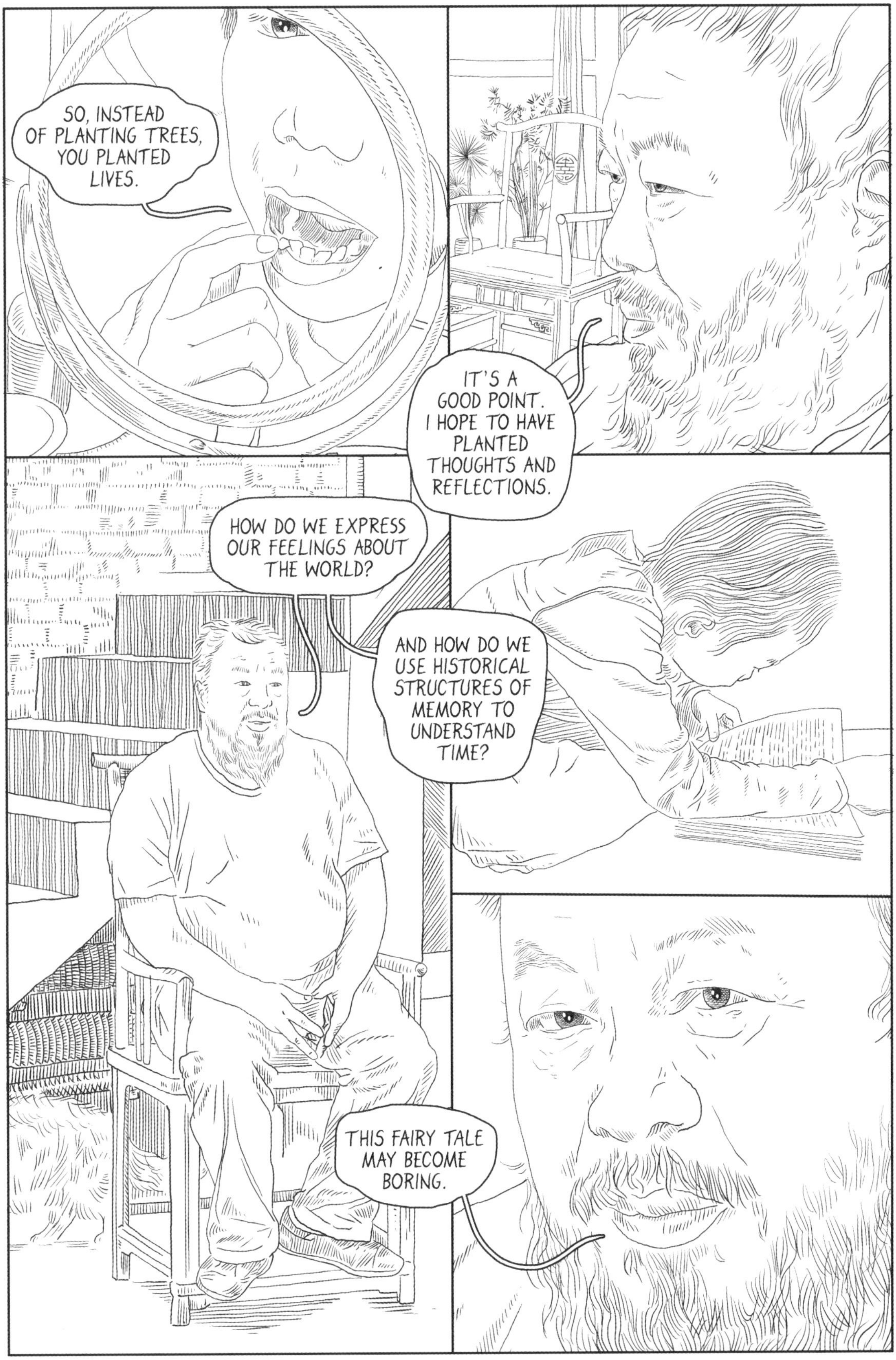
SO, INSTEAD OF PLANTING TREES, YOU PLANTED LIVES.
IT'S A GOOD POINT. I HOPE TO HAVE PLANTED THOUGHTS AND REFLECTIONS.
HOW DO WE EXPRESS OUR FEELINGS ABOUT THE WORLD?
AND HOW DO WE USE HISTORICAL STRUCTURES OF MEMORY TO UNDERSTAND TIME?
THIS FAIRY TALE MAY BECOME BORING.

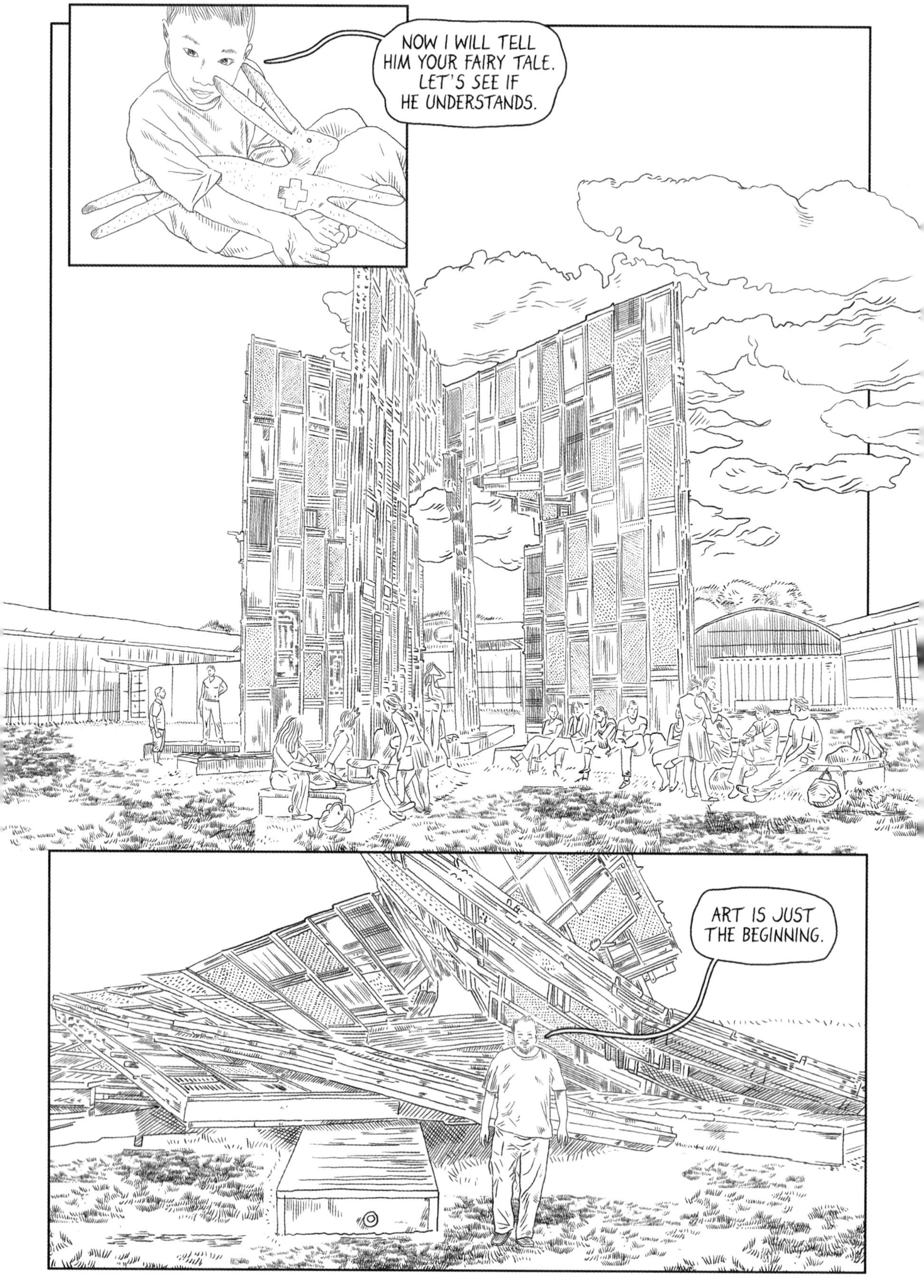
NOW I WILL TELL HIM YOUR FAIRY TALE. LET'S SEE IF HE UNDERSTANDS.
ART IS JUST THE BEGINNING.

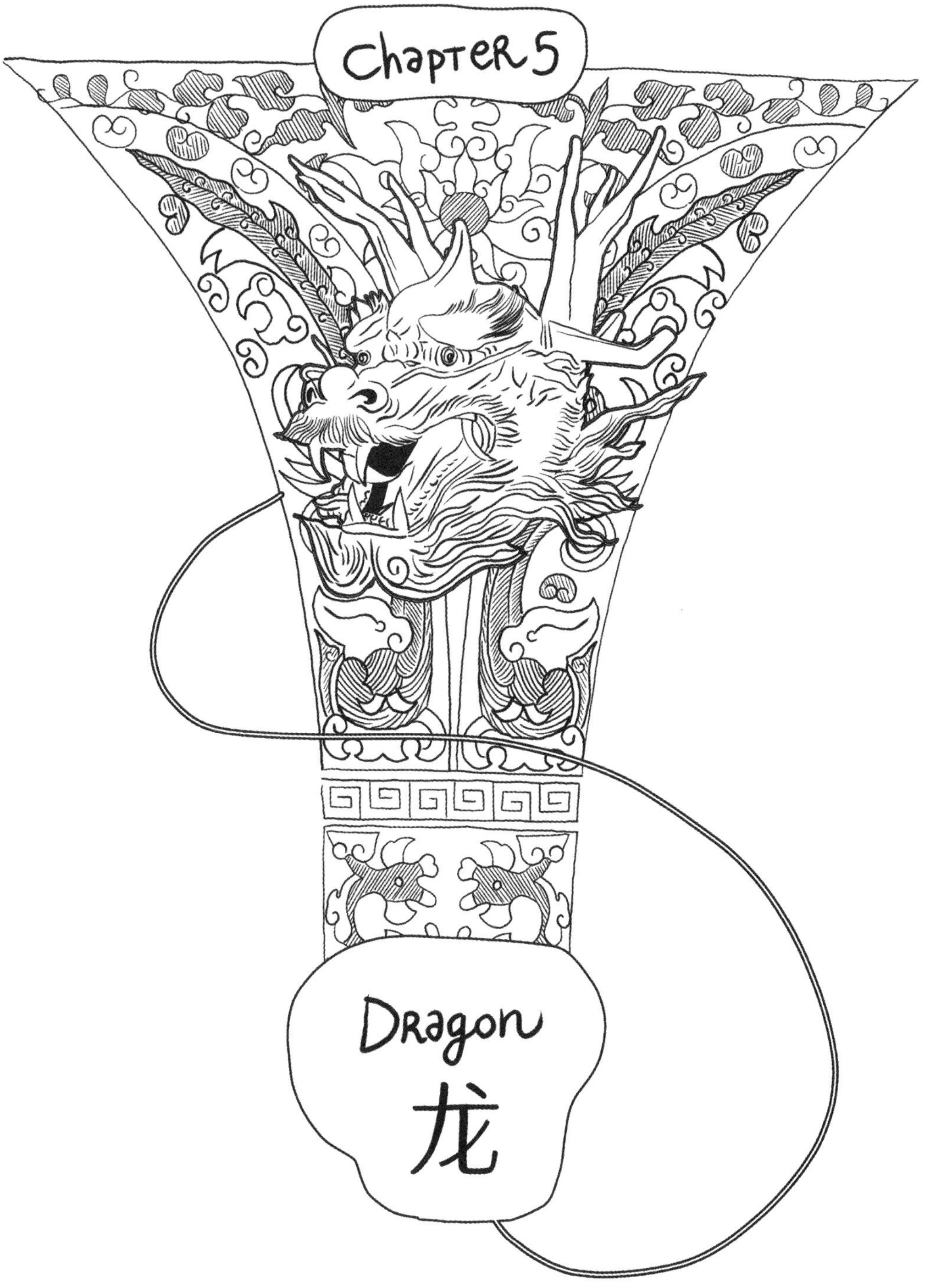
Chapter 5
Dragon
龙

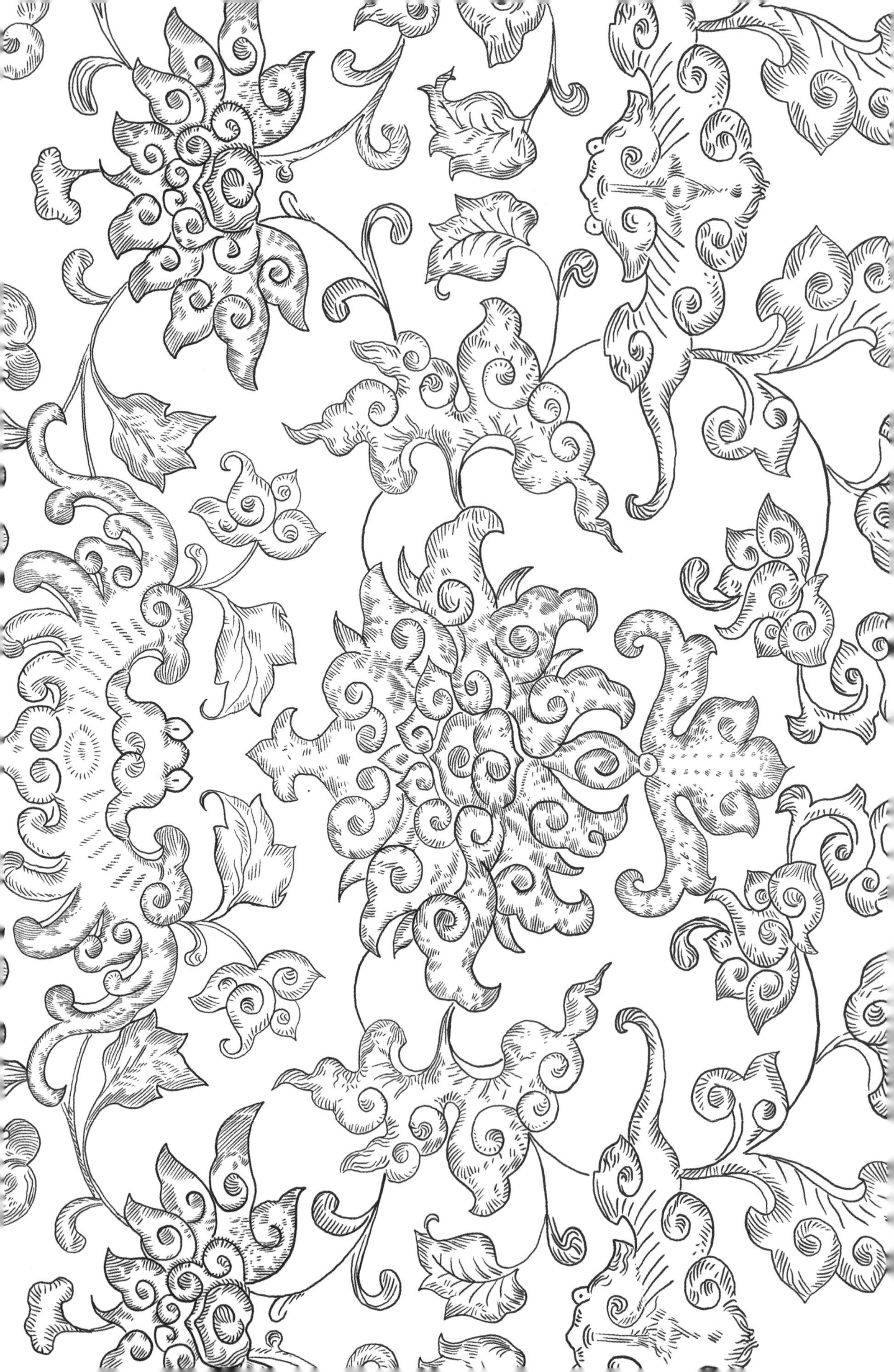

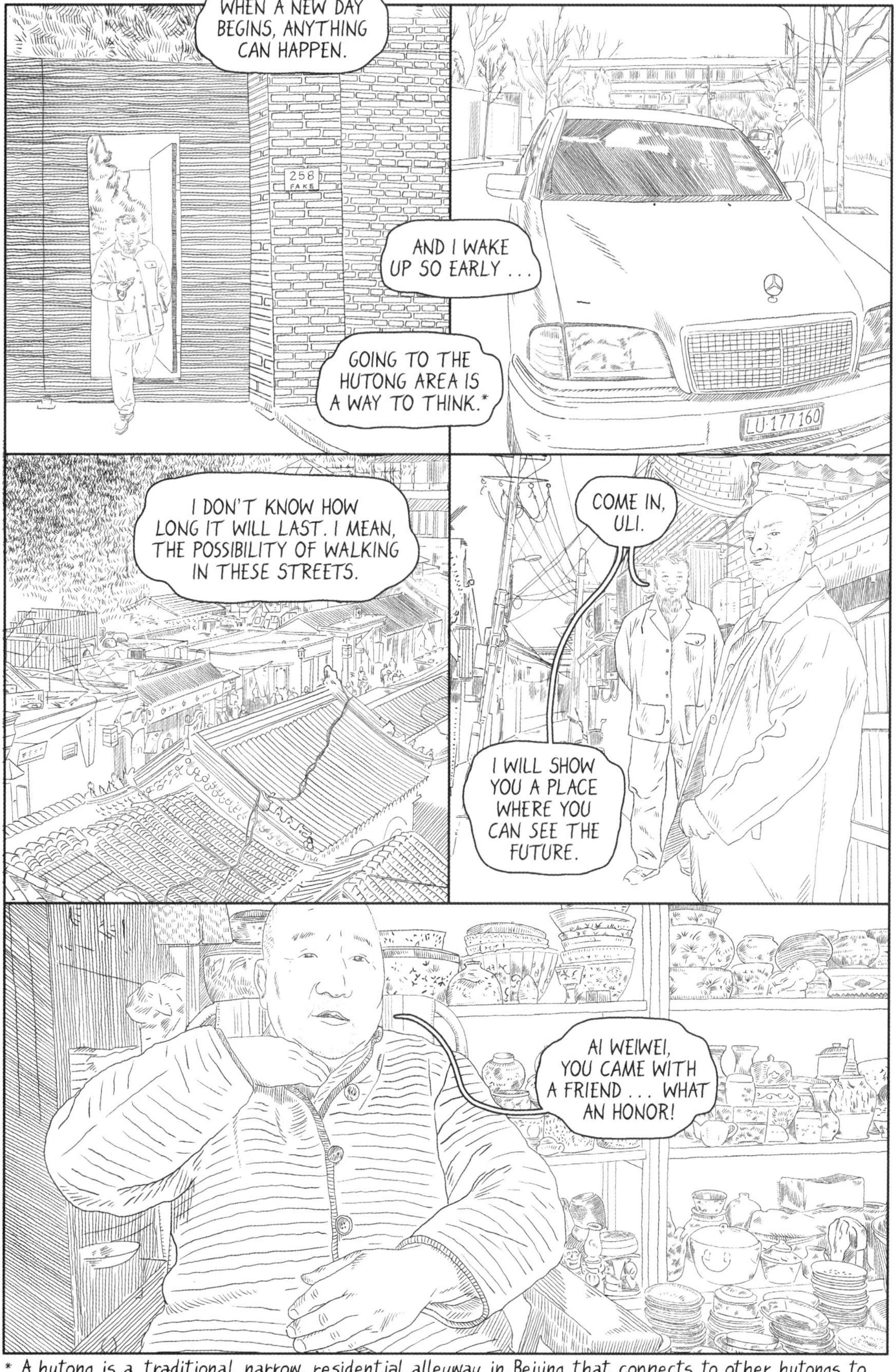

WHEN A NEW DAY BEGINS, ANYTHING CAN HAPPEN.
258 FAKE
AND I WAKE UP SO EARLY . . .
GOING TO THE HUTONG AREA IS A WAY TO THINK.*
LU·177160
I DON'T KNOW HOW LONG IT WILL LAST. I MEAN, THE POSSIBILITY OF WALKING IN THESE STREETS.
COME IN, ULI.
I WILL SHOW YOU A PLACE WHERE YOU CAN SEE THE FUTURE.
AI WEIWEI, YOU CAME WITH A FRIEND . . . WHAT AN HONOR!

* A hutong is a traditional, narrow, residential alleyway in Beijing that connects to other hutongs to form a neighborhood. It is also a system of traditional ethics.

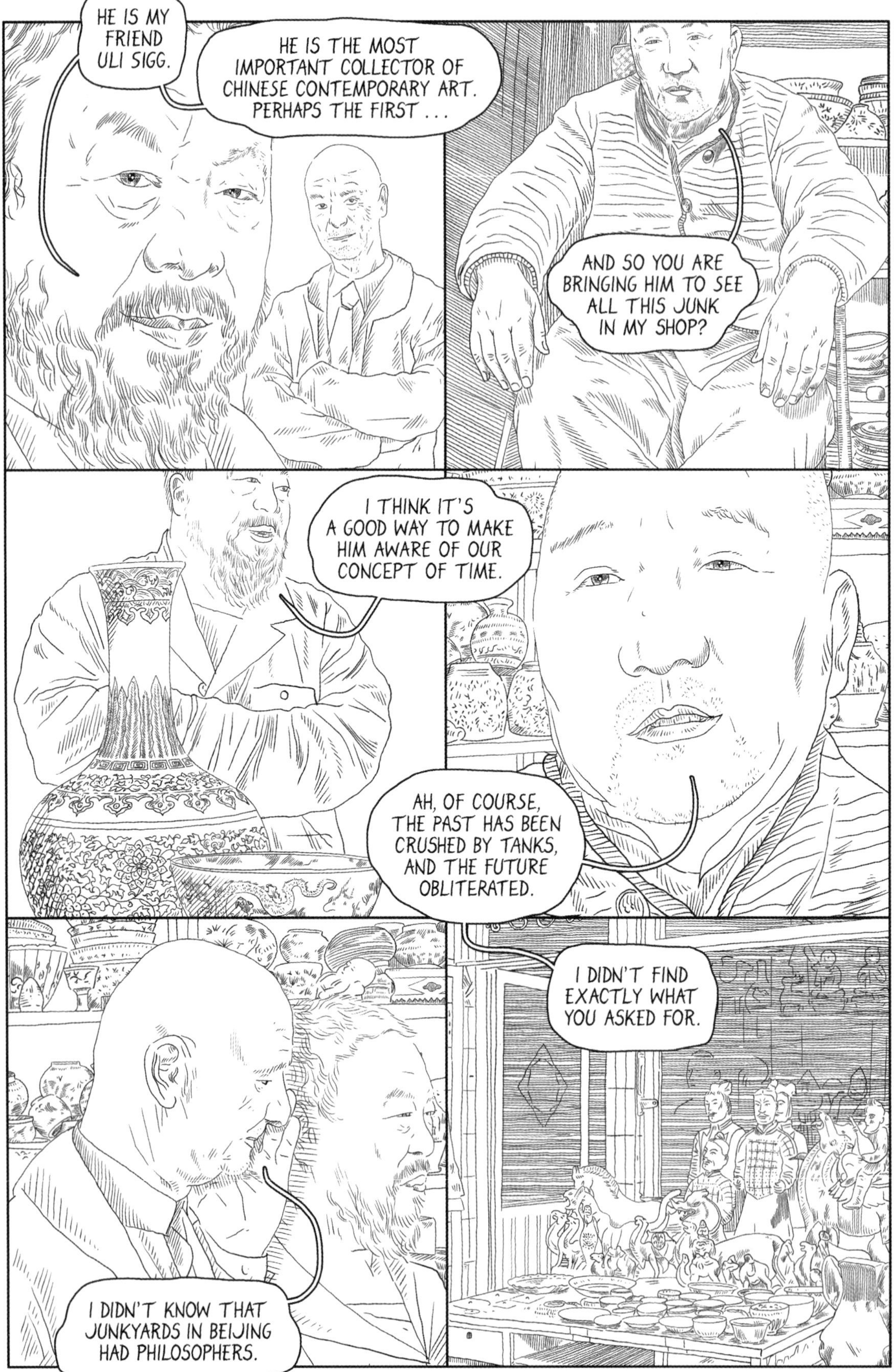
HE IS MY FRIEND ULI SIGG.
HE IS THE MOST IMPORTANT COLLECTOR OF CHINESE CONTEMPORARY ART. PERHAPS THE FIRST . . .
AND SO YOU ARE BRINGING HIM TO SEE ALL THIS JUNK IN MY SHOP?
I THINK IT'S A GOOD WAY TO MAKE HIM AWARE OF OUR CONCEPT OF TIME.
AH, OF COURSE, THE PAST HAS BEEN CRUSHED BY TANKS, AND THE FUTURE OBLITERATED.
I DIDN'T KNOW THAT JUNKYARDS IN BEIJING HAD PHILOSOPHERS.
I DIDN'T FIND EXACTLY WHAT YOU ASKED FOR.

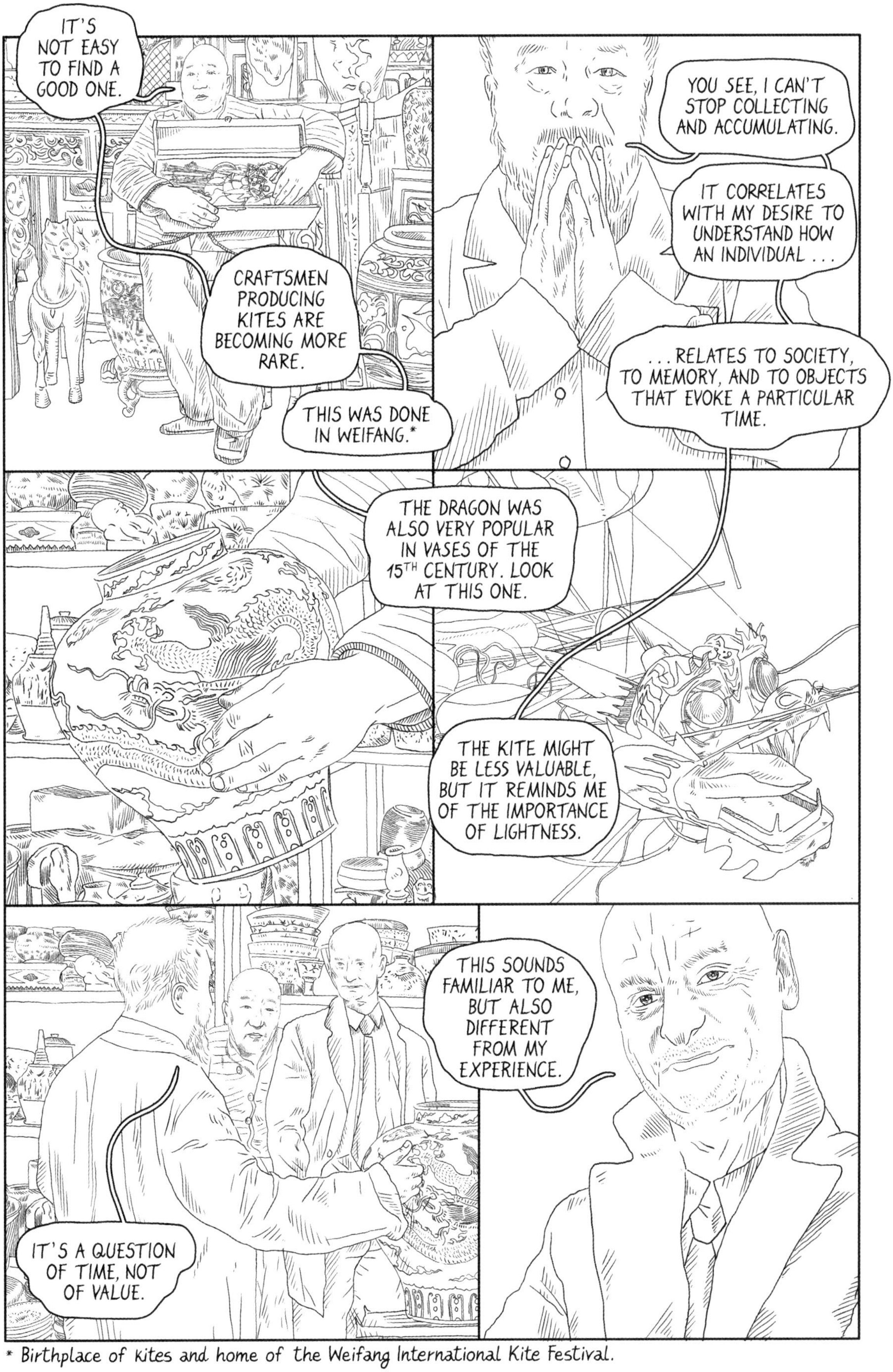
IT'S NOT EASY TO FIND A GOOD ONE.
CRAFTSMEN PRODUCING KITES ARE BECOMING MORE RARE.
THIS WAS DONE IN WEIFANG.*
YOU SEE, I CAN'T STOP COLLECTING AND ACCUMULATING.
IT CORRELATES WITH MY DESIRE TO UNDERSTAND HOW AN INDIVIDUAL . . .
. . . RELATES TO SOCIETY, TO MEMORY, AND TO OBJECTS THAT EVOKE A PARTICULAR TIME.
THE DRAGON WAS ALSO VERY POPULAR IN VASES OF THE 15TH CENTURY. LOOK AT THIS ONE.
THE KITE MIGHT BE LESS VALUABLE, BUT IT REMINDS ME OF THE IMPORTANCE OF LIGHTNESS.
IT'S A QUESTION OF TIME, NOT OF VALUE.
THIS SOUNDS FAMILIAR TO ME, BUT ALSO DIFFERENT FROM MY EXPERIENCE.

* Birthplace of kites and home of the Weifang International Kite Festival.

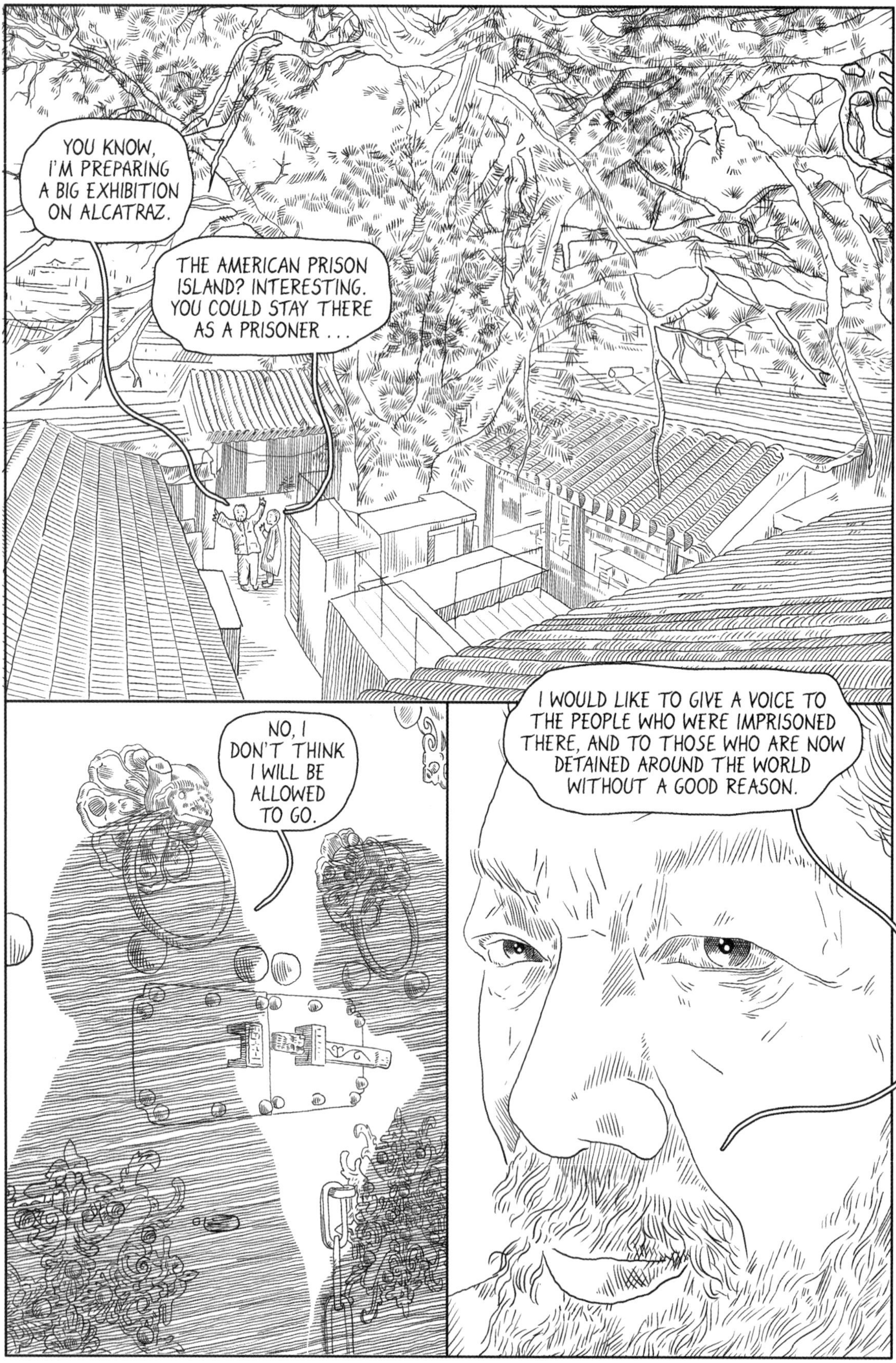
YOU KNOW, I'M PREPARING A BIG EXHIBITION ON ALCATRAZ.
THE AMERICAN PRISON ISLAND? INTERESTING. YOU COULD STAY THERE AS A PRISONER . . .
NO, I DON'T THINK I WILL BE ALLOWED TO GO.
I WOULD LIKE TO GIVE A VOICE TO THE PEOPLE WHO WERE IMPRISONED THERE, AND TO THOSE WHO ARE NOW DETAINED AROUND THE WORLD WITHOUT A GOOD REASON.

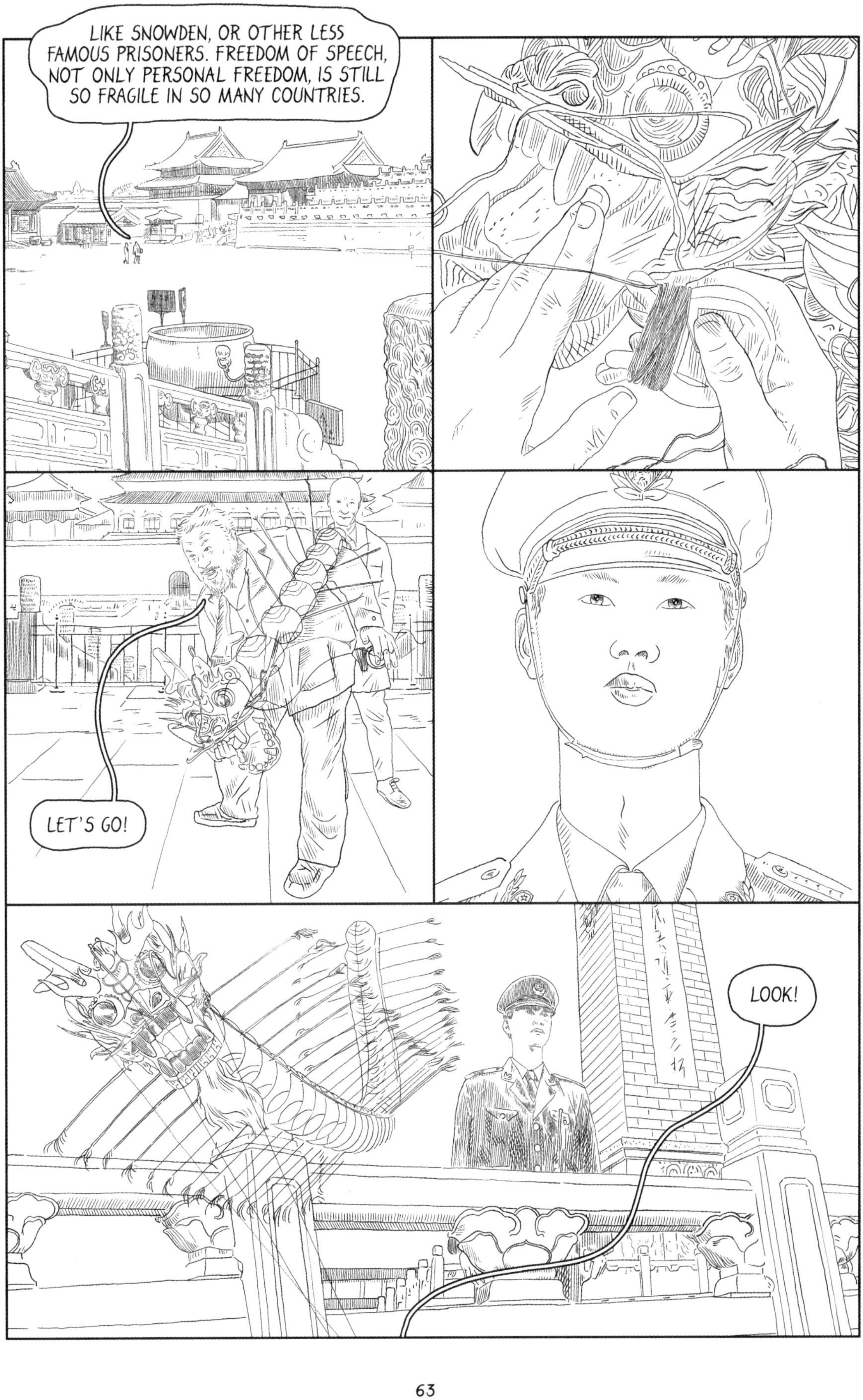
LIKE SNOWDEN, OR OTHER LESS FAMOUS PRISONERS. FREEDOM OF SPEECH, NOT ONLY PERSONAL FREEDOM, IS STILL SO FRAGILE IN SO MANY COUNTRIES.
LET'S GO!
LOOK!

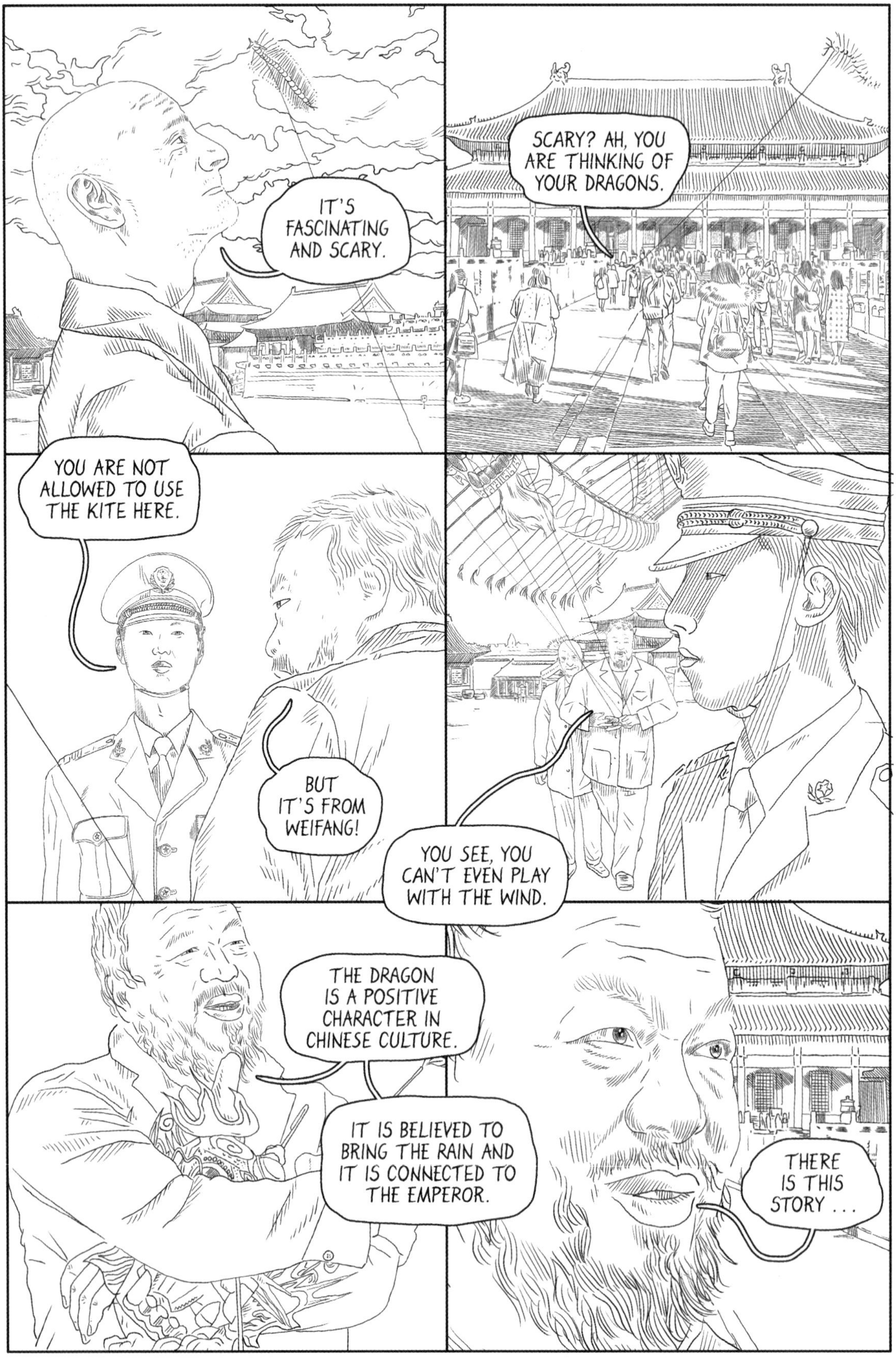
IT'S FASCINATING AND SCARY.
SCARY? AH, YOU ARE THINKING OF YOUR DRAGONS.
YOU ARE NOT ALLOWED TO USE THE KITE HERE.
BUT IT'S FROM WEIFANG!
YOU SEE, YOU CAN'T EVEN PLAY WITH THE WIND.
THE DRAGON IS A POSITIVE CHARACTER IN CHINESE CULTURE.
IT IS BELIEVED TO BRING THE RAIN AND IT IS CONNECTED TO THE EMPEROR.
THERE IS THIS STORY . . .

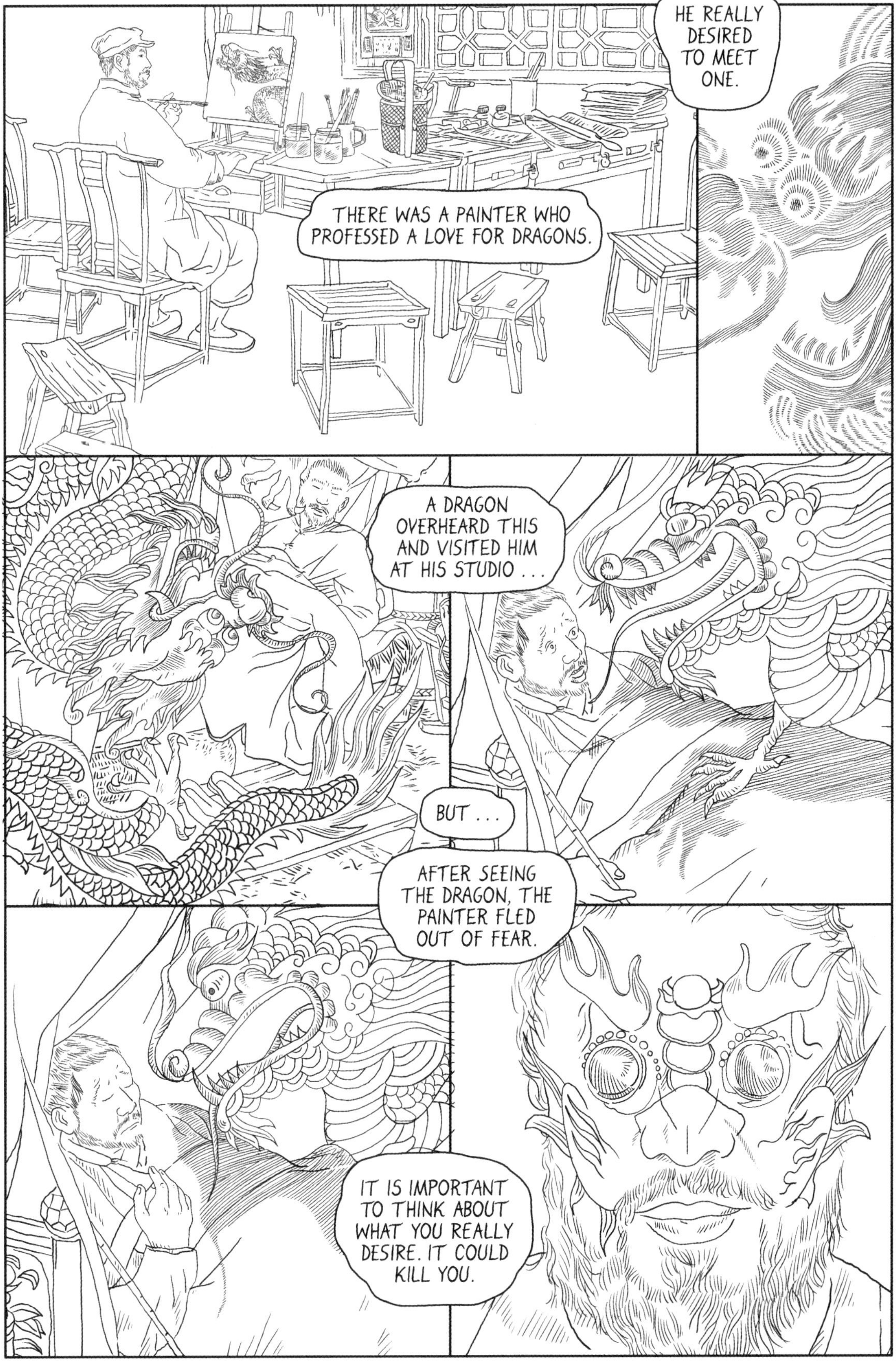
HE REALLY DESIRED TO MEET ONE.
THERE WAS A PAINTER WHO PROFESSED A LOVE FOR DRAGONS.
A DRAGON OVERHEARD THIS AND VISITED HIM AT HIS STUDIO . . .
BUT . . .
AFTER SEEING THE DRAGON, THE PAINTER FLED OUT OF FEAR.
IT IS IMPORTANT TO THINK ABOUT WHAT YOU REALLY DESIRE. IT COULD KILL YOU.

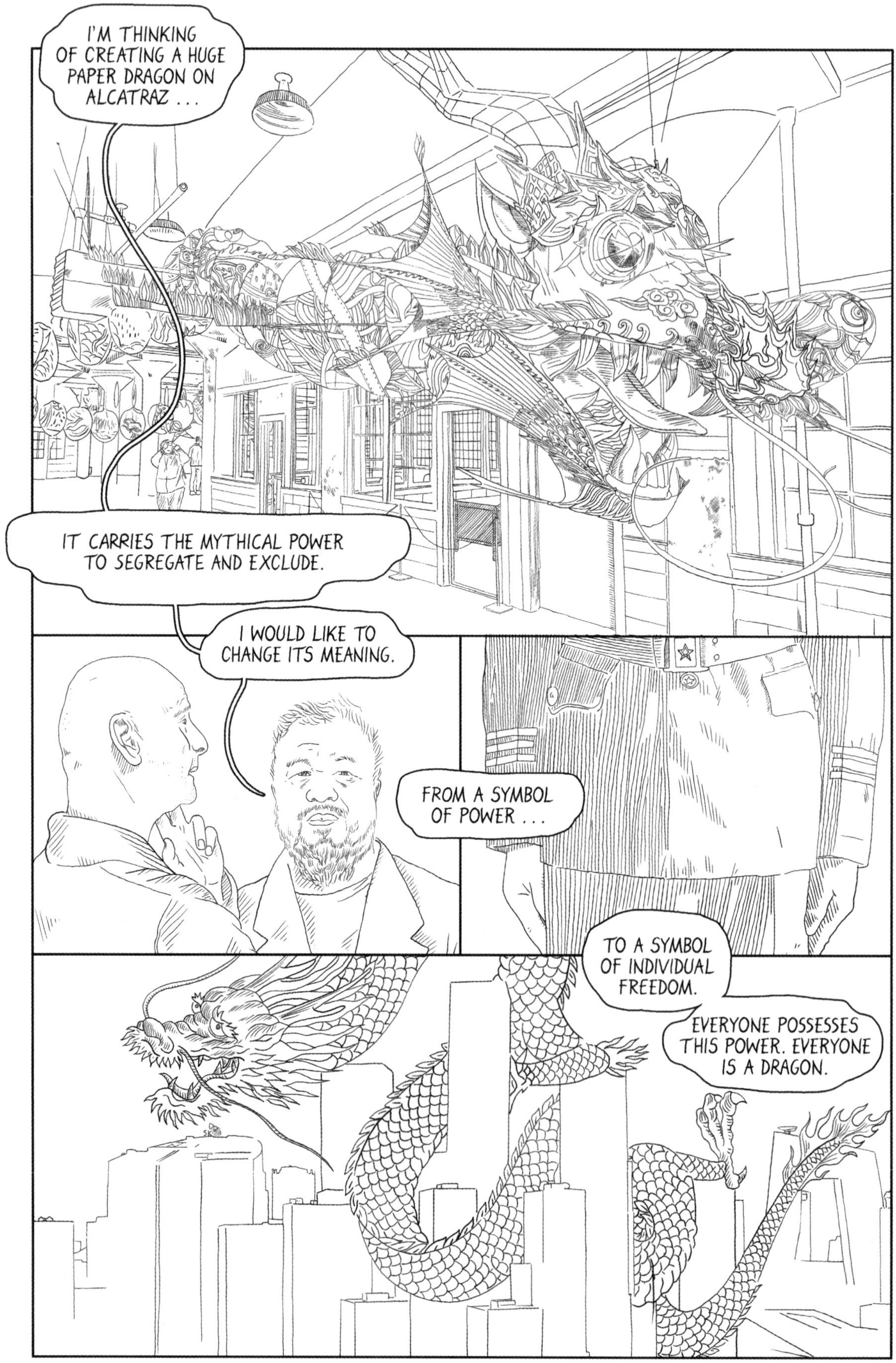
I'M THINKING OF CREATING A HUGE PAPER DRAGON ON ALCATRAZ . . .
IT CARRIES THE MYTHICAL POWER TO SEGREGATE AND EXCLUDE.
I WOULD LIKE TO CHANGE ITS MEANING.
FROM A SYMBOL OF POWER . . .
TO A SYMBOL OF INDIVIDUAL FREEDOM.
EVERYONE POSSESSES THIS POWER. EVERYONE IS A DRAGON.

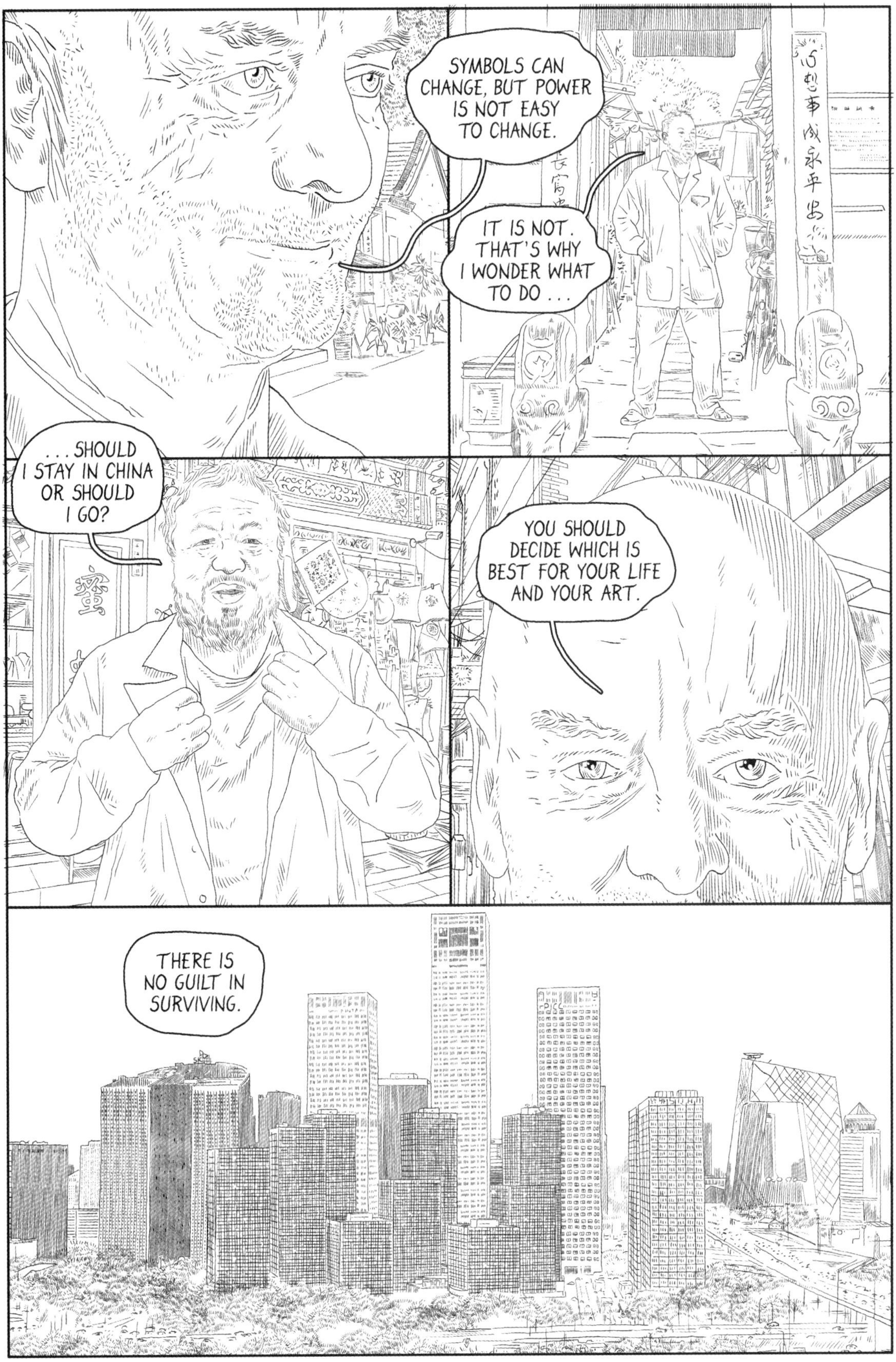
SYMBOLS CAN CHANGE, BUT POWER IS NOT EASY TO CHANGE.
IT IS NOT. THAT'S WHY I WONDER WHAT TO DO . . .
. . . SHOULD I STAY IN CHINA OR SHOULD I GO?
YOU SHOULD DECIDE WHICH IS BEST FOR YOUR LIFE AND YOUR ART.
THERE IS NO GUILT IN SURVIVING.

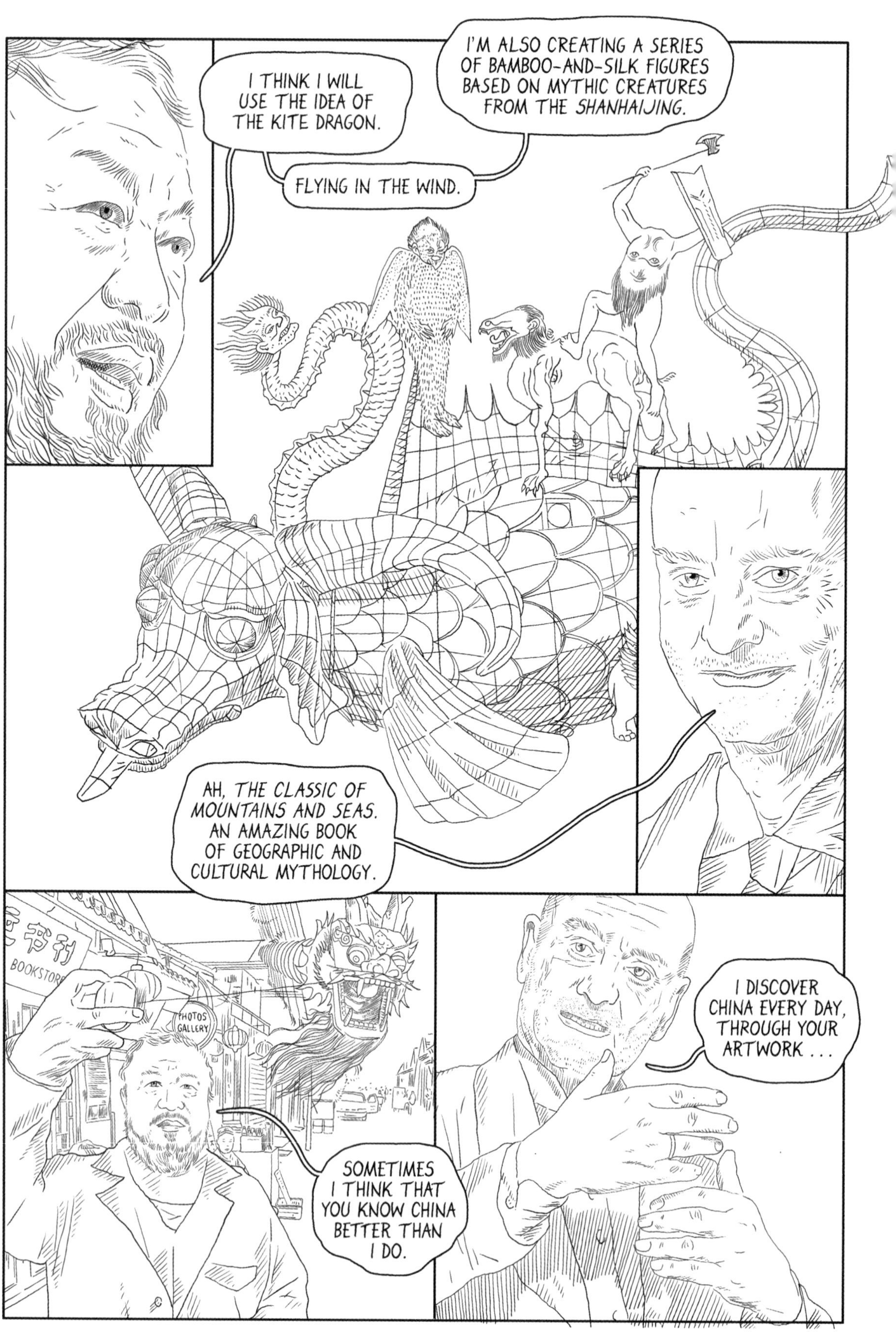
I THINK I WILL USE THE IDEA OF THE KITE DRAGON.
I'M ALSO CREATING A SERIES OF BAMBOO-AND-SILK FIGURES BASED ON MYTHIC CREATURES FROM THE *SHANHAIJING*.
FLYING IN THE WIND.
AH, *THE CLASSIC OF MOUNTAINS AND SEAS*. AN AMAZING BOOK OF GEOGRAPHIC AND CULTURAL MYTHOLOGY.
BOOKSTORE
PHOTOS GALLERY
SOMETIMES I THINK THAT YOU KNOW CHINA BETTER THAN I DO.
I DISCOVER CHINA EVERY DAY, THROUGH YOUR ARTWORK . . .

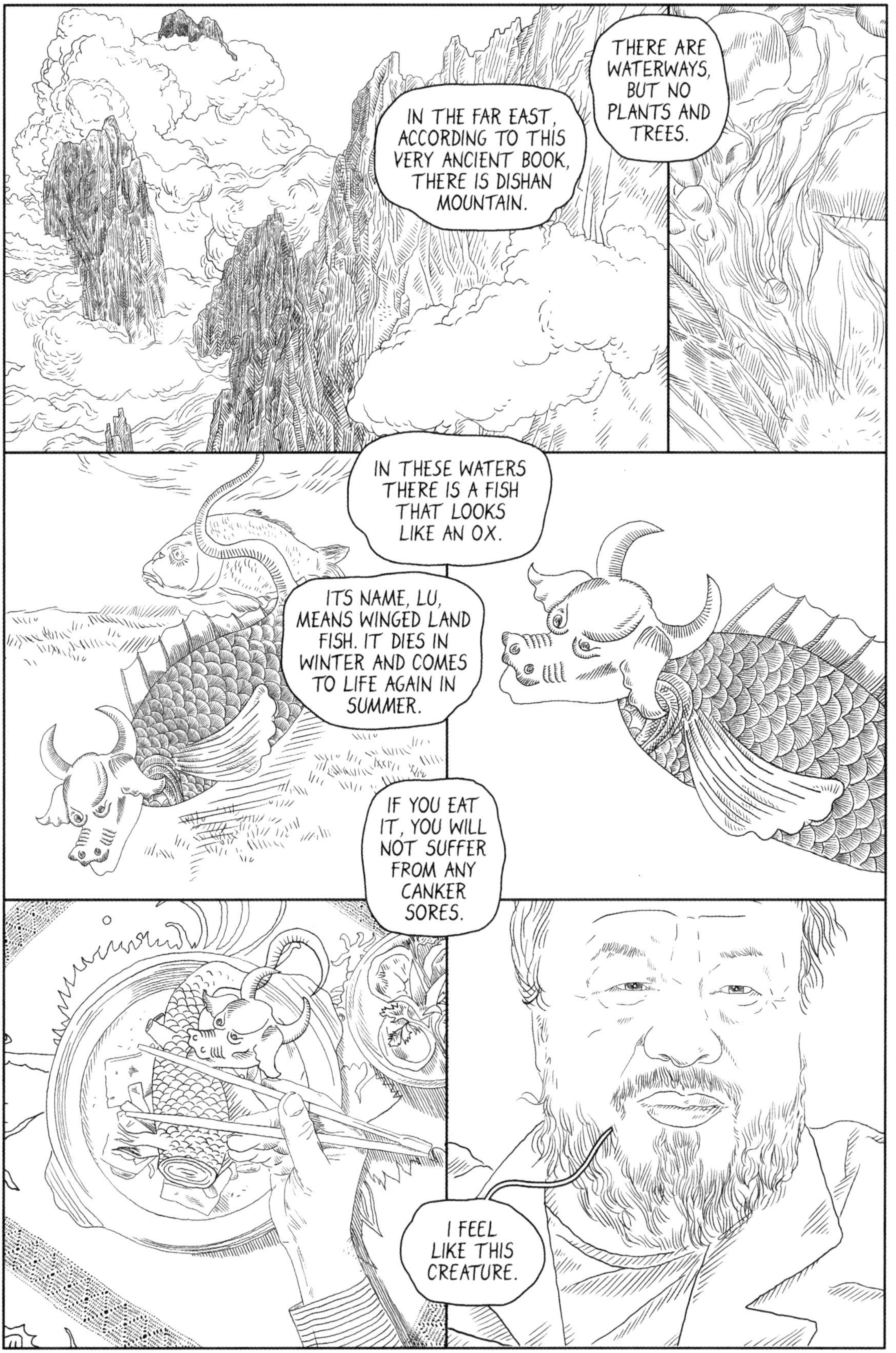
IN THE FAR EAST, ACCORDING TO THIS VERY ANCIENT BOOK, THERE IS DISHAN MOUNTAIN.
THERE ARE WATERWAYS, BUT NO PLANTS AND TREES.
IN THESE WATERS THERE IS A FISH THAT LOOKS LIKE AN OX.
ITS NAME, LU, MEANS WINGED LAND FISH. IT DIES IN WINTER AND COMES TO LIFE AGAIN IN SUMMER.
IF YOU EAT IT, YOU WILL NOT SUFFER FROM ANY CANKER SORES.
I FEEL LIKE THIS CREATURE.

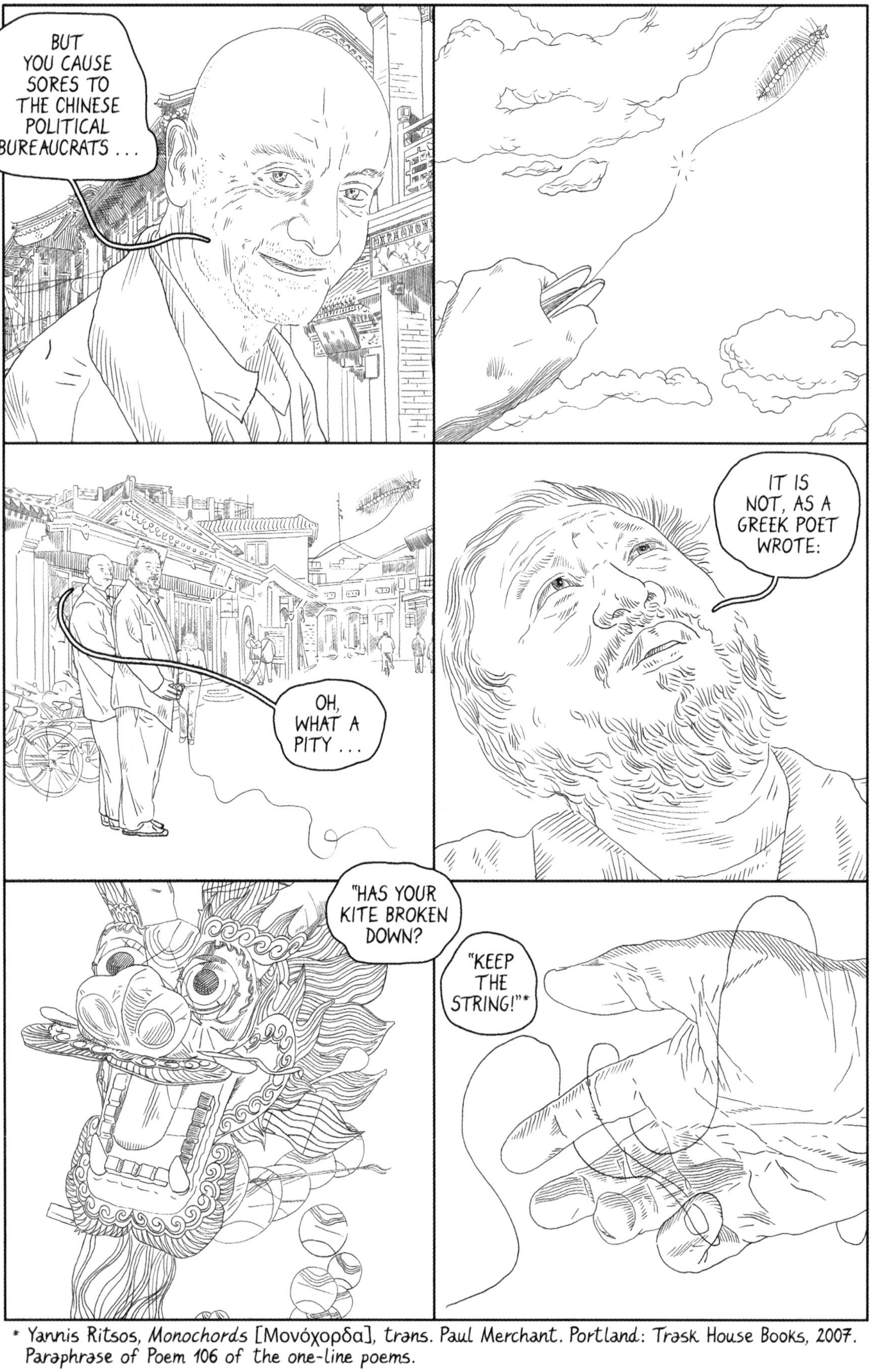
BUT YOU CAUSE SORES TO THE CHINESE POLITICAL BUREAUCRATS . . .
OH, WHAT A PITY . . .
IT IS NOT, AS A GREEK POET WROTE:
"HAS YOUR KITE BROKEN DOWN?
"KEEP THE STRING!"*

* Yannis Ritsos, *Monochords* [Μονόχορδα], trans. Paul Merchant. Portland: Trask House Books, 2007. Paraphrase of Poem 106 of the one-line poems.

CHAPTER 6

Snake
蛇

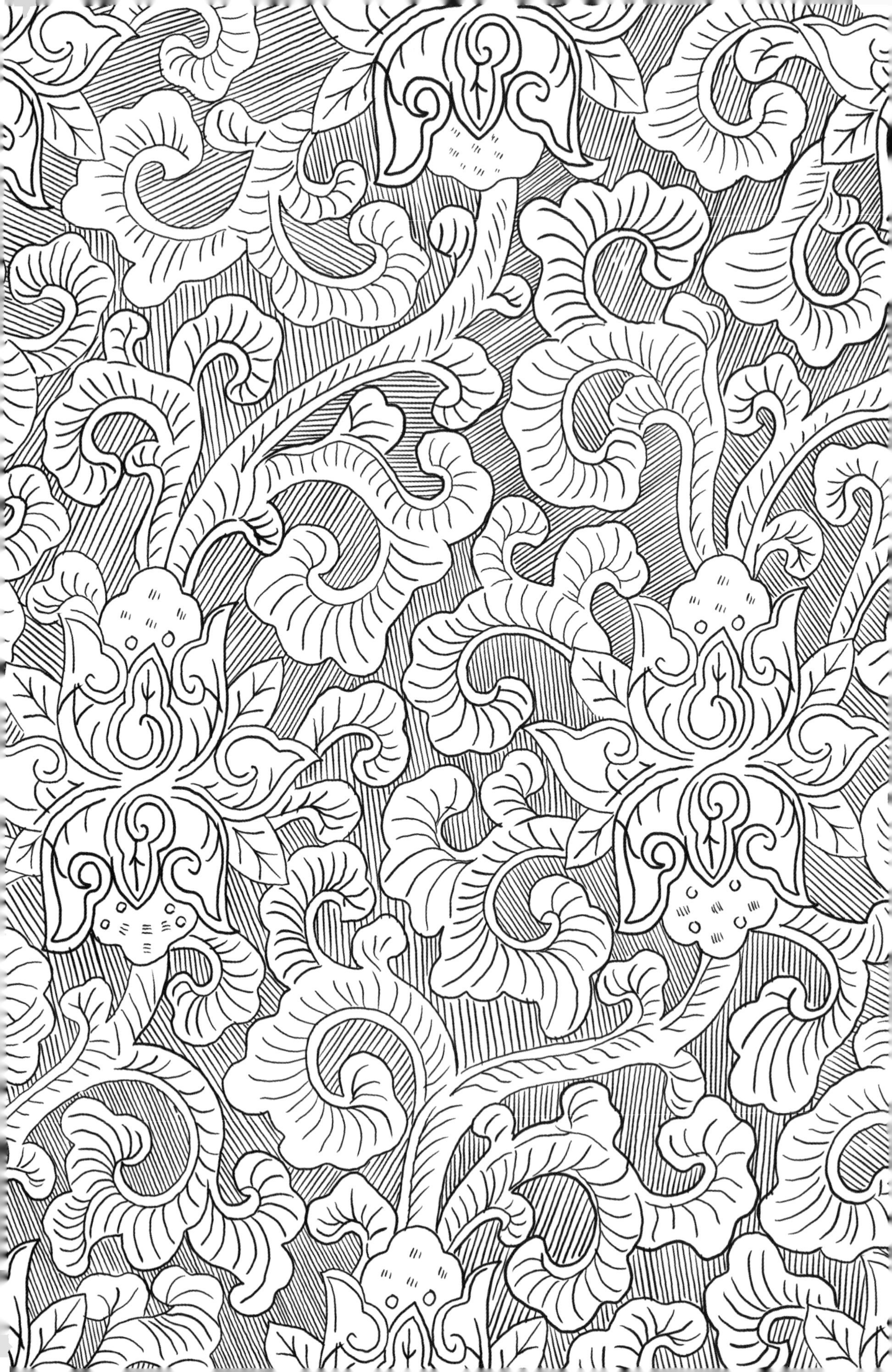

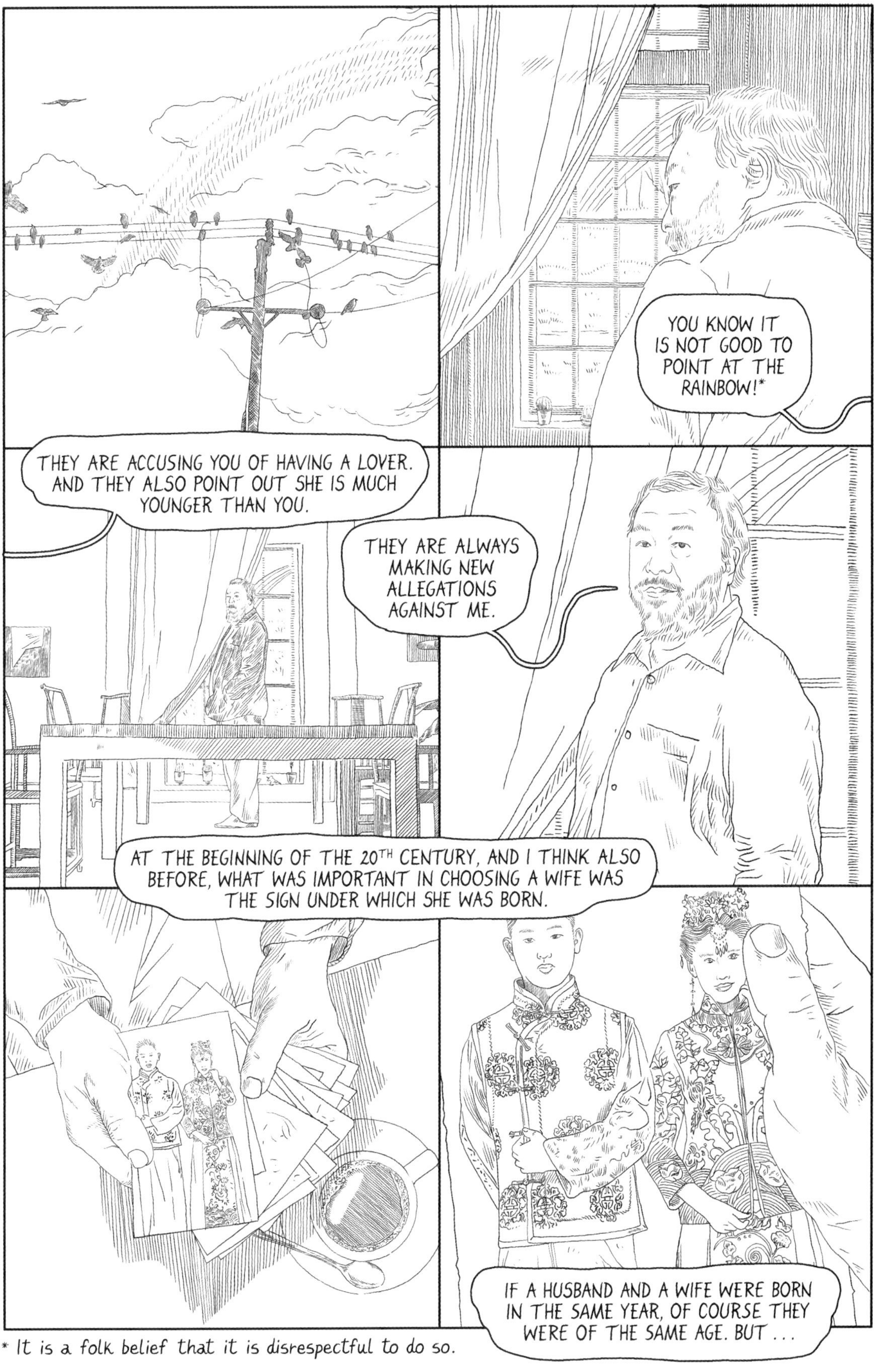
YOU KNOW IT IS NOT GOOD TO POINT AT THE RAINBOW!*
THEY ARE ACCUSING YOU OF HAVING A LOVER. AND THEY ALSO POINT OUT SHE IS MUCH YOUNGER THAN YOU.
THEY ARE ALWAYS MAKING NEW ALLEGATIONS AGAINST ME.
AT THE BEGINNING OF THE 20TH CENTURY, AND I THINK ALSO BEFORE, WHAT WAS IMPORTANT IN CHOOSING A WIFE WAS THE SIGN UNDER WHICH SHE WAS BORN.
IF A HUSBAND AND A WIFE WERE BORN IN THE SAME YEAR, OF COURSE THEY WERE OF THE SAME AGE. BUT . . .

* It is a folk belief that it is disrespectful to do so.

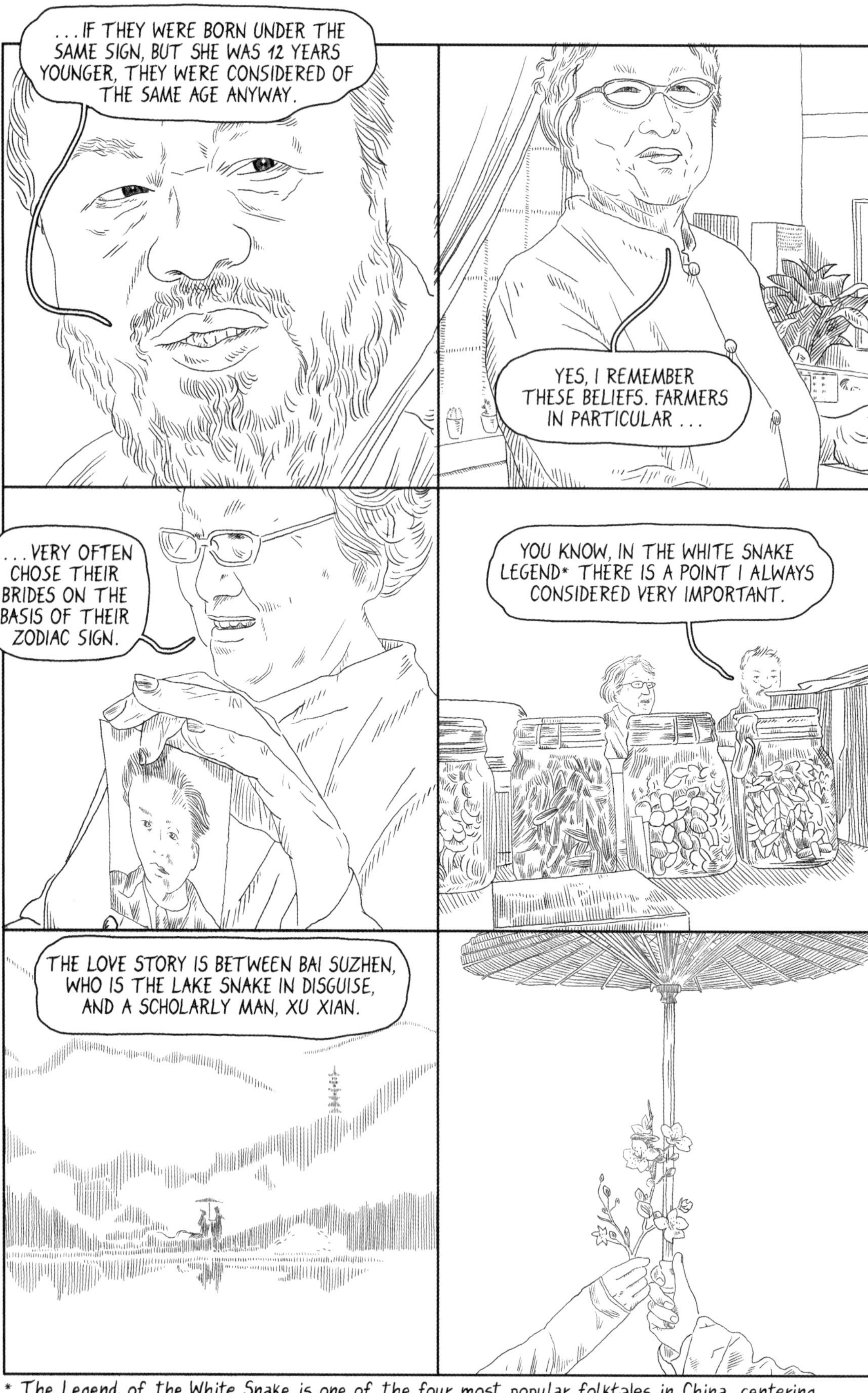
...IF THEY WERE BORN UNDER THE SAME SIGN, BUT SHE WAS 12 YEARS YOUNGER, THEY WERE CONSIDERED OF THE SAME AGE ANYWAY.
YES, I REMEMBER THESE BELIEFS. FARMERS IN PARTICULAR ...
...VERY OFTEN CHOSE THEIR BRIDES ON THE BASIS OF THEIR ZODIAC SIGN.
YOU KNOW, IN THE WHITE SNAKE LEGEND* THERE IS A POINT I ALWAYS CONSIDERED VERY IMPORTANT.
THE LOVE STORY IS BETWEEN BAI SUZHEN, WHO IS THE LAKE SNAKE IN DISGUISE, AND A SCHOLARLY MAN, XU XIAN.

* The Legend of the White Snake is one of the four most popular folktales in China, centering around a romance between a man and a snake spirit. There are many different versions of it in diverse art forms, including Chinese operas and television series.

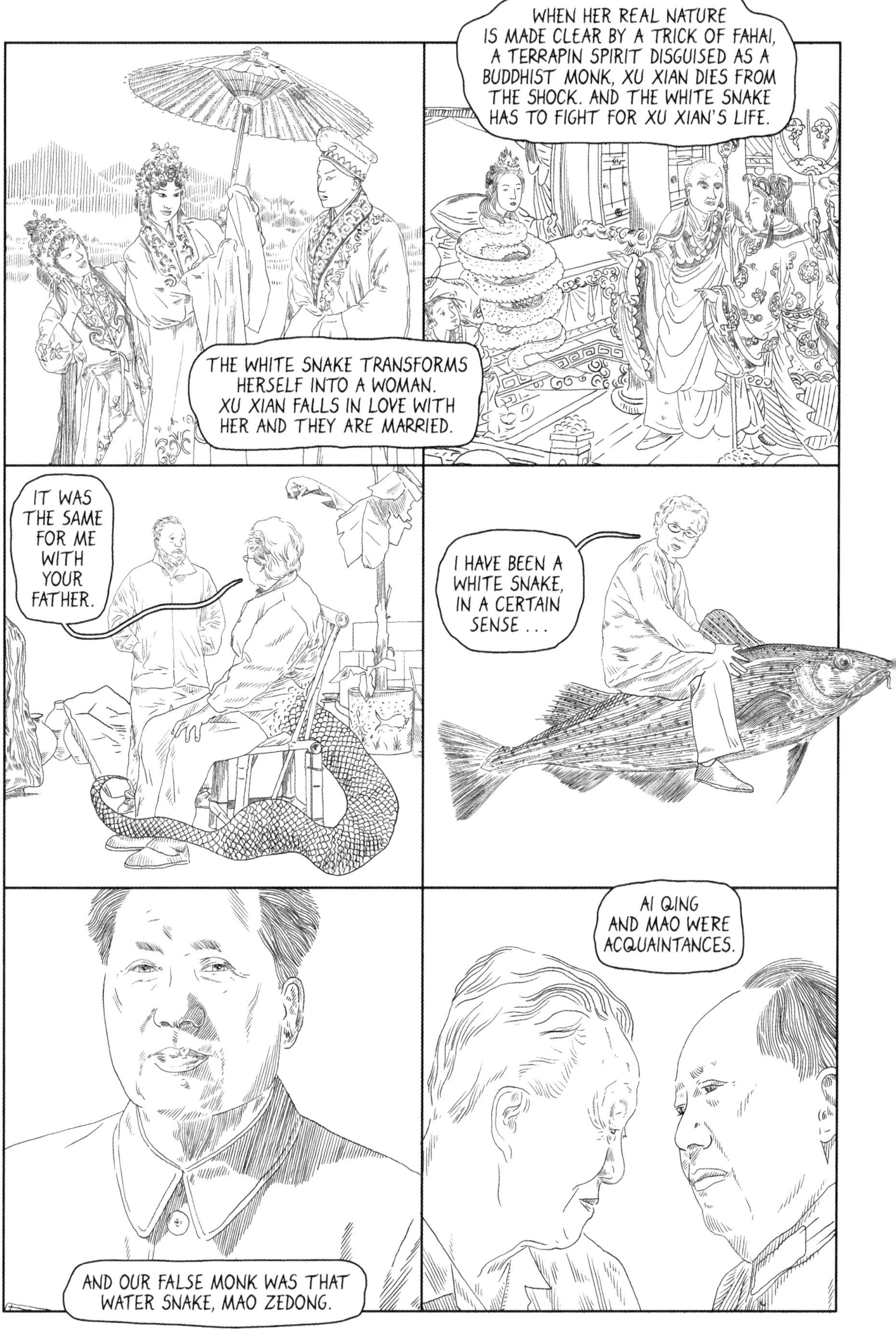
WHEN HER REAL NATURE IS MADE CLEAR BY A TRICK OF FAHAI, A TERRAPIN SPIRIT DISGUISED AS A BUDDHIST MONK, XU XIAN DIES FROM THE SHOCK. AND THE WHITE SNAKE HAS TO FIGHT FOR XU XIAN'S LIFE.
THE WHITE SNAKE TRANSFORMS HERSELF INTO A WOMAN. XU XIAN FALLS IN LOVE WITH HER AND THEY ARE MARRIED.
IT WAS THE SAME FOR ME WITH YOUR FATHER.
I HAVE BEEN A WHITE SNAKE, IN A CERTAIN SENSE . . .
AND OUR FALSE MONK WAS THAT WATER SNAKE, MAO ZEDONG.
AI QING AND MAO WERE ACQUAINTANCES.

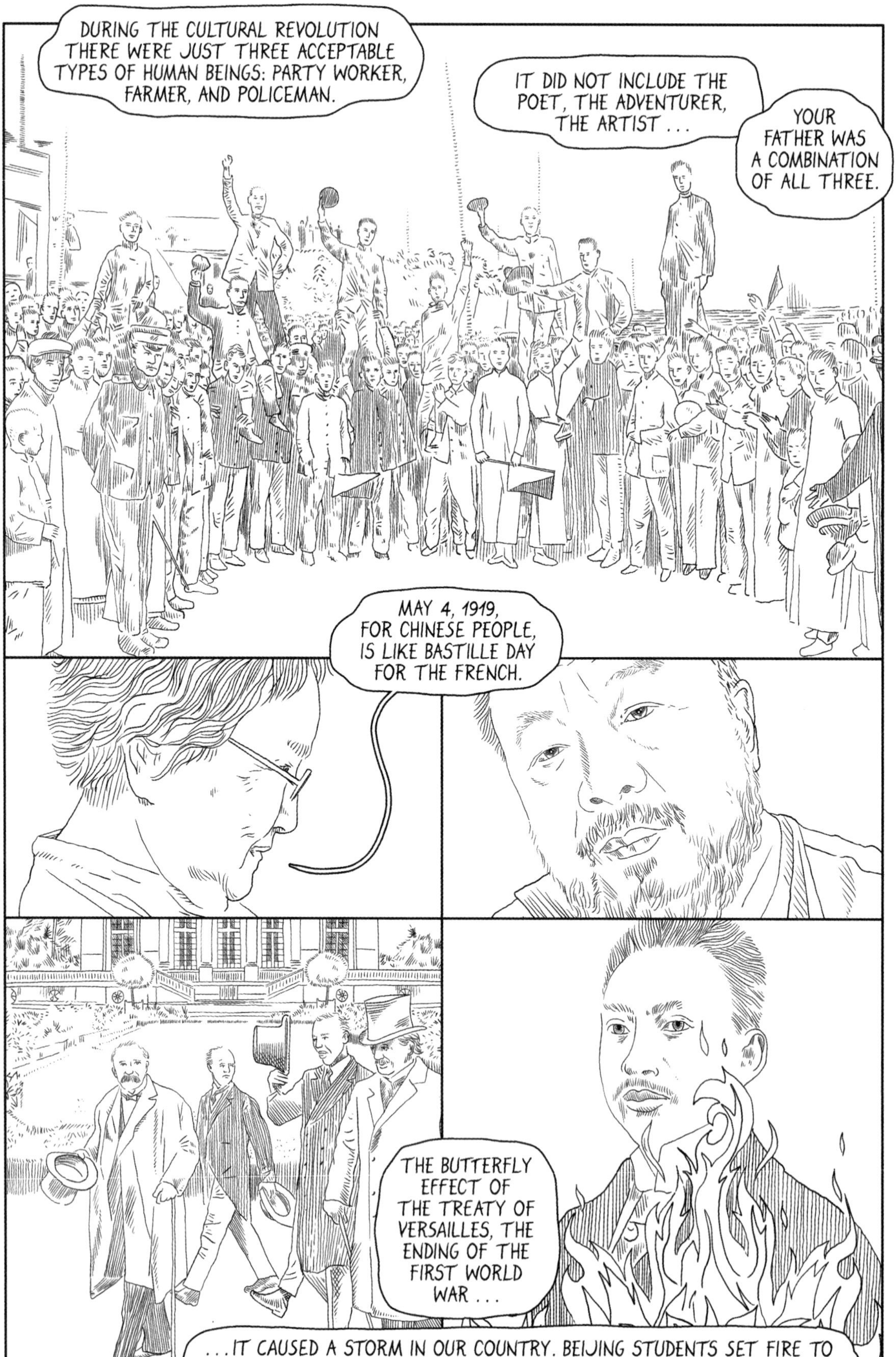
DURING THE CULTURAL REVOLUTION THERE WERE JUST THREE ACCEPTABLE TYPES OF HUMAN BEINGS: PARTY WORKER, FARMER, AND POLICEMAN.
IT DID NOT INCLUDE THE POET, THE ADVENTURER, THE ARTIST . . .
YOUR FATHER WAS A COMBINATION OF ALL THREE.
MAY 4, 1919, FOR CHINESE PEOPLE, IS LIKE BASTILLE DAY FOR THE FRENCH.
THE BUTTERFLY EFFECT OF THE TREATY OF VERSAILLES, THE ENDING OF THE FIRST WORLD WAR . . .
. . . IT CAUSED A STORM IN OUR COUNTRY. BEIJING STUDENTS SET FIRE TO THE HOUSE OF CAO RULIN, A MINISTER ACCUSED OF BEING PRO-JAPANESE.

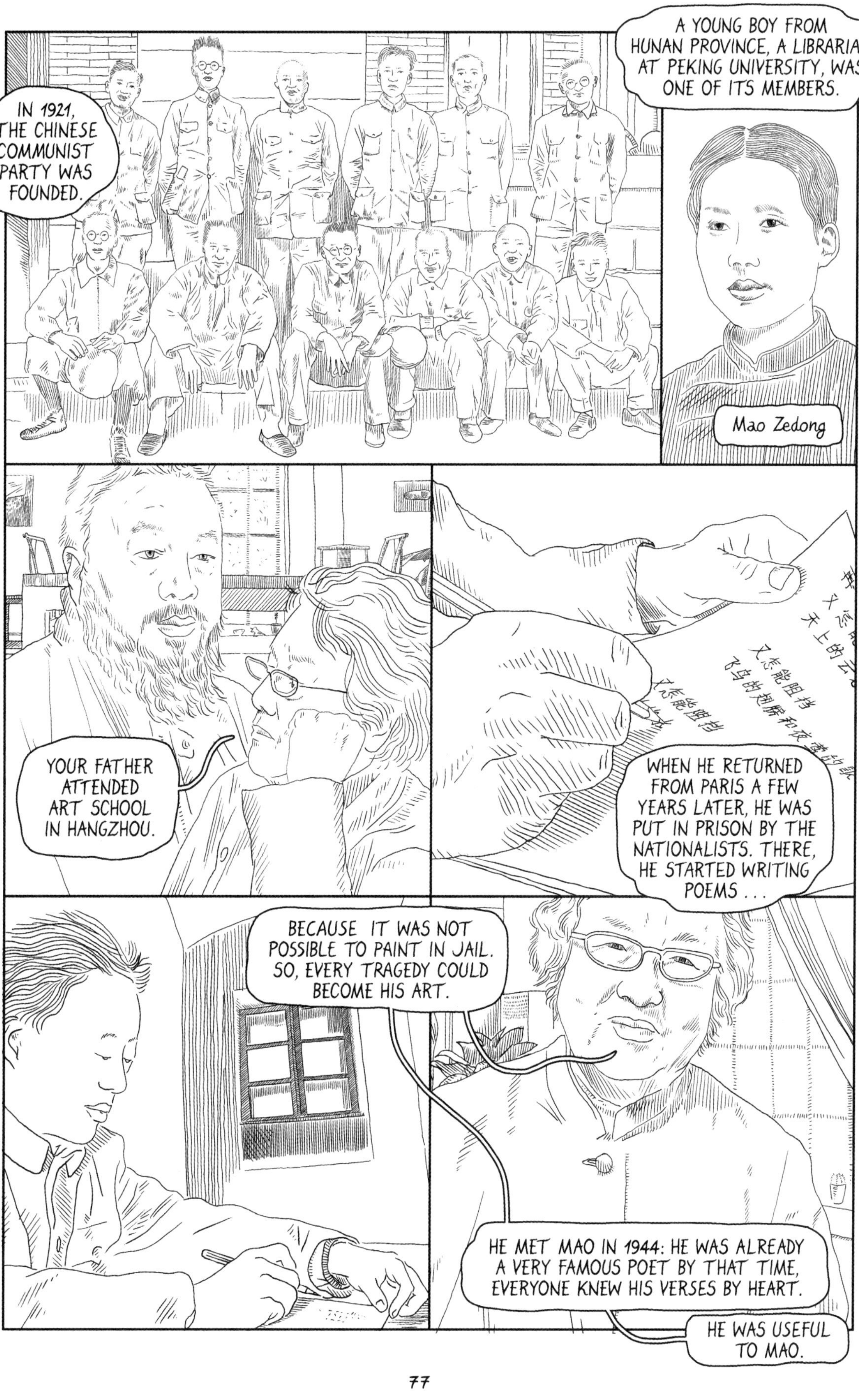
IN 1921, THE CHINESE COMMUNIST PARTY WAS FOUNDED.
A YOUNG BOY FROM HUNAN PROVINCE, A LIBRARIAN AT PEKING UNIVERSITY, WAS ONE OF ITS MEMBERS.
Mao Zedong
YOUR FATHER ATTENDED ART SCHOOL IN HANGZHOU.
又怎能阻挡
飞鸟的翅膀和夜莺的歌
WHEN HE RETURNED FROM PARIS A FEW YEARS LATER, HE WAS PUT IN PRISON BY THE NATIONALISTS. THERE, HE STARTED WRITING POEMS . . .
BECAUSE IT WAS NOT POSSIBLE TO PAINT IN JAIL. SO, EVERY TRAGEDY COULD BECOME HIS ART.
HE MET MAO IN 1944: HE WAS ALREADY A VERY FAMOUS POET BY THAT TIME, EVERYONE KNEW HIS VERSES BY HEART.
HE WAS USEFUL TO MAO.

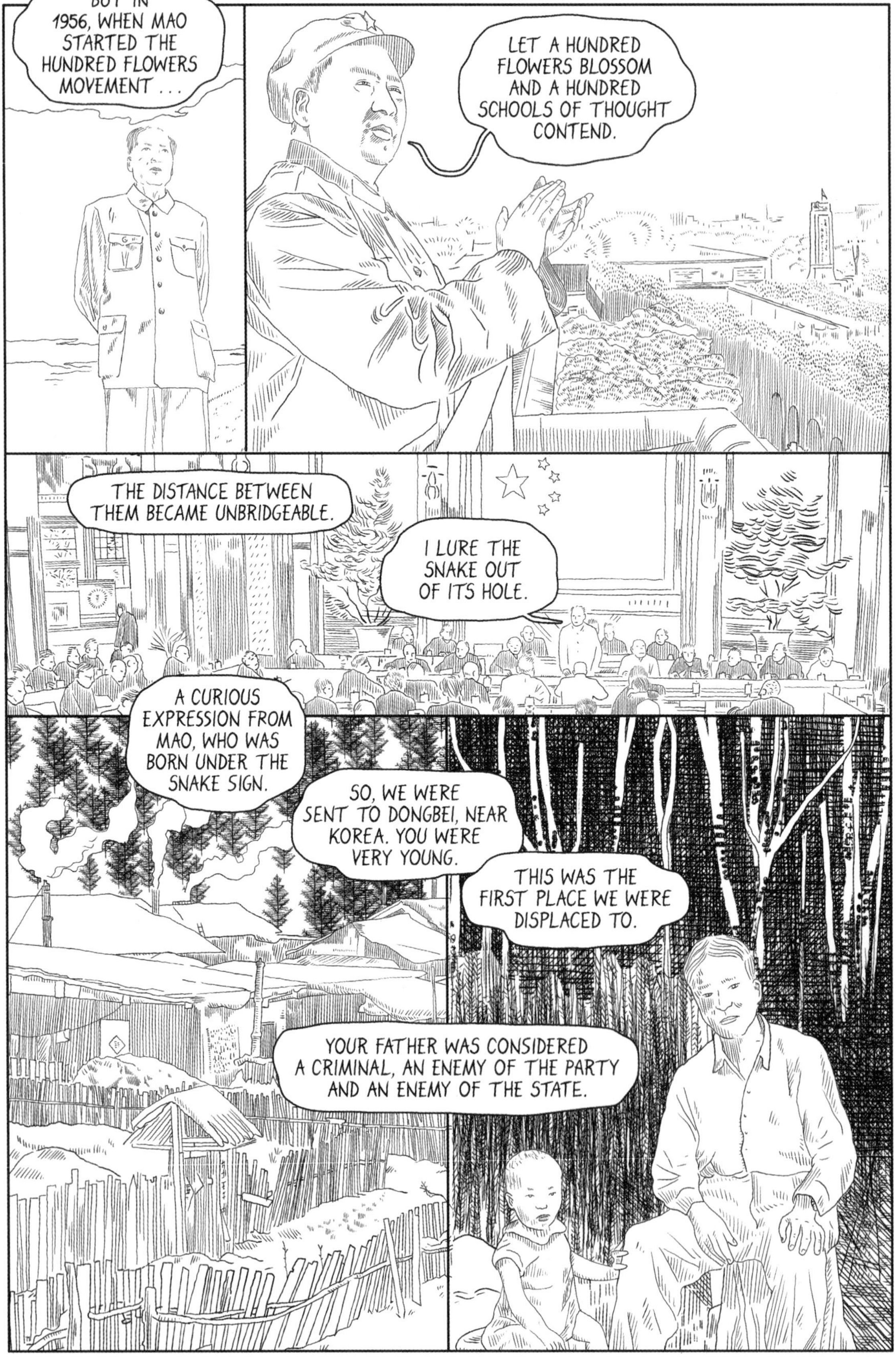
BUT IN 1956, WHEN MAO STARTED THE HUNDRED FLOWERS MOVEMENT . . .
LET A HUNDRED FLOWERS BLOSSOM AND A HUNDRED SCHOOLS OF THOUGHT CONTEND.
THE DISTANCE BETWEEN THEM BECAME UNBRIDGEABLE.
I LURE THE SNAKE OUT OF ITS HOLE.
A CURIOUS EXPRESSION FROM MAO, WHO WAS BORN UNDER THE SNAKE SIGN.
SO, WE WERE SENT TO DONGBEI, NEAR KOREA. YOU WERE VERY YOUNG.
THIS WAS THE FIRST PLACE WE WERE DISPLACED TO.
YOUR FATHER WAS CONSIDERED A CRIMINAL, AN ENEMY OF THE PARTY AND AN ENEMY OF THE STATE.

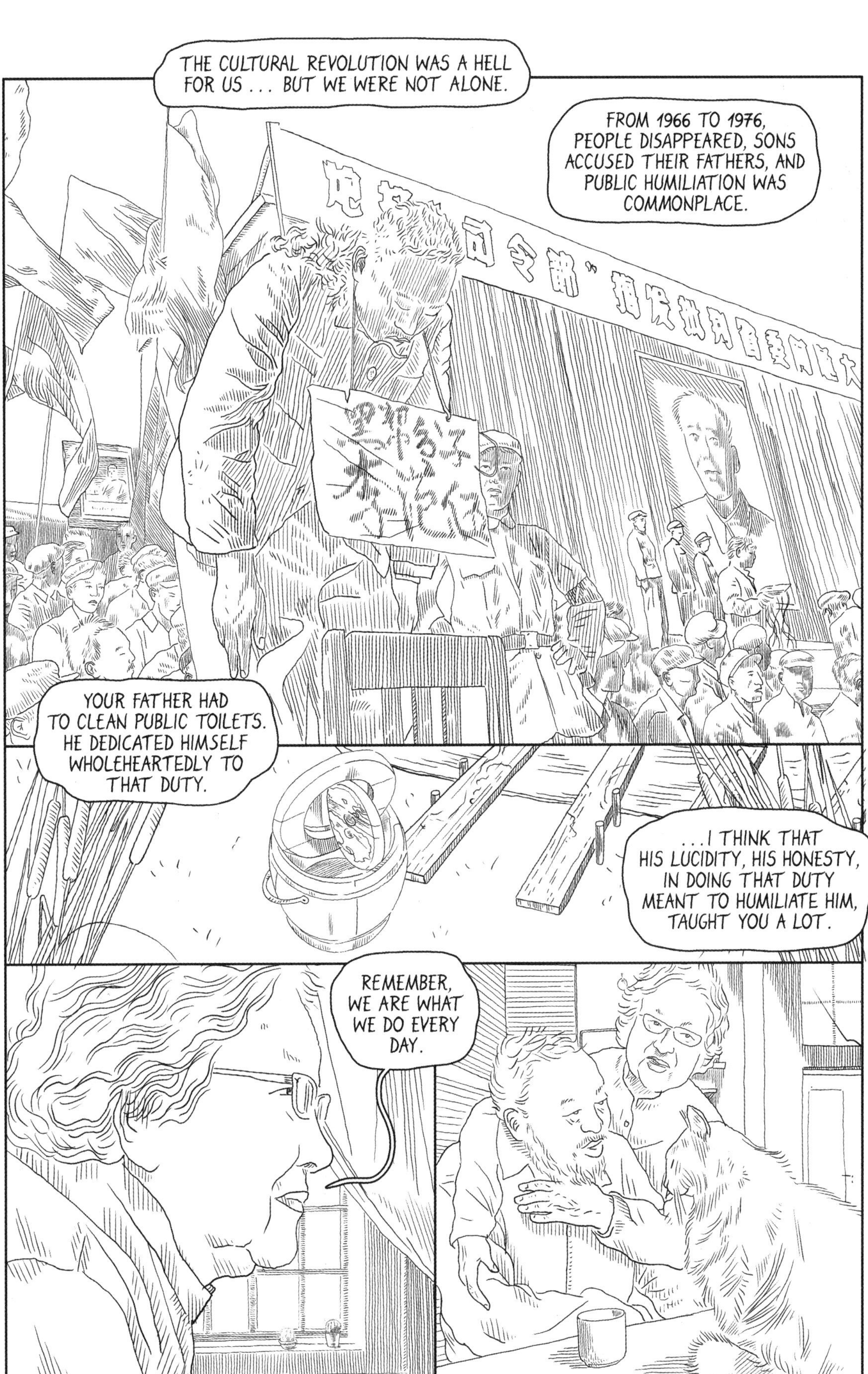
THE CULTURAL REVOLUTION WAS A HELL FOR US . . . BUT WE WERE NOT ALONE.
FROM 1966 TO 1976, PEOPLE DISAPPEARED, SONS ACCUSED THEIR FATHERS, AND PUBLIC HUMILIATION WAS COMMONPLACE.
YOUR FATHER HAD TO CLEAN PUBLIC TOILETS. HE DEDICATED HIMSELF WHOLEHEARTEDLY TO THAT DUTY.
. . . I THINK THAT HIS LUCIDITY, HIS HONESTY, IN DOING THAT DUTY MEANT TO HUMILIATE HIM, TAUGHT YOU A LOT.
REMEMBER, WE ARE WHAT WE DO EVERY DAY.

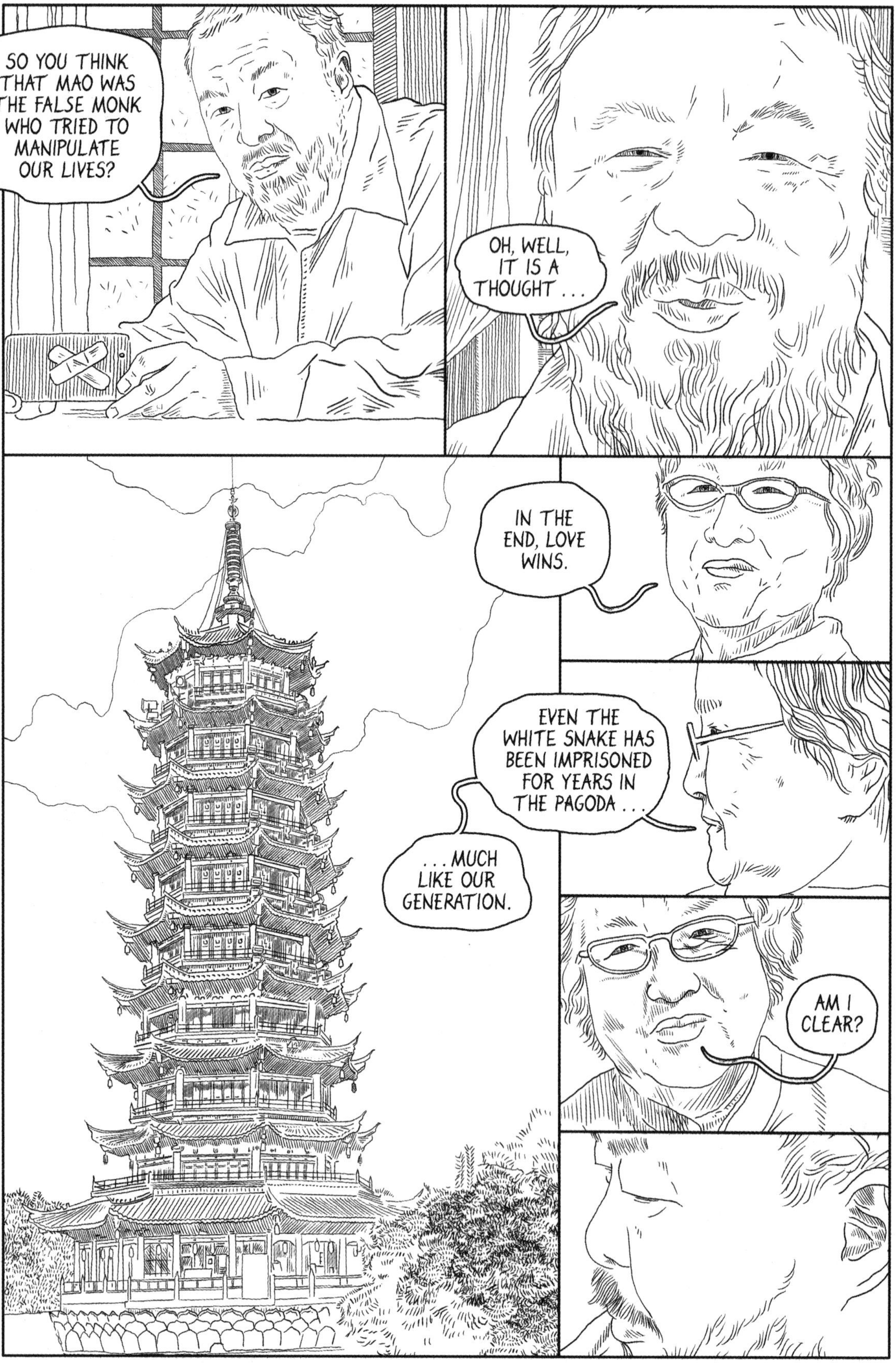
SO YOU THINK THAT MAO WAS THE FALSE MONK WHO TRIED TO MANIPULATE OUR LIVES?
OH, WELL, IT IS A THOUGHT . . .
IN THE END, LOVE WINS.
EVEN THE WHITE SNAKE HAS BEEN IMPRISONED FOR YEARS IN THE PAGODA . . .
. . . MUCH LIKE OUR GENERATION.
AM I CLEAR?

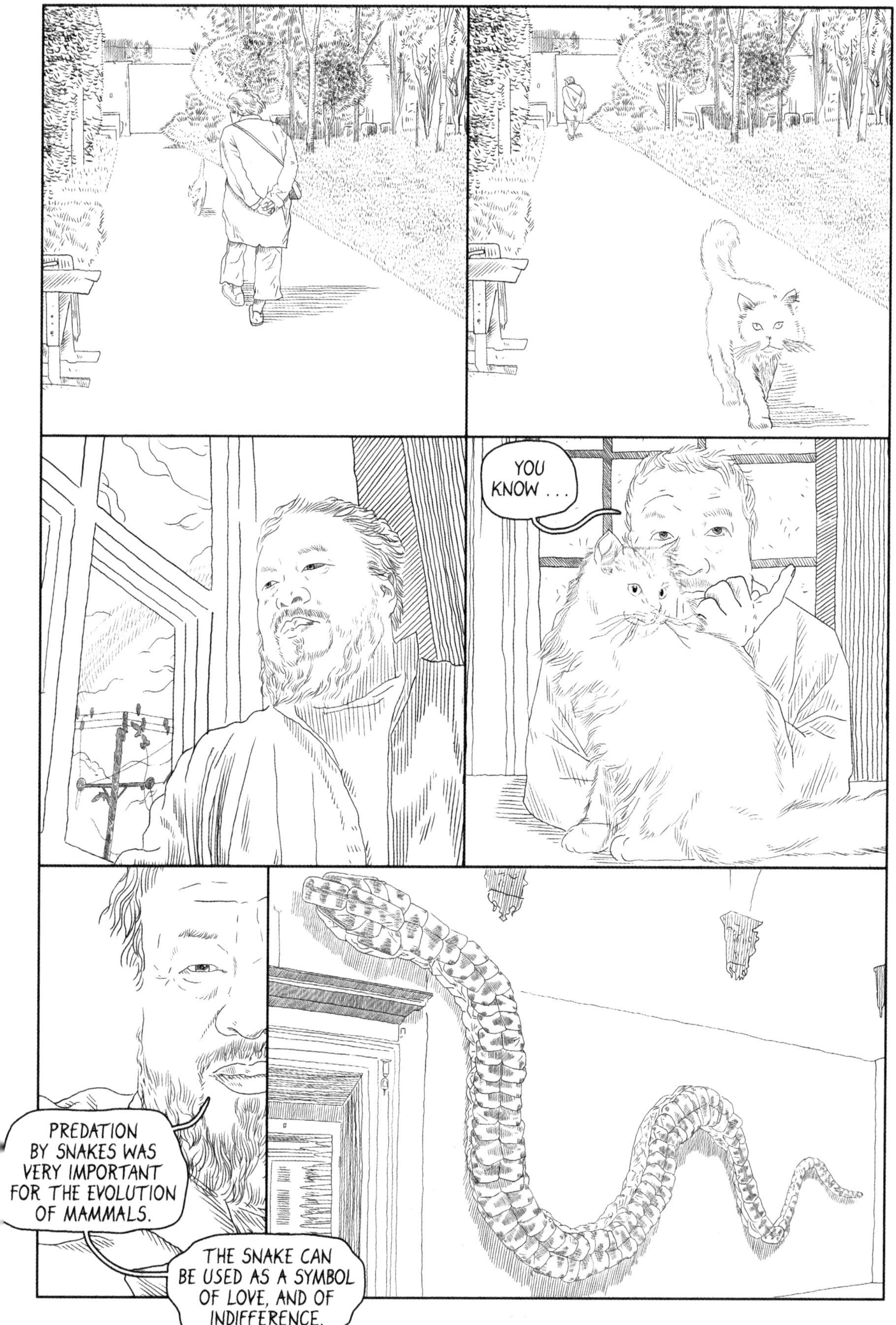
YOU KNOW . . .
PREDATION BY SNAKES WAS VERY IMPORTANT FOR THE EVOLUTION OF MAMMALS.
THE SNAKE CAN BE USED AS A SYMBOL OF LOVE, AND OF INDIFFERENCE.

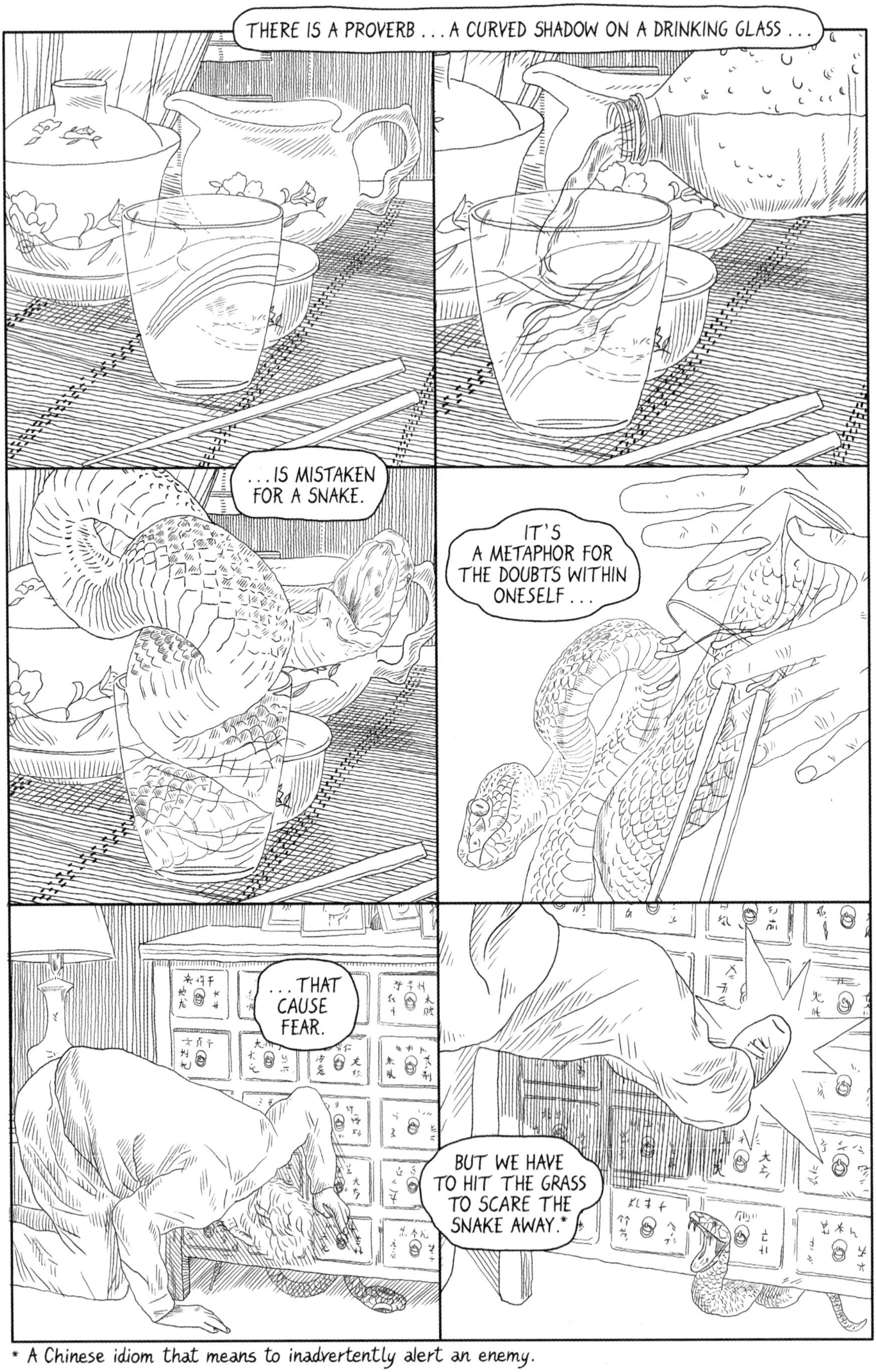
THERE IS A PROVERB . . . A CURVED SHADOW ON A DRINKING GLASS . . .
. . . IS MISTAKEN FOR A SNAKE.
IT'S A METAPHOR FOR THE DOUBTS WITHIN ONESELF . . .
. . . THAT CAUSE FEAR.
BUT WE HAVE TO HIT THE GRASS TO SCARE THE SNAKE AWAY.*

* A Chinese idiom that means to inadvertently alert an enemy.

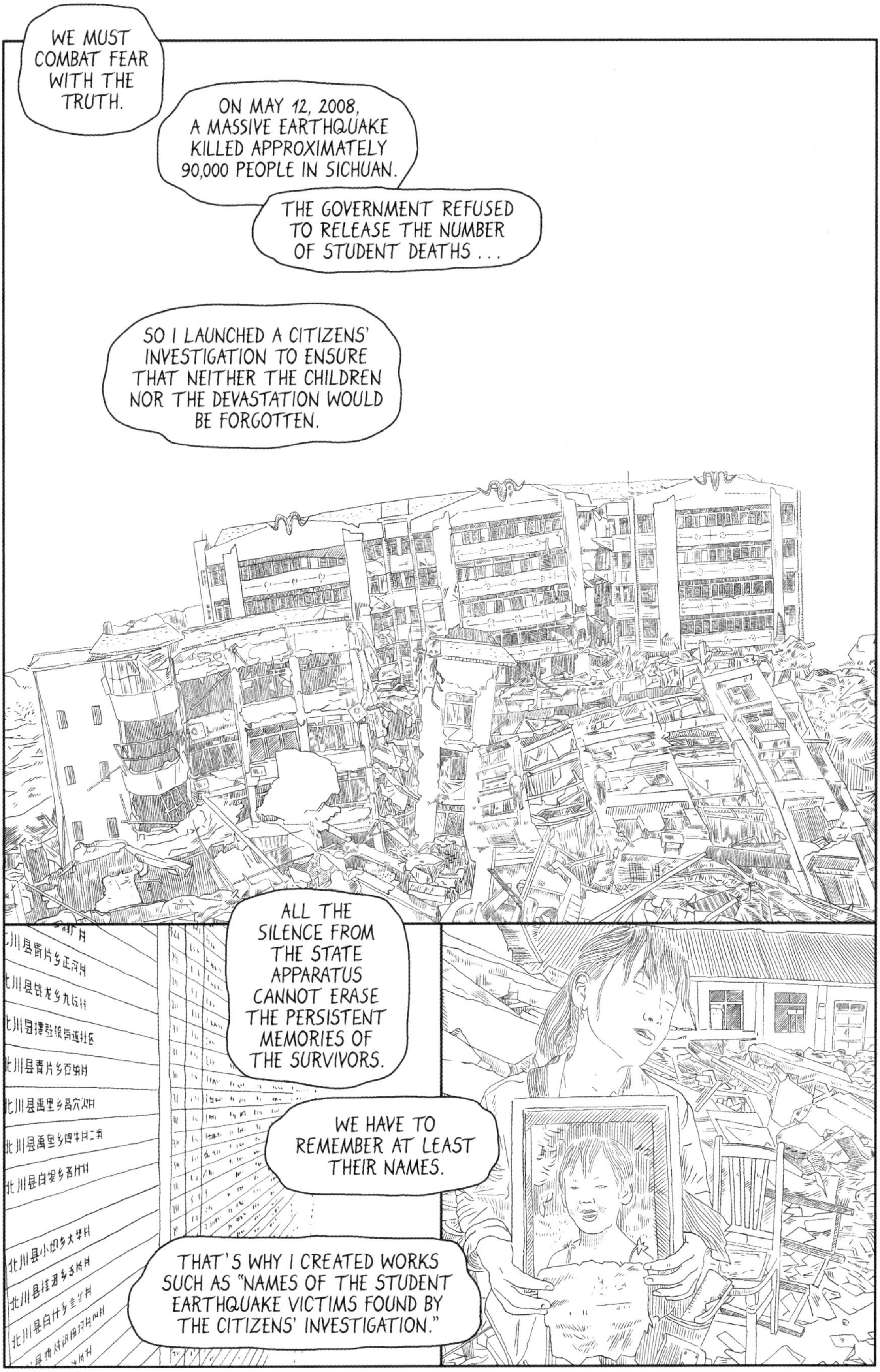
WE MUST COMBAT FEAR WITH THE TRUTH.
ON MAY 12, 2008, A MASSIVE EARTHQUAKE KILLED APPROXIMATELY 90,000 PEOPLE IN SICHUAN.
THE GOVERNMENT REFUSED TO RELEASE THE NUMBER OF STUDENT DEATHS . . .
SO I LAUNCHED A CITIZENS' INVESTIGATION TO ENSURE THAT NEITHER THE CHILDREN NOR THE DEVASTATION WOULD BE FORGOTTEN.
ALL THE SILENCE FROM THE STATE APPARATUS CANNOT ERASE THE PERSISTENT MEMORIES OF THE SURVIVORS.
WE HAVE TO REMEMBER AT LEAST THEIR NAMES.
THAT'S WHY I CREATED WORKS SUCH AS "NAMES OF THE STUDENT EARTHQUAKE VICTIMS FOUND BY THE CITIZENS' INVESTIGATION."

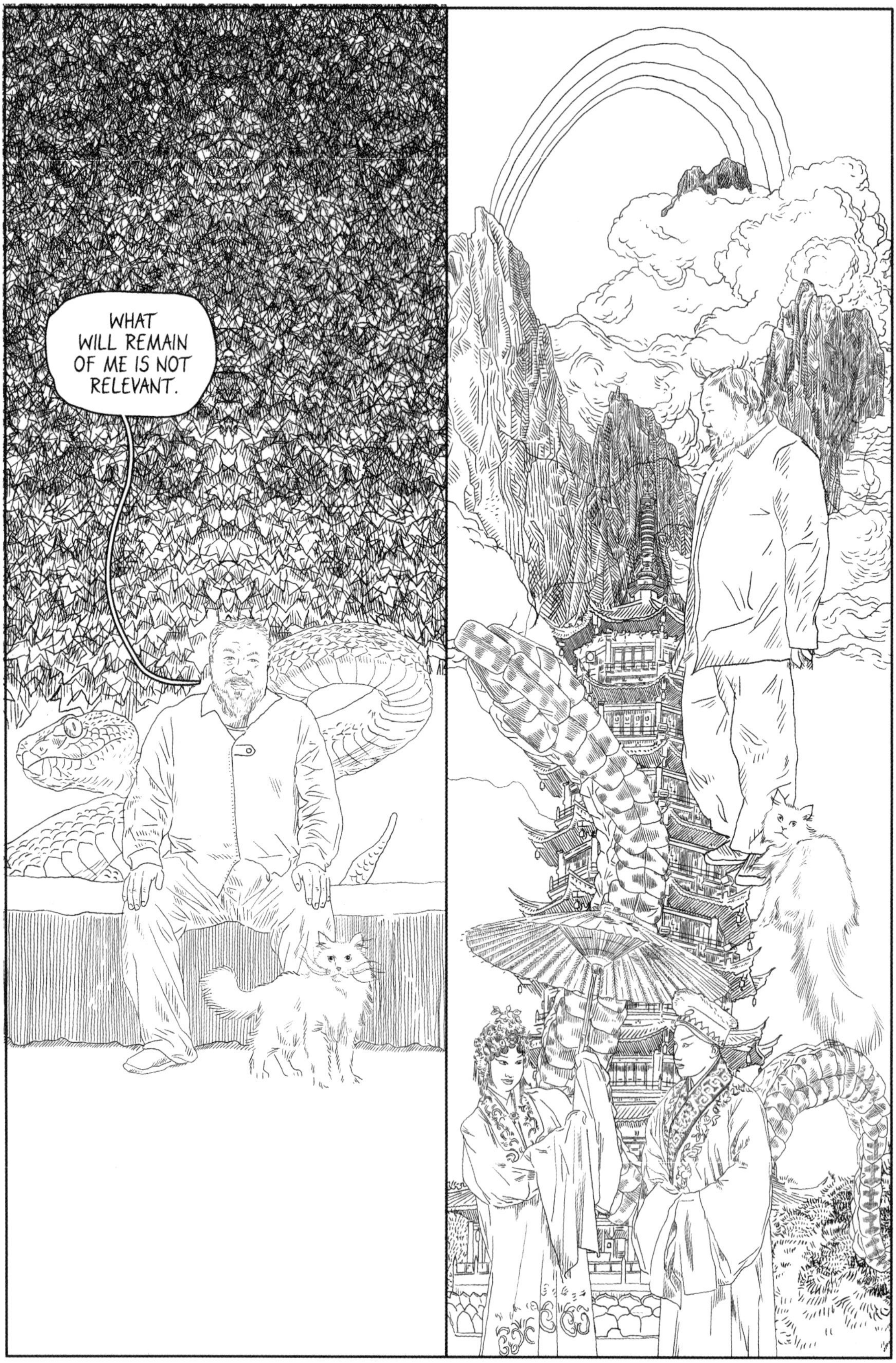
WHAT WILL REMAIN OF ME IS NOT RELEVANT.

Chapter 7

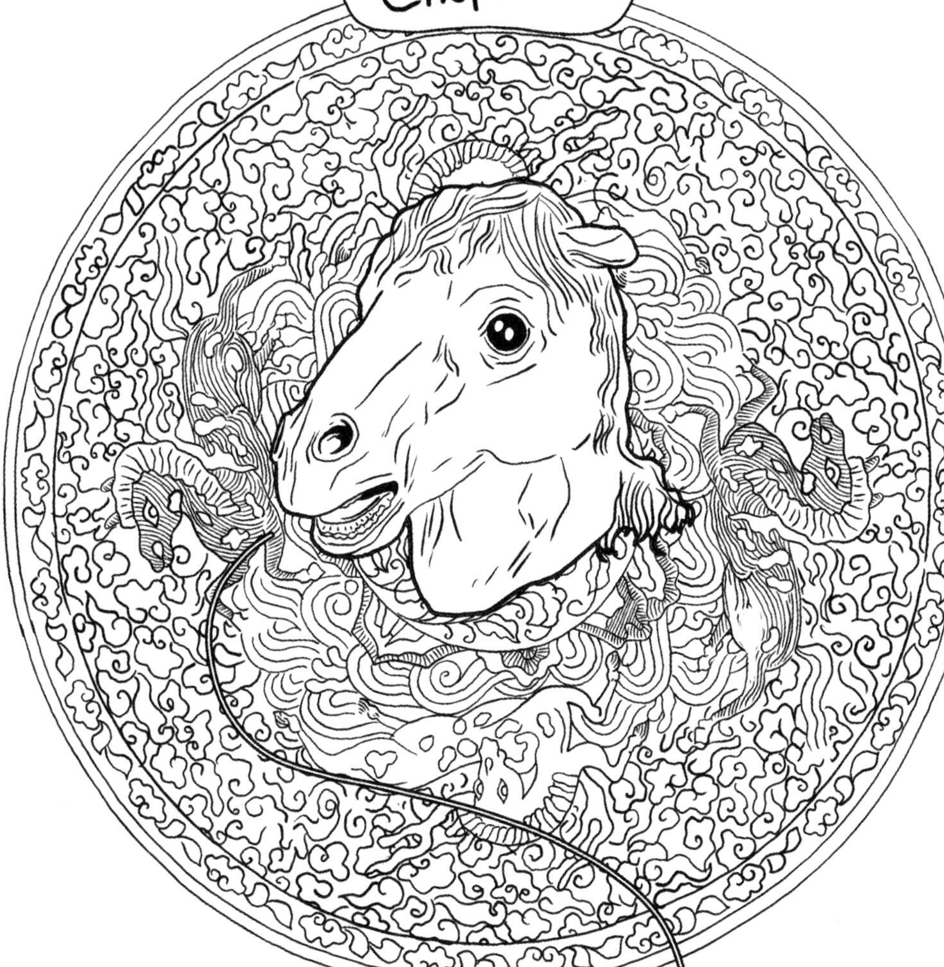

Horse 马

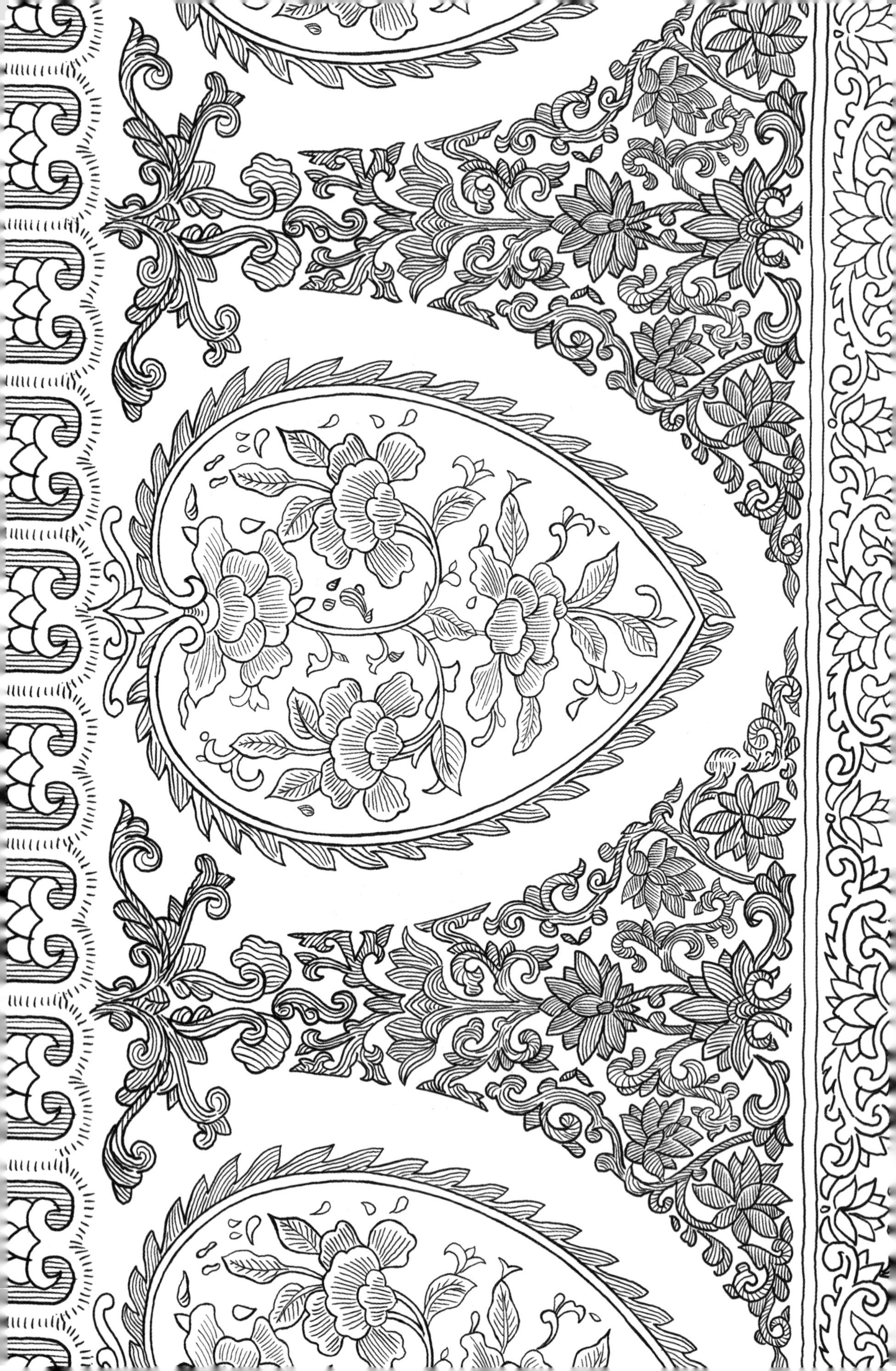

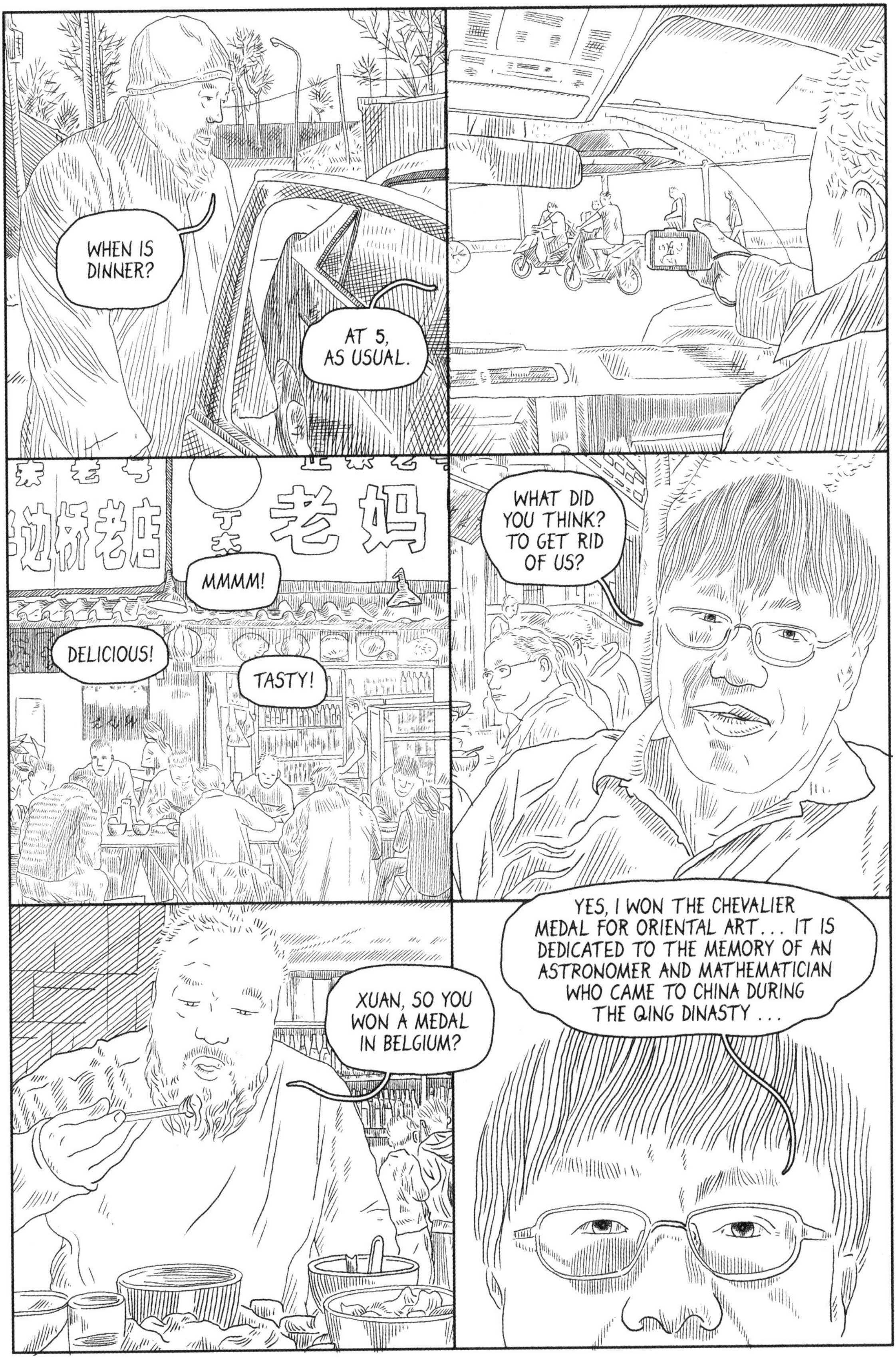
WHEN IS DINNER?
AT 5, AS USUAL.
边桥老店
老妈
MMMM!
DELICIOUS!
TASTY!
WHAT DID YOU THINK? TO GET RID OF US?
XUAN, SO YOU WON A MEDAL IN BELGIUM?
YES, I WON THE CHEVALIER MEDAL FOR ORIENTAL ART . . . IT IS DEDICATED TO THE MEMORY OF AN ASTRONOMER AND MATHEMATICIAN WHO CAME TO CHINA DURING THE QING DINASTY . . .

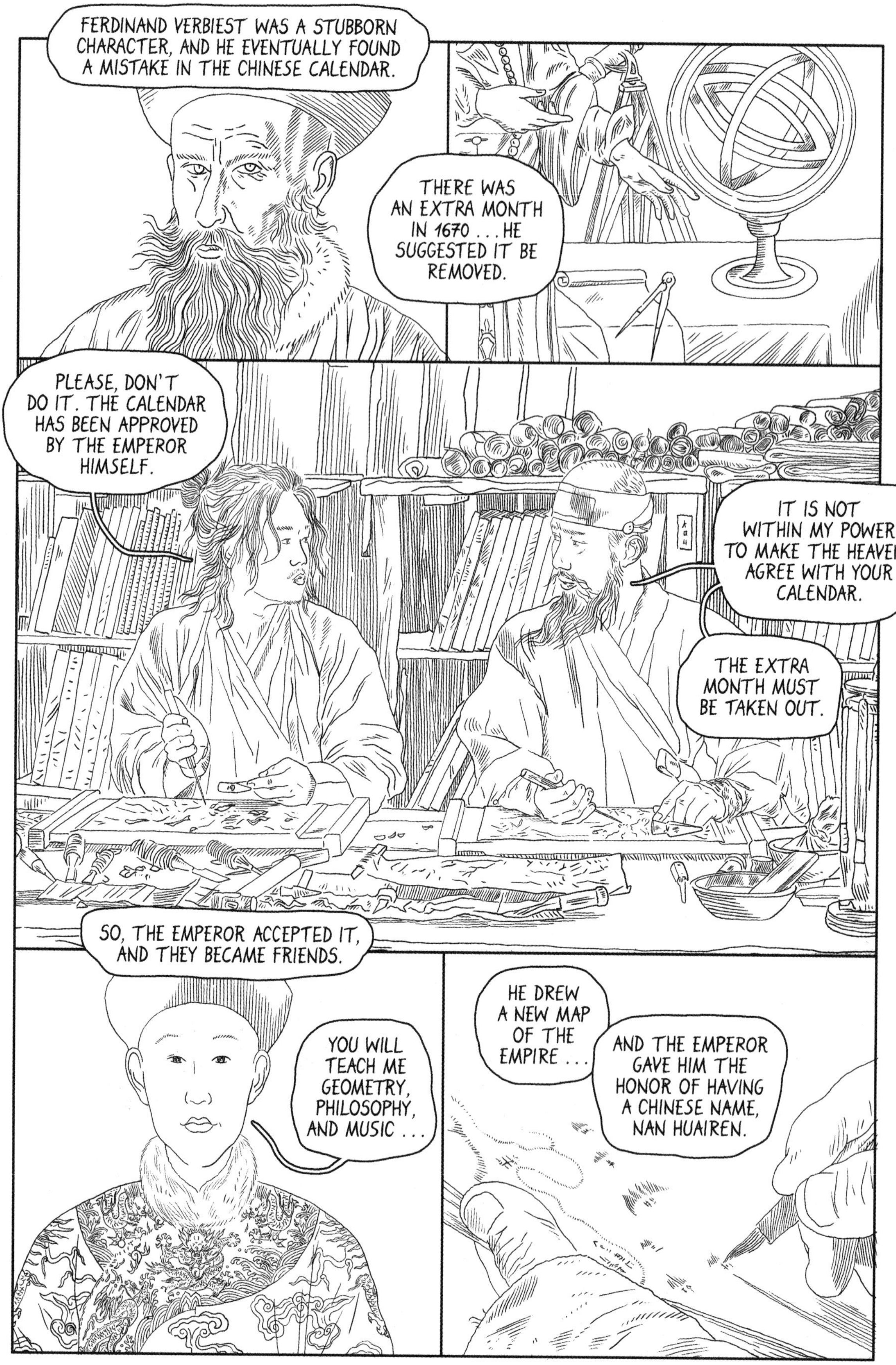
FERDINAND VERBIEST WAS A STUBBORN CHARACTER, AND HE EVENTUALLY FOUND A MISTAKE IN THE CHINESE CALENDAR.
THERE WAS AN EXTRA MONTH IN 1670 . . . HE SUGGESTED IT BE REMOVED.
PLEASE, DON'T DO IT. THE CALENDAR HAS BEEN APPROVED BY THE EMPEROR HIMSELF.
IT IS NOT WITHIN MY POWER TO MAKE THE HEAVENS AGREE WITH YOUR CALENDAR.
THE EXTRA MONTH MUST BE TAKEN OUT.
SO, THE EMPEROR ACCEPTED IT, AND THEY BECAME FRIENDS.
YOU WILL TEACH ME GEOMETRY, PHILOSOPHY, AND MUSIC . . .
HE DREW A NEW MAP OF THE EMPIRE . . .
AND THE EMPEROR GAVE HIM THE HONOR OF HAVING A CHINESE NAME, NAN HUAIREN.

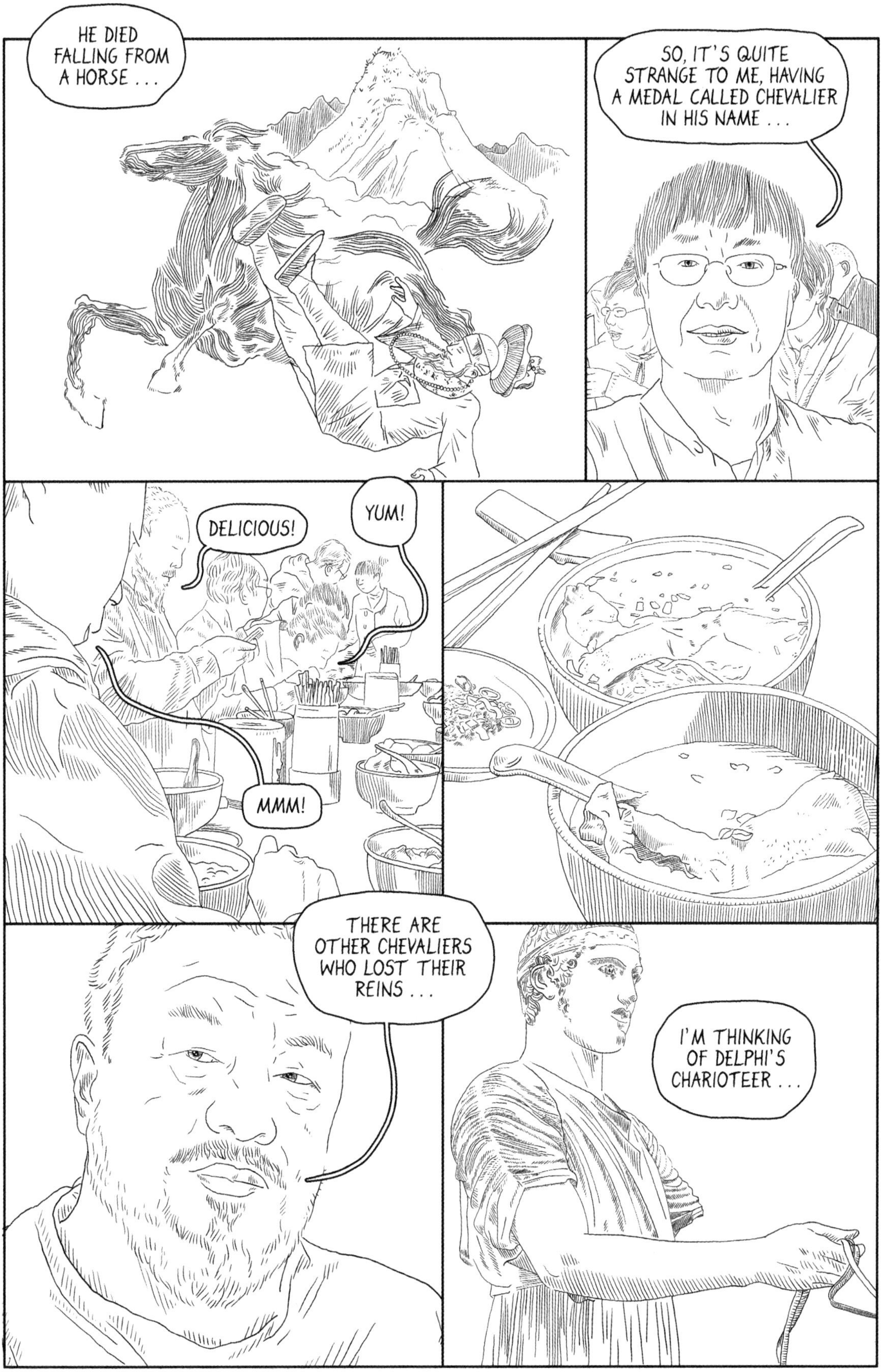
HE DIED FALLING FROM A HORSE . . .
SO, IT'S QUITE STRANGE TO ME, HAVING A MEDAL CALLED CHEVALIER IN HIS NAME . . .
DELICIOUS!
YUM!
MMM!
THERE ARE OTHER CHEVALIERS WHO LOST THEIR REINS . . .
I'M THINKING OF DELPHI'S CHARIOTEER . . .

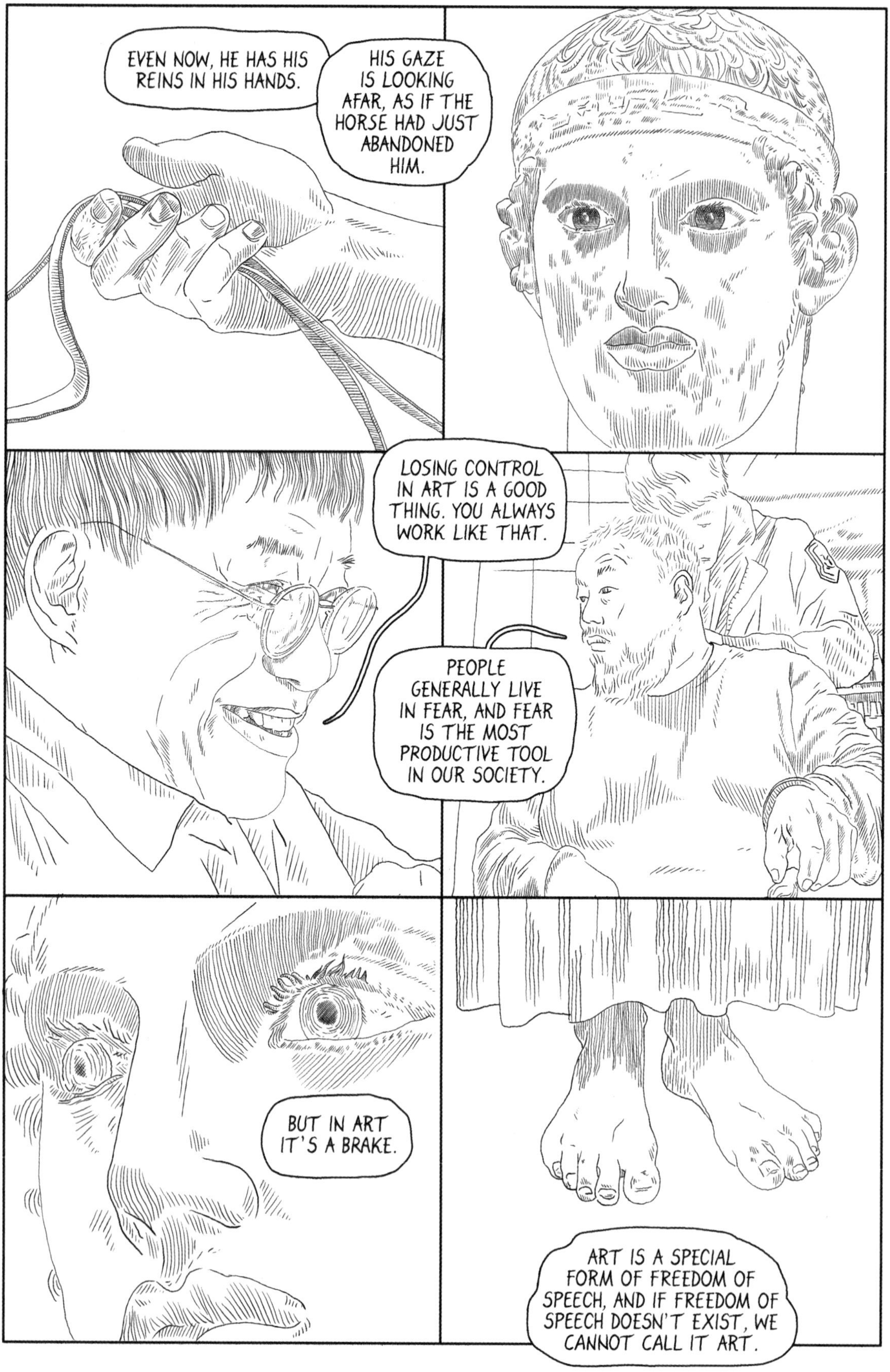
EVEN NOW, HE HAS HIS REINS IN HIS HANDS.
HIS GAZE IS LOOKING AFAR, AS IF THE HORSE HAD JUST ABANDONED HIM.
LOSING CONTROL IN ART IS A GOOD THING. YOU ALWAYS WORK LIKE THAT.
PEOPLE GENERALLY LIVE IN FEAR, AND FEAR IS THE MOST PRODUCTIVE TOOL IN OUR SOCIETY.
BUT IN ART IT'S A BRAKE.
ART IS A SPECIAL FORM OF FREEDOM OF SPEECH, AND IF FREEDOM OF SPEECH DOESN'T EXIST, WE CANNOT CALL IT ART.

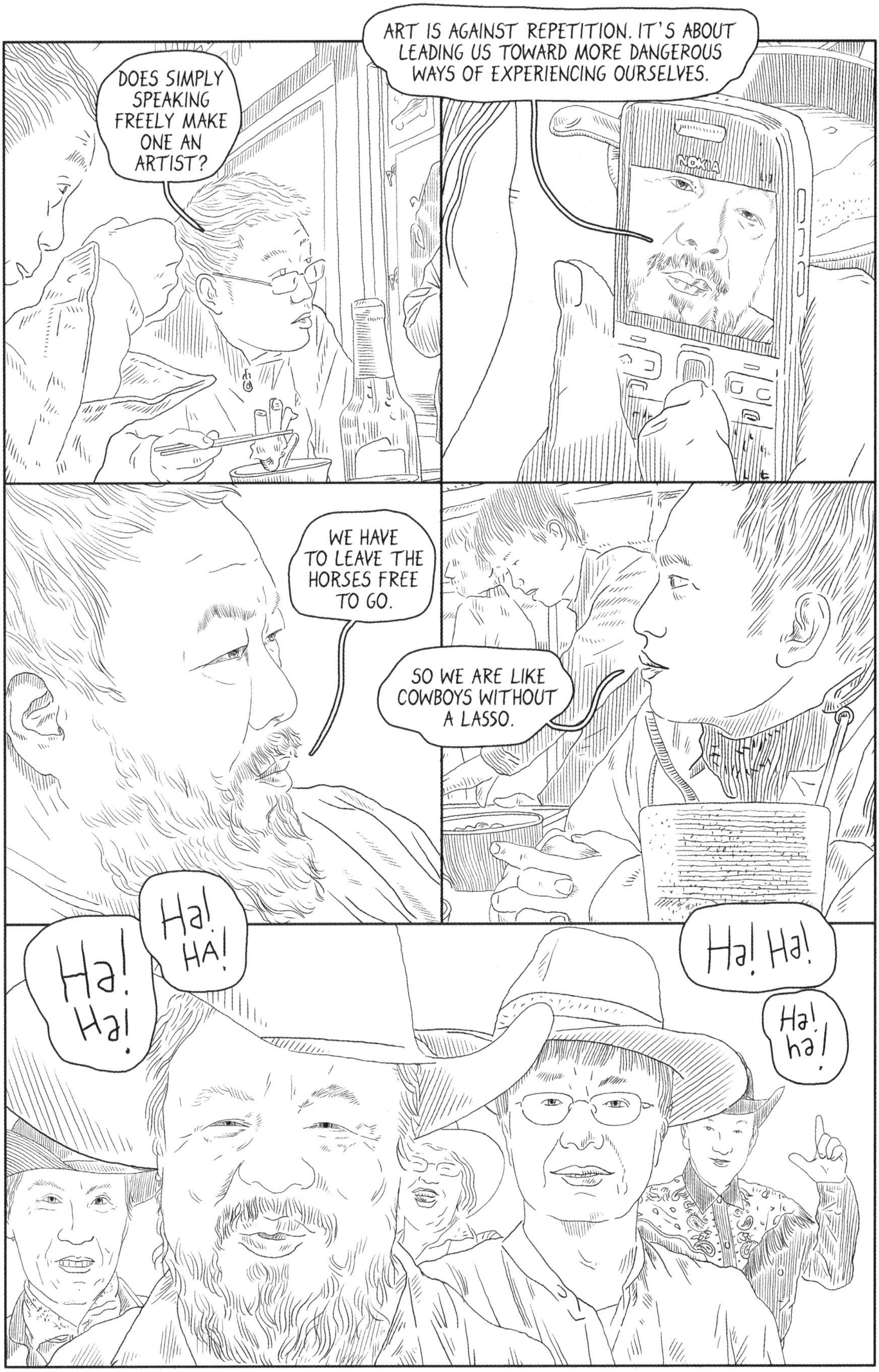
DOES SIMPLY SPEAKING FREELY MAKE ONE AN ARTIST?
ART IS AGAINST REPETITION. IT'S ABOUT LEADING US TOWARD MORE DANGEROUS WAYS OF EXPERIENCING OURSELVES.
NOKIA
WE HAVE TO LEAVE THE HORSES FREE TO GO.
SO WE ARE LIKE COWBOYS WITHOUT A LASSO.
Ha! Ha!
Ha! HA!
Ha! Ha!
Ha! ha!

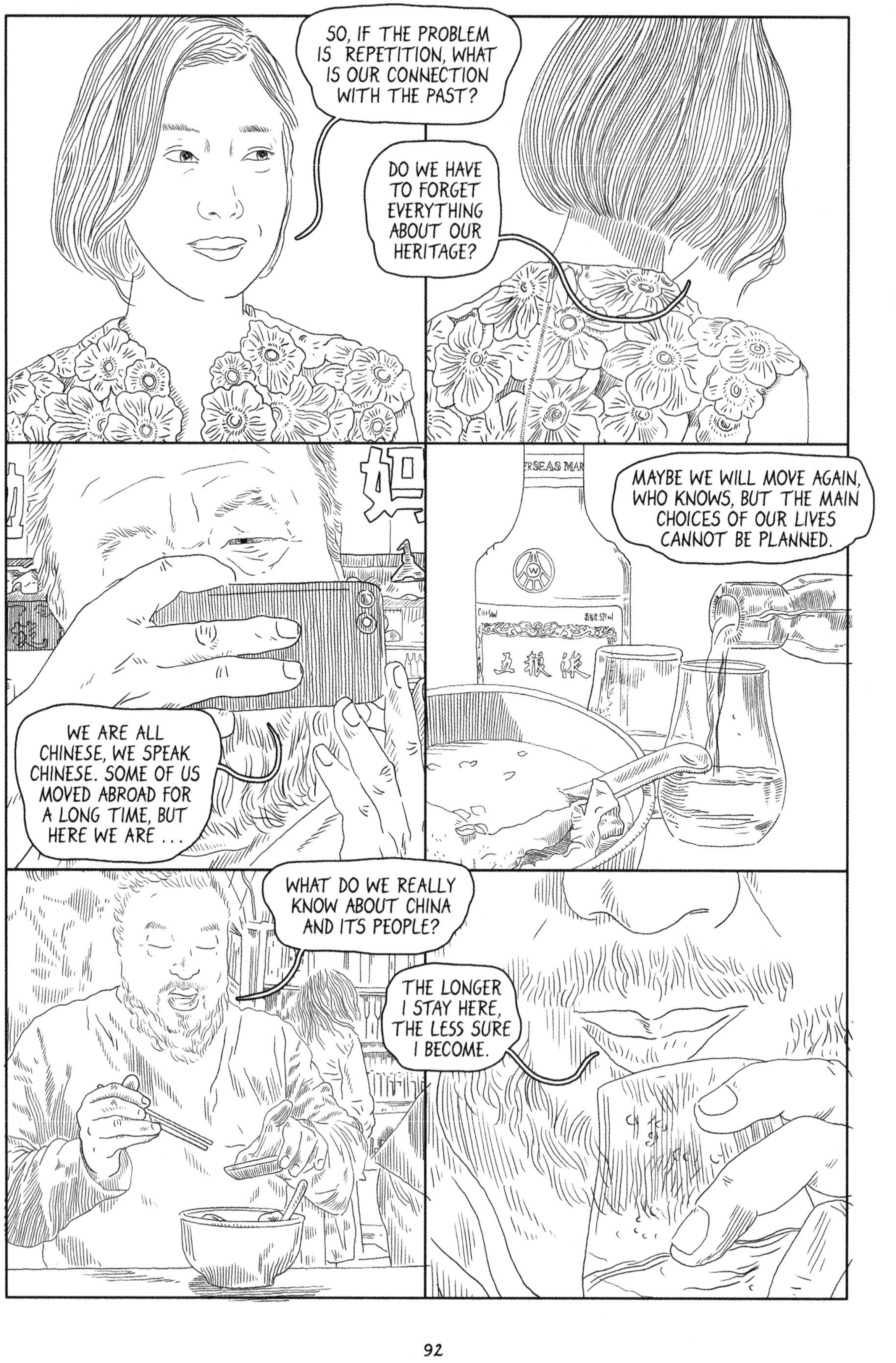
SO, IF THE PROBLEM IS REPETITION, WHAT IS OUR CONNECTION WITH THE PAST?
DO WE HAVE TO FORGET EVERYTHING ABOUT OUR HERITAGE?
WE ARE ALL CHINESE, WE SPEAK CHINESE. SOME OF US MOVED ABROAD FOR A LONG TIME, BUT HERE WE ARE . . .
MAYBE WE WILL MOVE AGAIN, WHO KNOWS, BUT THE MAIN CHOICES OF OUR LIVES CANNOT BE PLANNED.
五粮液
WHAT DO WE REALLY KNOW ABOUT CHINA AND ITS PEOPLE?
THE LONGER I STAY HERE, THE LESS SURE I BECOME.

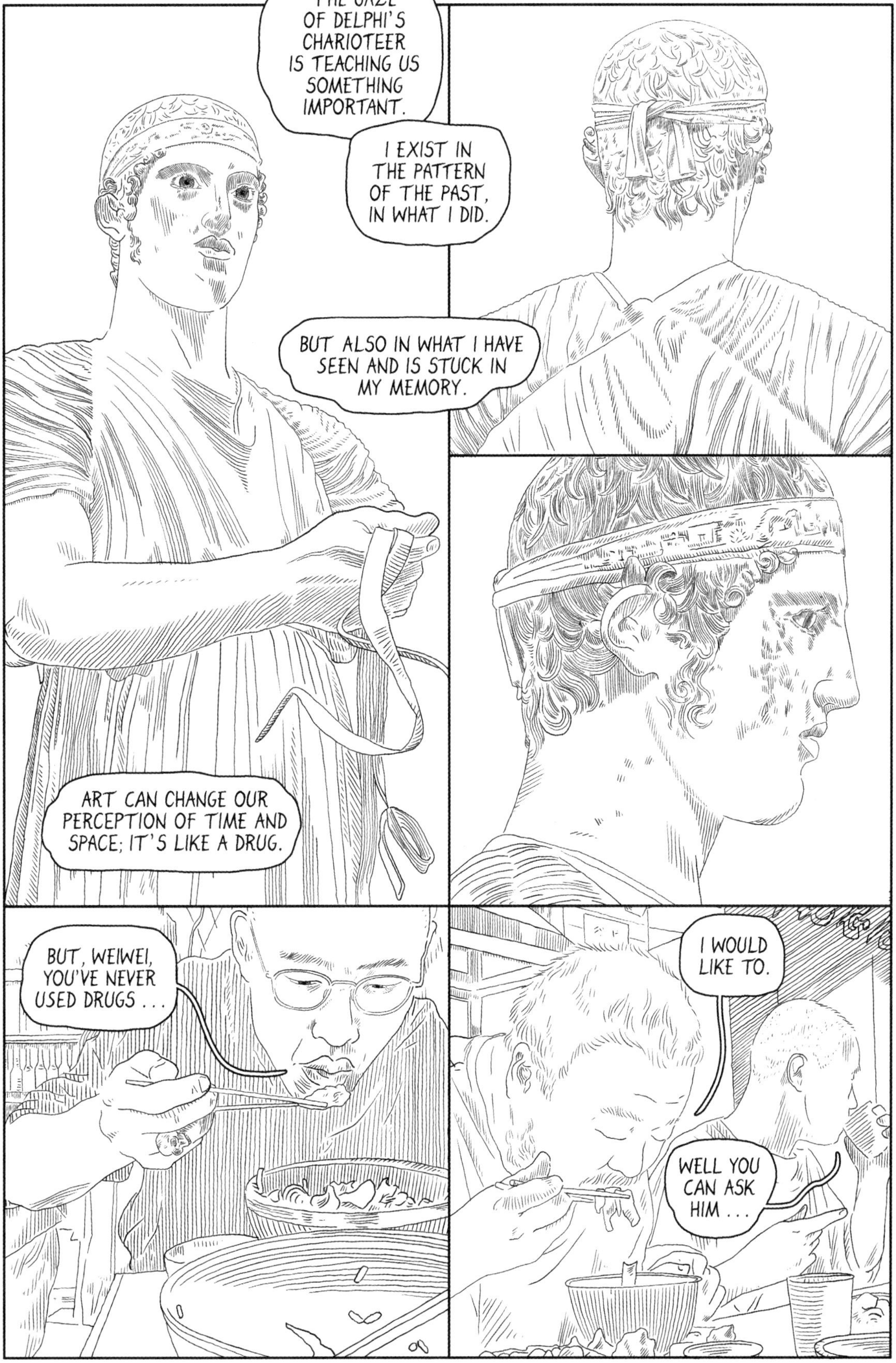
THE GAZE OF DELPHI'S CHARIOTEER IS TEACHING US SOMETHING IMPORTANT.
I EXIST IN THE PATTERN OF THE PAST, IN WHAT I DID.
BUT ALSO IN WHAT I HAVE SEEN AND IS STUCK IN MY MEMORY.
ART CAN CHANGE OUR PERCEPTION OF TIME AND SPACE; IT'S LIKE A DRUG.
BUT, WEIWEI, YOU'VE NEVER USED DRUGS . . .
I WOULD LIKE TO.
WELL YOU CAN ASK HIM . . .

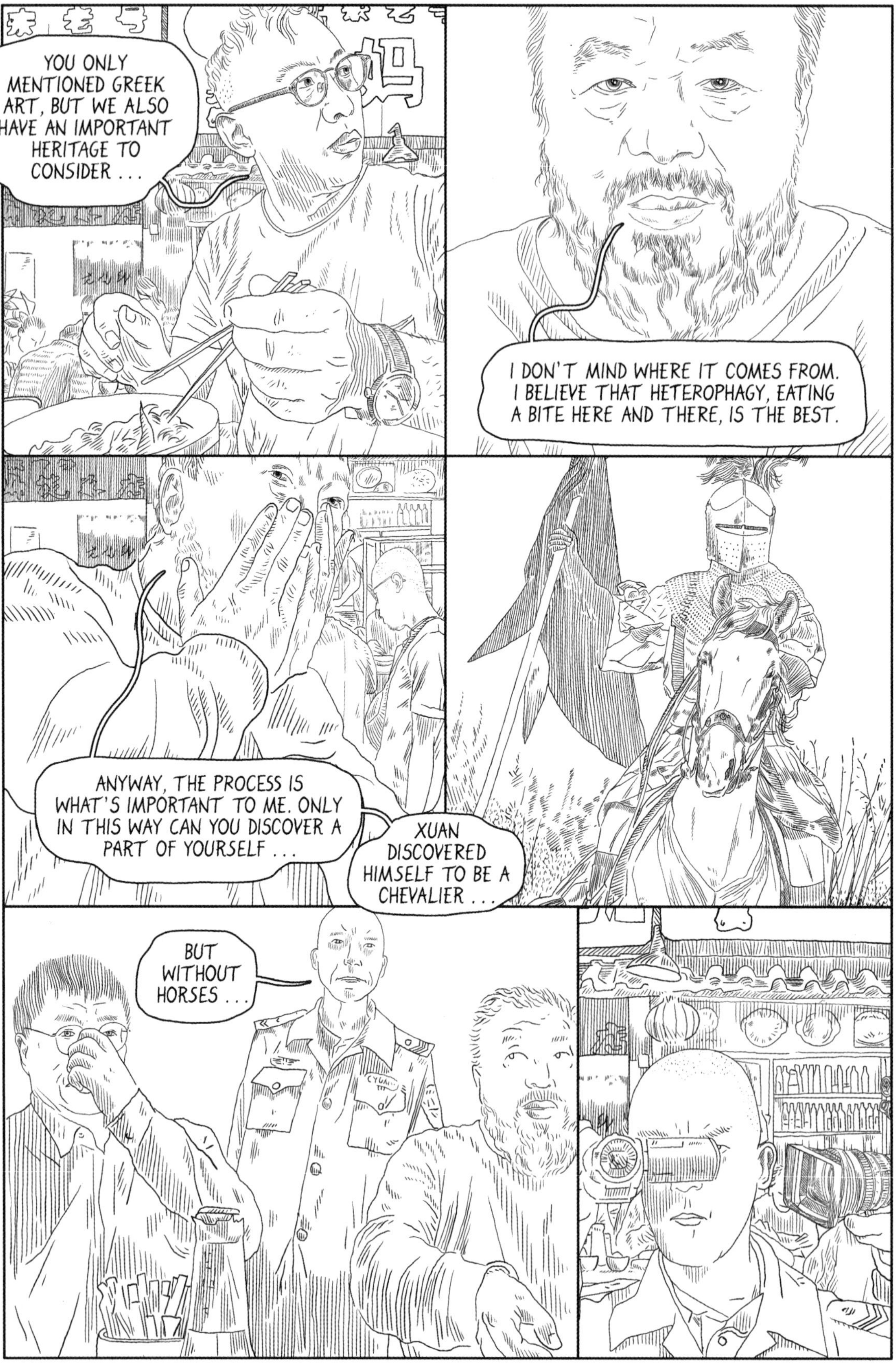
YOU ONLY MENTIONED GREEK ART, BUT WE ALSO HAVE AN IMPORTANT HERITAGE TO CONSIDER . . .
I DON'T MIND WHERE IT COMES FROM. I BELIEVE THAT HETEROPHAGY, EATING A BITE HERE AND THERE, IS THE BEST.
ANYWAY, THE PROCESS IS WHAT'S IMPORTANT TO ME. ONLY IN THIS WAY CAN YOU DISCOVER A PART OF YOURSELF . . .
XUAN DISCOVERED HIMSELF TO BE A CHEVALIER . . .
BUT WITHOUT HORSES . . .

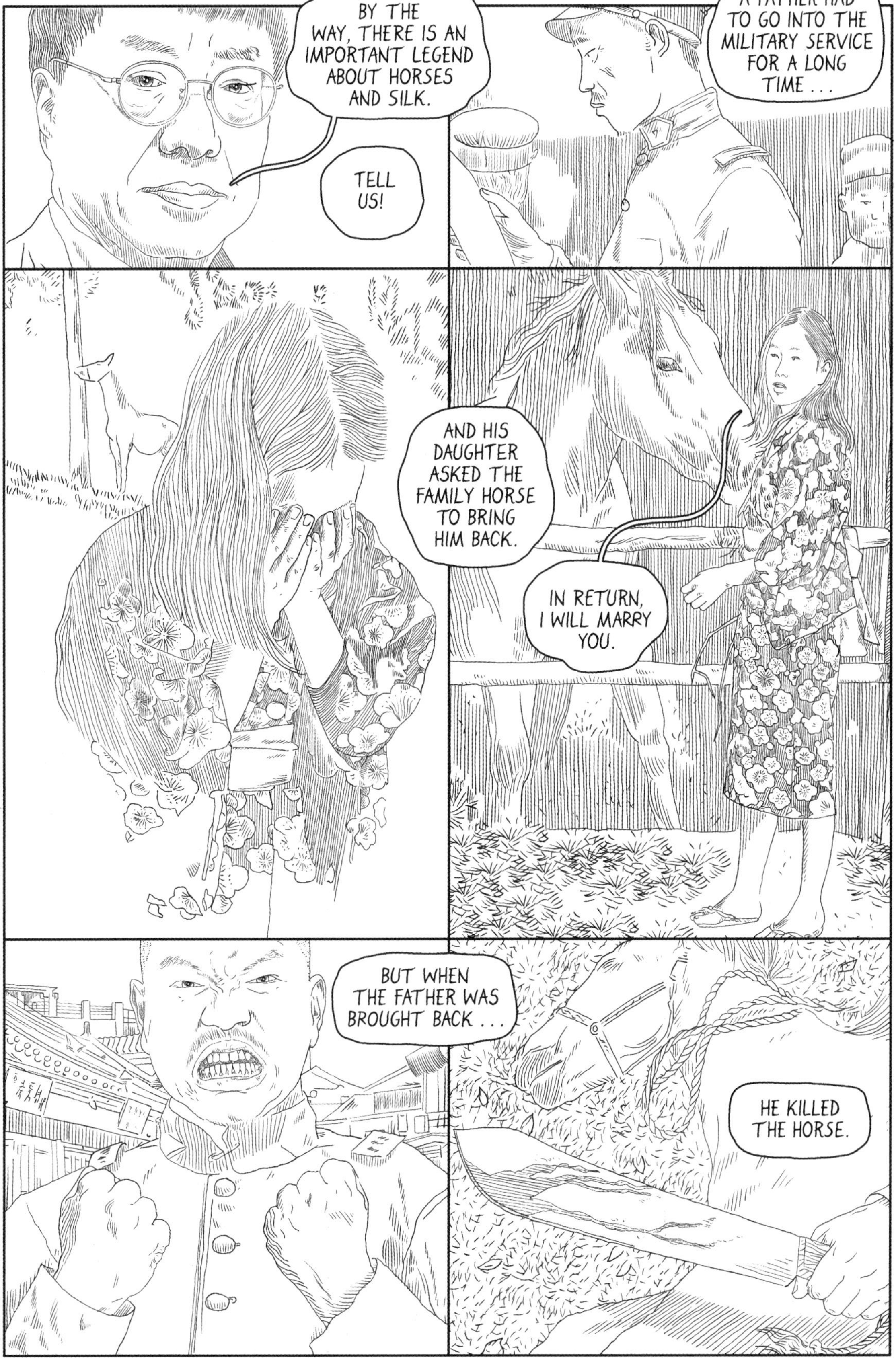
BY THE WAY, THERE IS AN IMPORTANT LEGEND ABOUT HORSES AND SILK.
TELL US!
A FATHER HAD TO GO INTO THE MILITARY SERVICE FOR A LONG TIME . . .
AND HIS DAUGHTER ASKED THE FAMILY HORSE TO BRING HIM BACK.
IN RETURN, I WILL MARRY YOU.
BUT WHEN THE FATHER WAS BROUGHT BACK . . .
HE KILLED THE HORSE.

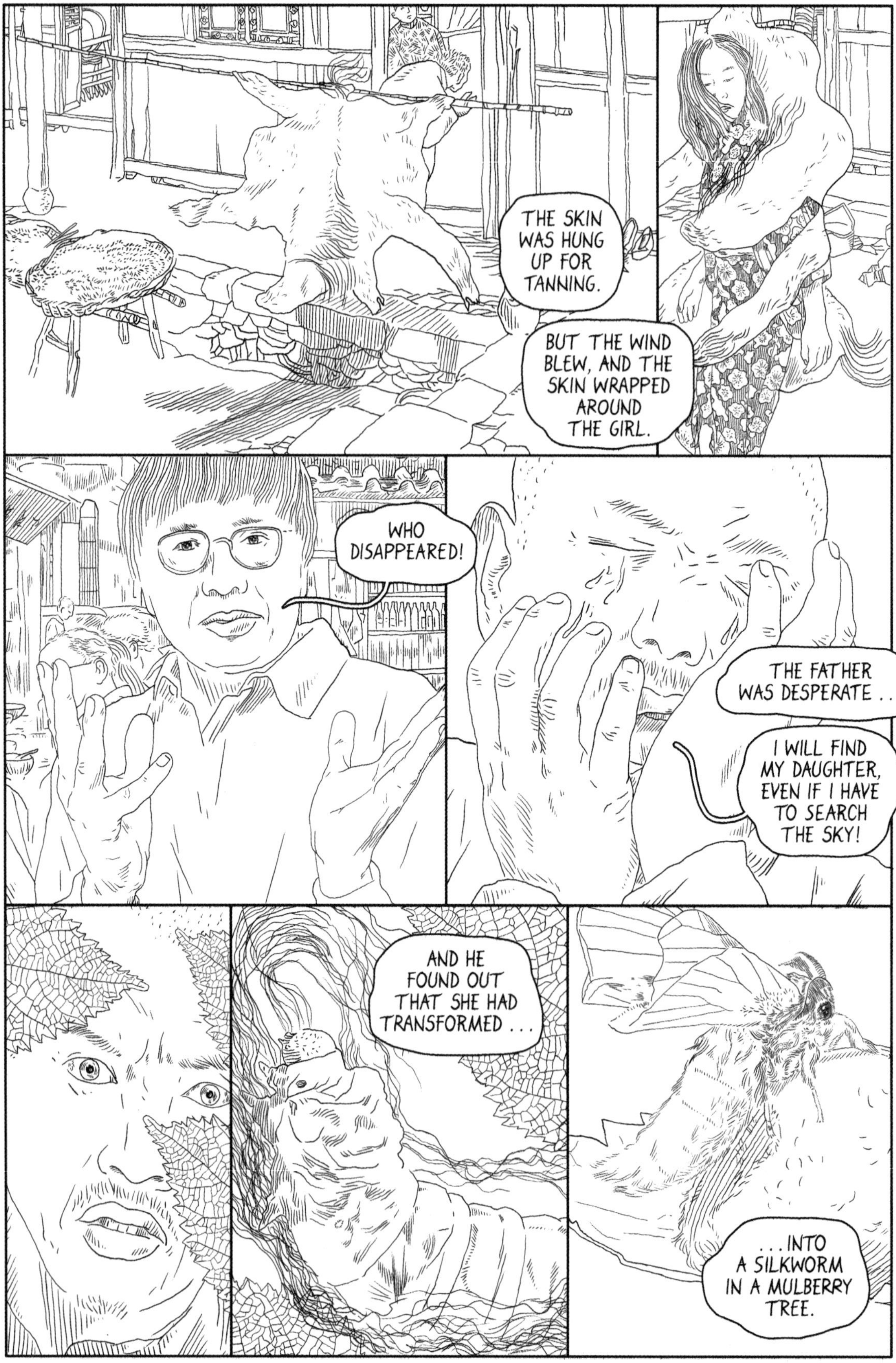
THE SKIN WAS HUNG UP FOR TANNING.
BUT THE WIND BLEW, AND THE SKIN WRAPPED AROUND THE GIRL.
WHO DISAPPEARED!
THE FATHER WAS DESPERATE . . .
I WILL FIND MY DAUGHTER, EVEN IF I HAVE TO SEARCH THE SKY!
AND HE FOUND OUT THAT SHE HAD TRANSFORMED . . .
. . . INTO A SILKWORM IN A MULBERRY TREE.

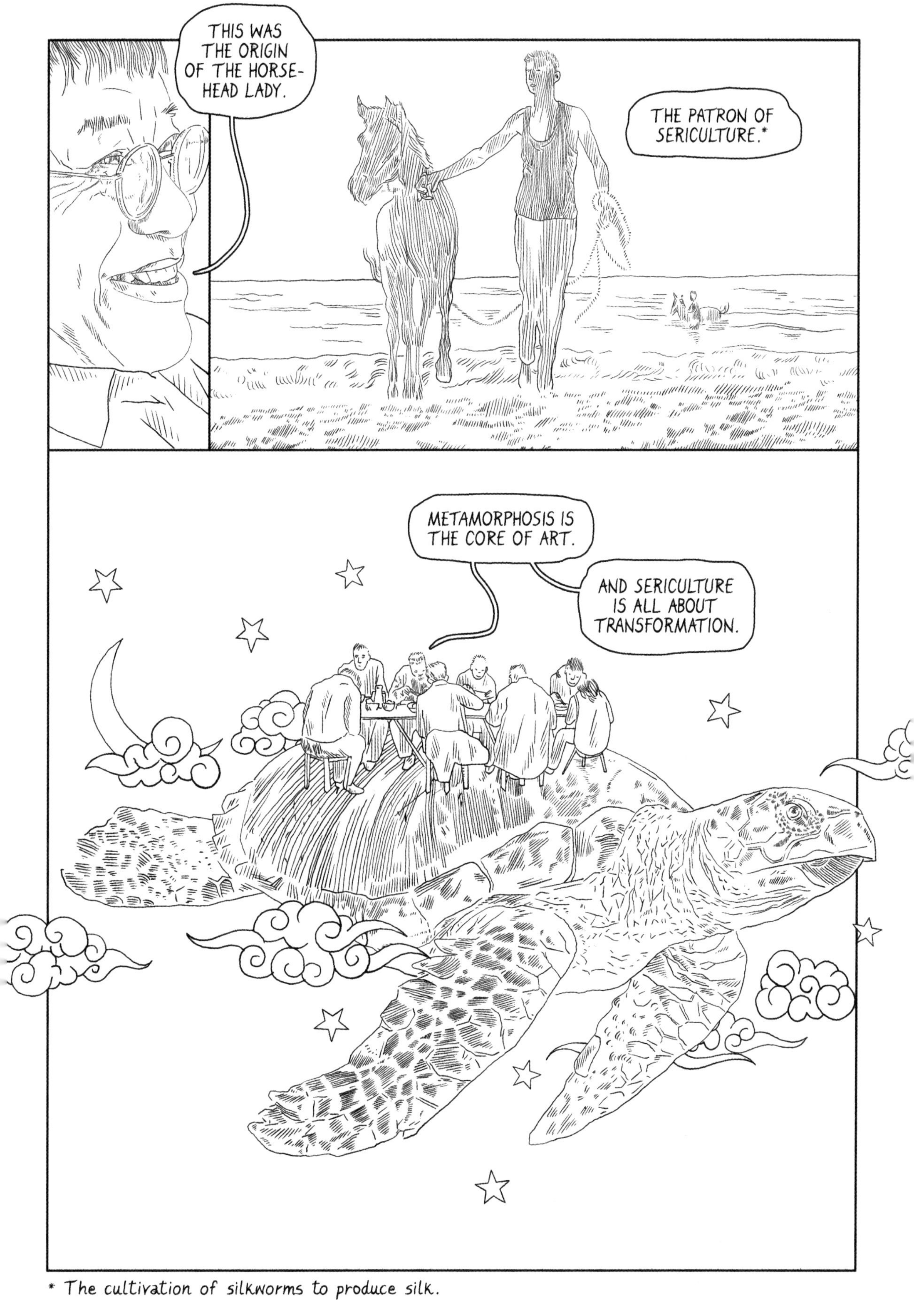
THIS WAS THE ORIGIN OF THE HORSE-HEAD LADY.
THE PATRON OF SERICULTURE.*
METAMORPHOSIS IS THE CORE OF ART.
AND SERICULTURE IS ALL ABOUT TRANSFORMATION.

* The cultivation of silkworms to produce silk.

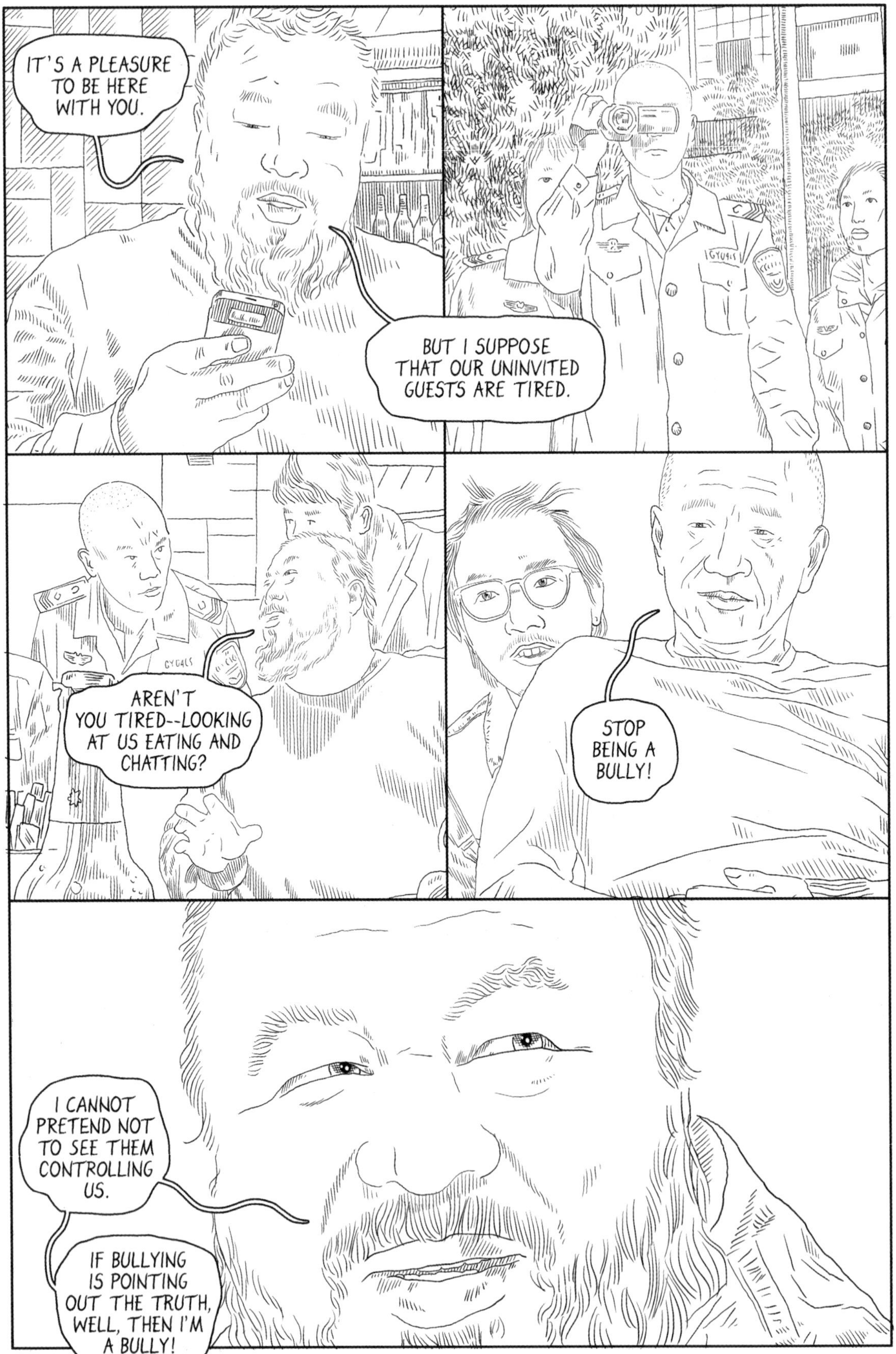
IT'S A PLEASURE TO BE HERE WITH YOU.
BUT I SUPPOSE THAT OUR UNINVITED GUESTS ARE TIRED.
AREN'T YOU TIRED--LOOKING AT US EATING AND CHATTING?
STOP BEING A BULLY!
I CANNOT PRETEND NOT TO SEE THEM CONTROLLING US.
IF BULLYING IS POINTING OUT THE TRUTH, WELL, THEN I'M A BULLY!

Chapter 8

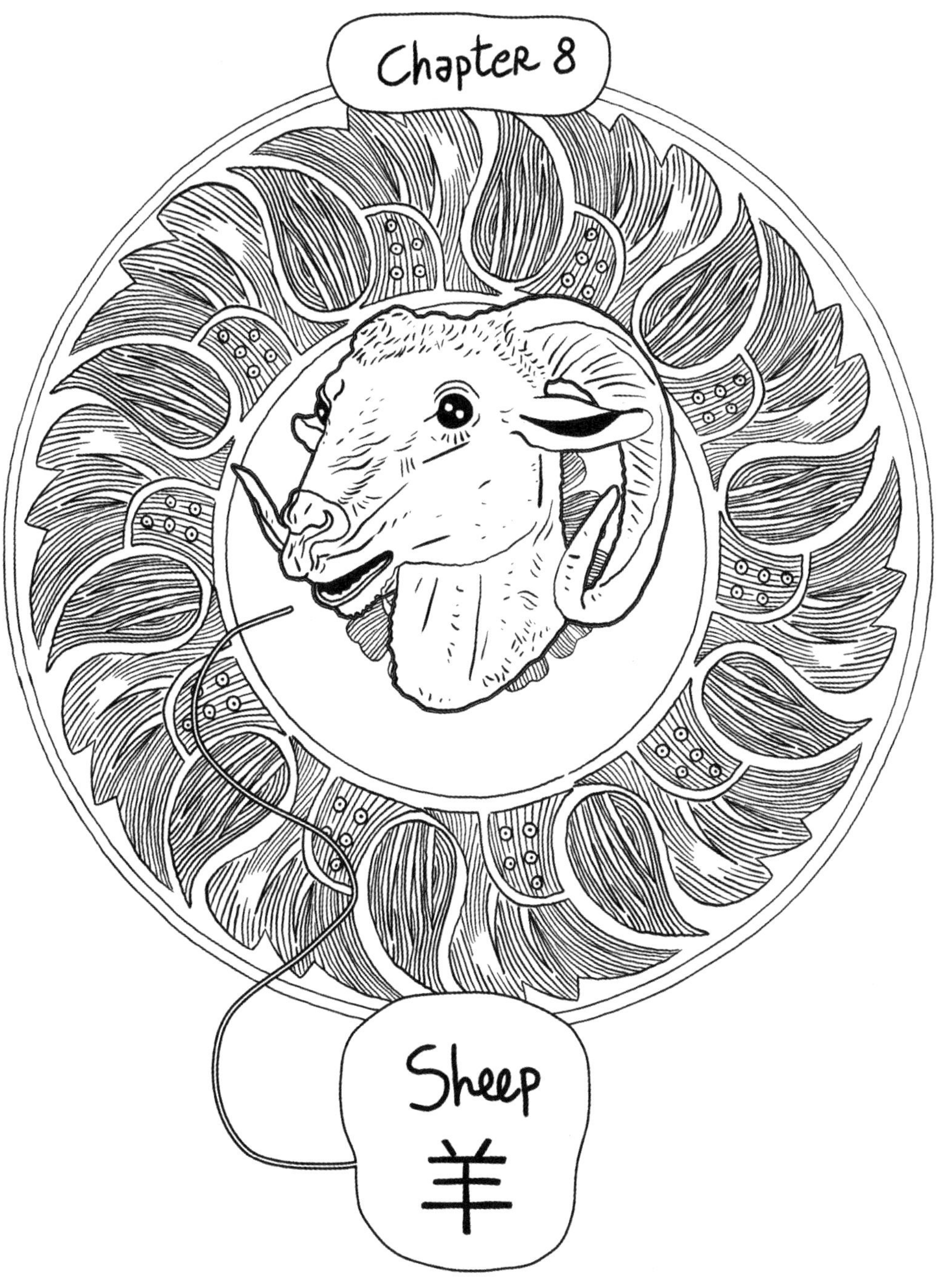

Sheep 羊

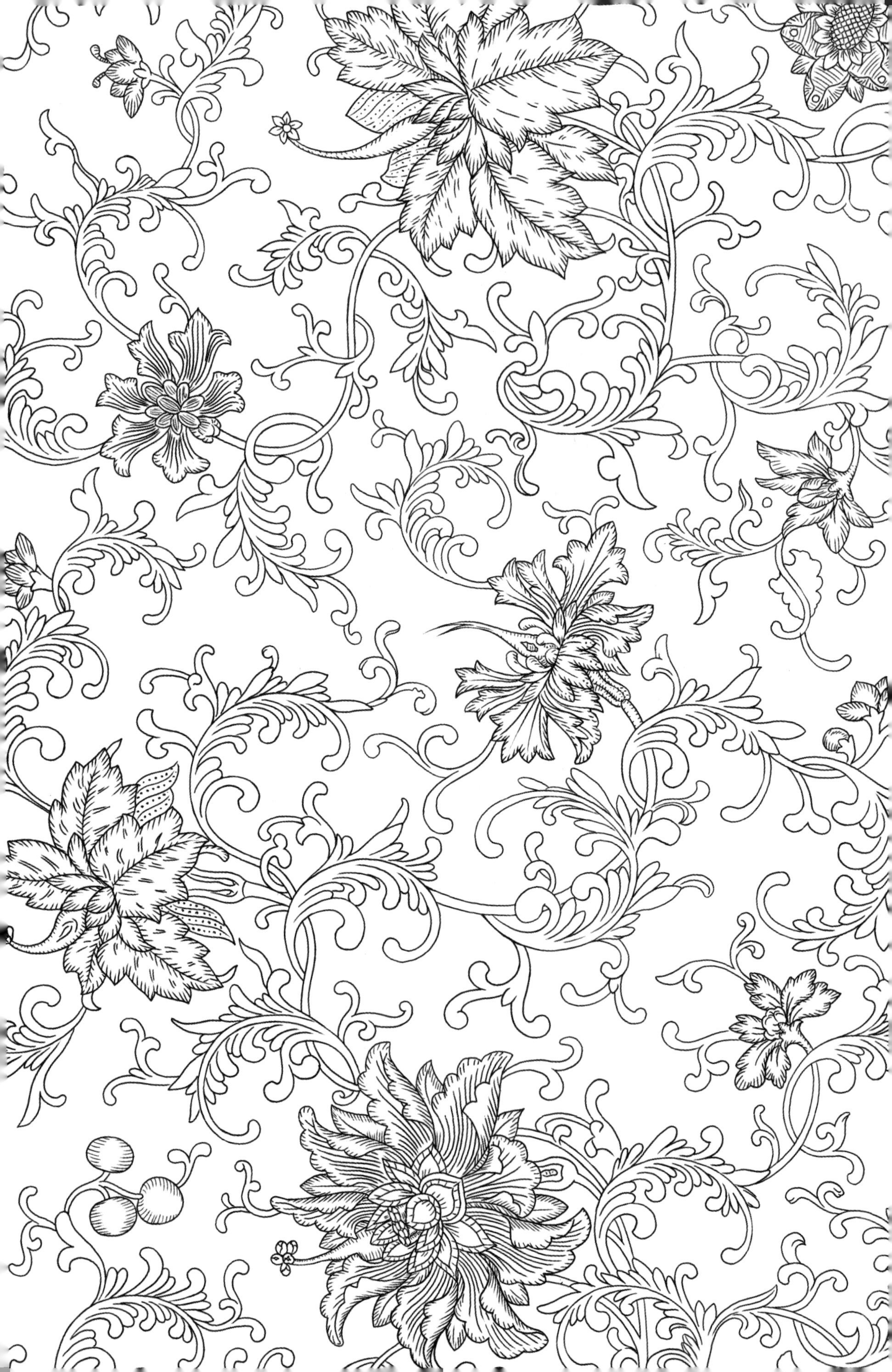

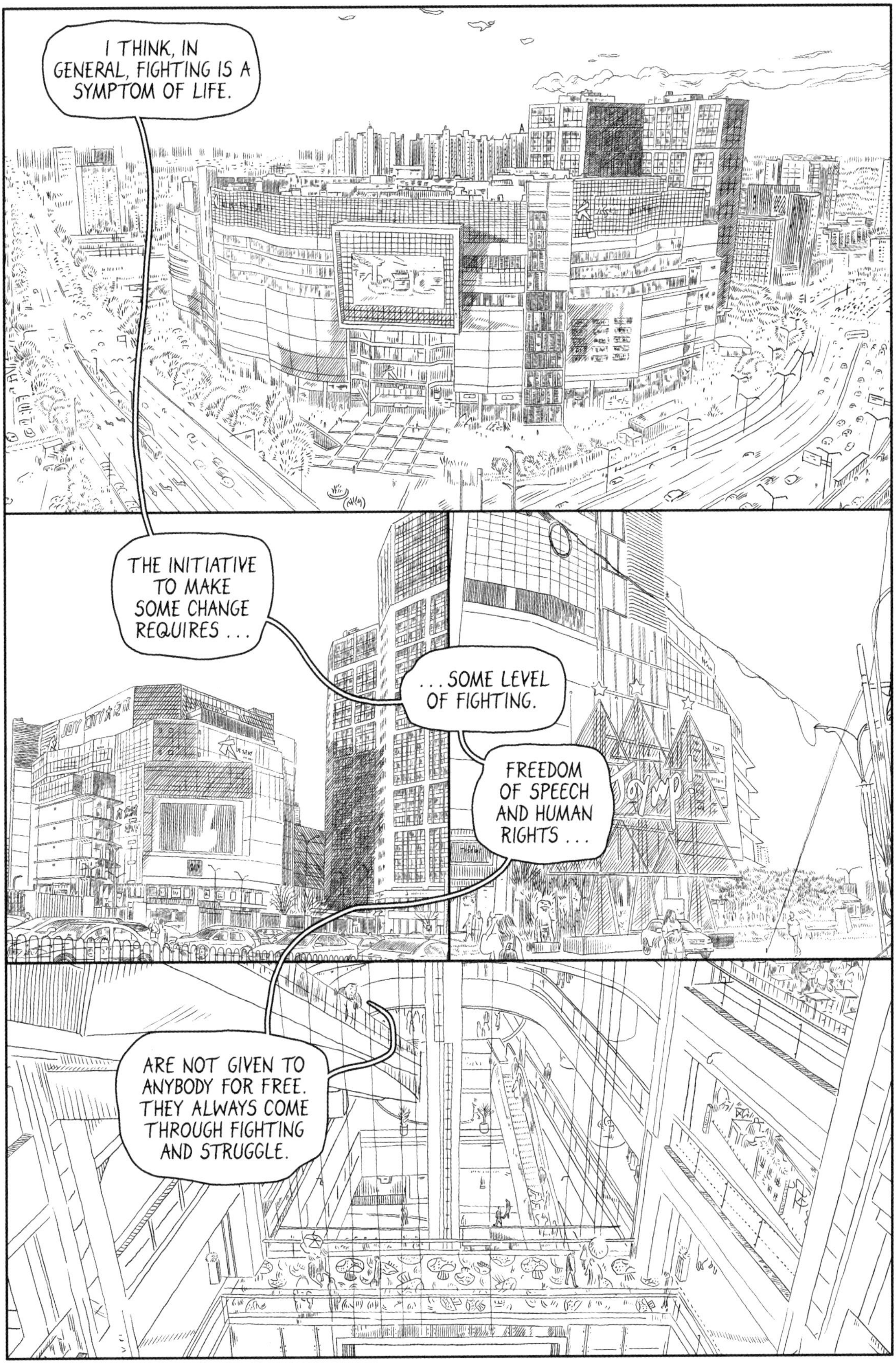
I THINK, IN GENERAL, FIGHTING IS A SYMPTOM OF LIFE.
THE INITIATIVE TO MAKE SOME CHANGE REQUIRES . . .
. . . SOME LEVEL OF FIGHTING.
FREEDOM OF SPEECH AND HUMAN RIGHTS . . .
ARE NOT GIVEN TO ANYBODY FOR FREE. THEY ALWAYS COME THROUGH FIGHTING AND STRUGGLE.

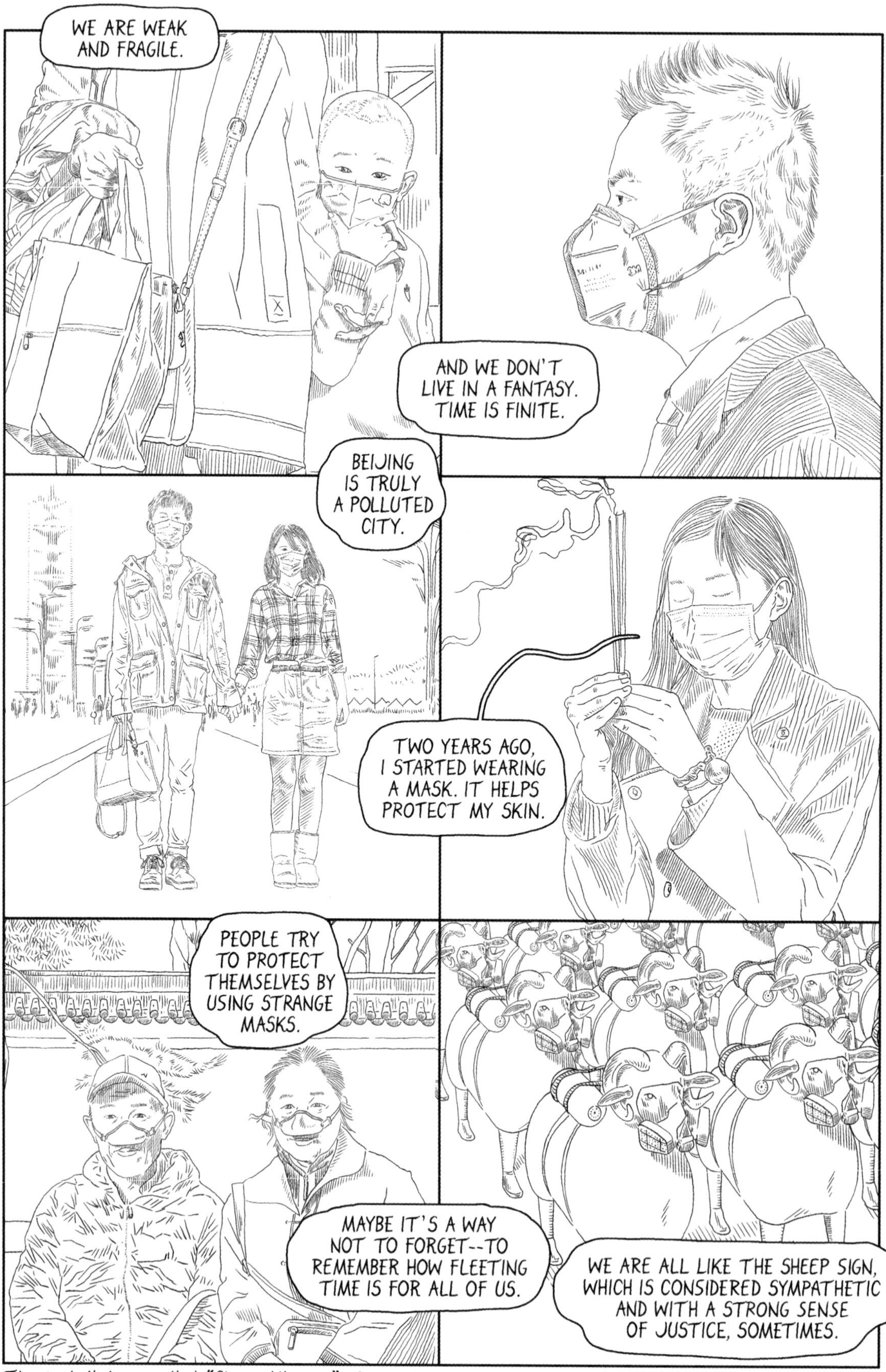
WE ARE WEAK AND FRAGILE.
AND WE DON'T LIVE IN A FANTASY. TIME IS FINITE.
BEIJING IS TRULY A POLLUTED CITY.
TWO YEARS AGO, I STARTED WEARING A MASK. IT HELPS PROTECT MY SKIN.
PEOPLE TRY TO PROTECT THEMSELVES BY USING STRANGE MASKS.
MAYBE IT'S A WAY NOT TO FORGET--TO REMEMBER HOW FLEETING TIME IS FOR ALL OF US.
WE ARE ALL LIKE THE SHEEP SIGN, WHICH IS CONSIDERED SYMPATHETIC AND WITH A STRONG SENSE OF JUSTICE, SOMETIMES.
The installation, called "Sheep Alliance," of 100 sheep statues with gas masks and oxygen bottles was on display and for sale in Beijing's Chaoyang Joy City Shopping Mall on May 12, 2015.

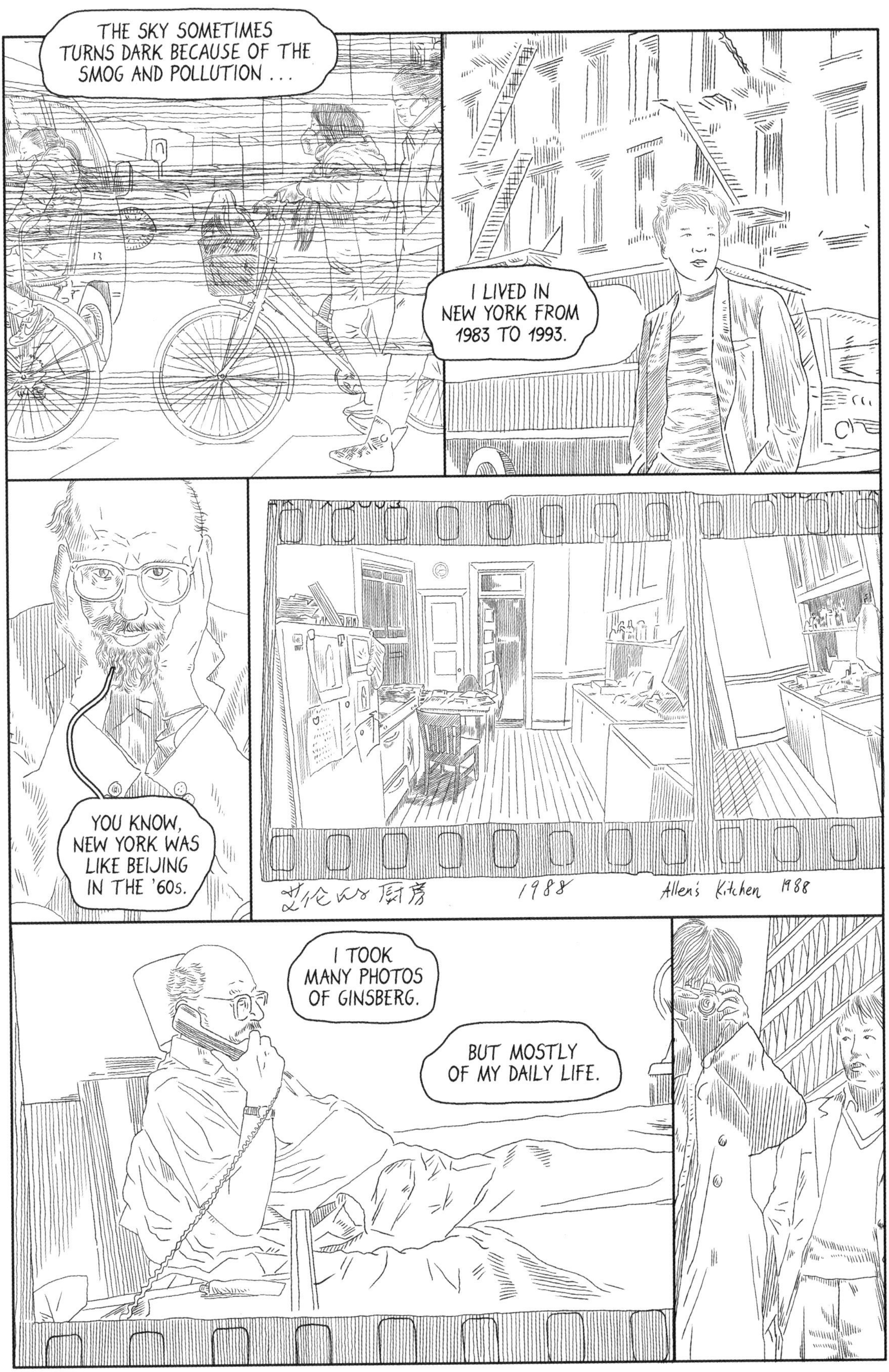
THE SKY SOMETIMES TURNS DARK BECAUSE OF THE SMOG AND POLLUTION . . .
I LIVED IN NEW YORK FROM 1983 TO 1993.
YOU KNOW, NEW YORK WAS LIKE BEIJING IN THE '60s.
艾伦的厨房 1988
Allen's Kitchen 1988
I TOOK MANY PHOTOS OF GINSBERG.
BUT MOSTLY OF MY DAILY LIFE.

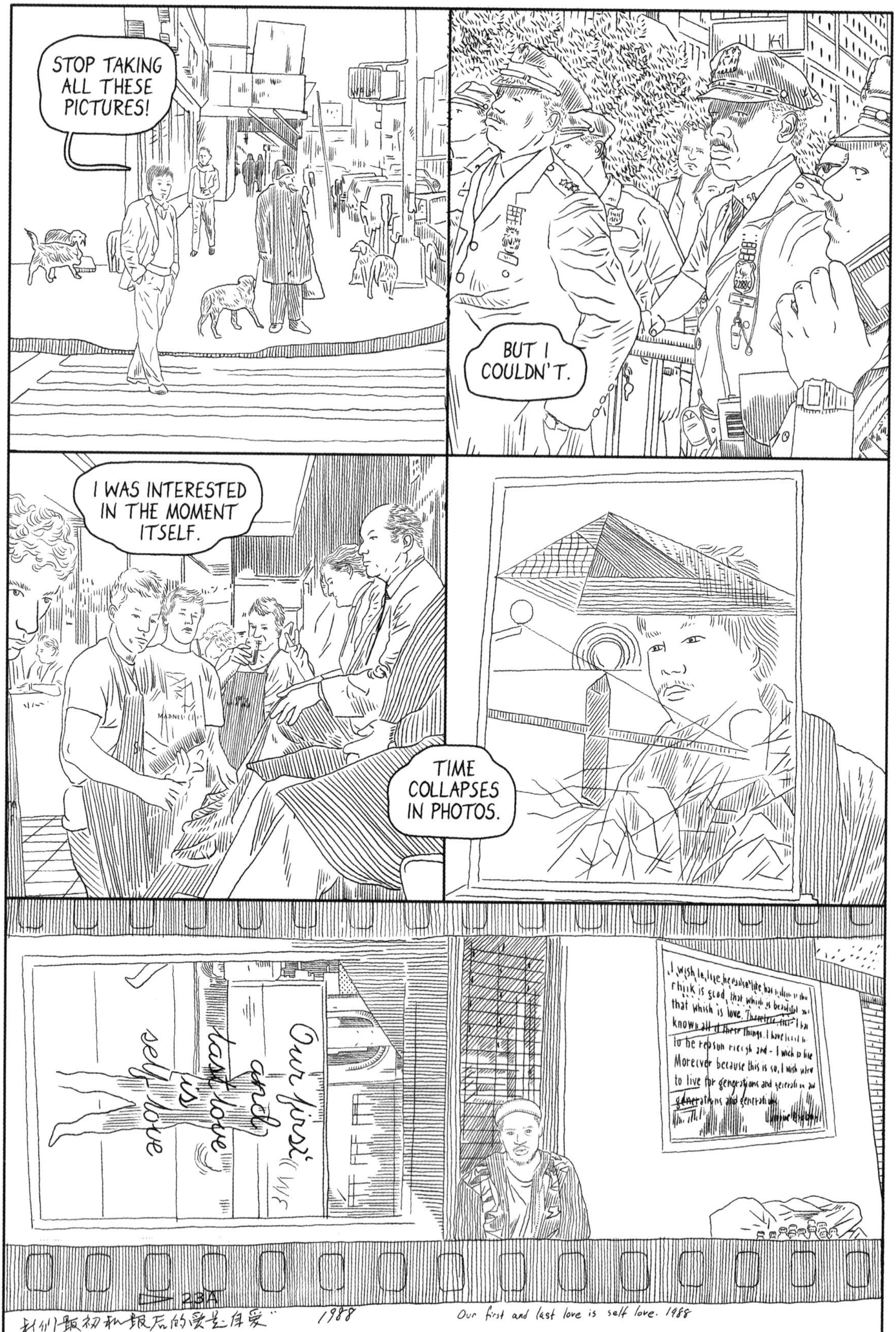
STOP TAKING ALL THESE PICTURES!
BUT I COULDN'T.
I WAS INTERESTED IN THE MOMENT ITSELF.
TIME COLLAPSES IN PHOTOS.
Our first and last love is self love
23A
1988
Our first and last love is self love. 1988

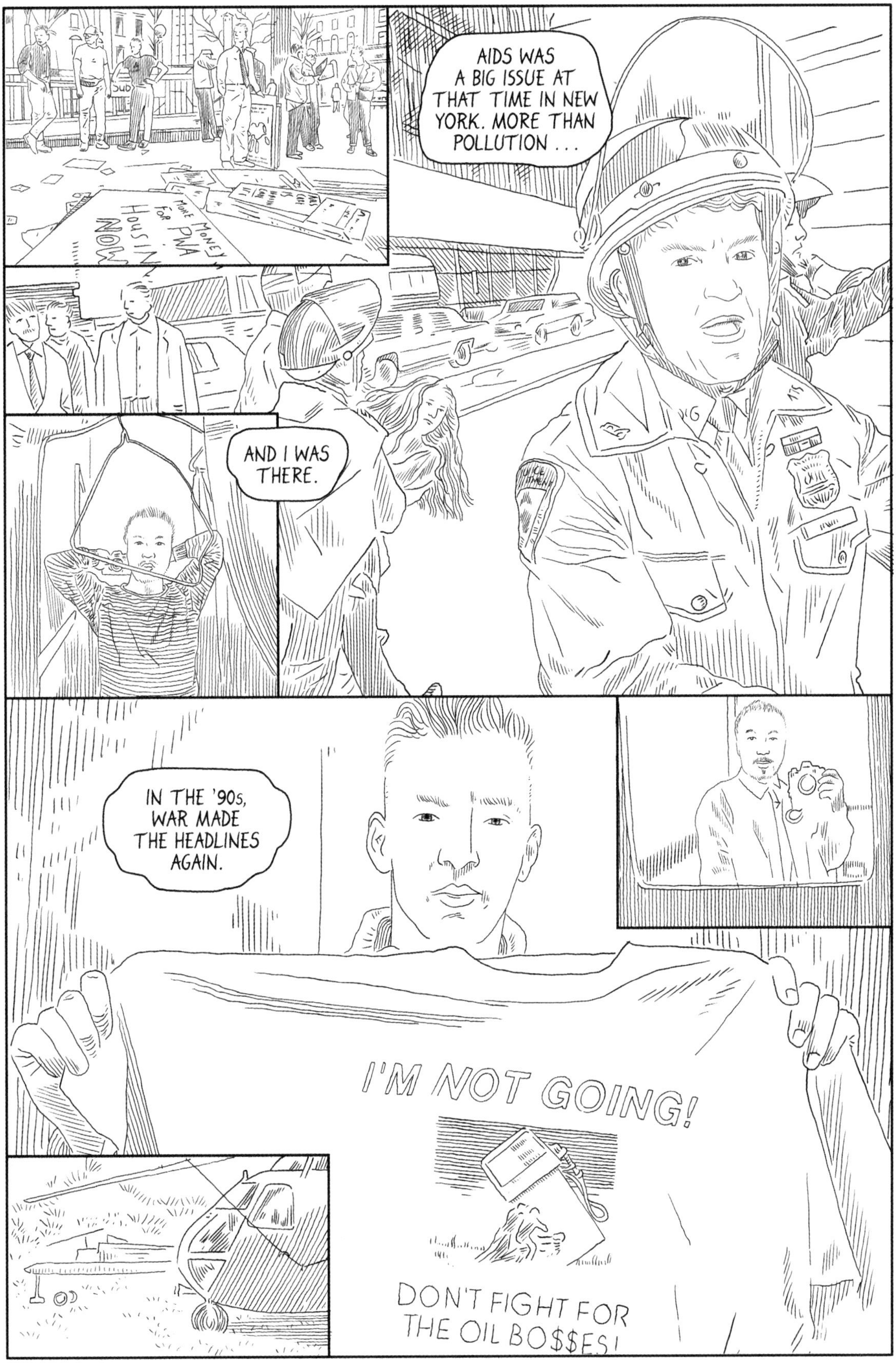
MORE MONEY FOR PWA HOUSIN NOW
AIDS WAS A BIG ISSUE AT THAT TIME IN NEW YORK. MORE THAN POLLUTION . . .
AND I WAS THERE.
IN THE '90s, WAR MADE THE HEADLINES AGAIN.
I'M NOT GOING!
DON'T FIGHT FOR THE OIL BO$$ES!

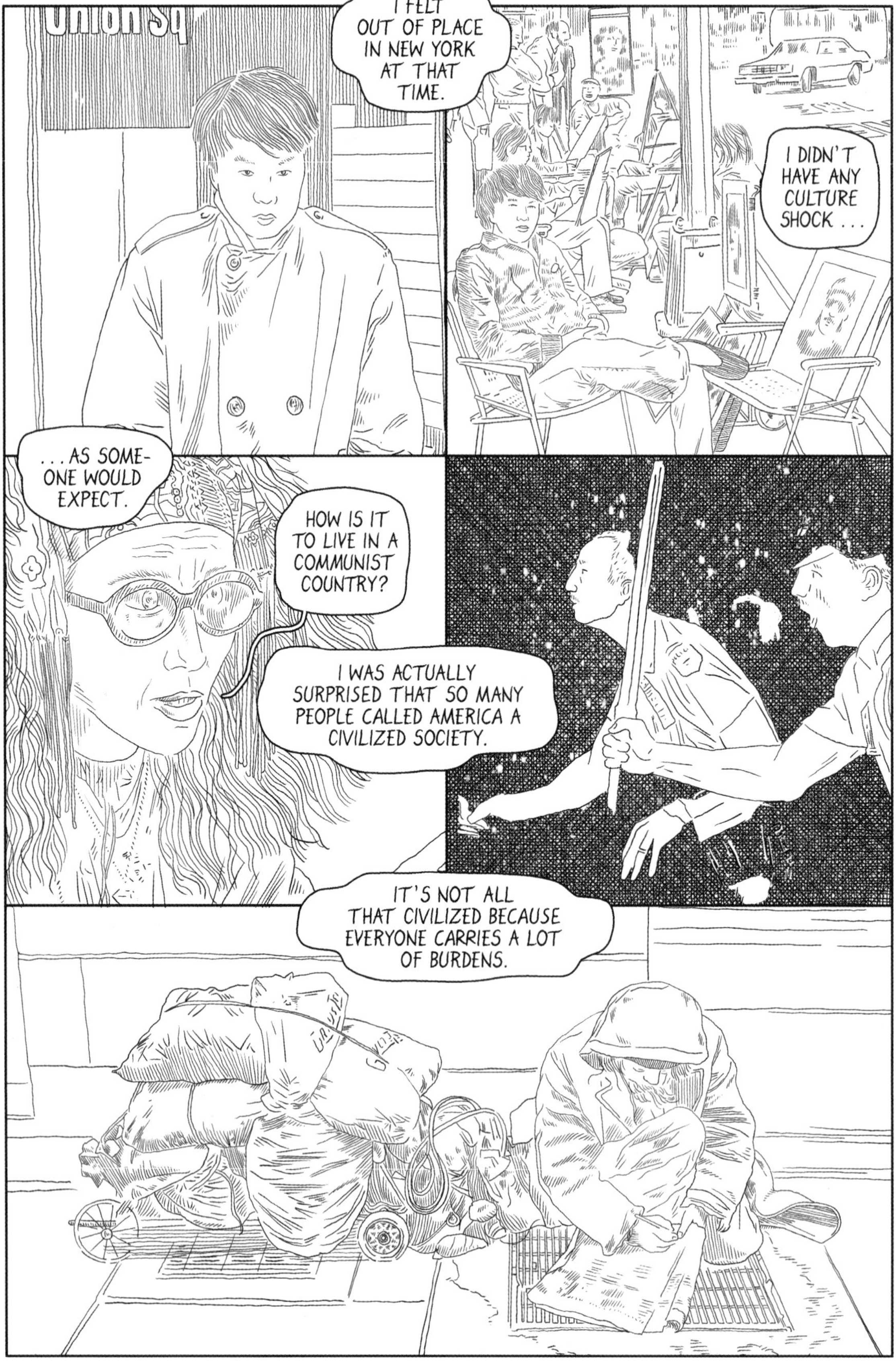
Union Sq
I FELT OUT OF PLACE IN NEW YORK AT THAT TIME.
I DIDN'T HAVE ANY CULTURE SHOCK . . .
. . . AS SOME-ONE WOULD EXPECT.
HOW IS IT TO LIVE IN A COMMUNIST COUNTRY?
I WAS ACTUALLY SURPRISED THAT SO MANY PEOPLE CALLED AMERICA A CIVILIZED SOCIETY.
IT'S NOT ALL THAT CIVILIZED BECAUSE EVERYONE CARRIES A LOT OF BURDENS.

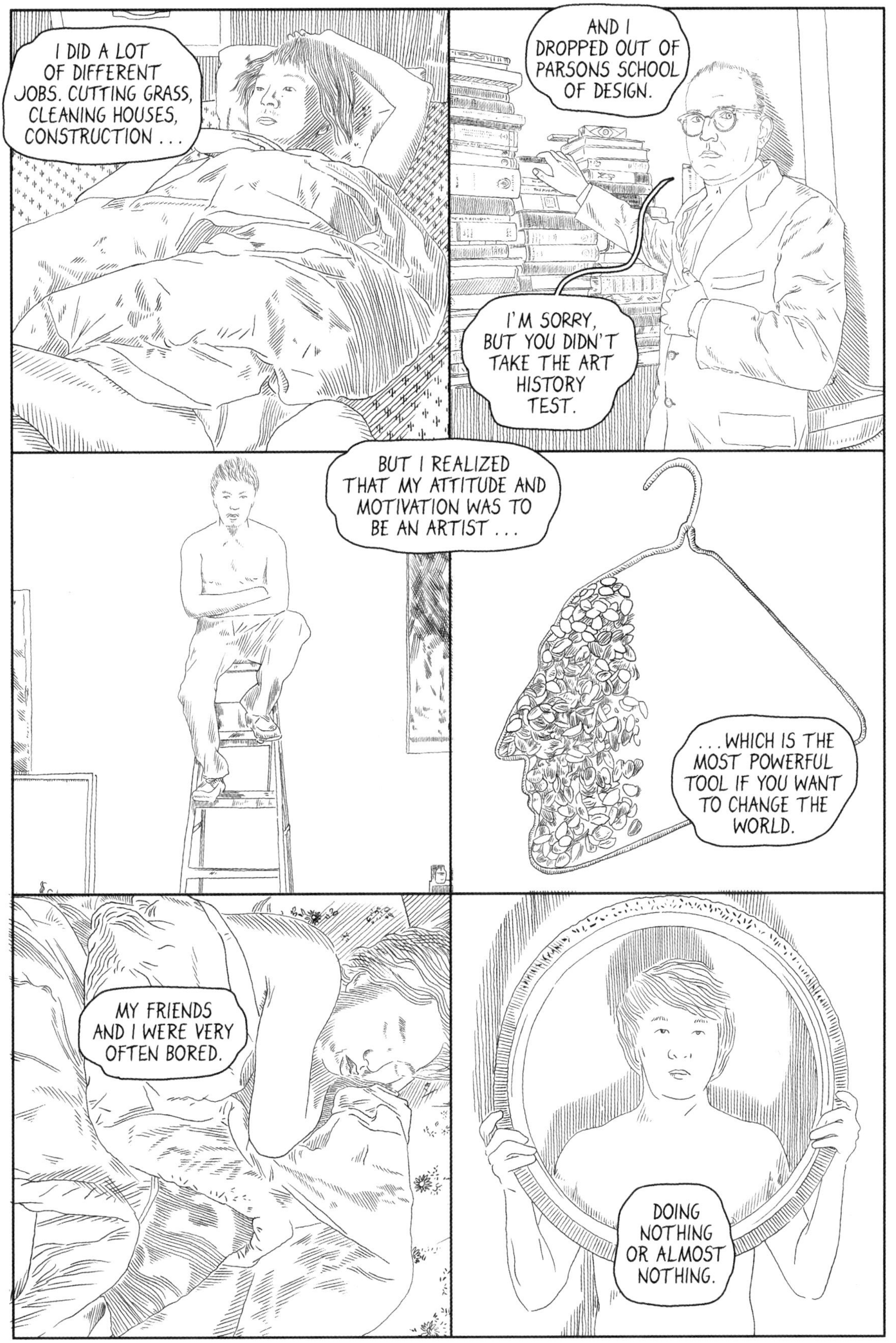
I DID A LOT OF DIFFERENT JOBS. CUTTING GRASS, CLEANING HOUSES, CONSTRUCTION . . .
AND I DROPPED OUT OF PARSONS SCHOOL OF DESIGN.
I'M SORRY, BUT YOU DIDN'T TAKE THE ART HISTORY TEST.
BUT I REALIZED THAT MY ATTITUDE AND MOTIVATION WAS TO BE AN ARTIST . . .
. . . WHICH IS THE MOST POWERFUL TOOL IF YOU WANT TO CHANGE THE WORLD.
MY FRIENDS AND I WERE VERY OFTEN BORED.
DOING NOTHING OR ALMOST NOTHING.

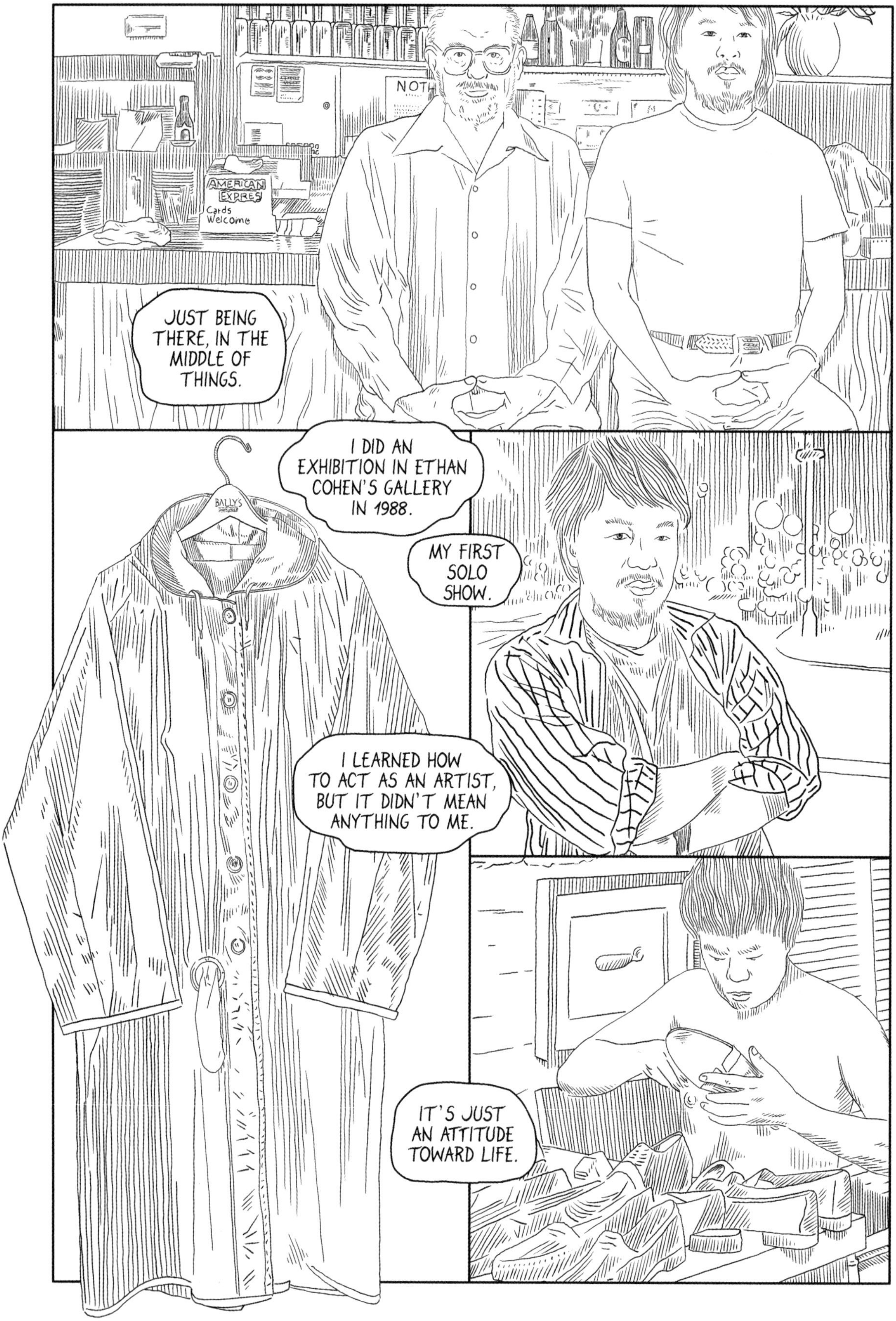
AMERICAN EXPRES
Cards Welcome
NOTH
JUST BEING THERE, IN THE MIDDLE OF THINGS.
BALLY'S
I DID AN EXHIBITION IN ETHAN COHEN'S GALLERY IN 1988.
MY FIRST SOLO SHOW.
I LEARNED HOW TO ACT AS AN ARTIST, BUT IT DIDN'T MEAN ANYTHING TO ME.
IT'S JUST AN ATTITUDE TOWARD LIFE.

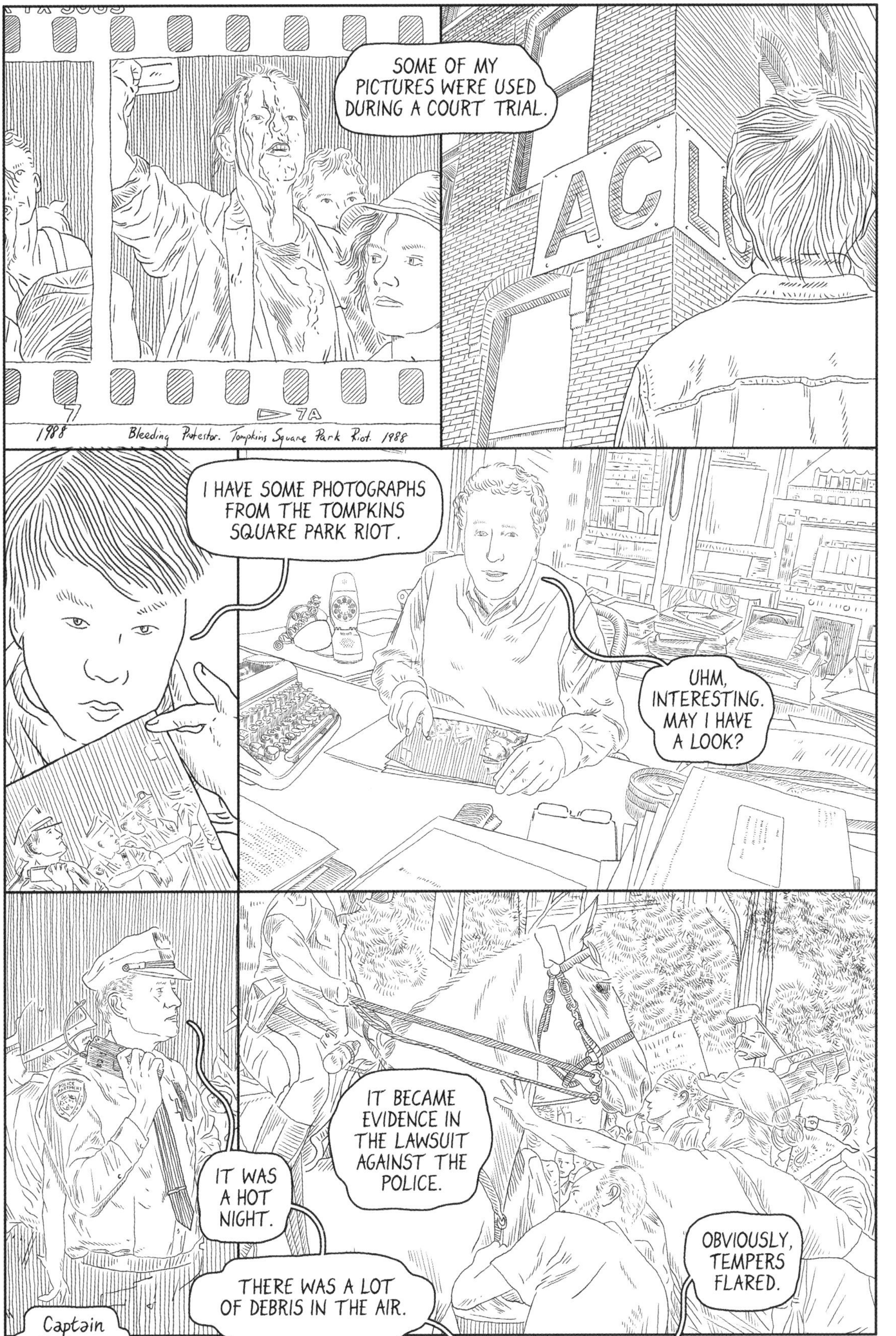

SOME OF MY PICTURES WERE USED DURING A COURT TRIAL.
7
7A
1988
Bleeding Protestor. Tompkins Square Park Riot. 1988
ACL
I HAVE SOME PHOTOGRAPHS FROM THE TOMPKINS SQUARE PARK RIOT.
UHM, INTERESTING. MAY I HAVE A LOOK?
IT BECAME EVIDENCE IN THE LAWSUIT AGAINST THE POLICE.
IT WAS A HOT NIGHT.
THERE WAS A LOT OF DEBRIS IN THE AIR.
OBVIOUSLY, TEMPERS FLARED.
Captain McNamara

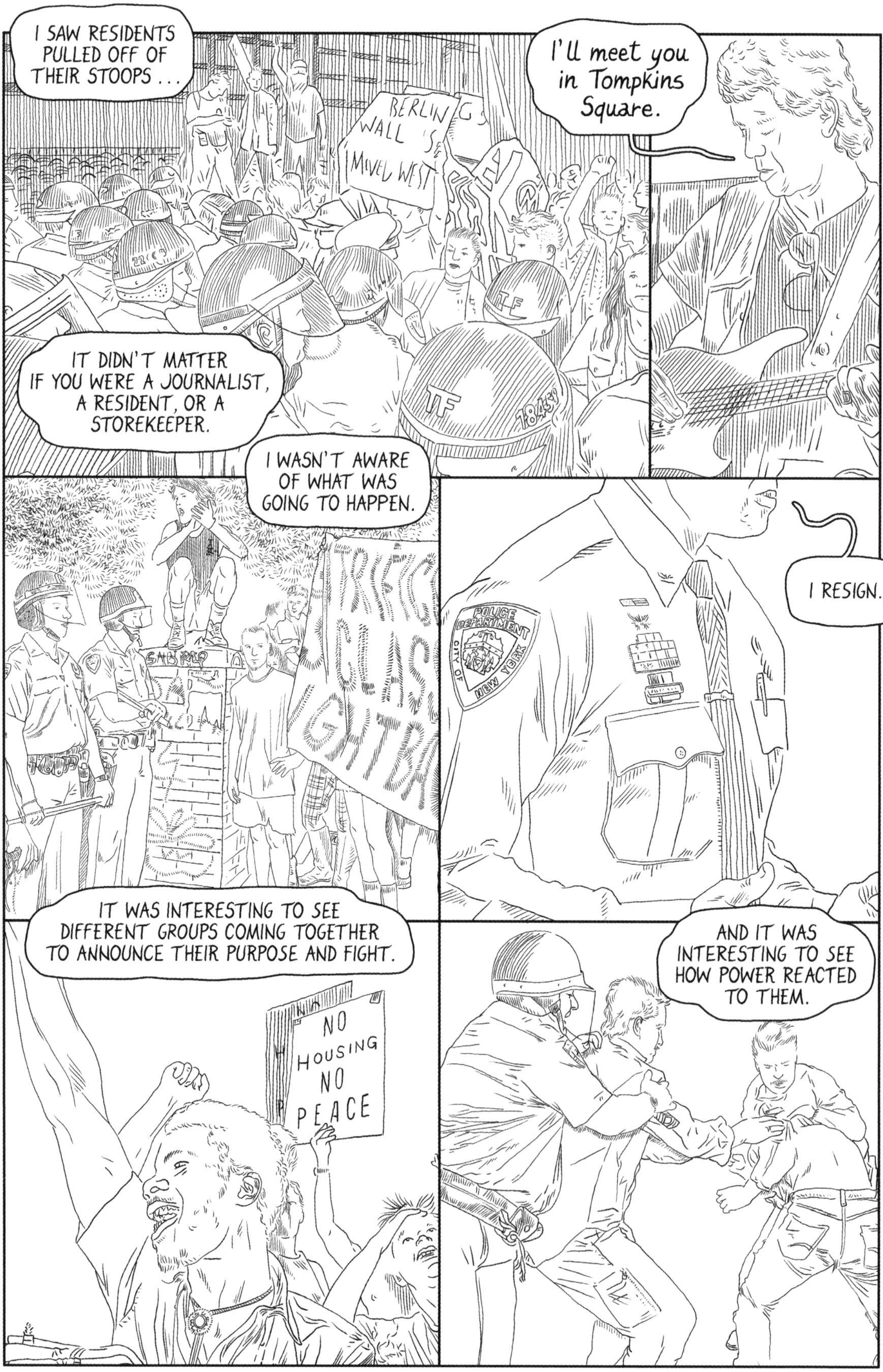
I SAW RESIDENTS PULLED OFF OF THEIR STOOPS . . .
BERLIN WALL IS MOVED WEST
IT DIDN'T MATTER IF YOU WERE A JOURNALIST, A RESIDENT, OR A STOREKEEPER.
I'll meet you in Tompkins Square.
I WASN'T AWARE OF WHAT WAS GOING TO HAPPEN.
I RESIGN.
POLICE DEPARTMENT CITY OF NEW YORK
IT WAS INTERESTING TO SEE DIFFERENT GROUPS COMING TOGETHER TO ANNOUNCE THEIR PURPOSE AND FIGHT.
NO HOUSING NO PEACE
AND IT WAS INTERESTING TO SEE HOW POWER REACTED TO THEM.

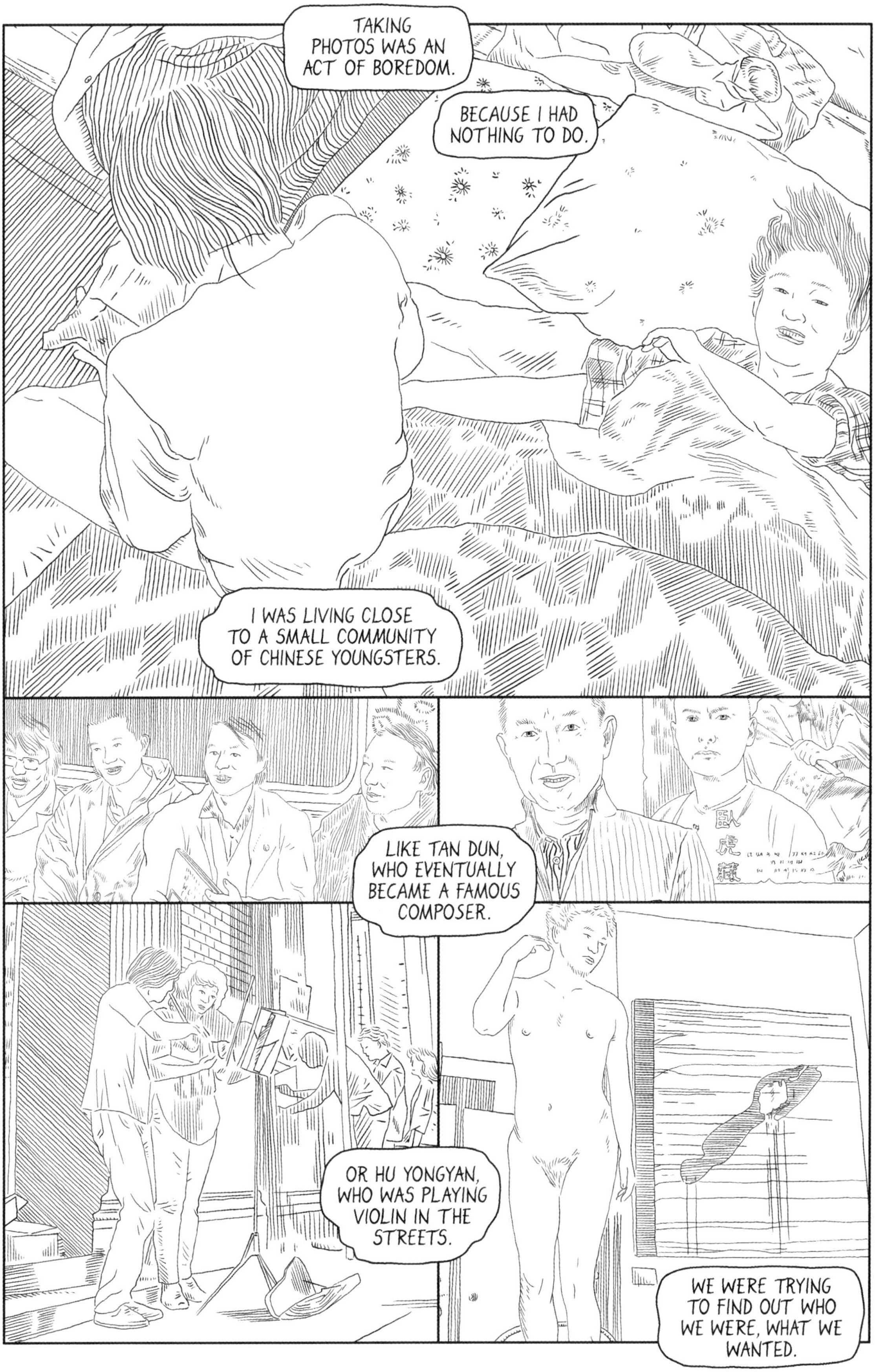
TAKING PHOTOS WAS AN ACT OF BOREDOM.
BECAUSE I HAD NOTHING TO DO.
I WAS LIVING CLOSE TO A SMALL COMMUNITY OF CHINESE YOUNGSTERS.
LIKE TAN DUN, WHO EVENTUALLY BECAME A FAMOUS COMPOSER.
OR HU YONGYAN, WHO WAS PLAYING VIOLIN IN THE STREETS.
WE WERE TRYING TO FIND OUT WHO WE WERE, WHAT WE WANTED.

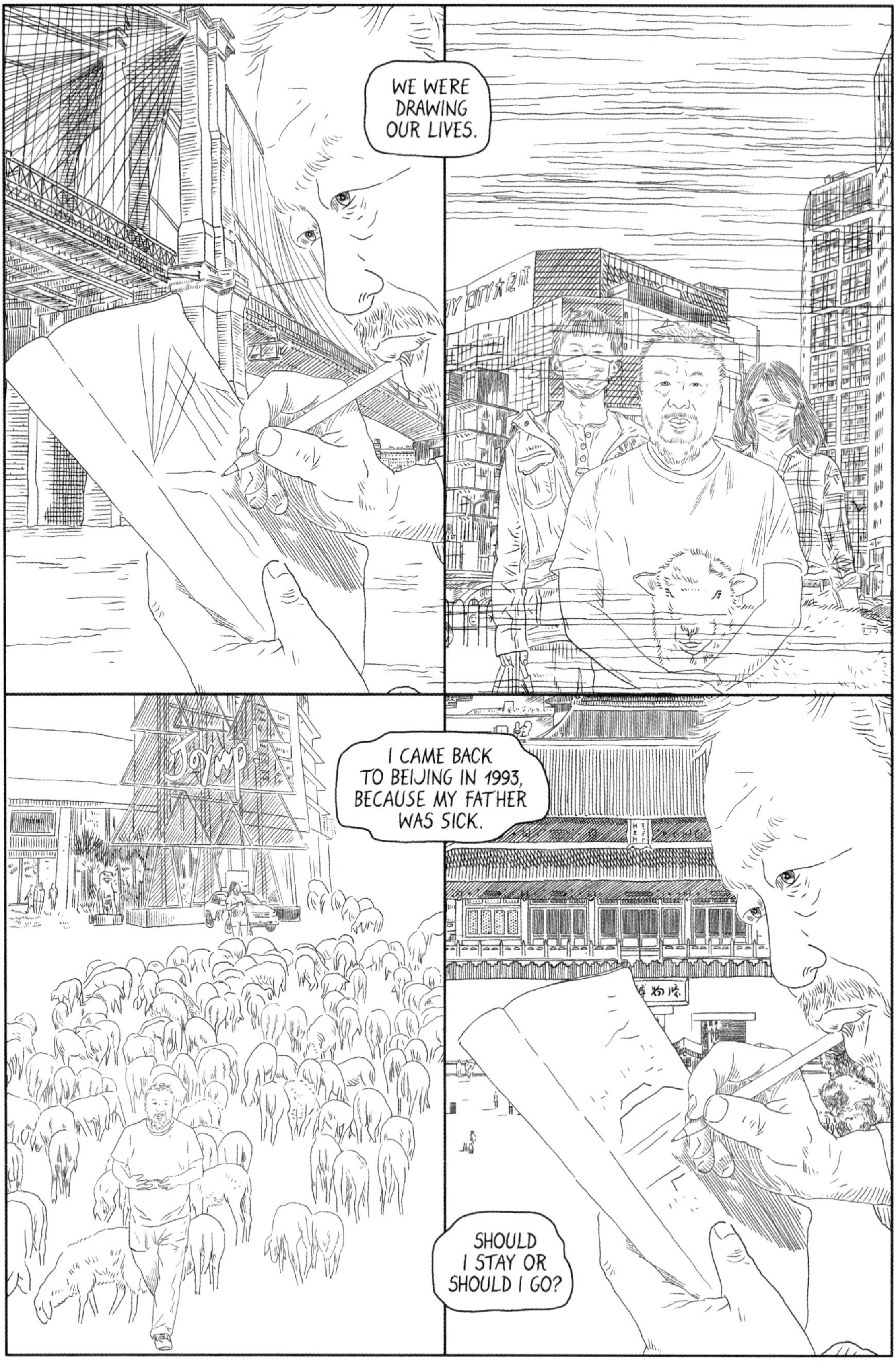
WE WERE DRAWING OUR LIVES.
I CAME BACK TO BEIJING IN 1993, BECAUSE MY FATHER WAS SICK.
SHOULD I STAY OR SHOULD I GO?

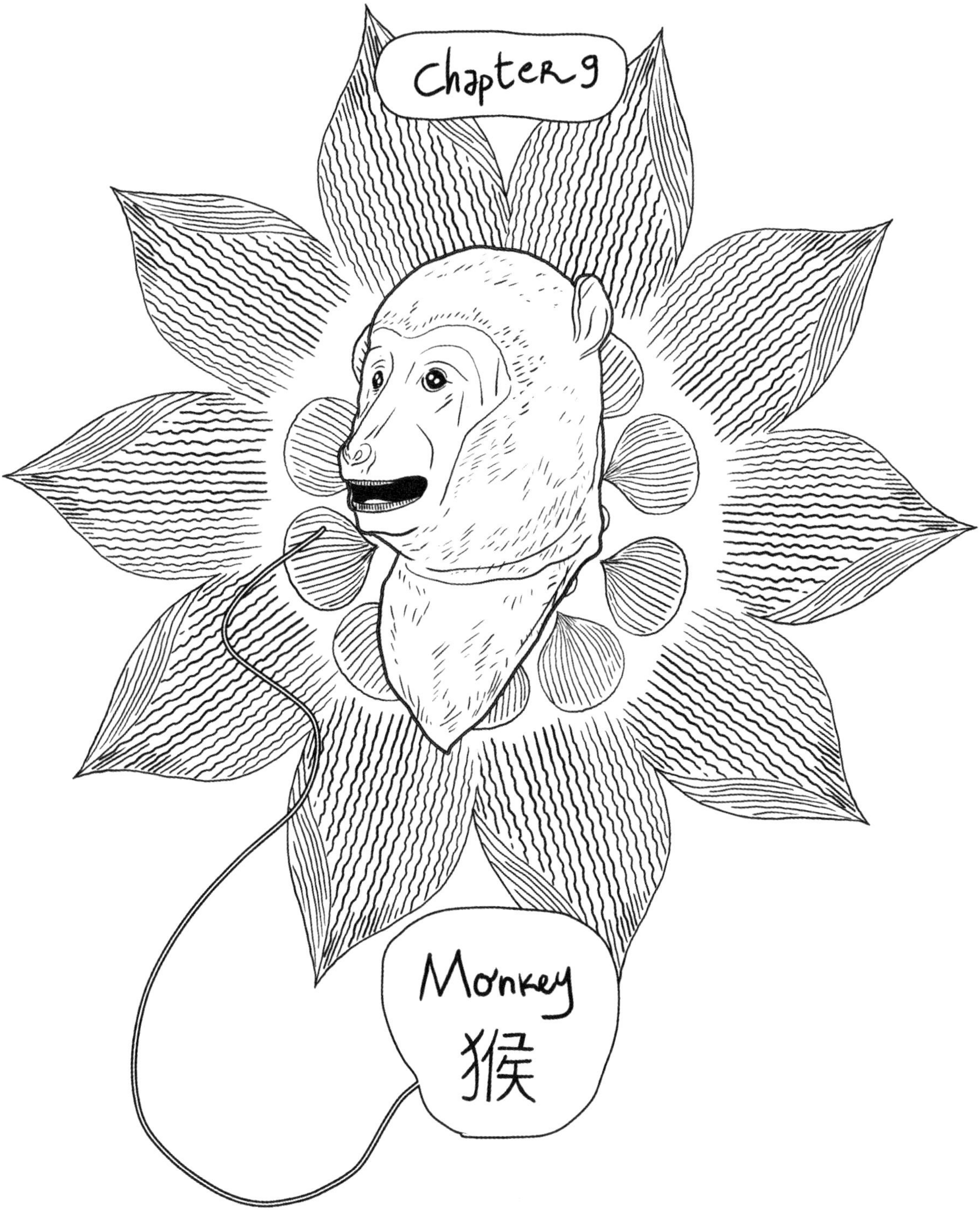
Chapter 9
Monkey
猴

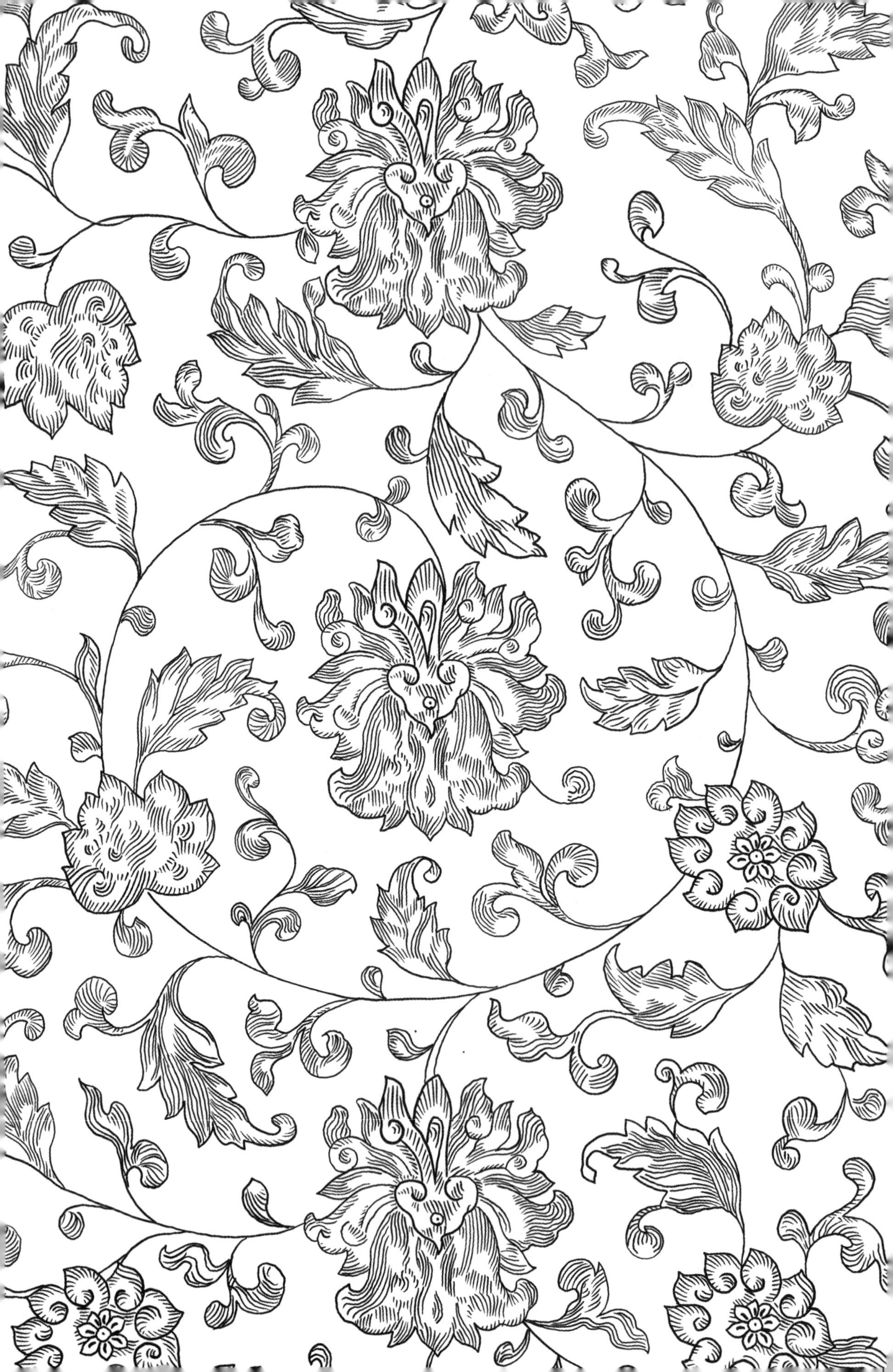

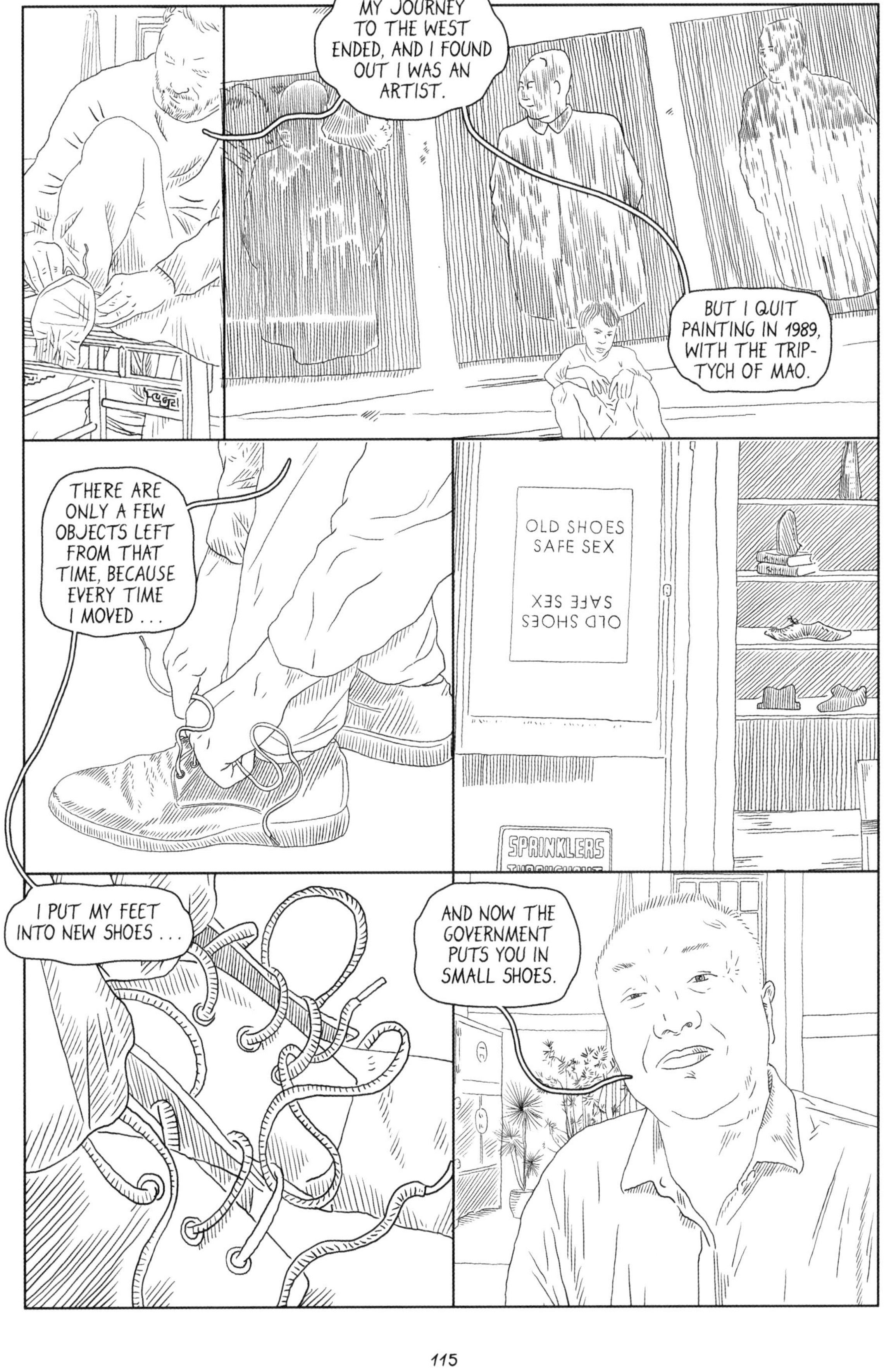
MY JOURNEY TO THE WEST ENDED, AND I FOUND OUT I WAS AN ARTIST.
BUT I QUIT PAINTING IN 1989, WITH THE TRIP-TYCH OF MAO.
THERE ARE ONLY A FEW OBJECTS LEFT FROM THAT TIME, BECAUSE EVERY TIME I MOVED . . .
OLD SHOES SAFE SEX
SPRINKLERS
I PUT MY FEET INTO NEW SHOES . . .
AND NOW THE GOVERNMENT PUTS YOU IN SMALL SHOES.

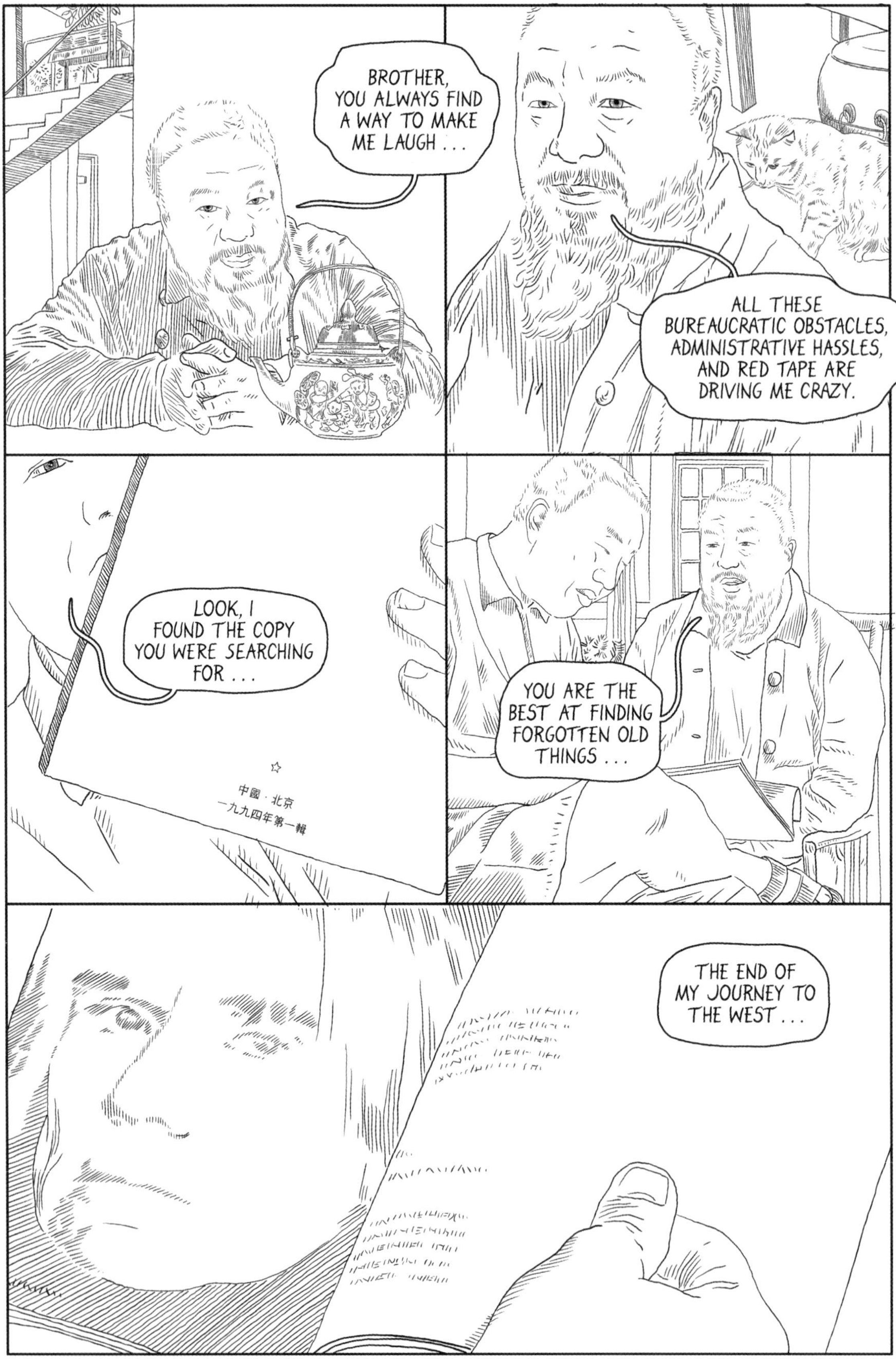
BROTHER, YOU ALWAYS FIND A WAY TO MAKE ME LAUGH . . .
ALL THESE BUREAUCRATIC OBSTACLES, ADMINISTRATIVE HASSLES, AND RED TAPE ARE DRIVING ME CRAZY.
LOOK, I FOUND THE COPY YOU WERE SEARCHING FOR . . .
中國・北京
一九九四年第一輯
YOU ARE THE BEST AT FINDING FORGOTTEN OLD THINGS . . .
THE END OF MY JOURNEY TO THE WEST . . .

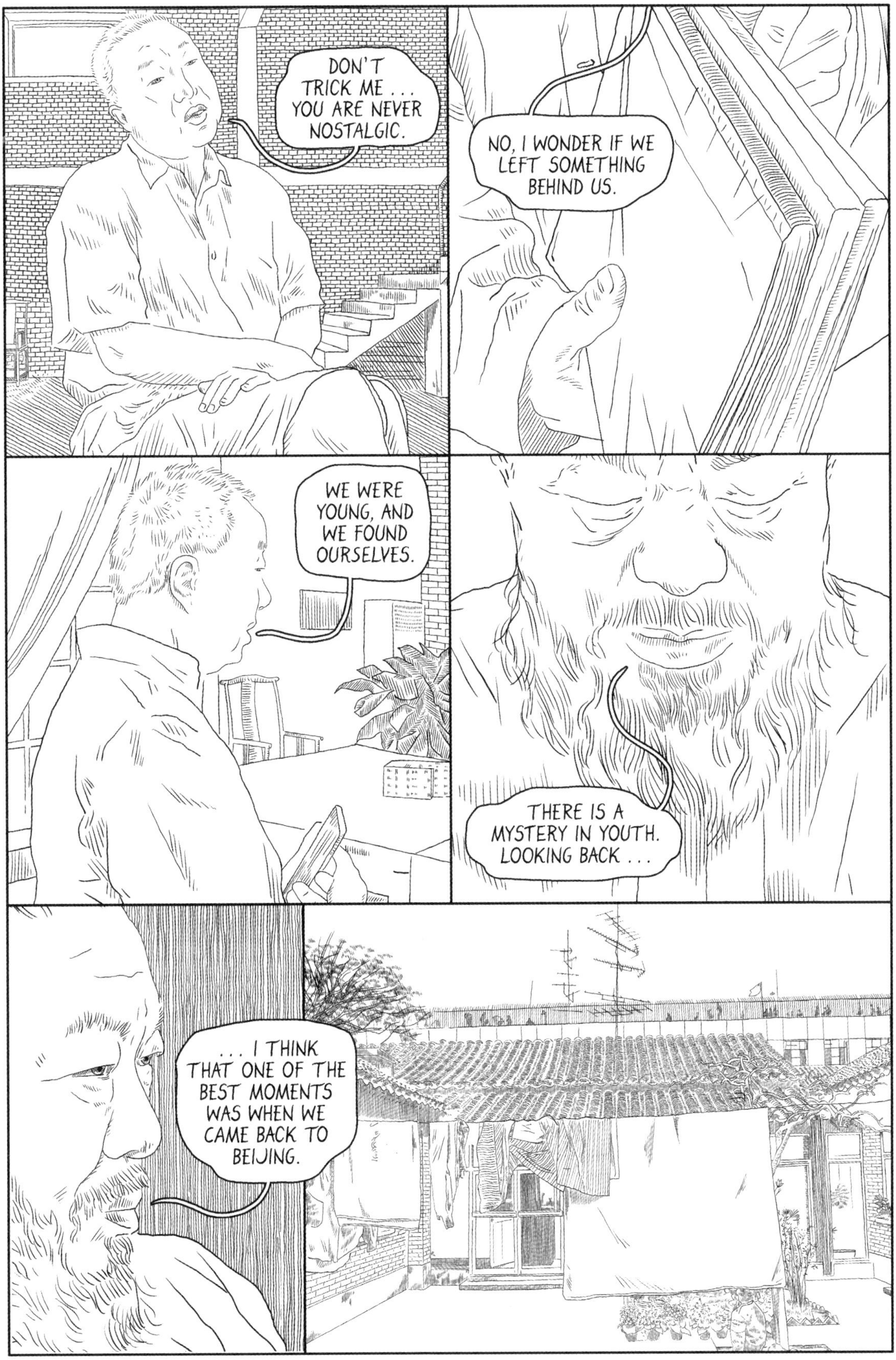
DON'T TRICK ME . . . YOU ARE NEVER NOSTALGIC.
NO, I WONDER IF WE LEFT SOMETHING BEHIND US.
WE WERE YOUNG, AND WE FOUND OURSELVES.
THERE IS A MYSTERY IN YOUTH. LOOKING BACK . . .
. . . I THINK THAT ONE OF THE BEST MOMENTS WAS WHEN WE CAME BACK TO BEIJING.

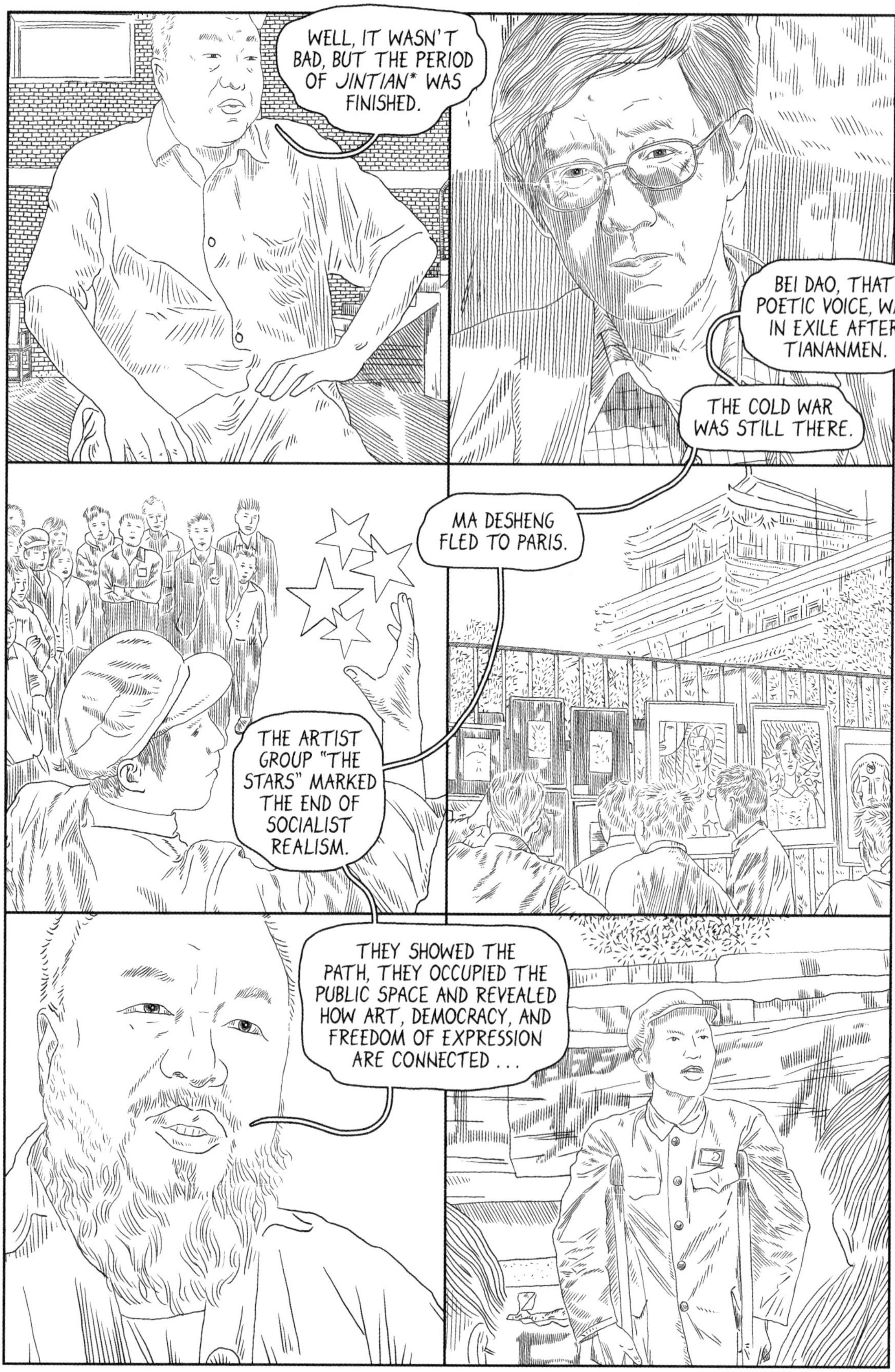
WELL, IT WASN'T BAD, BUT THE PERIOD OF JINTIAN* WAS FINISHED.
BEI DAO, THAT POETIC VOICE, WAS IN EXILE AFTER TIANANMEN.
THE COLD WAR WAS STILL THERE.
MA DESHENG FLED TO PARIS.
THE ARTIST GROUP "THE STARS" MARKED THE END OF SOCIALIST REALISM.
THEY SHOWED THE PATH, THEY OCCUPIED THE PUBLIC SPACE AND REVEALED HOW ART, DEMOCRACY, AND FREEDOM OF EXPRESSION ARE CONNECTED . . .

* *Jintian* was the revolutionary literary journal founded in 1978.

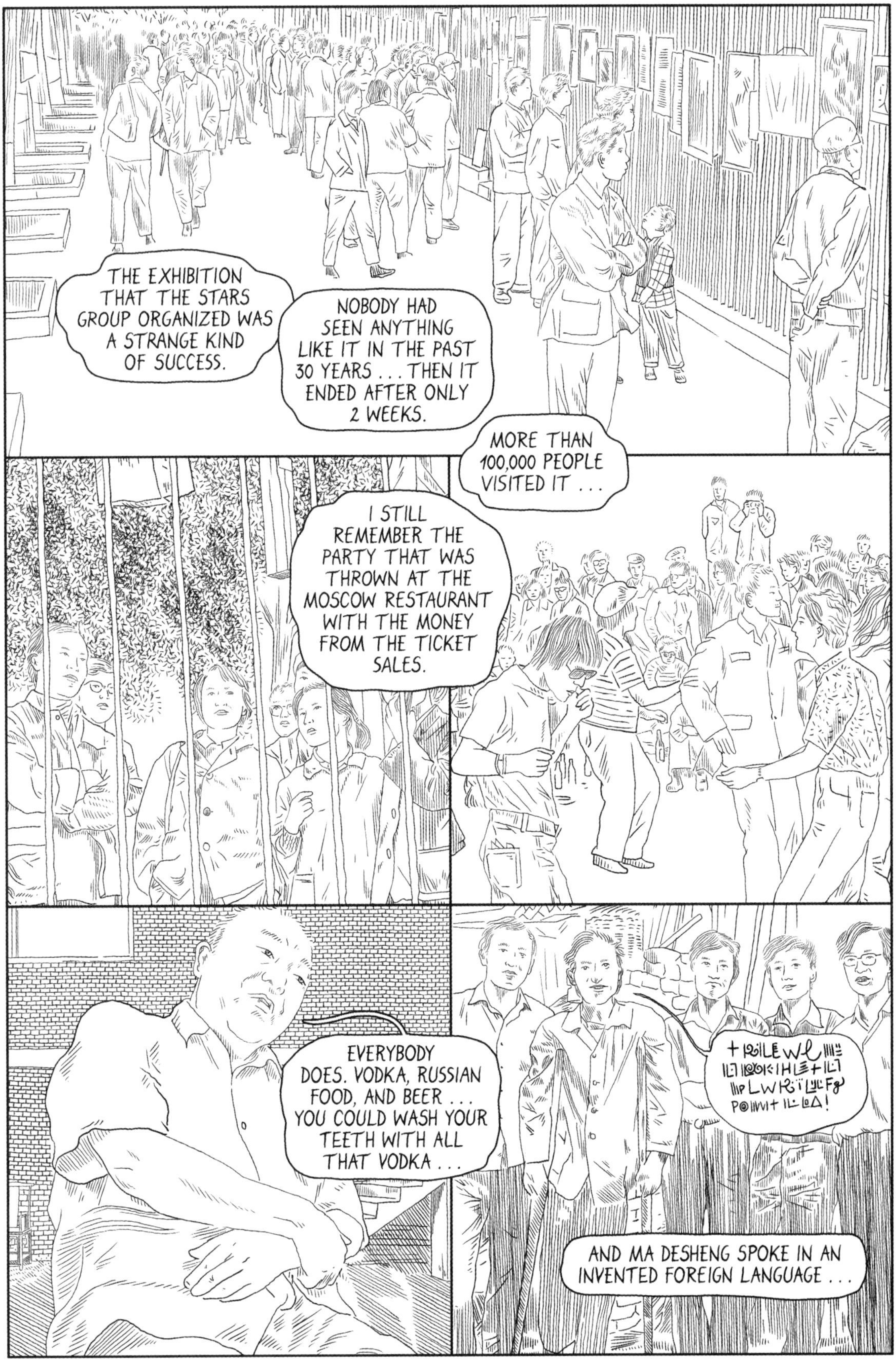
THE EXHIBITION THAT THE STARS GROUP ORGANIZED WAS A STRANGE KIND OF SUCCESS.
NOBODY HAD SEEN ANYTHING LIKE IT IN THE PAST 30 YEARS . . . THEN IT ENDED AFTER ONLY 2 WEEKS.
MORE THAN 100,000 PEOPLE VISITED IT . . .
I STILL REMEMBER THE PARTY THAT WAS THROWN AT THE MOSCOW RESTAURANT WITH THE MONEY FROM THE TICKET SALES.
EVERYBODY DOES. VODKA, RUSSIAN FOOD, AND BEER . . . YOU COULD WASH YOUR TEETH WITH ALL THAT VODKA . . .
AND MA DESHENG SPOKE IN AN INVENTED FOREIGN LANGUAGE . . .

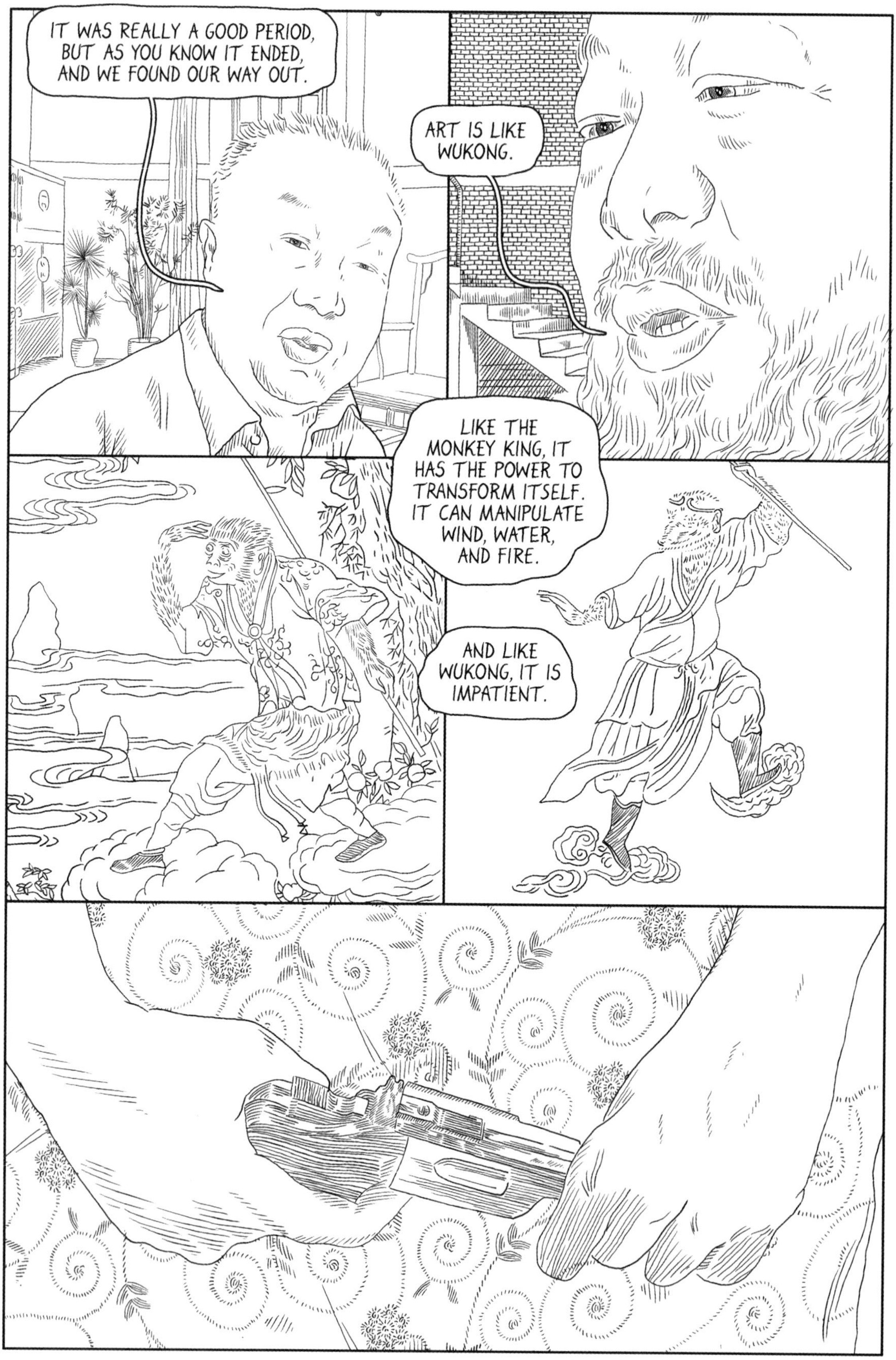
IT WAS REALLY A GOOD PERIOD, BUT AS YOU KNOW IT ENDED, AND WE FOUND OUR WAY OUT.
ART IS LIKE WUKONG.
LIKE THE MONKEY KING, IT HAS THE POWER TO TRANSFORM ITSELF. IT CAN MANIPULATE WIND, WATER, AND FIRE.
AND LIKE WUKONG, IT IS IMPATIENT.

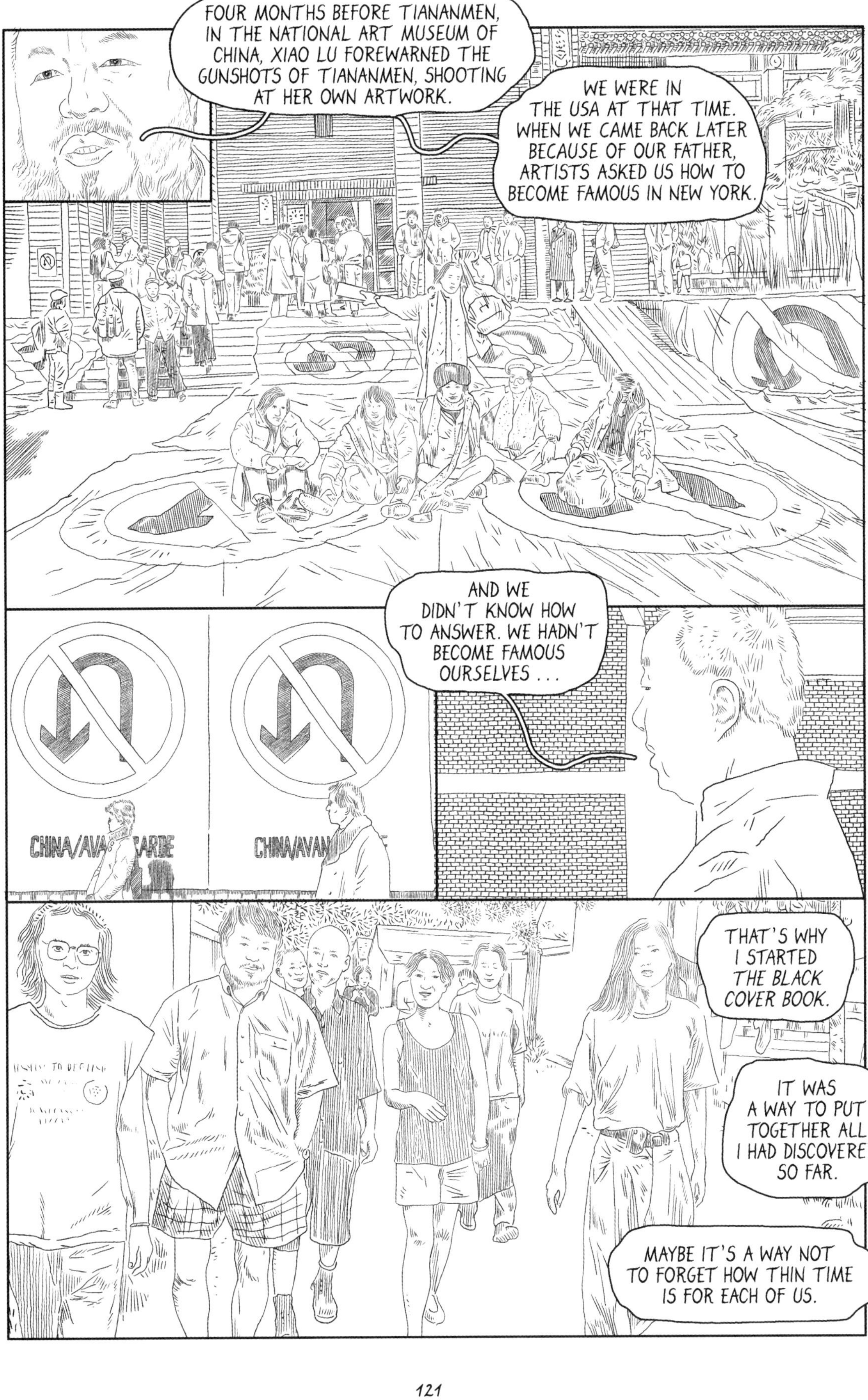
FOUR MONTHS BEFORE TIANANMEN, IN THE NATIONAL ART MUSEUM OF CHINA, XIAO LU FOREWARNED THE GUNSHOTS OF TIANANMEN, SHOOTING AT HER OWN ARTWORK.
WE WERE IN THE USA AT THAT TIME. WHEN WE CAME BACK LATER BECAUSE OF OUR FATHER, ARTISTS ASKED US HOW TO BECOME FAMOUS IN NEW YORK.
AND WE DIDN'T KNOW HOW TO ANSWER. WE HADN'T BECOME FAMOUS OURSELVES . . .
THAT'S WHY I STARTED *THE BLACK COVER BOOK.*
IT WAS A WAY TO PUT TOGETHER ALL I HAD DISCOVERED SO FAR.
MAYBE IT'S A WAY NOT TO FORGET HOW THIN TIME IS FOR EACH OF US.

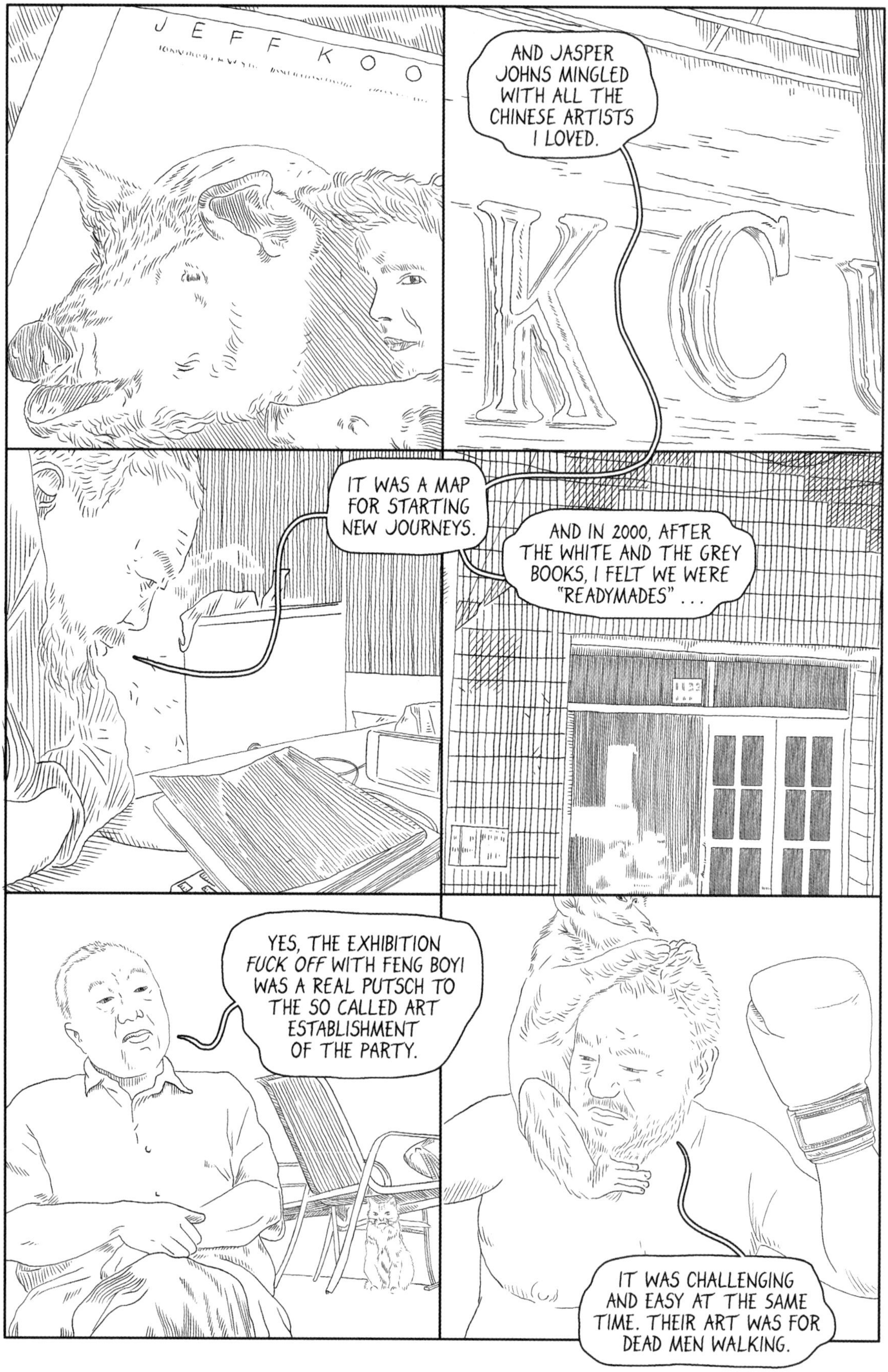
JEFF KOO
AND JASPER JOHNS MINGLED WITH ALL THE CHINESE ARTISTS I LOVED.
IT WAS A MAP FOR STARTING NEW JOURNEYS.
AND IN 2000, AFTER THE WHITE AND THE GREY BOOKS, I FELT WE WERE "READYMADES" . . .
YES, THE EXHIBITION *FUCK OFF* WITH FENG BOYI WAS A REAL PUTSCH TO THE SO CALLED ART ESTABLISHMENT OF THE PARTY.
IT WAS CHALLENGING AND EASY AT THE SAME TIME. THEIR ART WAS FOR DEAD MEN WALKING.

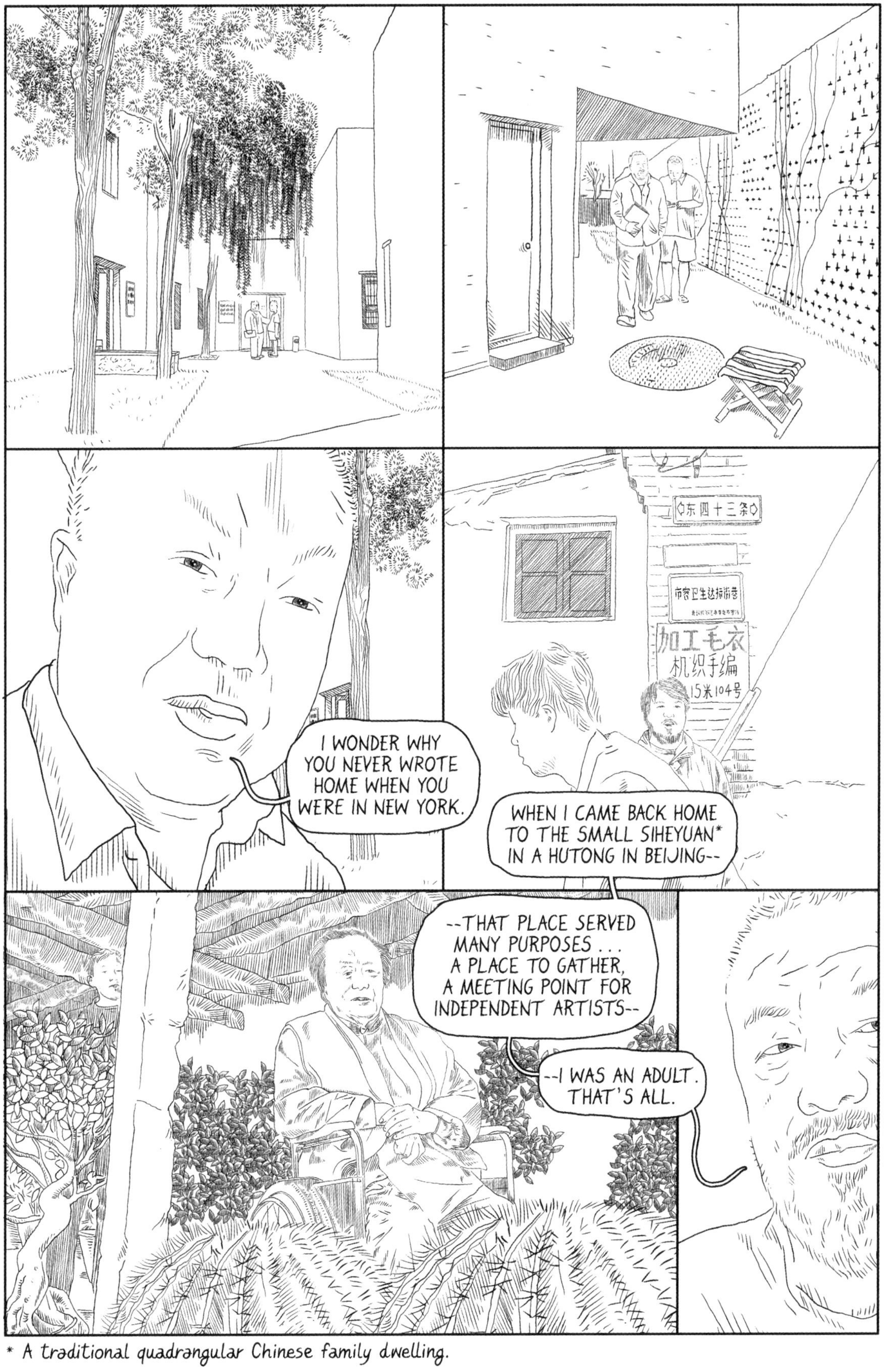
东四十三条
市容卫生达标街巷
加工毛衣
机织手编
15米104号
I WONDER WHY YOU NEVER WROTE HOME WHEN YOU WERE IN NEW YORK.
WHEN I CAME BACK HOME TO THE SMALL SIHEYUAN* IN A HUTONG IN BEIJING--
--THAT PLACE SERVED MANY PURPOSES . . . A PLACE TO GATHER, A MEETING POINT FOR INDEPENDENT ARTISTS--
--I WAS AN ADULT. THAT'S ALL.

* A traditional quadrangular Chinese family dwelling.

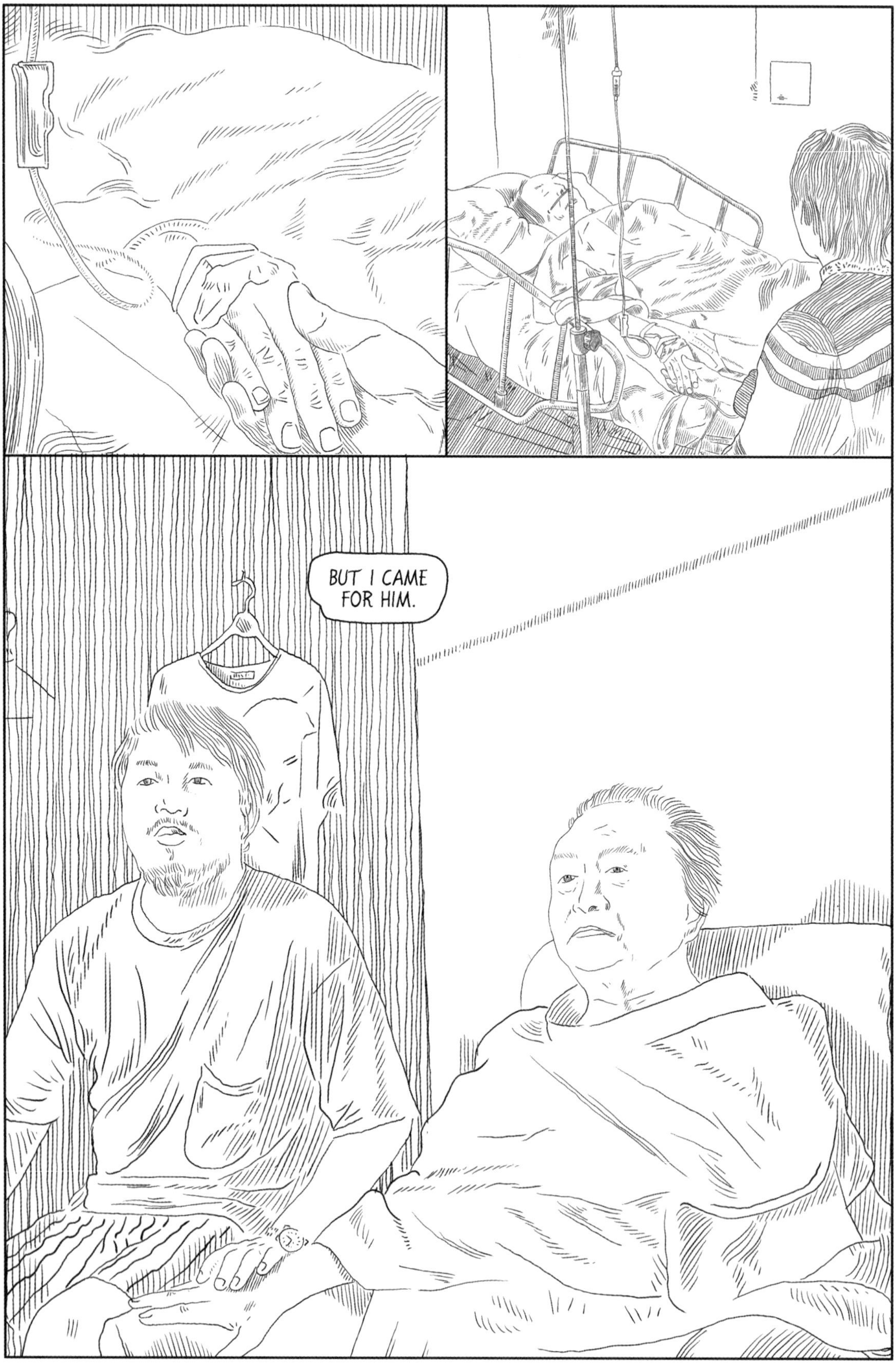
BUT I CAME FOR HIM.

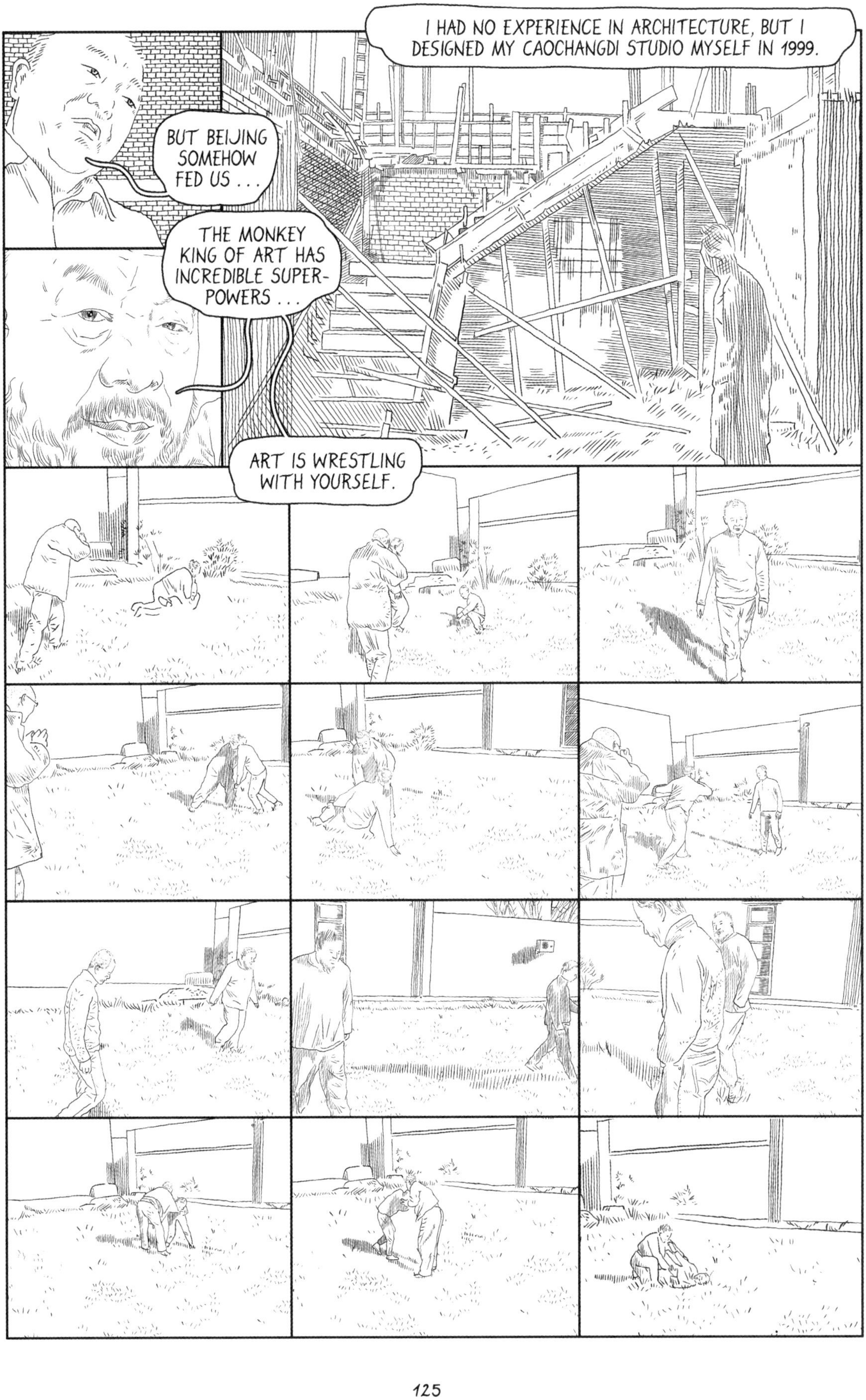

I HAD NO EXPERIENCE IN ARCHITECTURE, BUT I DESIGNED MY CAOCHANGDI STUDIO MYSELF IN 1999.
BUT BEIJING SOMEHOW FED US . . .
THE MONKEY KING OF ART HAS INCREDIBLE SUPER-POWERS . . .
ART IS WRESTLING WITH YOURSELF.

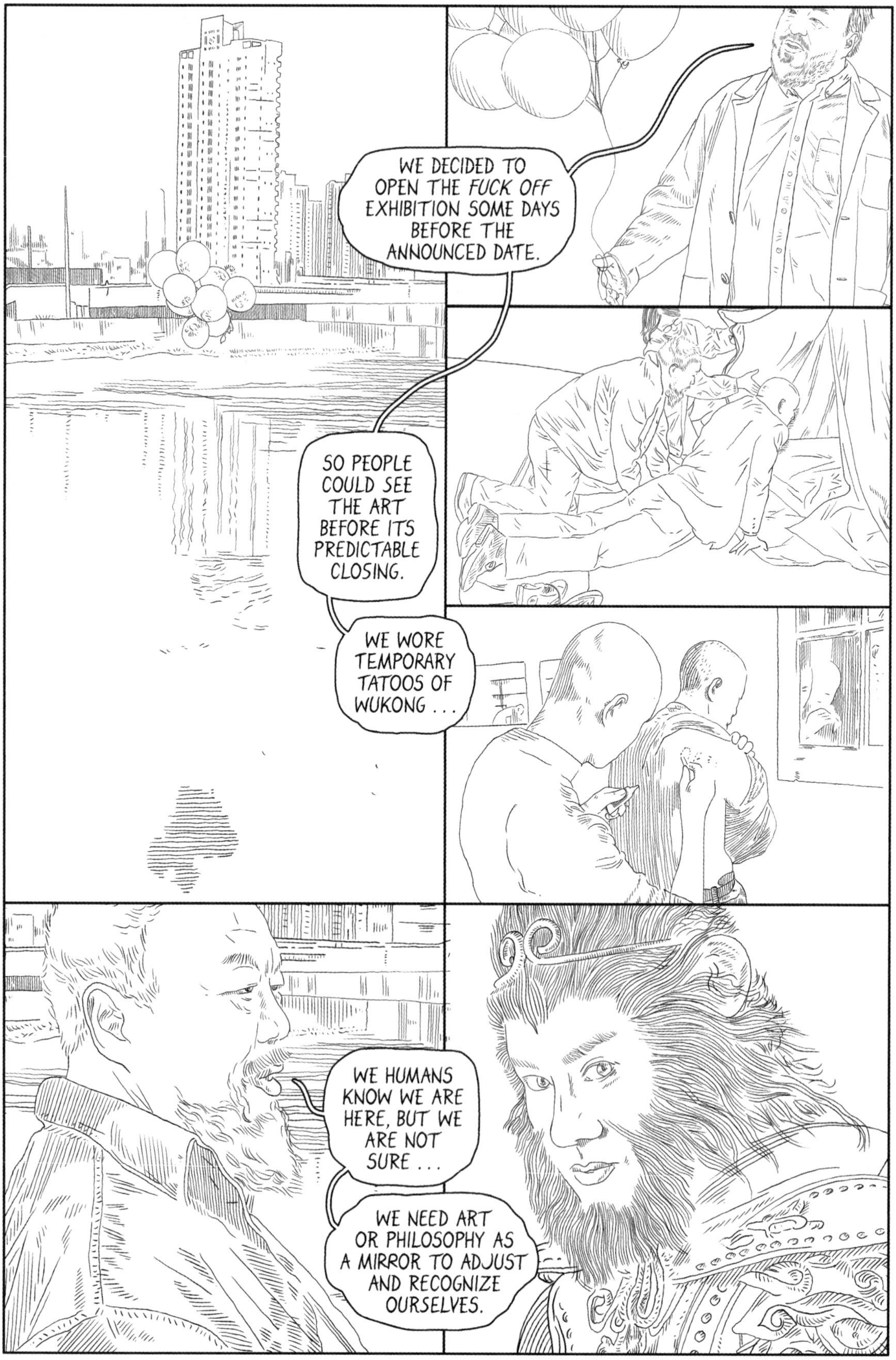
WE DECIDED TO OPEN THE *FUCK OFF* EXHIBITION SOME DAYS BEFORE THE ANNOUNCED DATE.
SO PEOPLE COULD SEE THE ART BEFORE ITS PREDICTABLE CLOSING.
WE WORE TEMPORARY TATOOS OF WUKONG . . .
WE HUMANS KNOW WE ARE HERE, BUT WE ARE NOT SURE . . .
WE NEED ART OR PHILOSOPHY AS A MIRROR TO ADJUST AND RECOGNIZE OURSELVES.

CHAPTER 10

Rooster
鸡

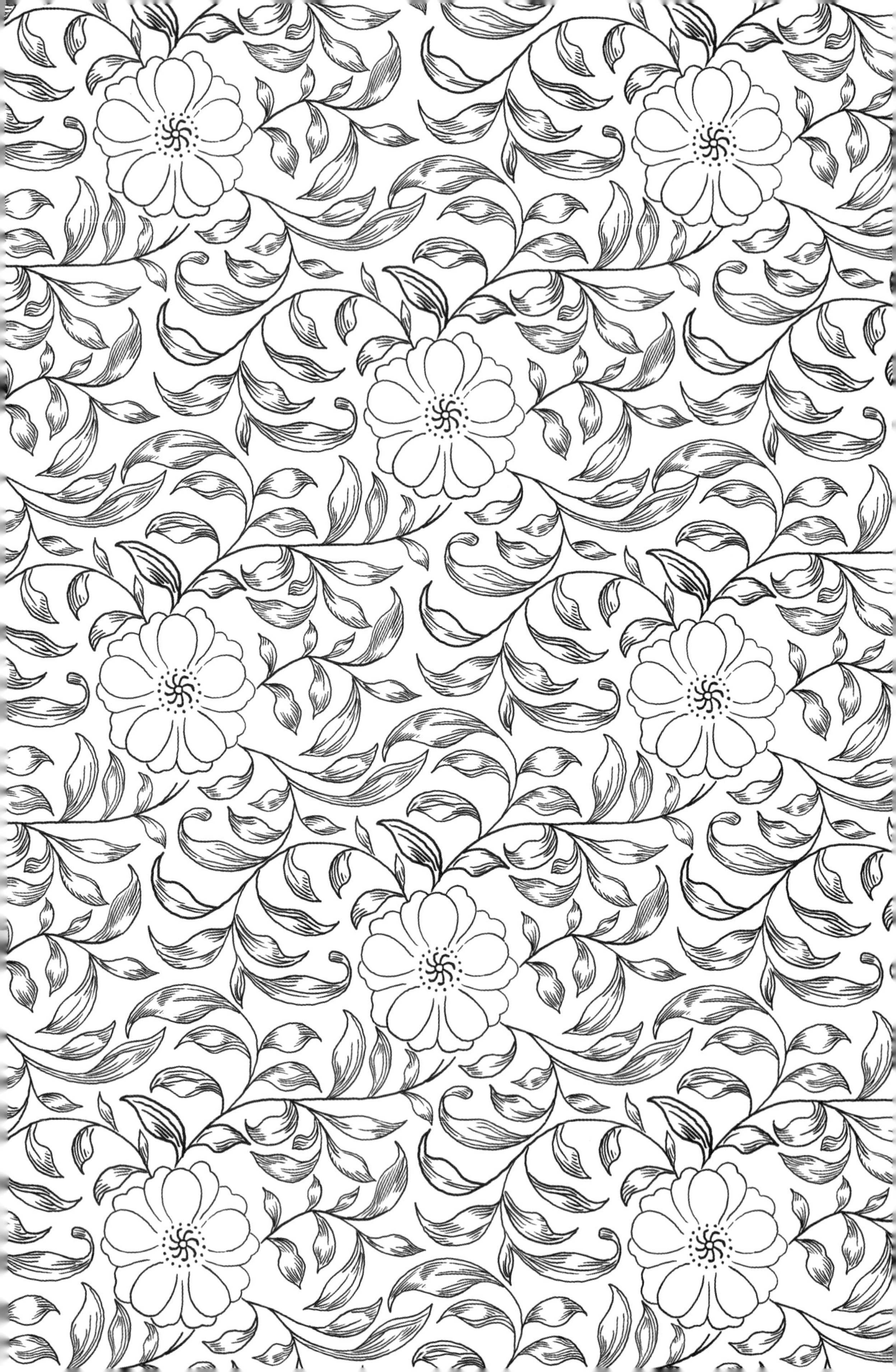

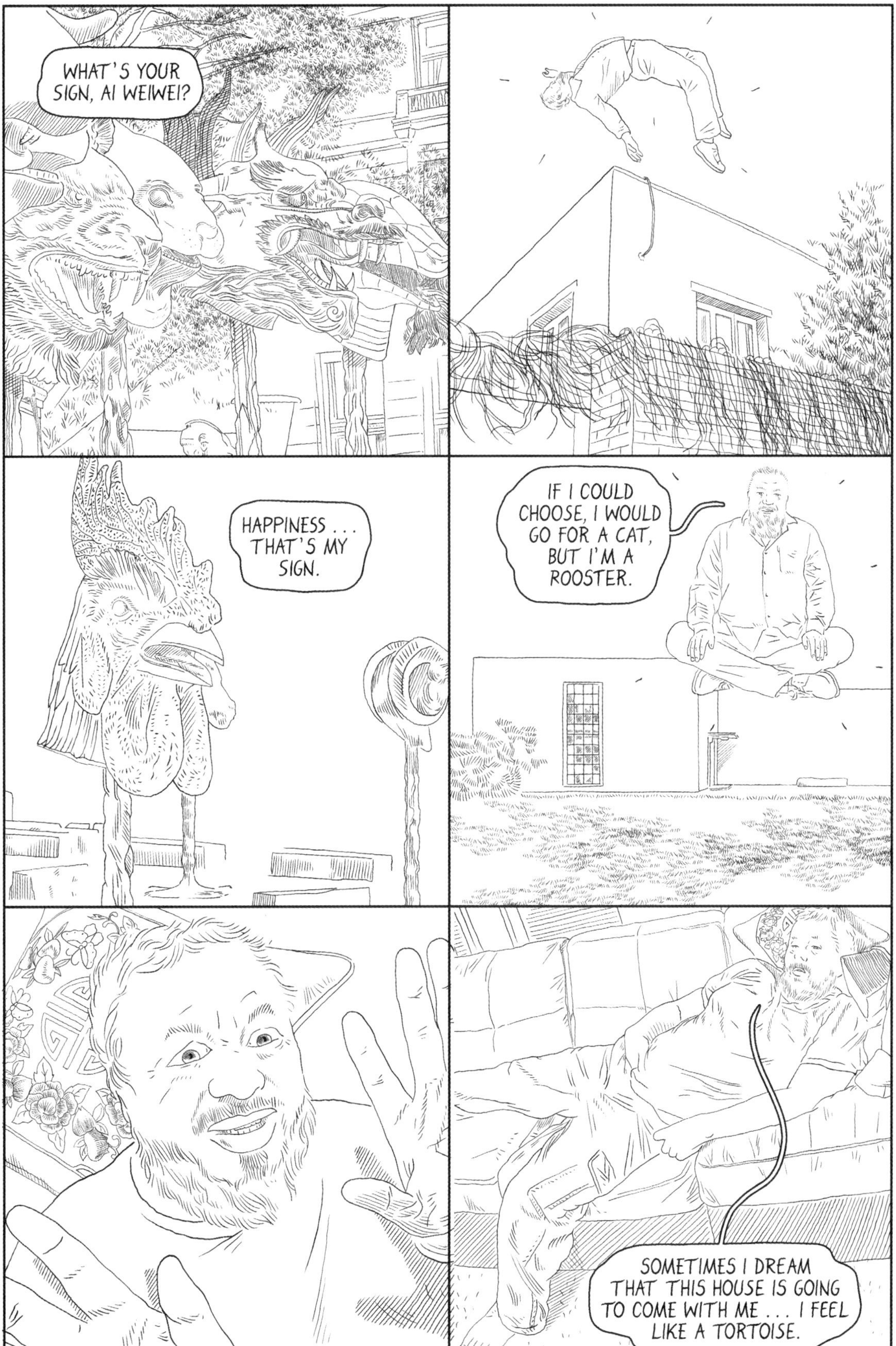
WHAT'S YOUR SIGN, AI WEIWEI?
HAPPINESS . . . THAT'S MY SIGN.
IF I COULD CHOOSE, I WOULD GO FOR A CAT, BUT I'M A ROOSTER.
SOMETIMES I DREAM THAT THIS HOUSE IS GOING TO COME WITH ME . . . I FEEL LIKE A TORTOISE.

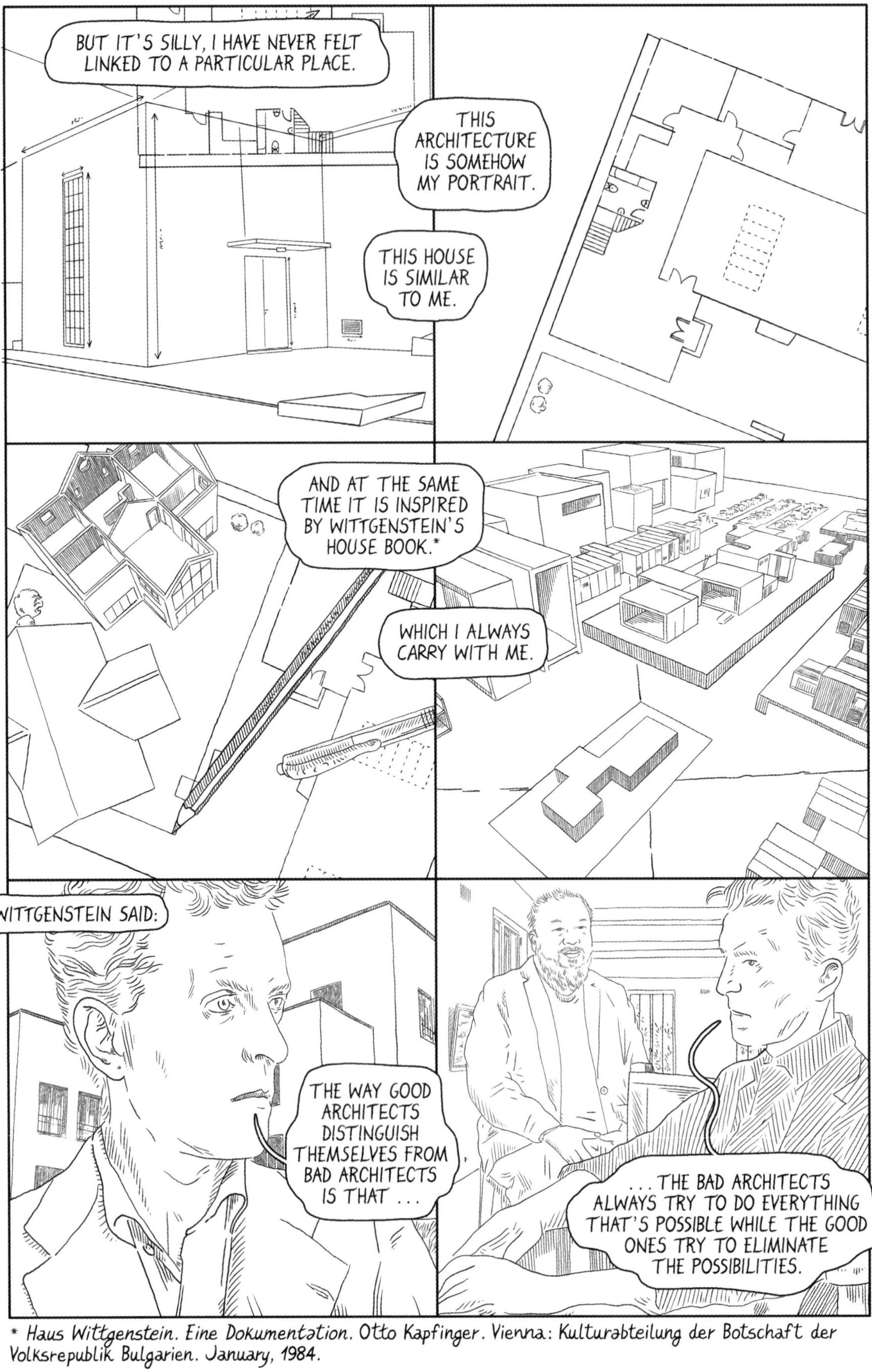
BUT IT'S SILLY, I HAVE NEVER FELT LINKED TO A PARTICULAR PLACE.
THIS ARCHITECTURE IS SOMEHOW MY PORTRAIT.
THIS HOUSE IS SIMILAR TO ME.
AND AT THE SAME TIME IT IS INSPIRED BY WITTGENSTEIN'S HOUSE BOOK.*
WHICH I ALWAYS CARRY WITH ME.
WITTGENSTEIN SAID:
THE WAY GOOD ARCHITECTS DISTINGUISH THEMSELVES FROM BAD ARCHITECTS IS THAT . . .
. . . THE BAD ARCHITECTS ALWAYS TRY TO DO EVERYTHING THAT'S POSSIBLE WHILE THE GOOD ONES TRY TO ELIMINATE THE POSSIBILITIES.

* *Haus Wittgenstein. Eine Dokumentation.* Otto Kapfinger. Vienna: Kulturabteilung der Botschaft der Volksrepublik Bulgarien. January, 1984.

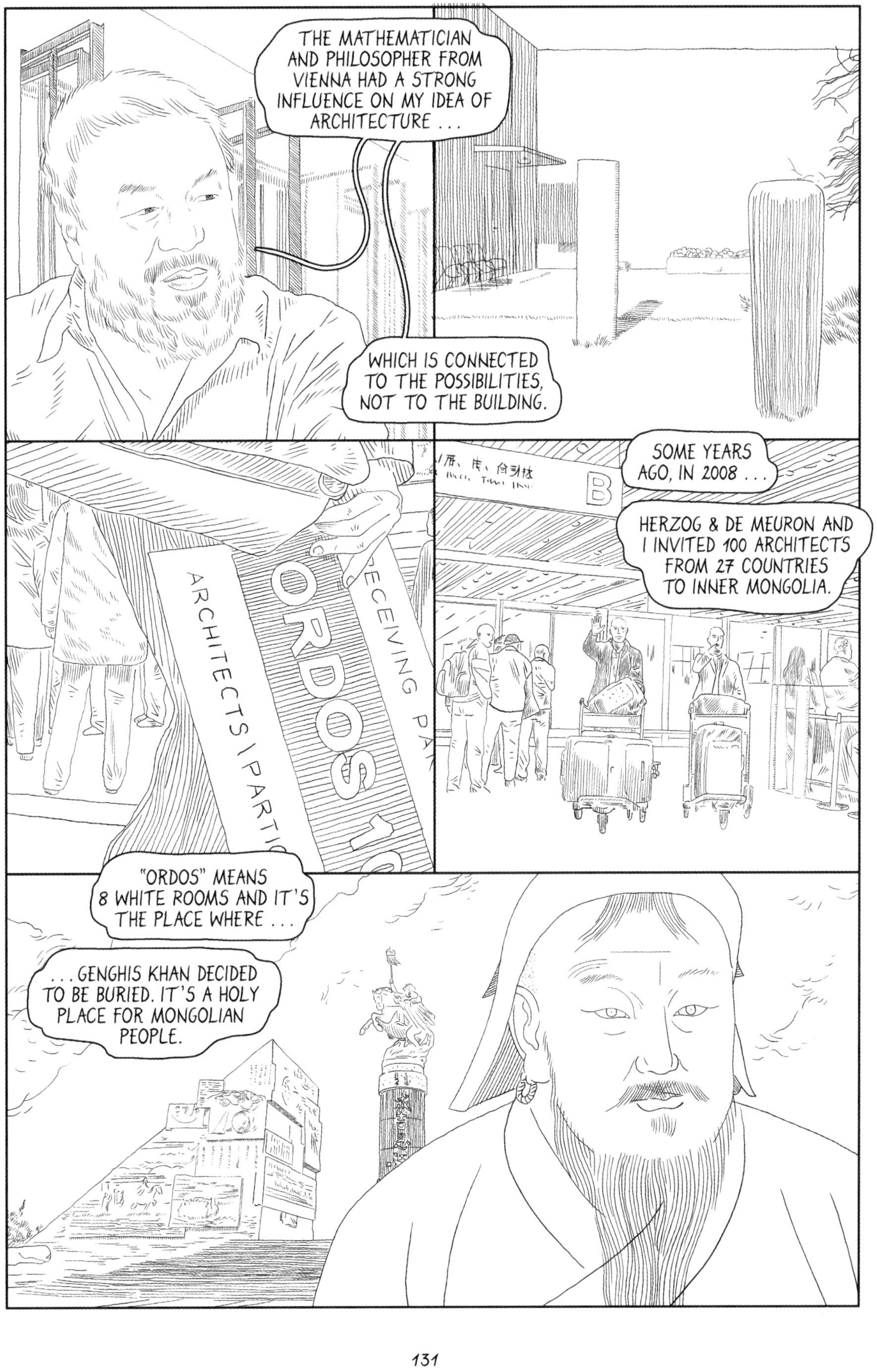
THE MATHEMATICIAN AND PHILOSOPHER FROM VIENNA HAD A STRONG INFLUENCE ON MY IDEA OF ARCHITECTURE . . .
WHICH IS CONNECTED TO THE POSSIBILITIES, NOT TO THE BUILDING.
RECEIVING
ORDOS
ARCHITECTS
B
SOME YEARS AGO, IN 2008 . . .
HERZOG & DE MEURON AND I INVITED 100 ARCHITECTS FROM 27 COUNTRIES TO INNER MONGOLIA.
"ORDOS" MEANS 8 WHITE ROOMS AND IT'S THE PLACE WHERE . . .
. . . GENGHIS KHAN DECIDED TO BE BURIED. IT'S A HOLY PLACE FOR MONGOLIAN PEOPLE.

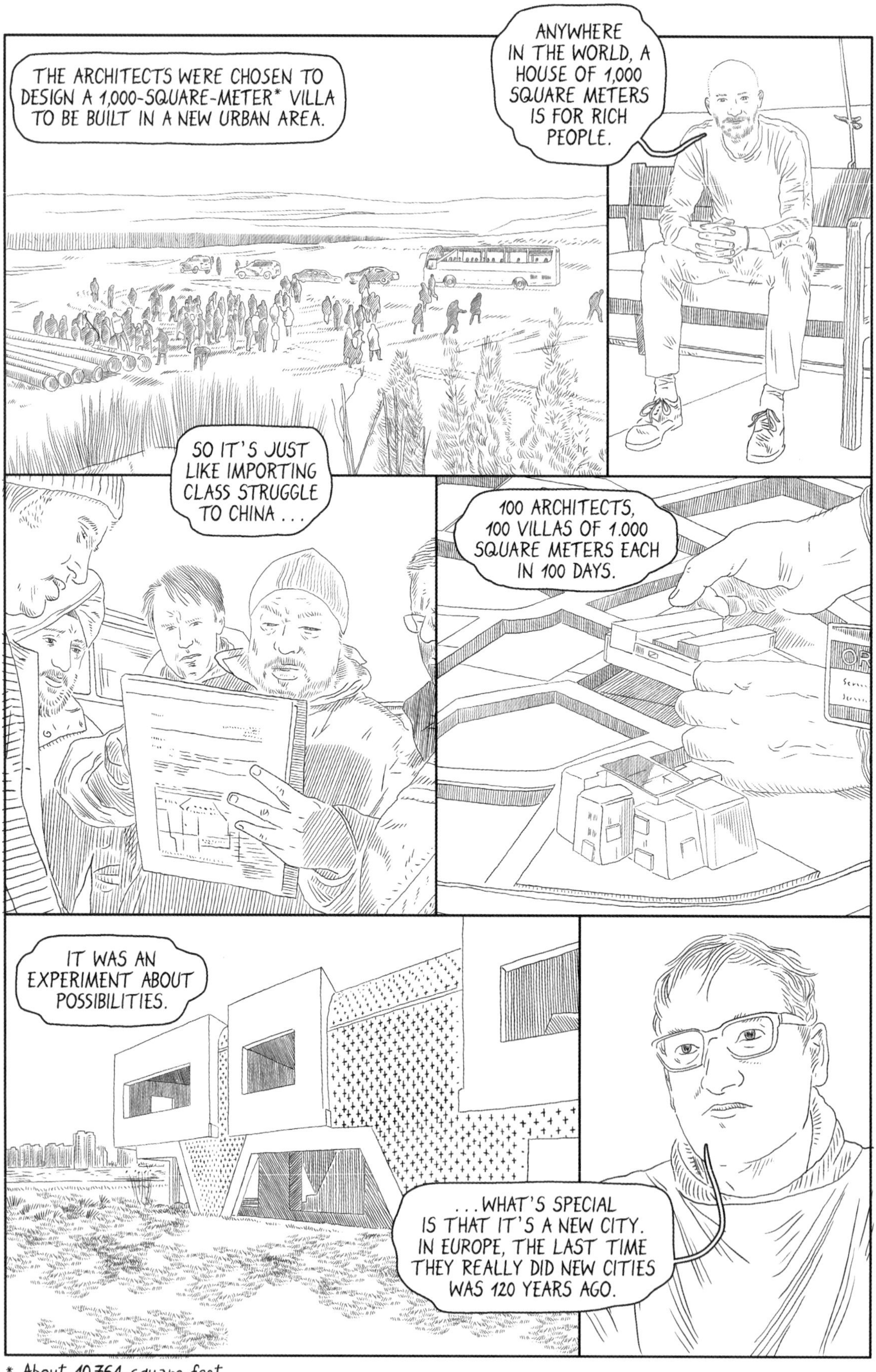
THE ARCHITECTS WERE CHOSEN TO DESIGN A 1,000-SQUARE-METER* VILLA TO BE BUILT IN A NEW URBAN AREA.
ANYWHERE IN THE WORLD, A HOUSE OF 1,000 SQUARE METERS IS FOR RICH PEOPLE.
SO IT'S JUST LIKE IMPORTING CLASS STRUGGLE TO CHINA . . .
100 ARCHITECTS, 100 VILLAS OF 1.000 SQUARE METERS EACH IN 100 DAYS.
IT WAS AN EXPERIMENT ABOUT POSSIBILITIES.
. . . WHAT'S SPECIAL IS THAT IT'S A NEW CITY. IN EUROPE, THE LAST TIME THEY REALLY DID NEW CITIES WAS 120 YEARS AGO.

* About 10,764 square feet.

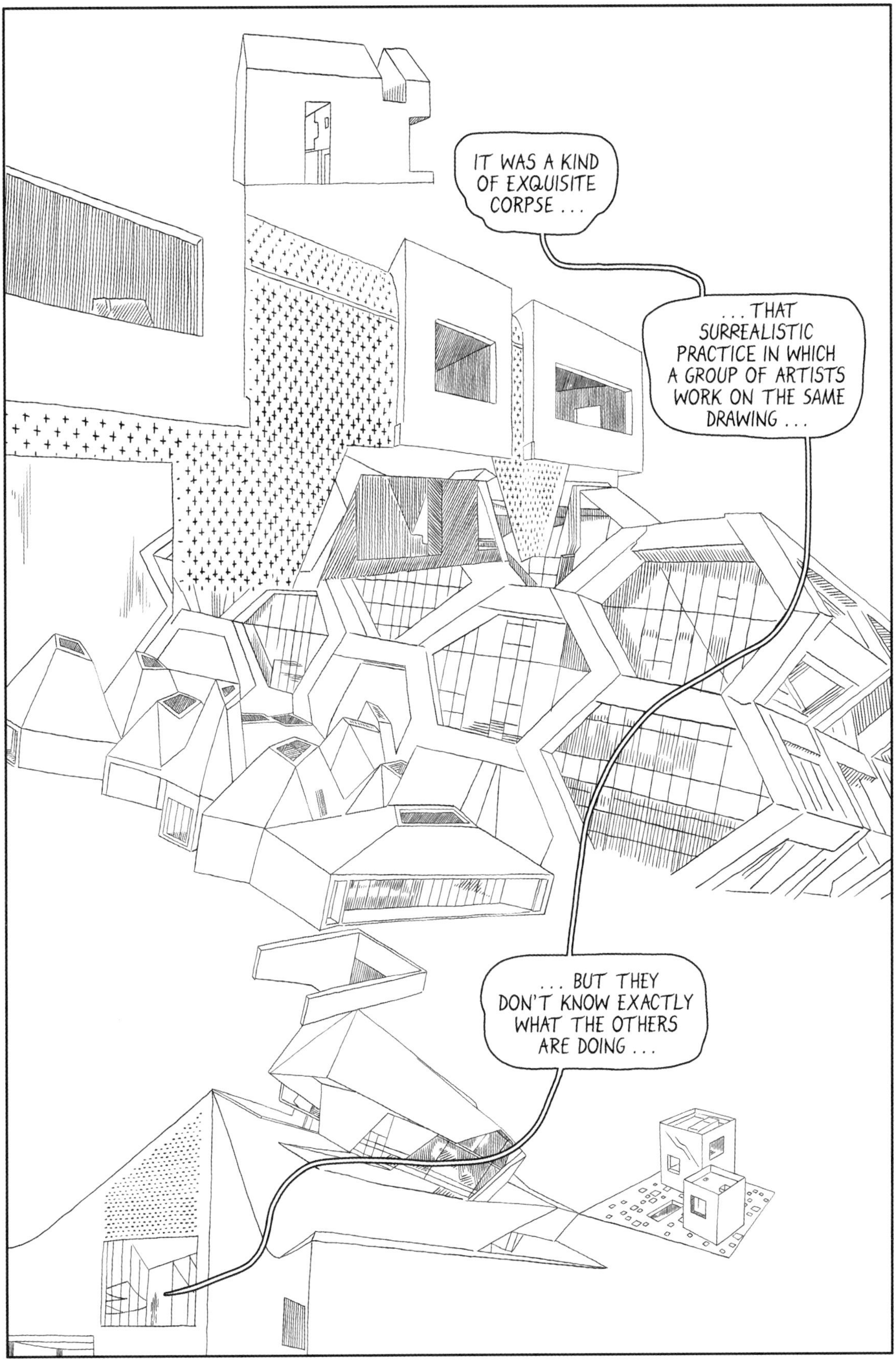
IT WAS A KIND OF EXQUISITE CORPSE . . .
. . . THAT SURREALISTIC PRACTICE IN WHICH A GROUP OF ARTISTS WORK ON THE SAME DRAWING . . .
. . . BUT THEY DON'T KNOW EXACTLY WHAT THE OTHERS ARE DOING . . .

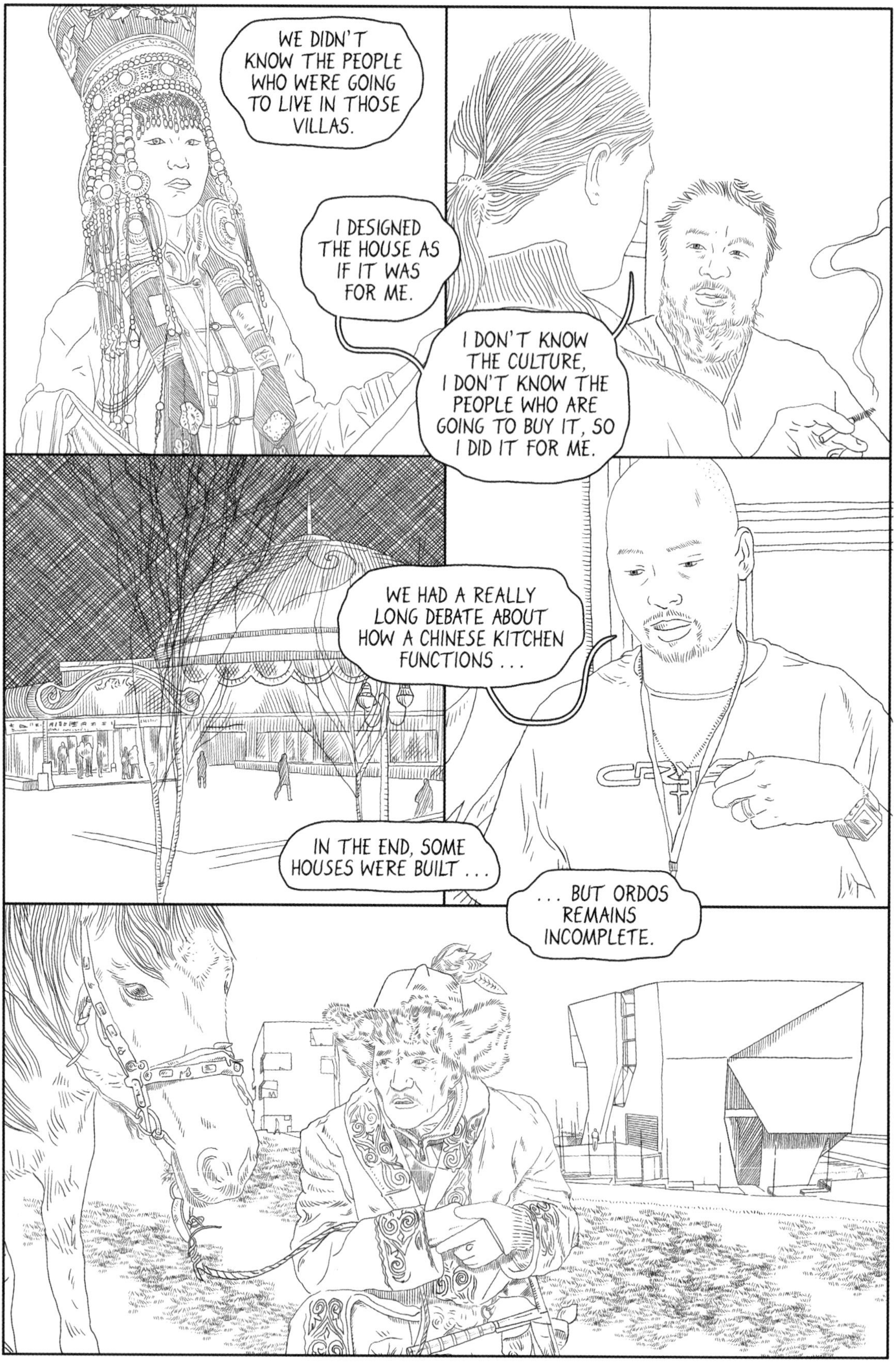
WE DIDN'T KNOW THE PEOPLE WHO WERE GOING TO LIVE IN THOSE VILLAS.
I DESIGNED THE HOUSE AS IF IT WAS FOR ME.
I DON'T KNOW THE CULTURE, I DON'T KNOW THE PEOPLE WHO ARE GOING TO BUY IT, SO I DID IT FOR ME.
WE HAD A REALLY LONG DEBATE ABOUT HOW A CHINESE KITCHEN FUNCTIONS . . .
IN THE END, SOME HOUSES WERE BUILT . . .
. . . BUT ORDOS REMAINS INCOMPLETE.

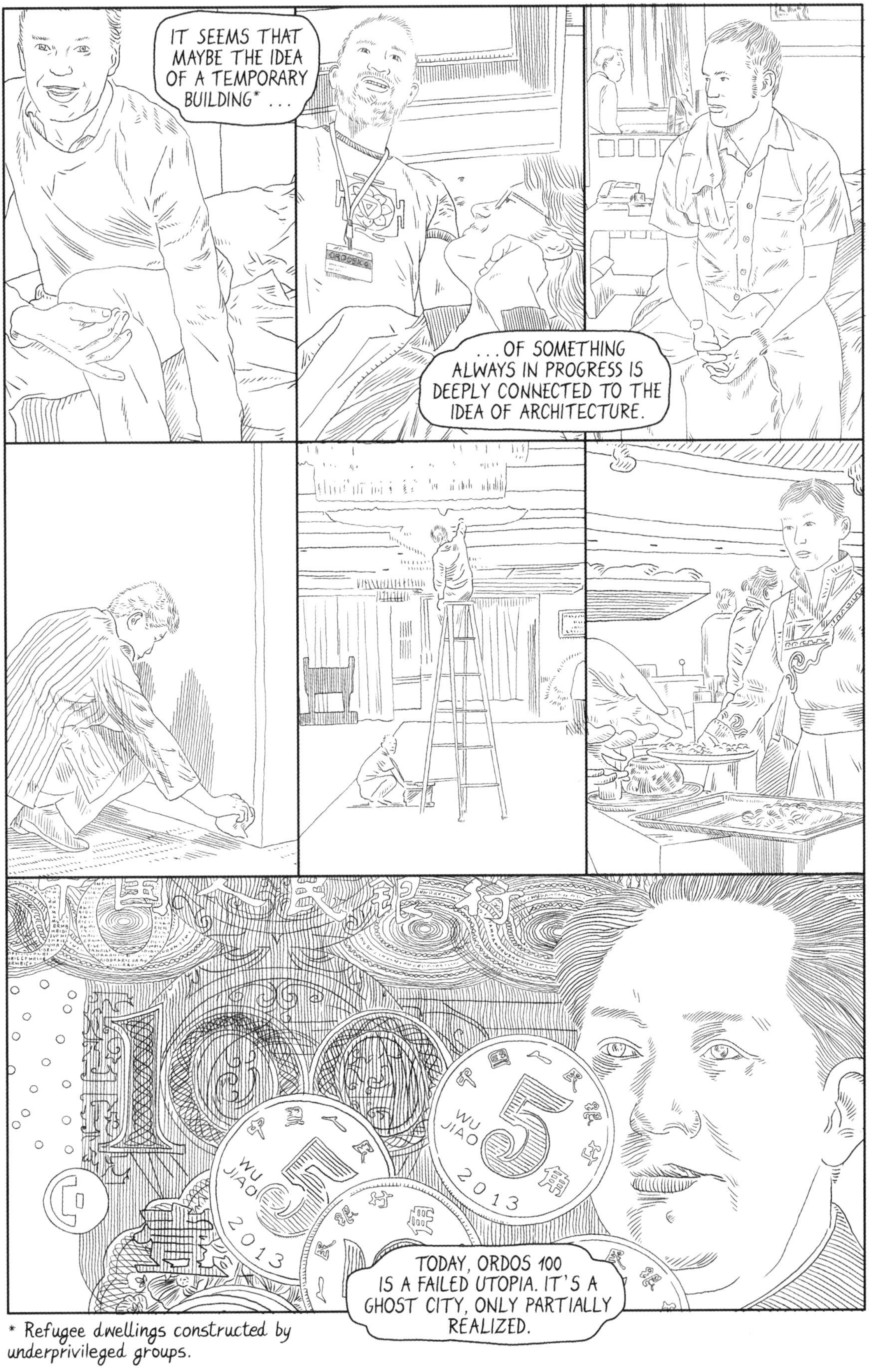
IT SEEMS THAT MAYBE THE IDEA OF A TEMPORARY BUILDING* . . .
. . .OF SOMETHING ALWAYS IN PROGRESS IS DEEPLY CONNECTED TO THE IDEA OF ARCHITECTURE.
TODAY, ORDOS 100 IS A FAILED UTOPIA. IT'S A GHOST CITY, ONLY PARTIALLY REALIZED.

* Refugee dwellings constructed by underprivileged groups.

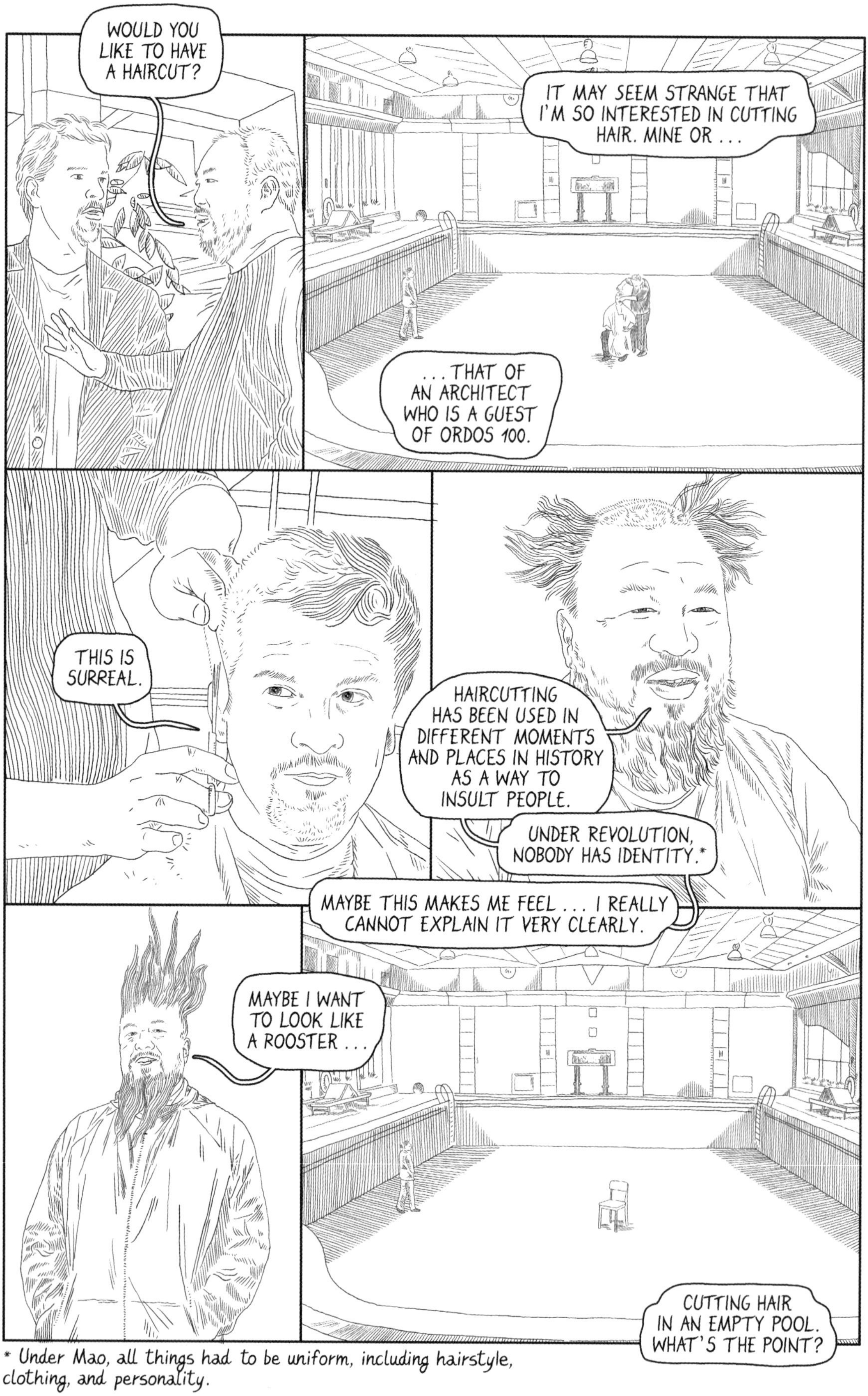
WOULD YOU LIKE TO HAVE A HAIRCUT?
IT MAY SEEM STRANGE THAT I'M SO INTERESTED IN CUTTING HAIR. MINE OR . . .
. . . THAT OF AN ARCHITECT WHO IS A GUEST OF ORDOS 100.
THIS IS SURREAL.
HAIRCUTTING HAS BEEN USED IN DIFFERENT MOMENTS AND PLACES IN HISTORY AS A WAY TO INSULT PEOPLE.
UNDER REVOLUTION, NOBODY HAS IDENTITY.*
MAYBE THIS MAKES ME FEEL . . . I REALLY CANNOT EXPLAIN IT VERY CLEARLY.
MAYBE I WANT TO LOOK LIKE A ROOSTER . . .
CUTTING HAIR IN AN EMPTY POOL. WHAT'S THE POINT?

* Under Mao, all things had to be uniform, including hairstyle, clothing, and personality.

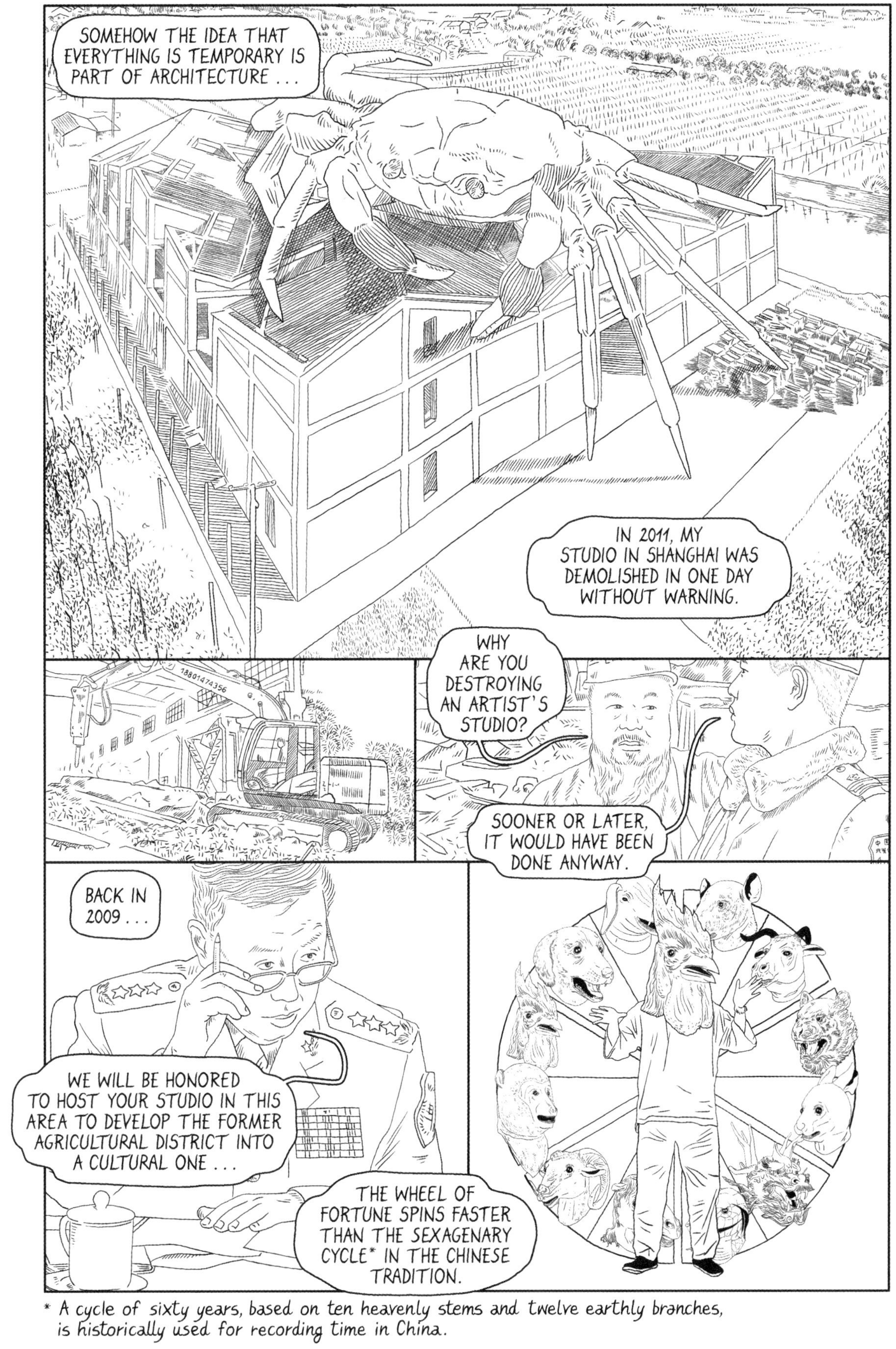
SOMEHOW THE IDEA THAT EVERYTHING IS TEMPORARY IS PART OF ARCHITECTURE . . .
IN 2011, MY STUDIO IN SHANGHAI WAS DEMOLISHED IN ONE DAY WITHOUT WARNING.
18801474356
WHY ARE YOU DESTROYING AN ARTIST'S STUDIO?
SOONER OR LATER, IT WOULD HAVE BEEN DONE ANYWAY.
BACK IN 2009 . . .
WE WILL BE HONORED TO HOST YOUR STUDIO IN THIS AREA TO DEVELOP THE FORMER AGRICULTURAL DISTRICT INTO A CULTURAL ONE . . .
THE WHEEL OF FORTUNE SPINS FASTER THAN THE SEXAGENARY CYCLE* IN THE CHINESE TRADITION.

* A cycle of sixty years, based on ten heavenly stems and twelve earthly branches, is historically used for recording time in China.

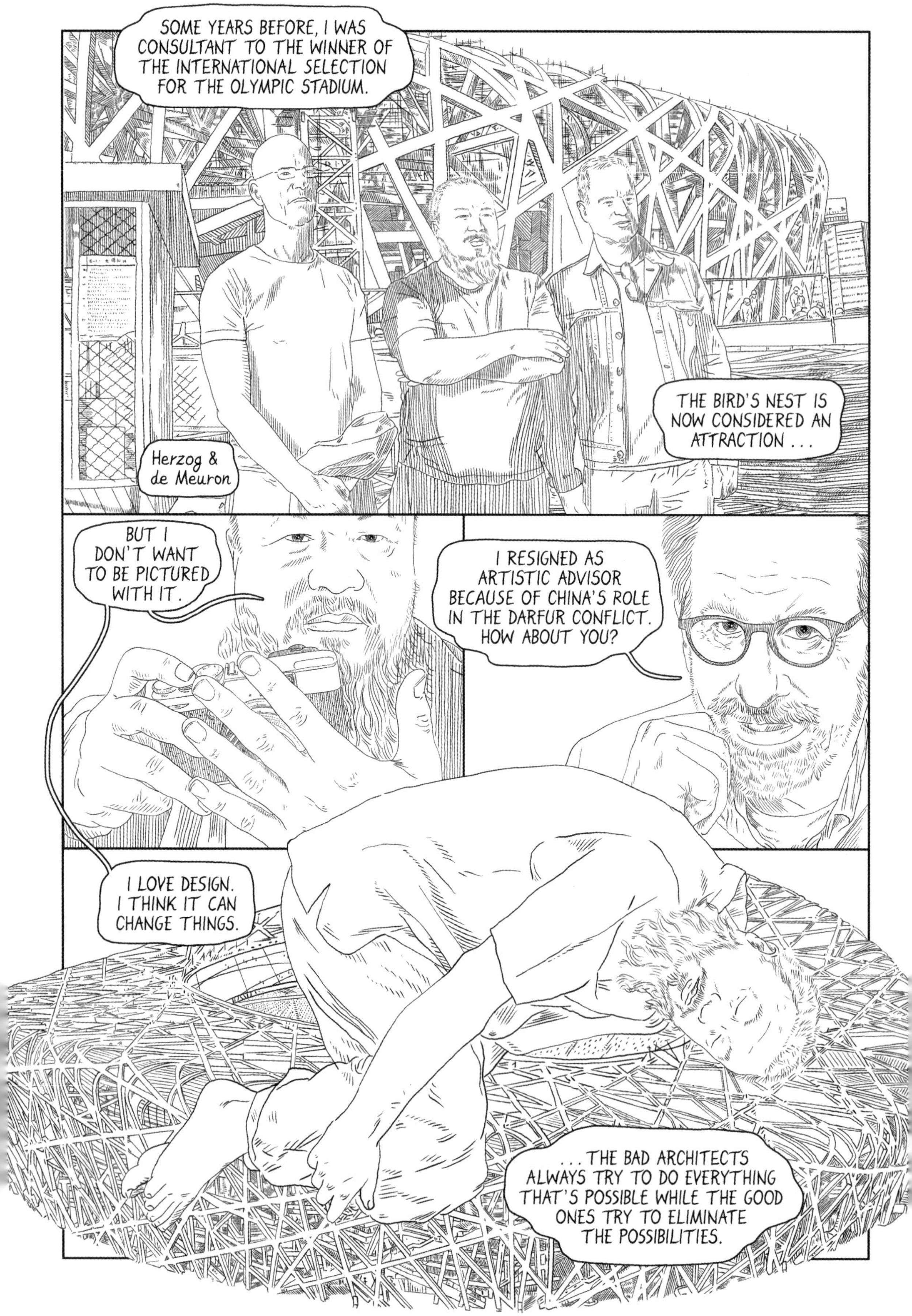
SOME YEARS BEFORE, I WAS CONSULTANT TO THE WINNER OF THE INTERNATIONAL SELECTION FOR THE OLYMPIC STADIUM.
Herzog & de Meuron
THE BIRD'S NEST IS NOW CONSIDERED AN ATTRACTION . . .
BUT I DON'T WANT TO BE PICTURED WITH IT.
I RESIGNED AS ARTISTIC ADVISOR BECAUSE OF CHINA'S ROLE IN THE DARFUR CONFLICT. HOW ABOUT YOU?
I LOVE DESIGN. I THINK IT CAN CHANGE THINGS.
. . . THE BAD ARCHITECTS ALWAYS TRY TO DO EVERYTHING THAT'S POSSIBLE WHILE THE GOOD ONES TRY TO ELIMINATE THE POSSIBILITIES.

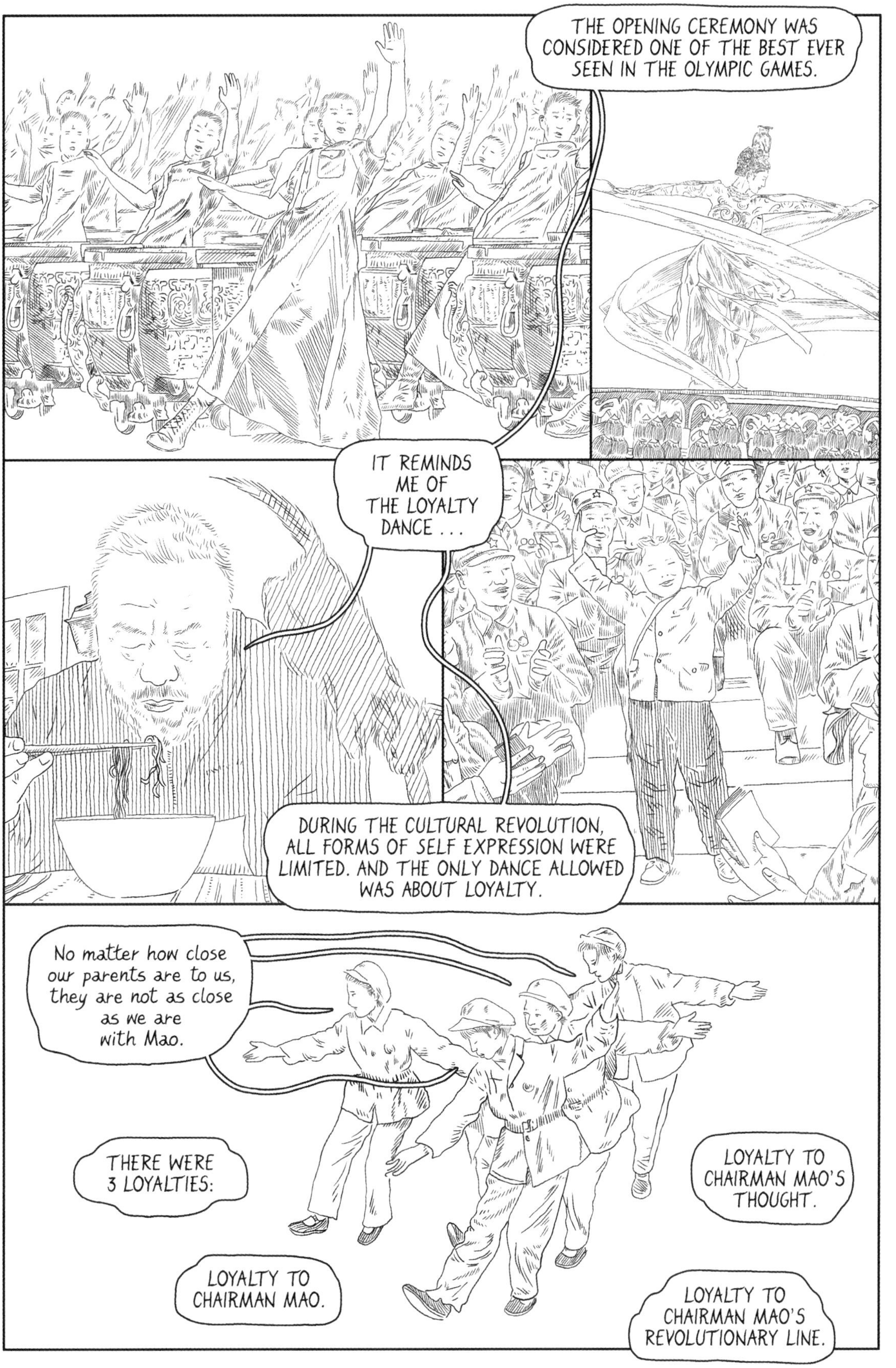
THE OPENING CEREMONY WAS CONSIDERED ONE OF THE BEST EVER SEEN IN THE OLYMPIC GAMES.
IT REMINDS ME OF THE LOYALTY DANCE . . .
DURING THE CULTURAL REVOLUTION, ALL FORMS OF SELF EXPRESSION WERE LIMITED. AND THE ONLY DANCE ALLOWED WAS ABOUT LOYALTY.
No matter how close our parents are to us, they are not as close as we are with Mao.
THERE WERE 3 LOYALTIES:
LOYALTY TO CHAIRMAN MAO.
LOYALTY TO CHAIRMAN MAO'S THOUGHT.
LOYALTY TO CHAIRMAN MAO'S REVOLUTIONARY LINE.

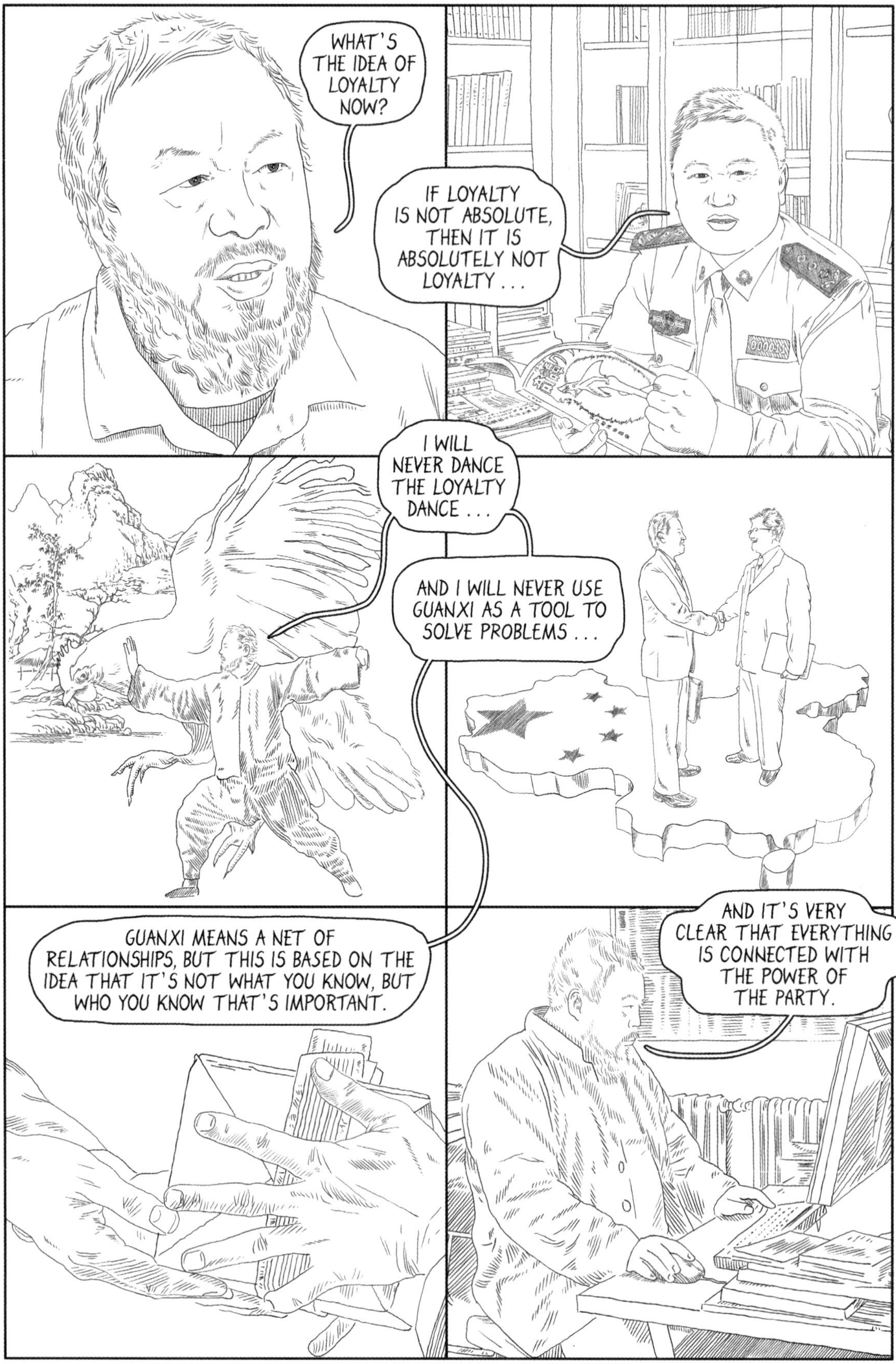
WHAT'S THE IDEA OF LOYALTY NOW?
IF LOYALTY IS NOT ABSOLUTE, THEN IT IS ABSOLUTELY NOT LOYALTY . . .
I WILL NEVER DANCE THE LOYALTY DANCE . . .
AND I WILL NEVER USE GUANXI AS A TOOL TO SOLVE PROBLEMS . . .
GUANXI MEANS A NET OF RELATIONSHIPS, BUT THIS IS BASED ON THE IDEA THAT IT'S NOT WHAT YOU KNOW, BUT WHO YOU KNOW THAT'S IMPORTANT.
AND IT'S VERY CLEAR THAT EVERYTHING IS CONNECTED WITH THE POWER OF THE PARTY.

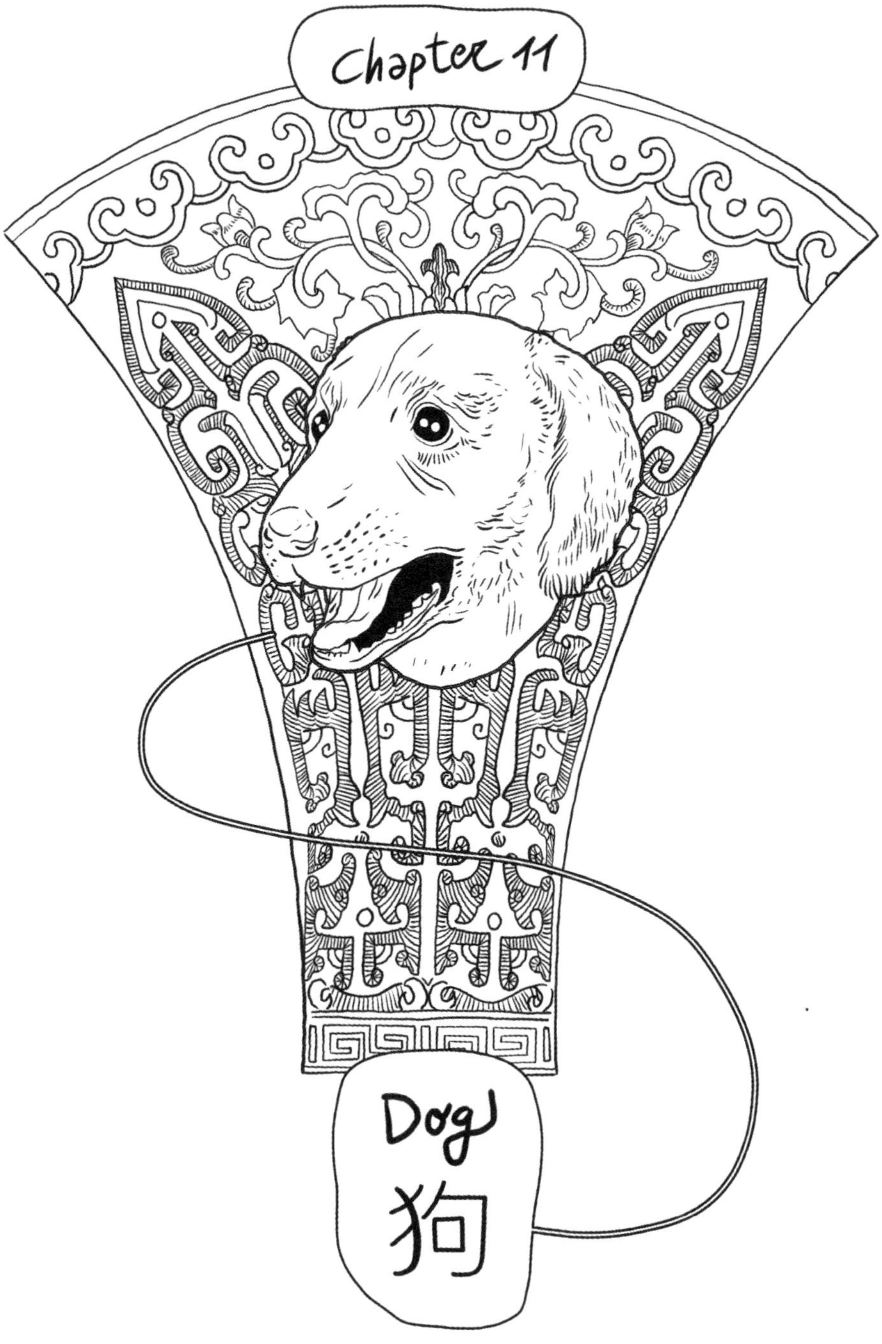
Chapter 11
Dog
狗

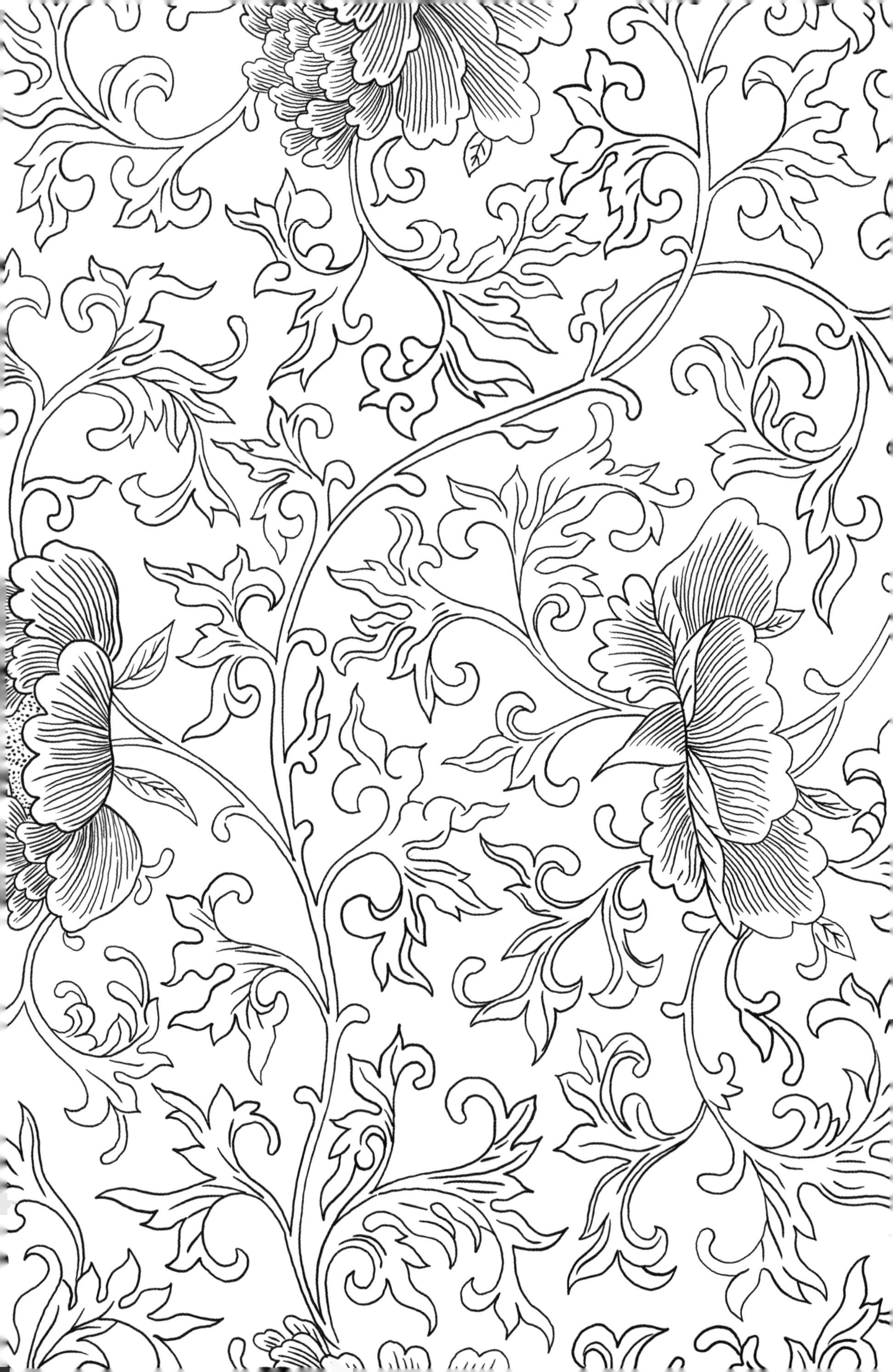

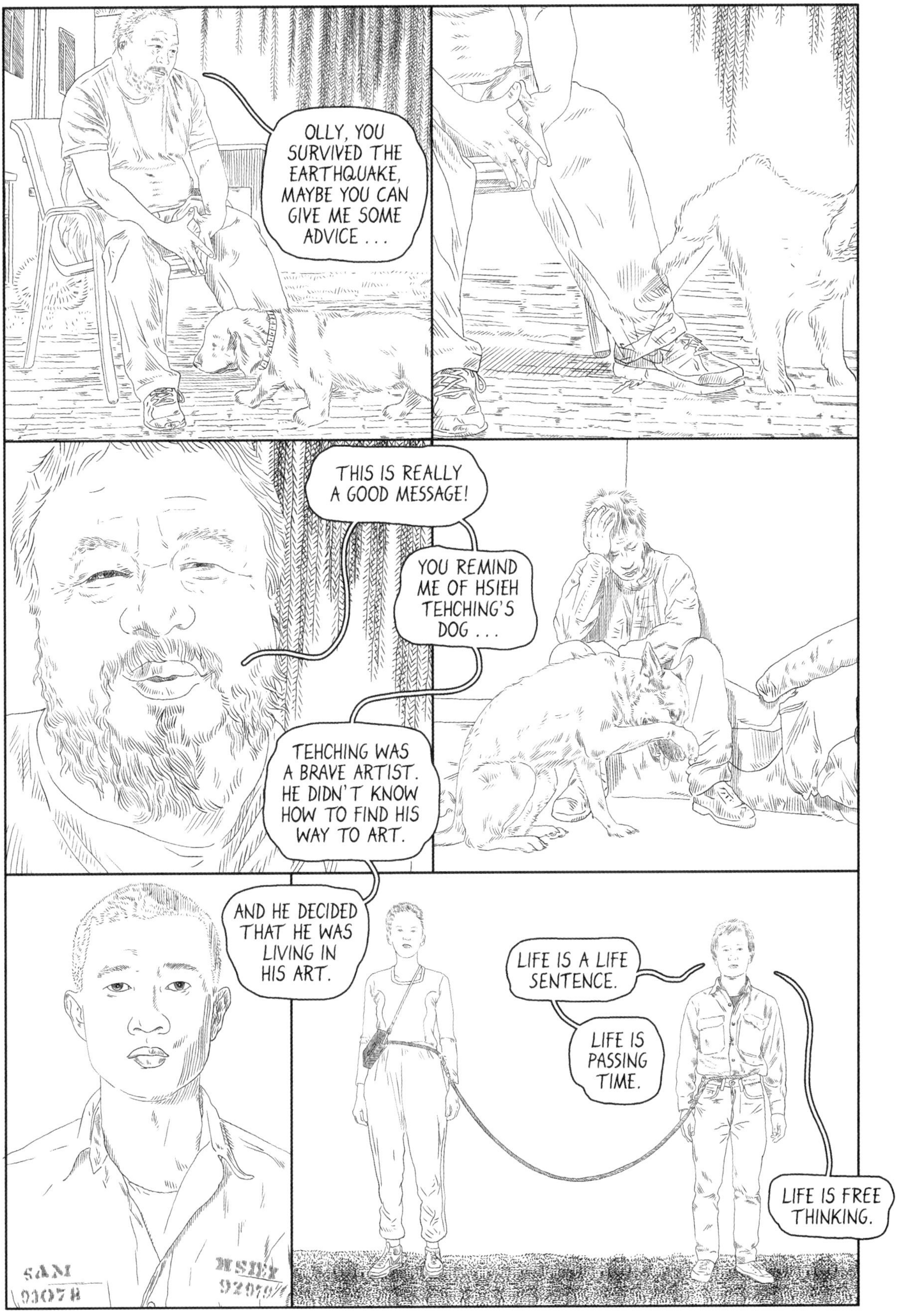
OLLY, YOU SURVIVED THE EARTHQUAKE, MAYBE YOU CAN GIVE ME SOME ADVICE . . .
THIS IS REALLY A GOOD MESSAGE!
YOU REMIND ME OF HSIEH TEHCHING'S DOG . . .
TEHCHING WAS A BRAVE ARTIST. HE DIDN'T KNOW HOW TO FIND HIS WAY TO ART.
AND HE DECIDED THAT HE WAS LIVING IN HIS ART.
SAM
91078
HSIEH
92979
LIFE IS A LIFE SENTENCE.
LIFE IS PASSING TIME.
LIFE IS FREE THINKING.

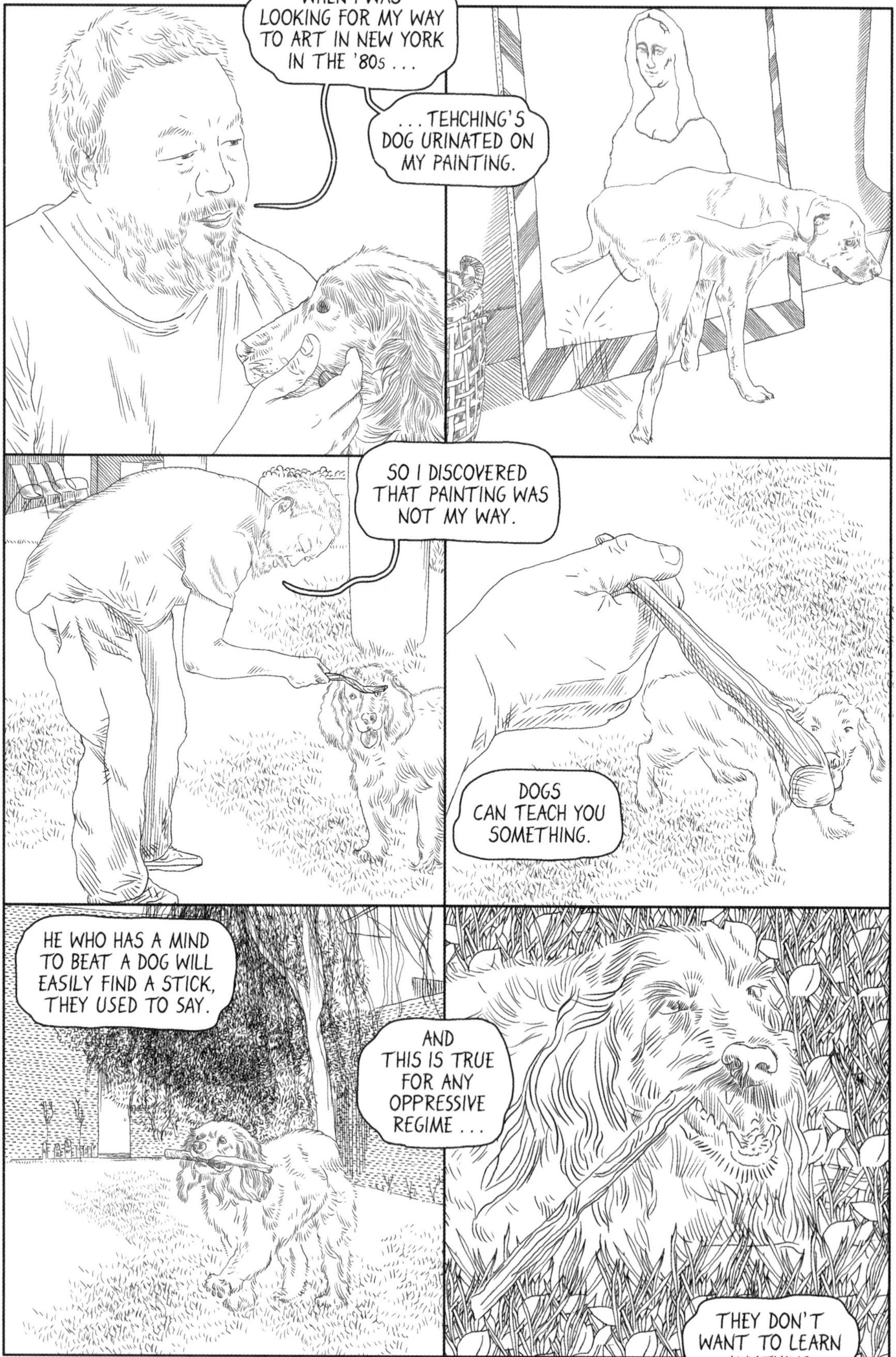
WHEN I WAS LOOKING FOR MY WAY TO ART IN NEW YORK IN THE '80s . . .
. . . TEHCHING'S DOG URINATED ON MY PAINTING.
SO I DISCOVERED THAT PAINTING WAS NOT MY WAY.
DOGS CAN TEACH YOU SOMETHING.
HE WHO HAS A MIND TO BEAT A DOG WILL EASILY FIND A STICK, THEY USED TO SAY.
AND THIS IS TRUE FOR ANY OPPRESSIVE REGIME . . .
THEY DON'T WANT TO LEARN ANYTHING.

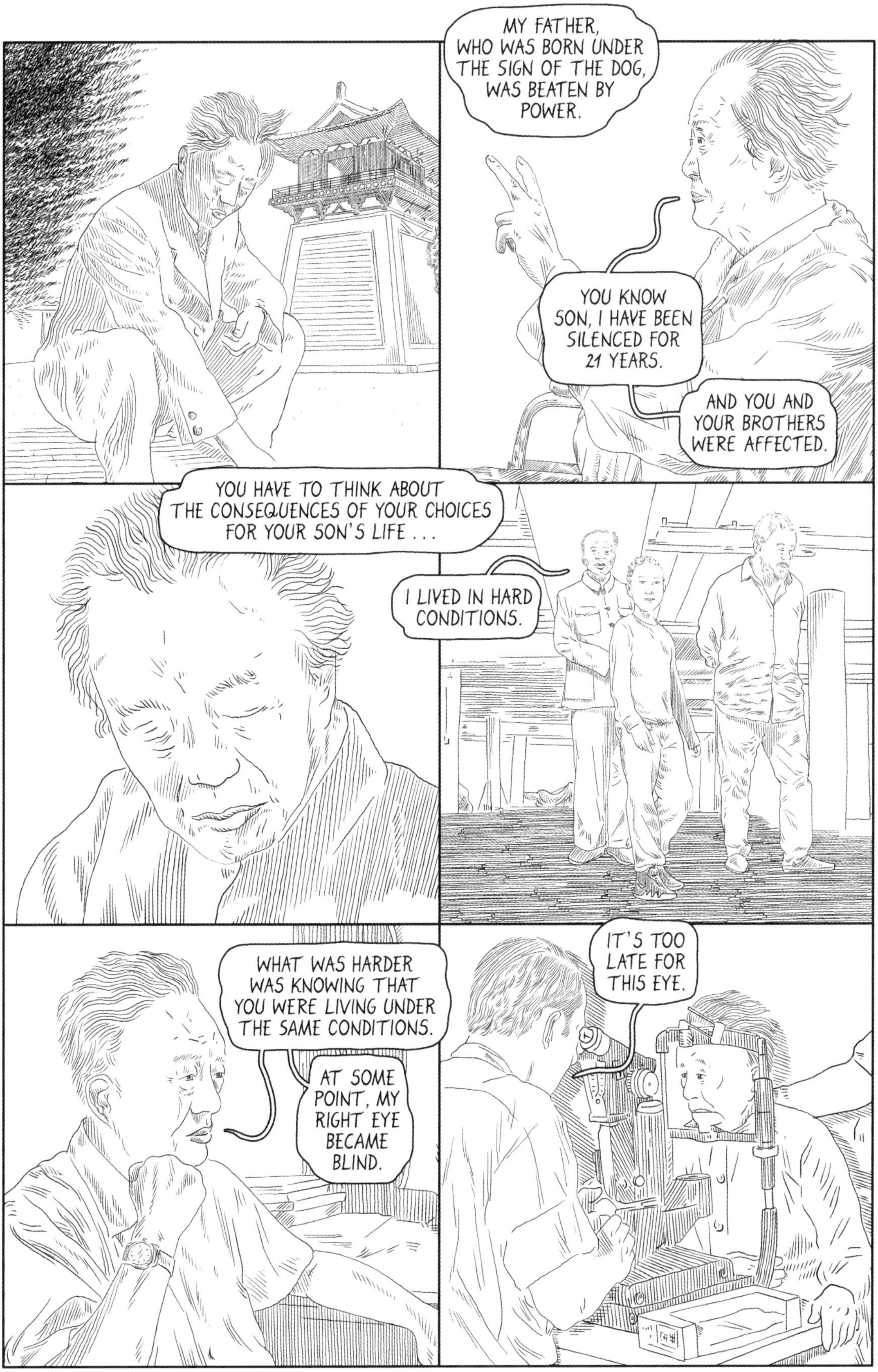
MY FATHER, WHO WAS BORN UNDER THE SIGN OF THE DOG, WAS BEATEN BY POWER.
YOU KNOW SON, I HAVE BEEN SILENCED FOR 21 YEARS.
AND YOU AND YOUR BROTHERS WERE AFFECTED.
YOU HAVE TO THINK ABOUT THE CONSEQUENCES OF YOUR CHOICES FOR YOUR SON'S LIFE . . .
I LIVED IN HARD CONDITIONS.
WHAT WAS HARDER WAS KNOWING THAT YOU WERE LIVING UNDER THE SAME CONDITIONS.
AT SOME POINT, MY RIGHT EYE BECAME BLIND.
IT'S TOO LATE FOR THIS EYE.

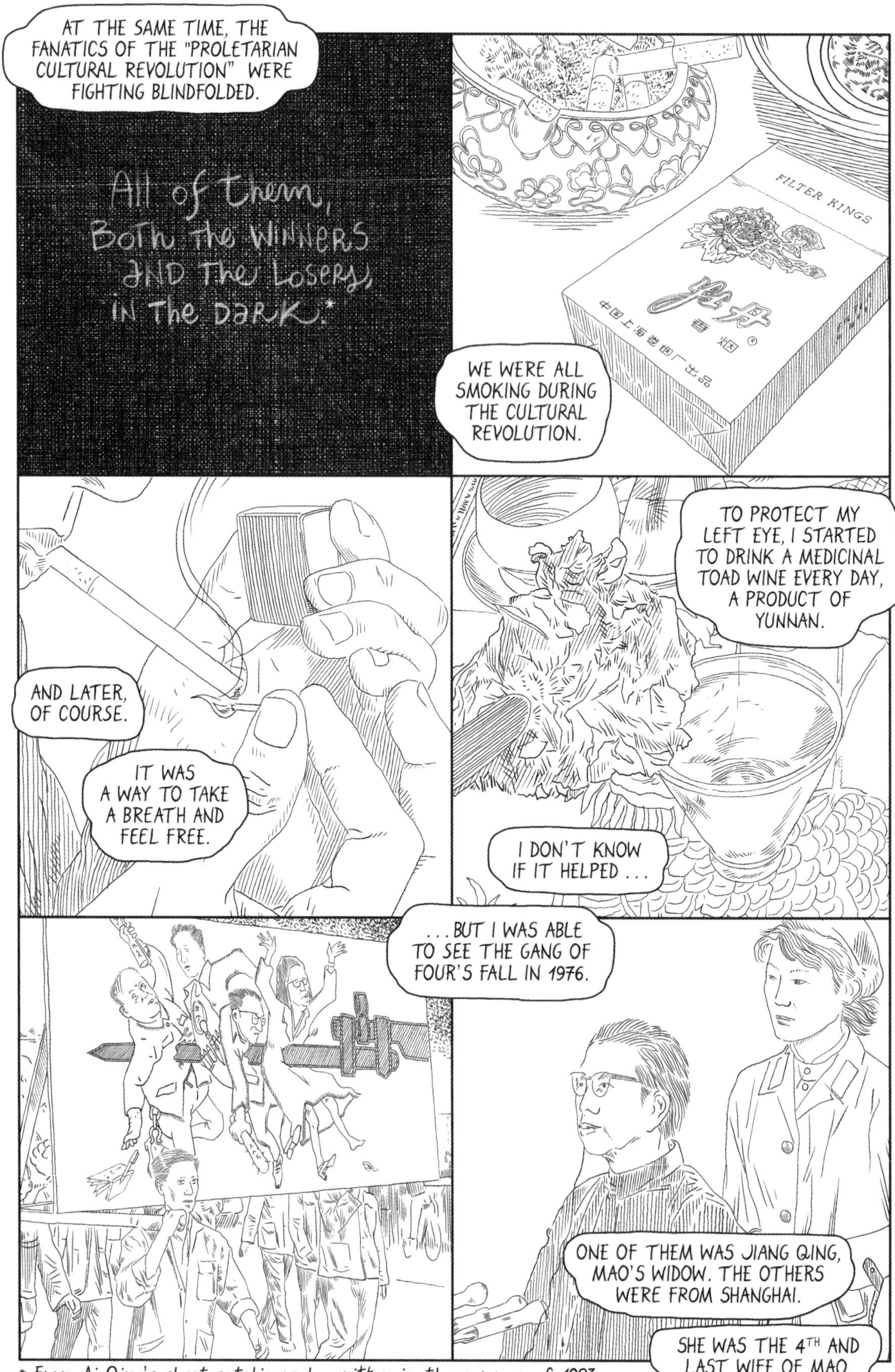
AT THE SAME TIME, THE FANATICS OF THE "PROLETARIAN CULTURAL REVOLUTION" WERE FIGHTING BLINDFOLDED.
All of them, Both the winners and the losers, in the dark.*
FILTER KINGS
牡丹
香烟
中国上海卷烟厂出品
WE WERE ALL SMOKING DURING THE CULTURAL REVOLUTION.
AND LATER, OF COURSE.
IT WAS A WAY TO TAKE A BREATH AND FEEL FREE.
TO PROTECT MY LEFT EYE, I STARTED TO DRINK A MEDICINAL TOAD WINE EVERY DAY, A PRODUCT OF YUNNAN.
I DON'T KNOW IF IT HELPED . . .
. . . BUT I WAS ABLE TO SEE THE GANG OF FOUR'S FALL IN 1976.
ONE OF THEM WAS JIANG QING, MAO'S WIDOW. THE OTHERS WERE FROM SHANGHAI.
SHE WAS THE 4TH AND LAST WIFE OF MAO.

* From Ai Qing's short autobiography written in the summer of 1983.

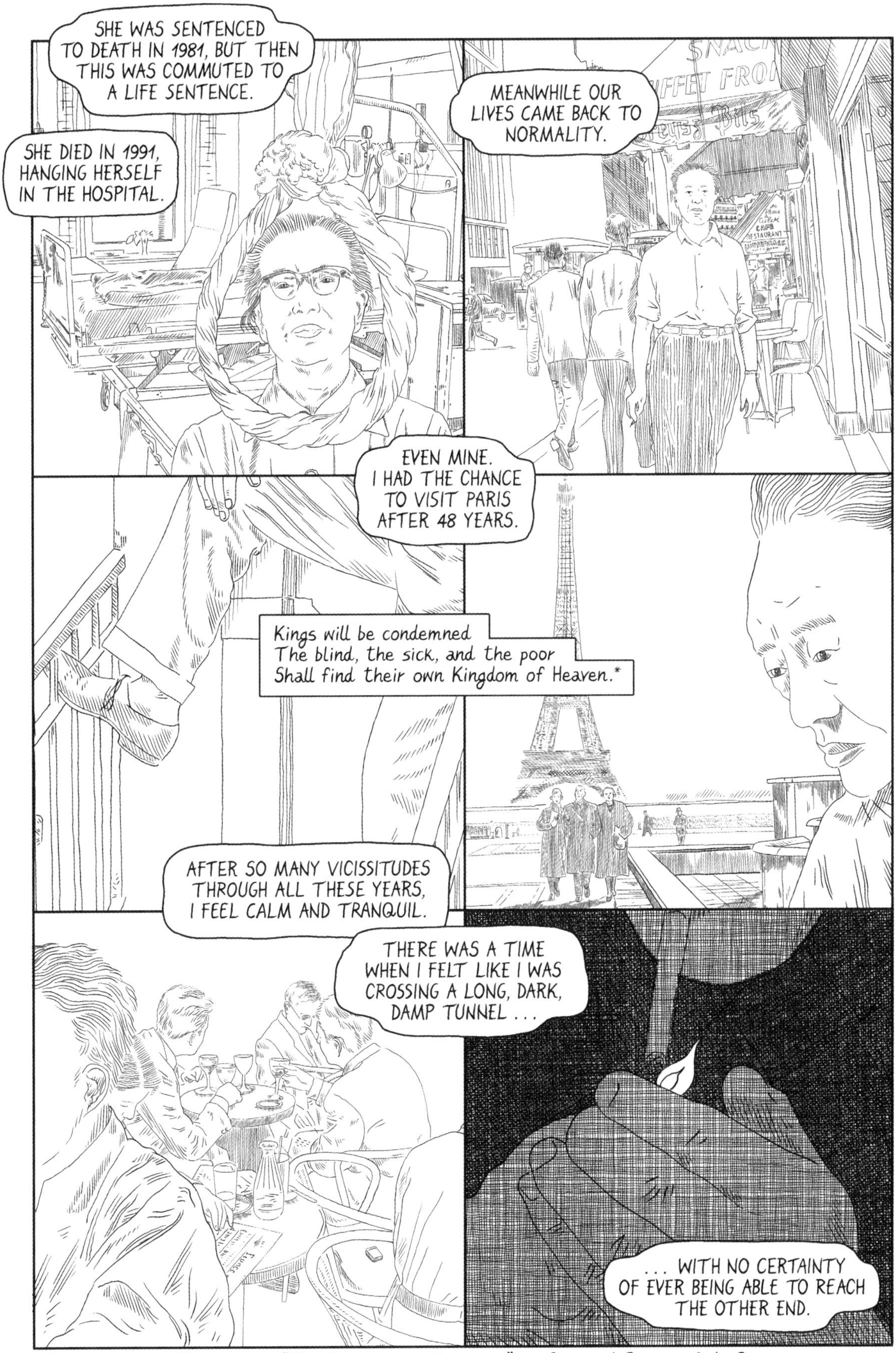
SHE WAS SENTENCED TO DEATH IN 1981, BUT THEN THIS WAS COMMUTED TO A LIFE SENTENCE.
SHE DIED IN 1991, HANGING HERSELF IN THE HOSPITAL.
MEANWHILE OUR LIVES CAME BACK TO NORMALITY.
EVEN MINE. I HAD THE CHANCE TO VISIT PARIS AFTER 48 YEARS.
Kings will be condemned
The blind, the sick, and the poor
Shall find their own Kingdom of Heaven.*
AFTER SO MANY VICISSITUDES THROUGH ALL THESE YEARS, I FEEL CALM AND TRANQUIL.
THERE WAS A TIME WHEN I FELT LIKE I WAS CROSSING A LONG, DARK, DAMP TUNNEL . . .
. . . WITH NO CERTAINTY OF EVER BEING ABLE TO REACH THE OTHER END.

* Verses from Ai Qing's poem "The Death of a Nazarene" in *Selected Poems of Ai Qing*. Eugene Chen Eoyang, ed., Bloomington: Indiana University Press, 1982.

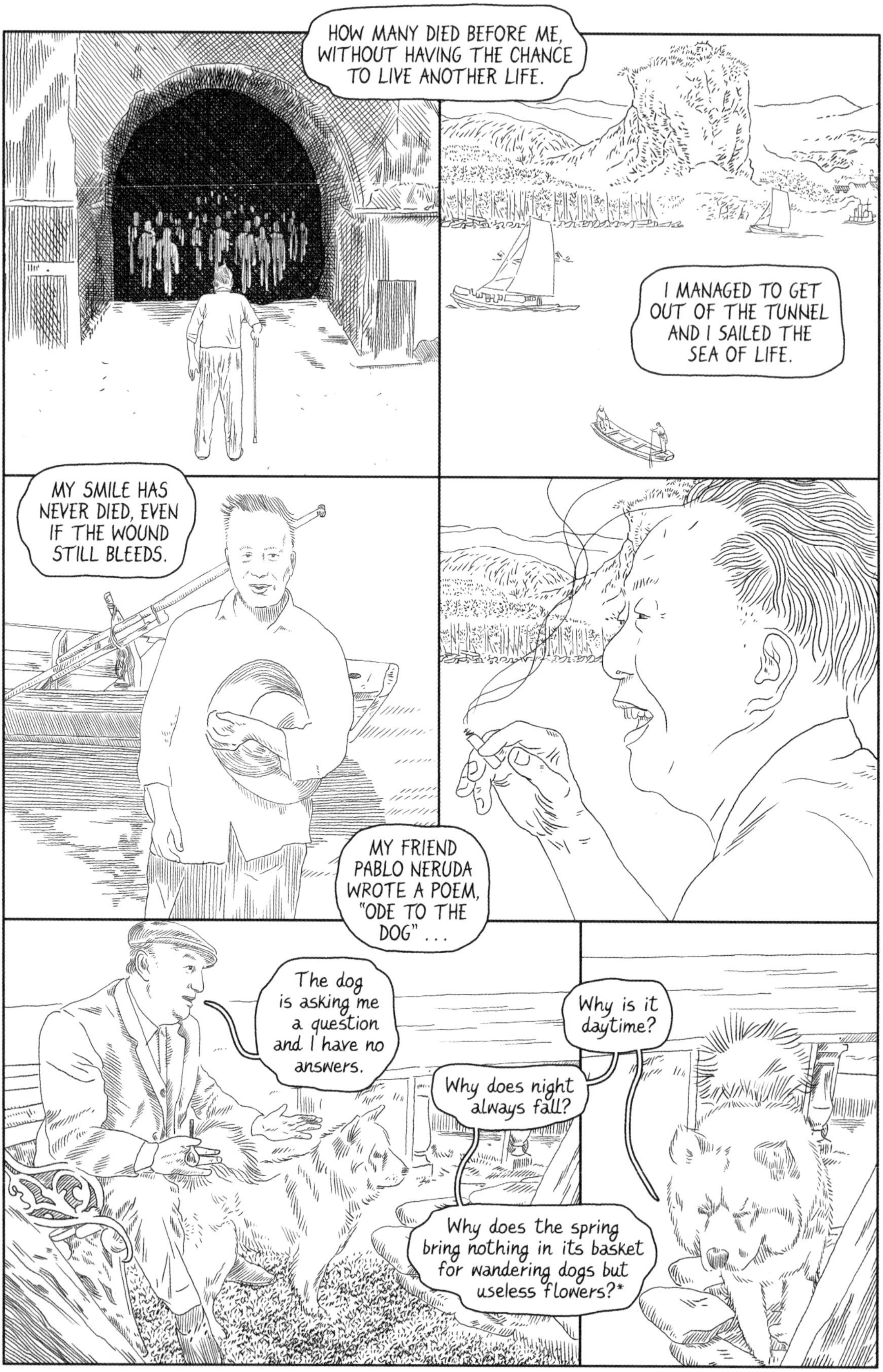

HOW MANY DIED BEFORE ME, WITHOUT HAVING THE CHANCE TO LIVE ANOTHER LIFE.
I MANAGED TO GET OUT OF THE TUNNEL AND I SAILED THE SEA OF LIFE.
MY SMILE HAS NEVER DIED, EVEN IF THE WOUND STILL BLEEDS.
MY FRIEND PABLO NERUDA WROTE A POEM, "ODE TO THE DOG" . . .
The dog is asking me a question and I have no answers.
Why is it daytime?
Why does night always fall?
Why does the spring bring nothing in its basket for wandering dogs but useless flowers?*

* Free selection of paraphrased verses from Pablo Neruda, "Ode to the Dog," in *Fifty Odes*. trans. George Schade. Austin: Host Publications, 1996.

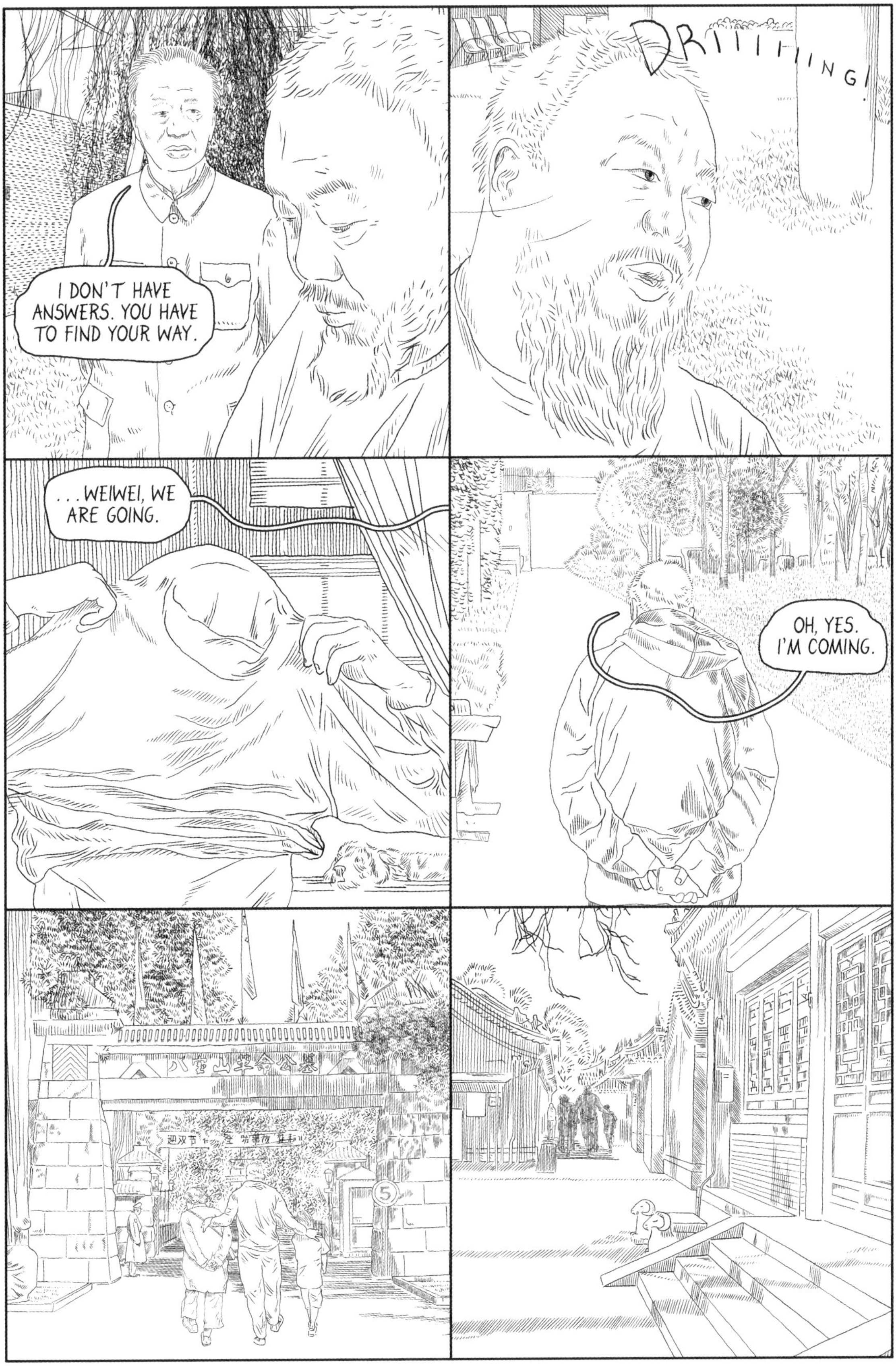
I DON'T HAVE ANSWERS. YOU HAVE TO FIND YOUR WAY.
DRIIIIIING!
...WEIWEI, WE ARE GOING.
OH, YES. I'M COMING.

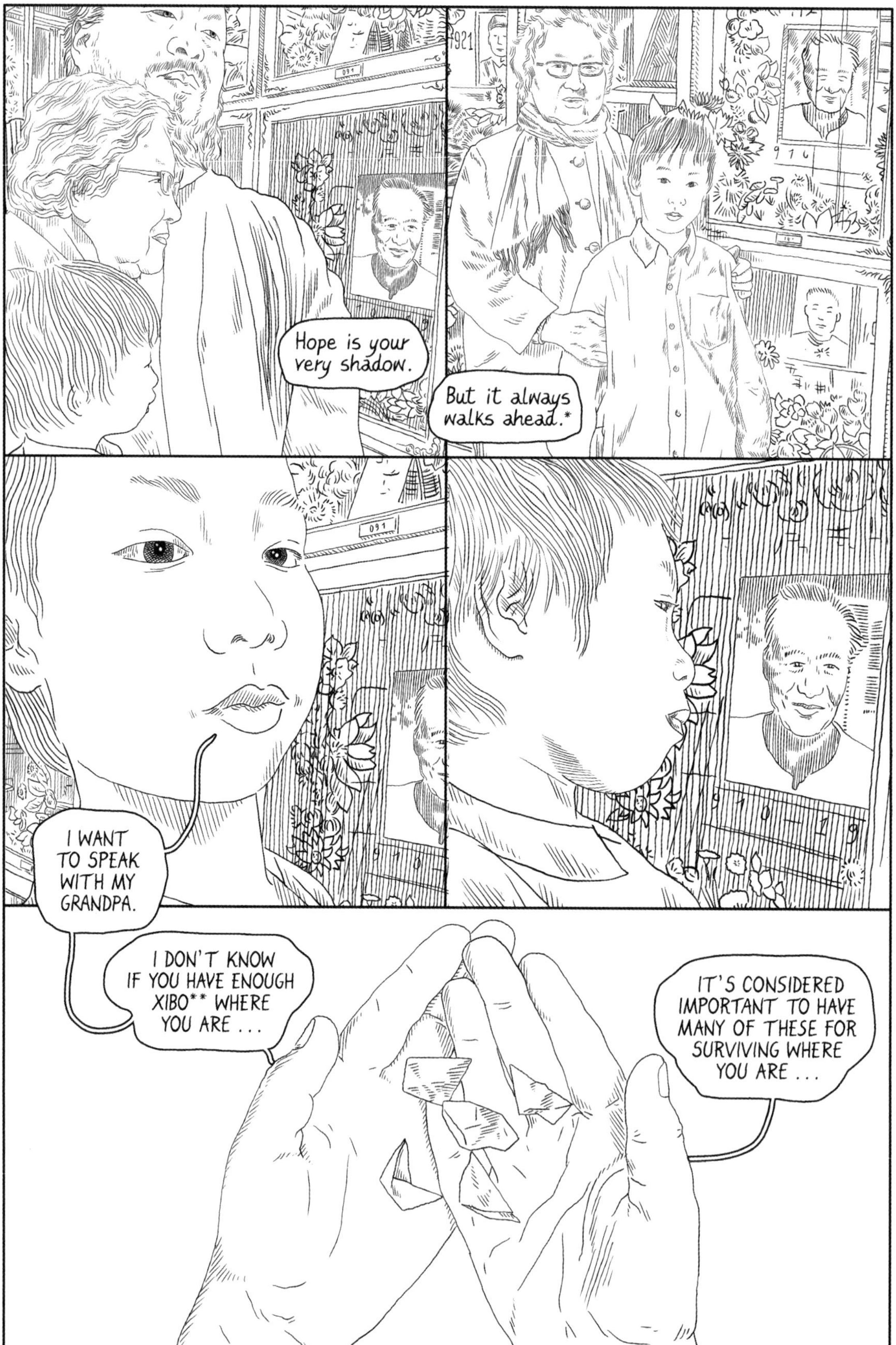
Hope is your very shadow.
But it always walks ahead.*
I WANT TO SPEAK WITH MY GRANDPA.
I DON'T KNOW IF YOU HAVE ENOUGH XIBO** WHERE YOU ARE . . .
IT'S CONSIDERED IMPORTANT TO HAVE MANY OF THESE FOR SURVIVING WHERE YOU ARE . . .

* From Ai Qing's poem "Hope" in *The Red Azalea: Chinese Poetry Since the Cultural Revolution*, Edward Morin, ed., trans. by Fang Dai, Dennis Ding, and Edward Morin. Honolulu: University of Hawai'i Press, November 1990.
** Xibo are burnt offerings common in Chinese ancestral worship.

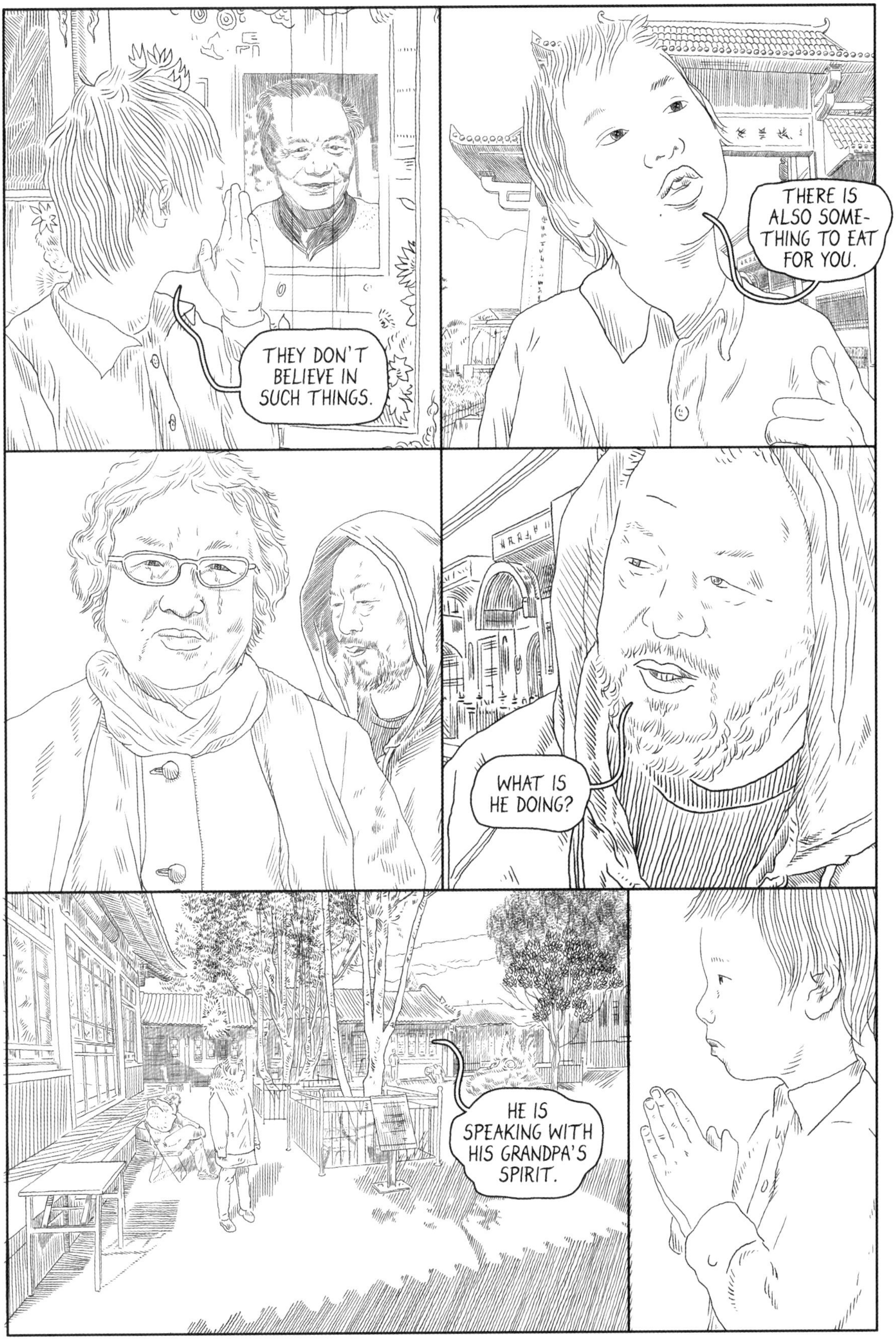
THEY DON'T BELIEVE IN SUCH THINGS.
THERE IS ALSO SOME-THING TO EAT FOR YOU.
WHAT IS HE DOING?
HE IS SPEAKING WITH HIS GRANDPA'S SPIRIT.

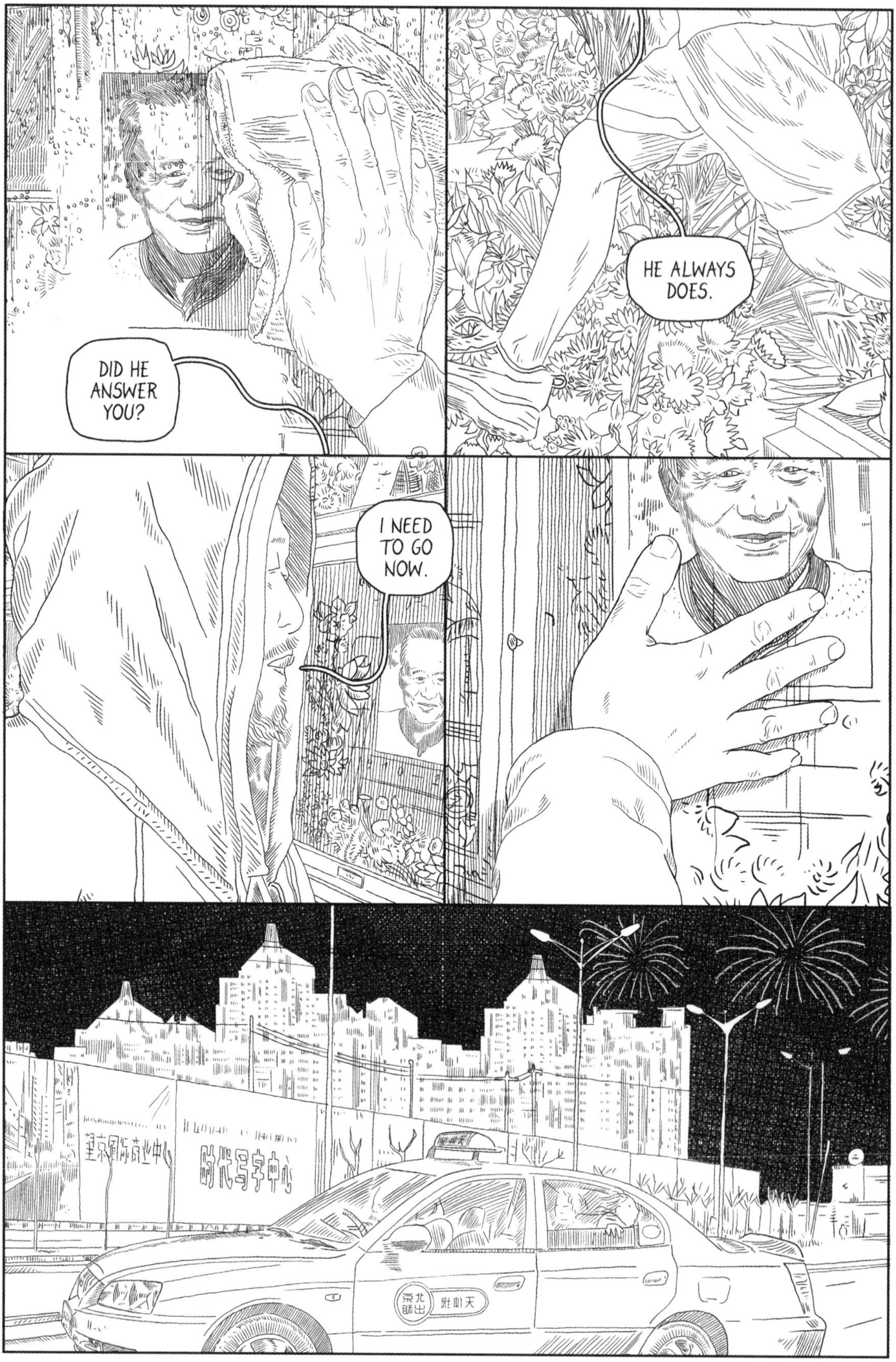
DID HE ANSWER YOU?
HE ALWAYS DOES.
I NEED TO GO NOW.
时代写字中心

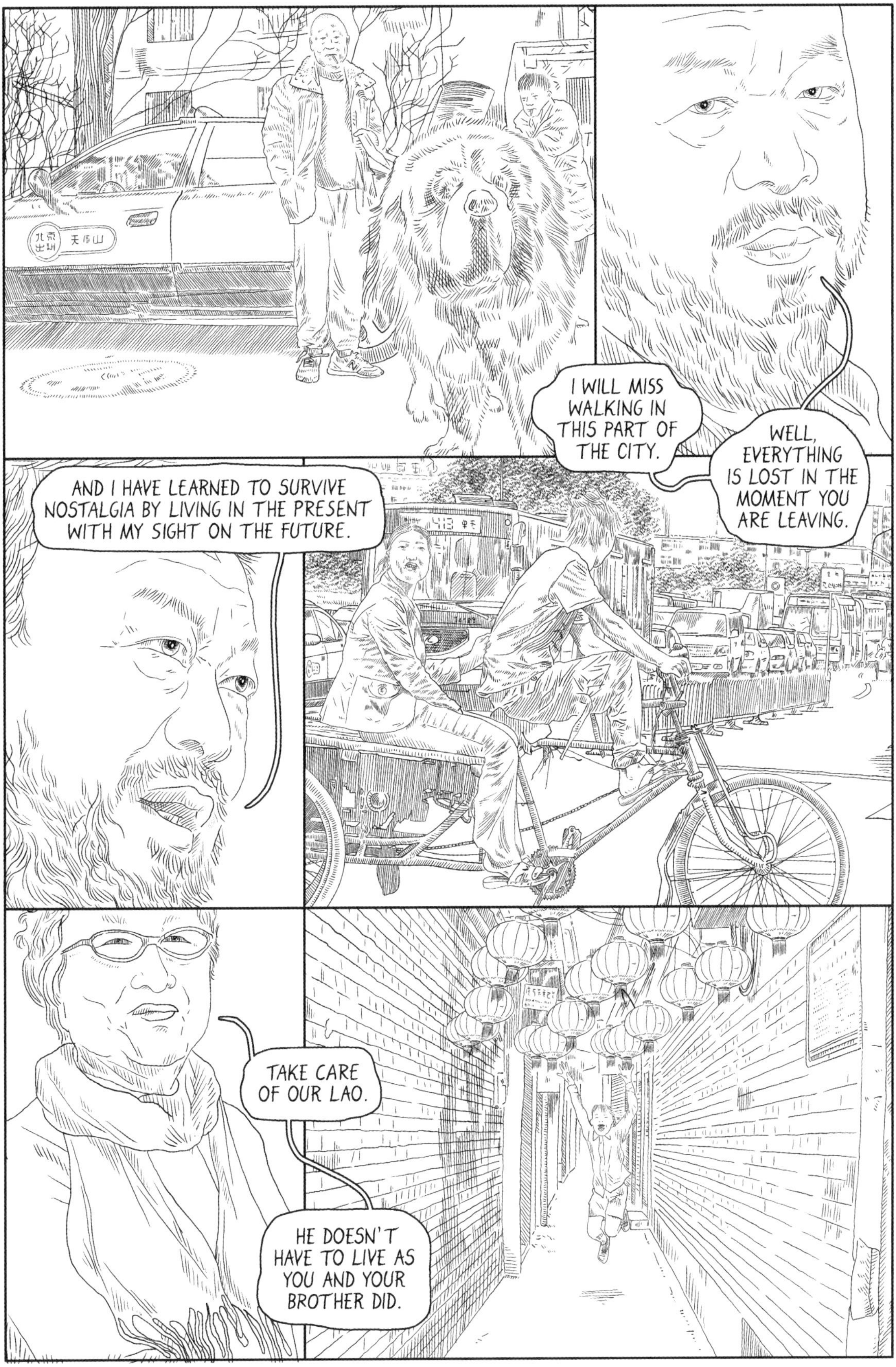

I WILL MISS WALKING IN THIS PART OF THE CITY.
WELL, EVERYTHING IS LOST IN THE MOMENT YOU ARE LEAVING.
AND I HAVE LEARNED TO SURVIVE NOSTALGIA BY LIVING IN THE PRESENT WITH MY SIGHT ON THE FUTURE.
TAKE CARE OF OUR LAO.
HE DOESN'T HAVE TO LIVE AS YOU AND YOUR BROTHER DID.

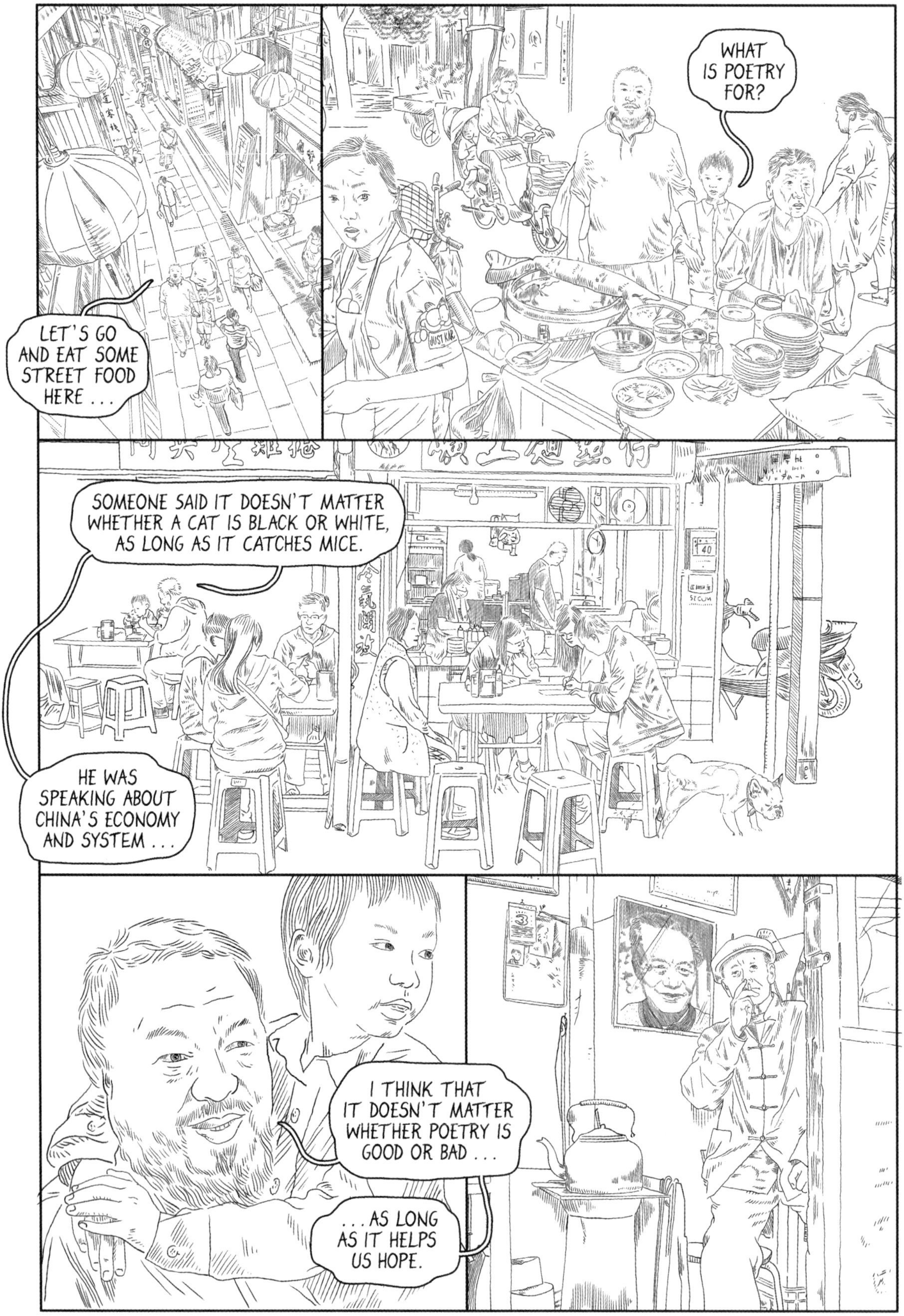

LET'S GO AND EAT SOME STREET FOOD HERE . . .
WHAT IS POETRY FOR?
SOMEONE SAID IT DOESN'T MATTER WHETHER A CAT IS BLACK OR WHITE, AS LONG AS IT CATCHES MICE.
HE WAS SPEAKING ABOUT CHINA'S ECONOMY AND SYSTEM . . .
I THINK THAT IT DOESN'T MATTER WHETHER POETRY IS GOOD OR BAD . . .
. . . AS LONG AS IT HELPS US HOPE.

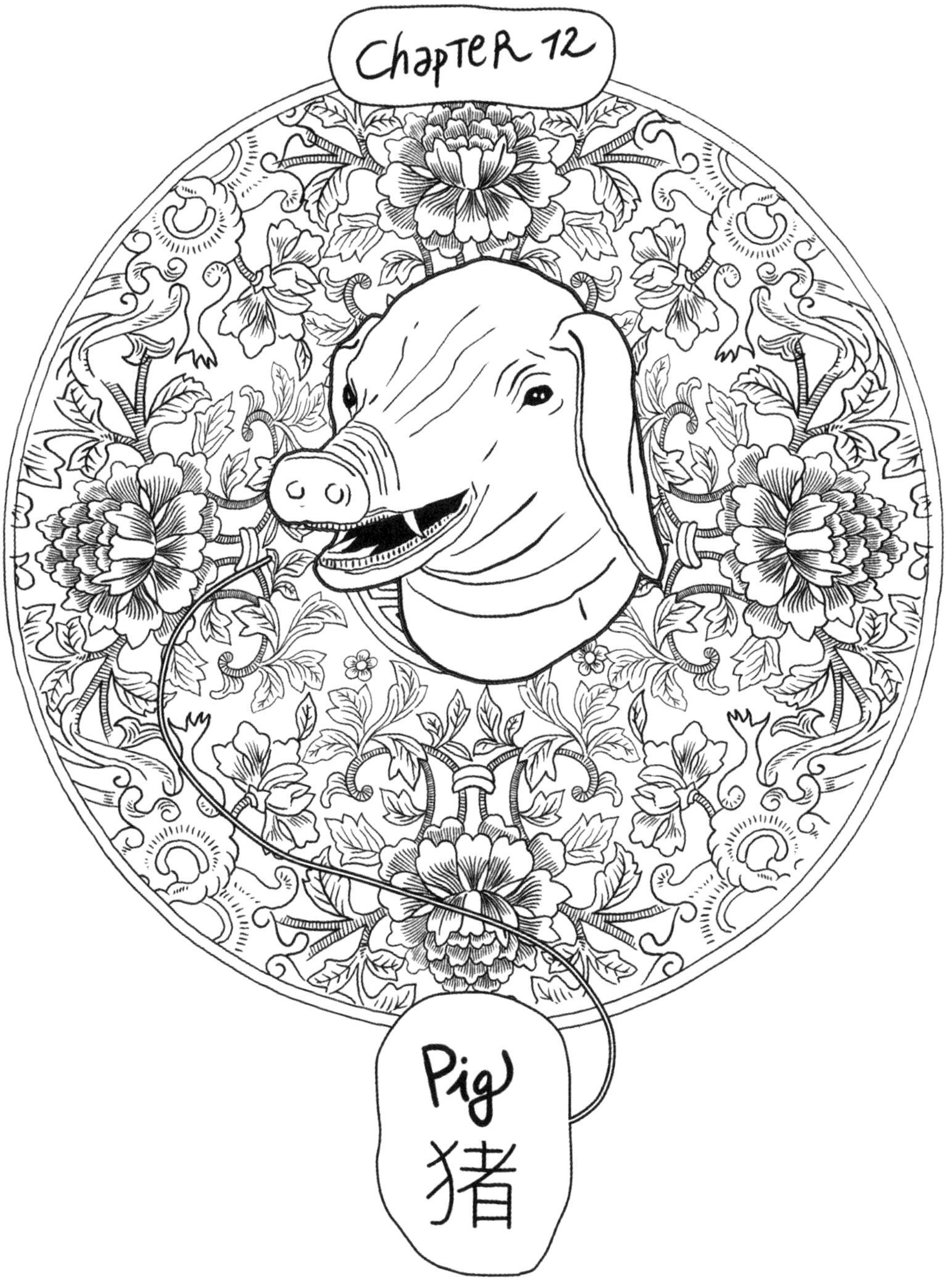
Chapter 12
Pig
猪

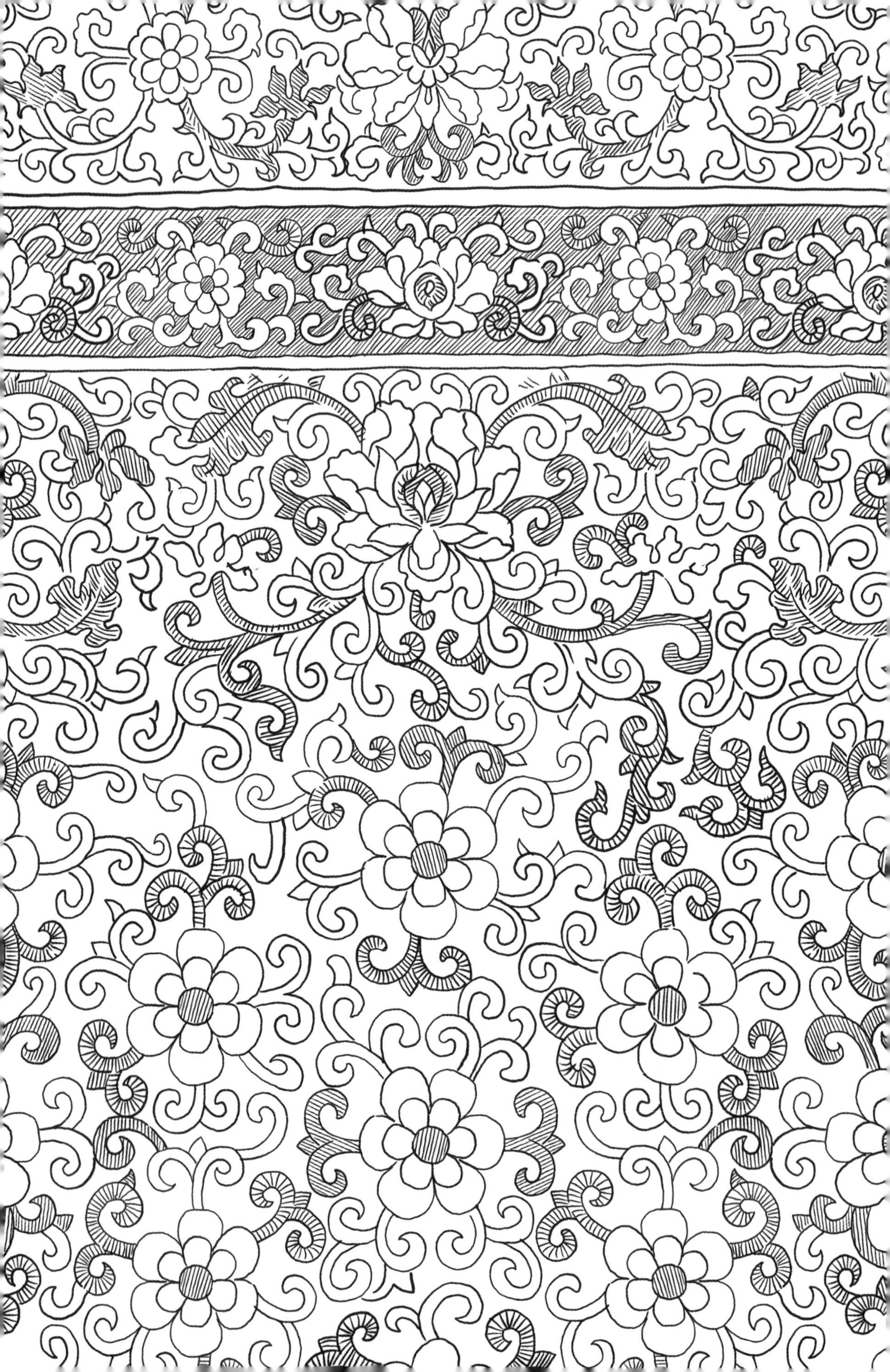

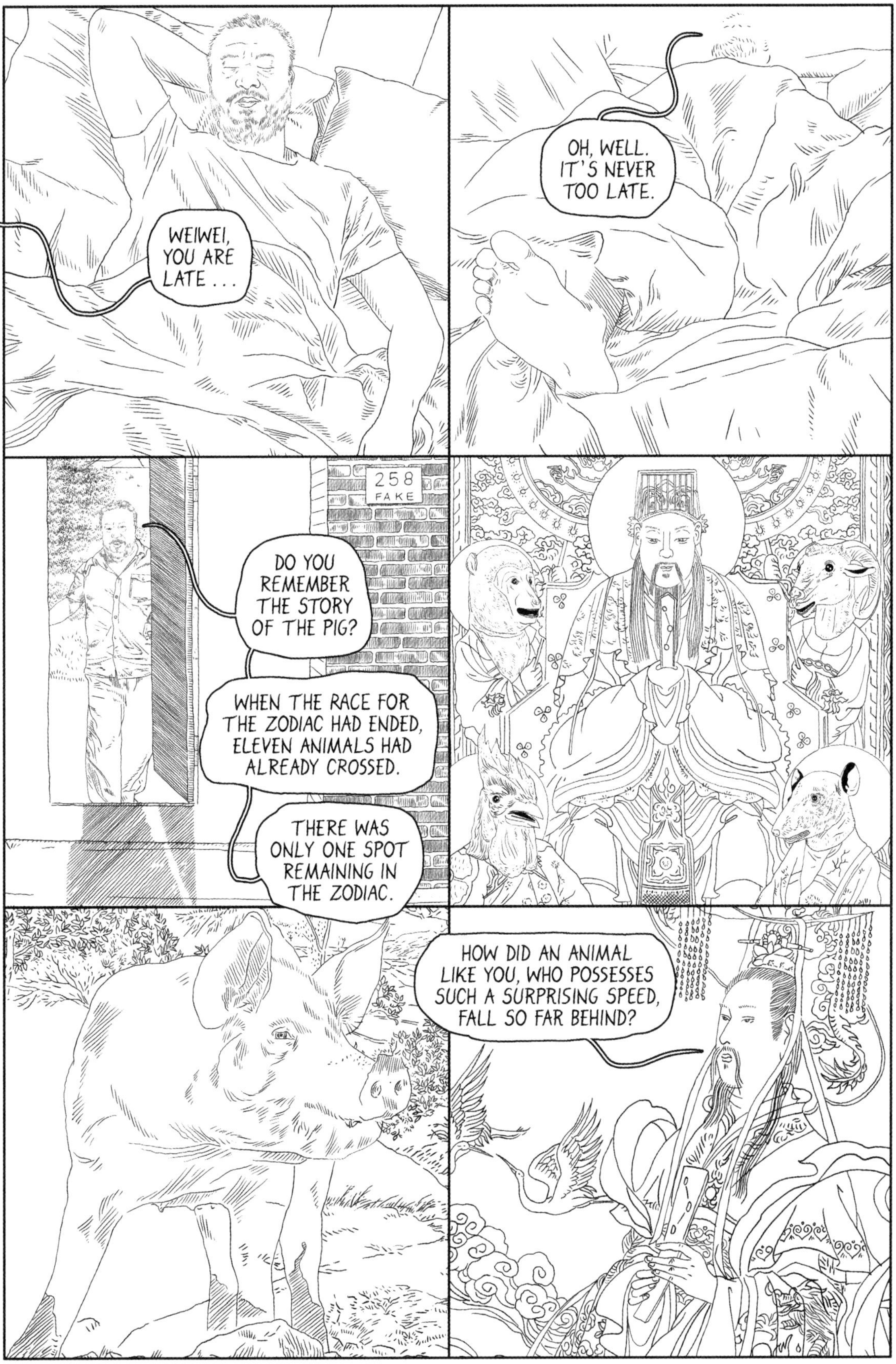
WEIWEI, YOU ARE LATE . . .
OH, WELL. IT'S NEVER TOO LATE.
258
FAKE
DO YOU REMEMBER THE STORY OF THE PIG?
WHEN THE RACE FOR THE ZODIAC HAD ENDED, ELEVEN ANIMALS HAD ALREADY CROSSED.
THERE WAS ONLY ONE SPOT REMAINING IN THE ZODIAC.
HOW DID AN ANIMAL LIKE YOU, WHO POSSESSES SUCH A SURPRISING SPEED, FALL SO FAR BEHIND?

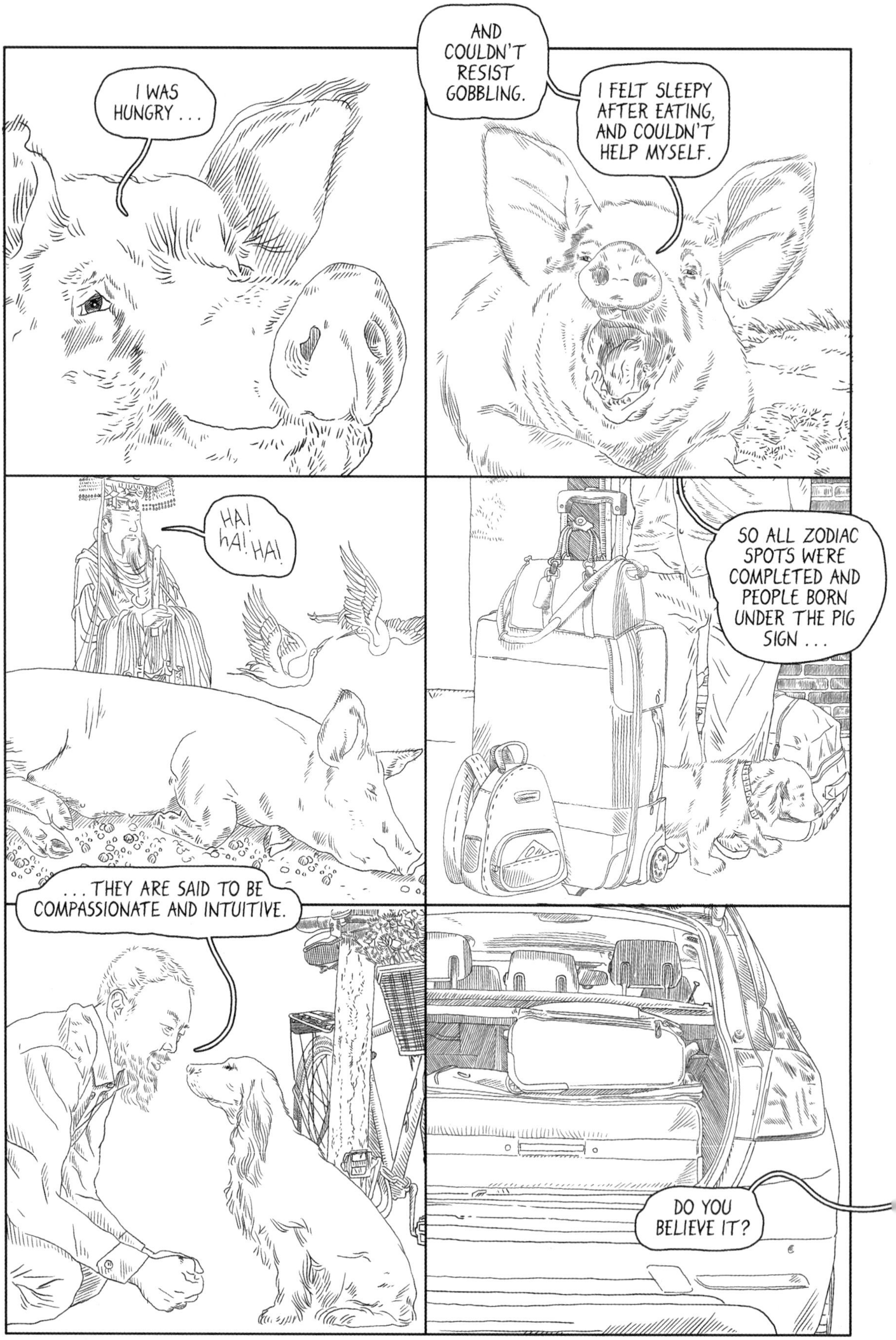
I WAS HUNGRY . . .
AND COULDN'T RESIST GOBBLING.
I FELT SLEEPY AFTER EATING, AND COULDN'T HELP MYSELF.
HA! hA! HA!
SO ALL ZODIAC SPOTS WERE COMPLETED AND PEOPLE BORN UNDER THE PIG SIGN . . .
. . . THEY ARE SAID TO BE COMPASSIONATE AND INTUITIVE.
DO YOU BELIEVE IT?

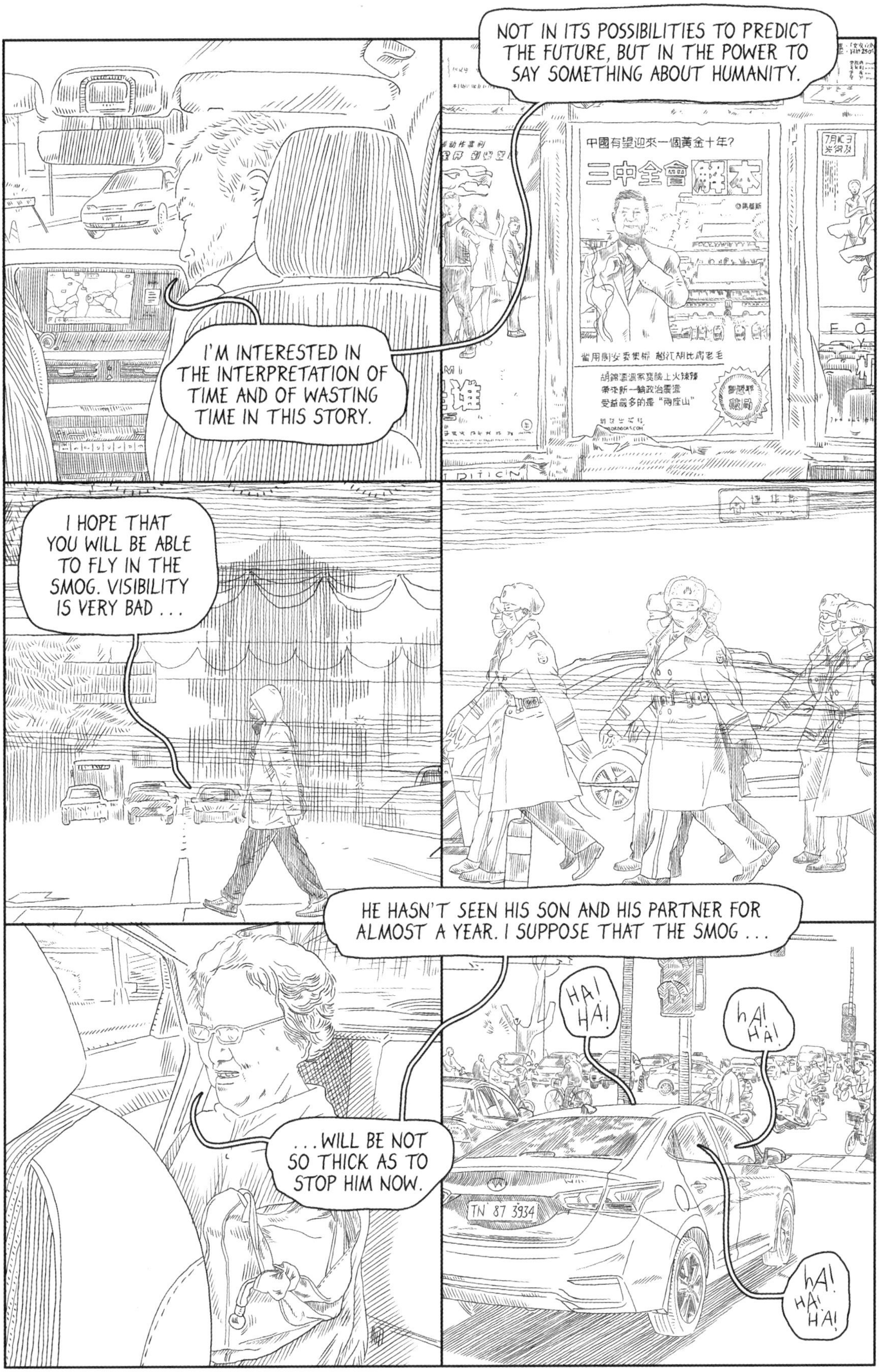
I'M INTERESTED IN THE INTERPRETATION OF TIME AND OF WASTING TIME IN THIS STORY.
NOT IN ITS POSSIBILITIES TO PREDICT THE FUTURE, BUT IN THE POWER TO SAY SOMETHING ABOUT HUMANITY.
中國有望迎來一個黃金十年?
三中全會解本
I HOPE THAT YOU WILL BE ABLE TO FLY IN THE SMOG. VISIBILITY IS VERY BAD . . .
HE HASN'T SEEN HIS SON AND HIS PARTNER FOR ALMOST A YEAR. I SUPPOSE THAT THE SMOG . . .
. . . WILL BE NOT SO THICK AS TO STOP HIM NOW.
HA! HA!
hA! HA!
TN 87 3934
hA! HA! HA!

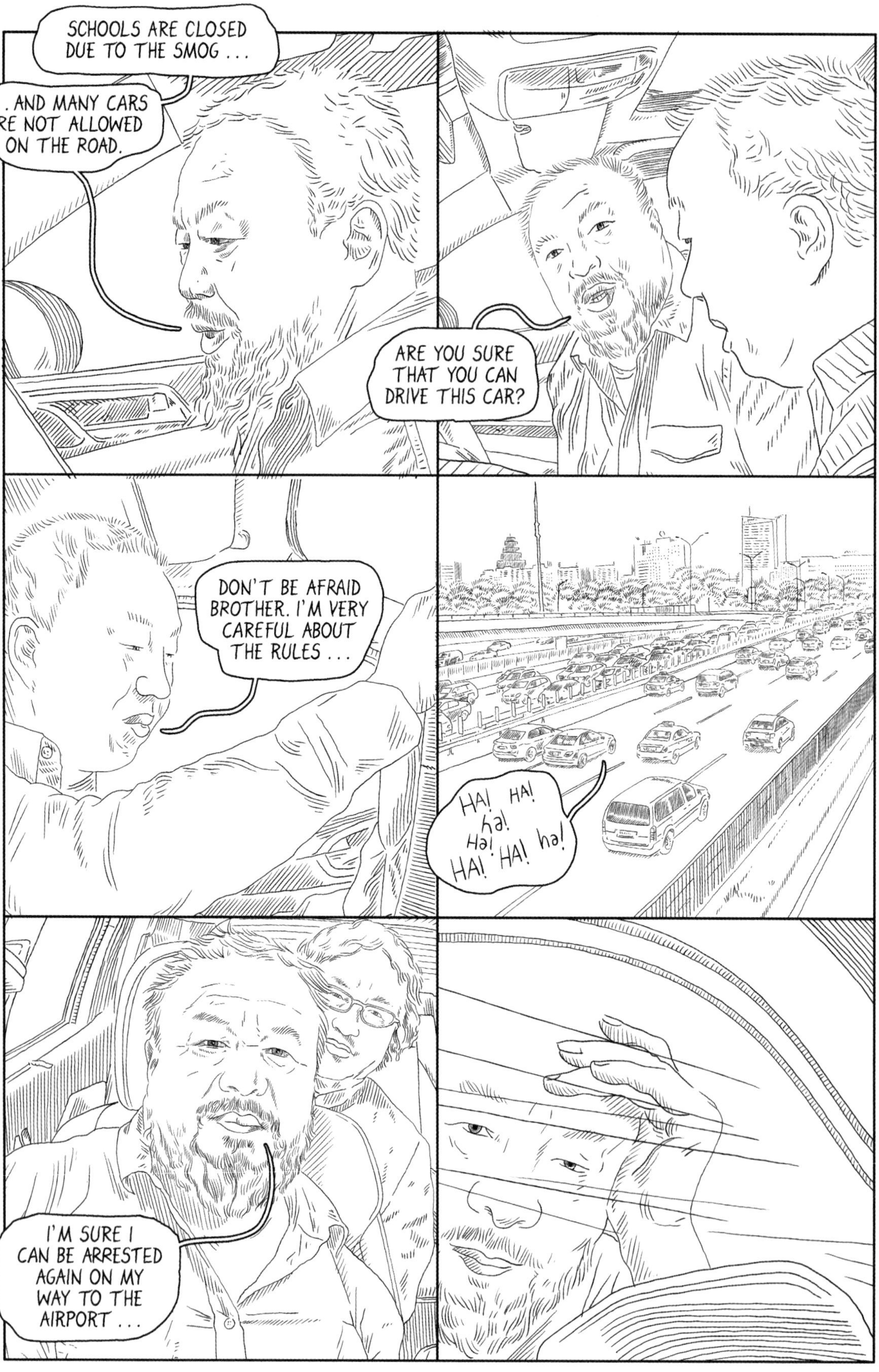
SCHOOLS ARE CLOSED DUE TO THE SMOG . . .
. . . AND MANY CARS ARE NOT ALLOWED ON THE ROAD.
ARE YOU SURE THAT YOU CAN DRIVE THIS CAR?
DON'T BE AFRAID BROTHER. I'M VERY CAREFUL ABOUT THE RULES . . .
HA! HA! ha! Ha! HA! HA! ha!
I'M SURE I CAN BE ARRESTED AGAIN ON MY WAY TO THE AIRPORT . . .

Chengdu, August 12, 2009

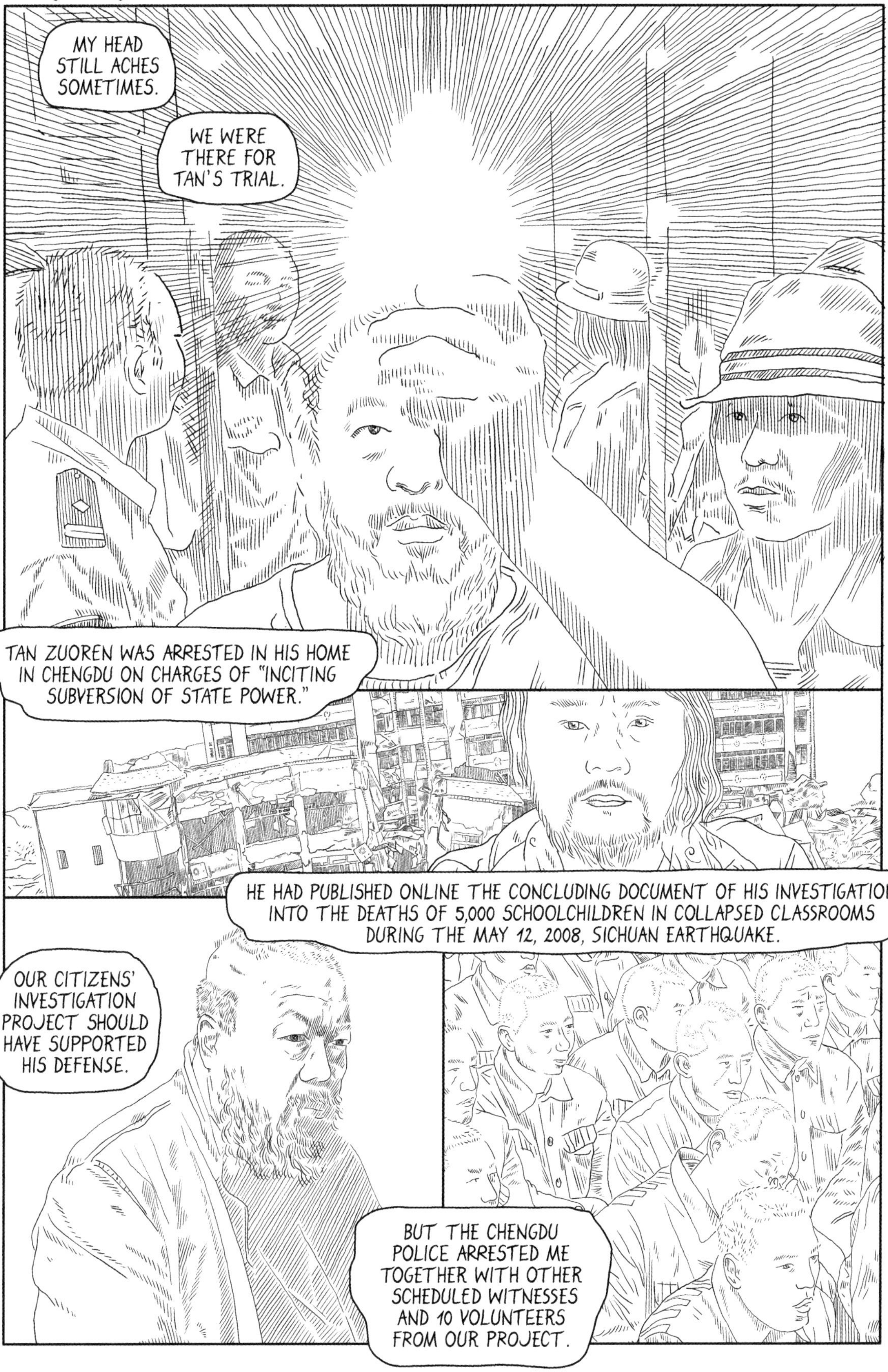
MY HEAD STILL ACHES SOMETIMES.
WE WERE THERE FOR TAN'S TRIAL.
TAN ZUOREN WAS ARRESTED IN HIS HOME IN CHENGDU ON CHARGES OF "INCITING SUBVERSION OF STATE POWER."
HE HAD PUBLISHED ONLINE THE CONCLUDING DOCUMENT OF HIS INVESTIGATION INTO THE DEATHS OF 5,000 SCHOOLCHILDREN IN COLLAPSED CLASSROOMS DURING THE MAY 12, 2008, SICHUAN EARTHQUAKE.
OUR CITIZENS' INVESTIGATION PROJECT SHOULD HAVE SUPPORTED HIS DEFENSE.
BUT THE CHENGDU POLICE ARRESTED ME TOGETHER WITH OTHER SCHEDULED WITNESSES AND 10 VOLUNTEERS FROM OUR PROJECT.

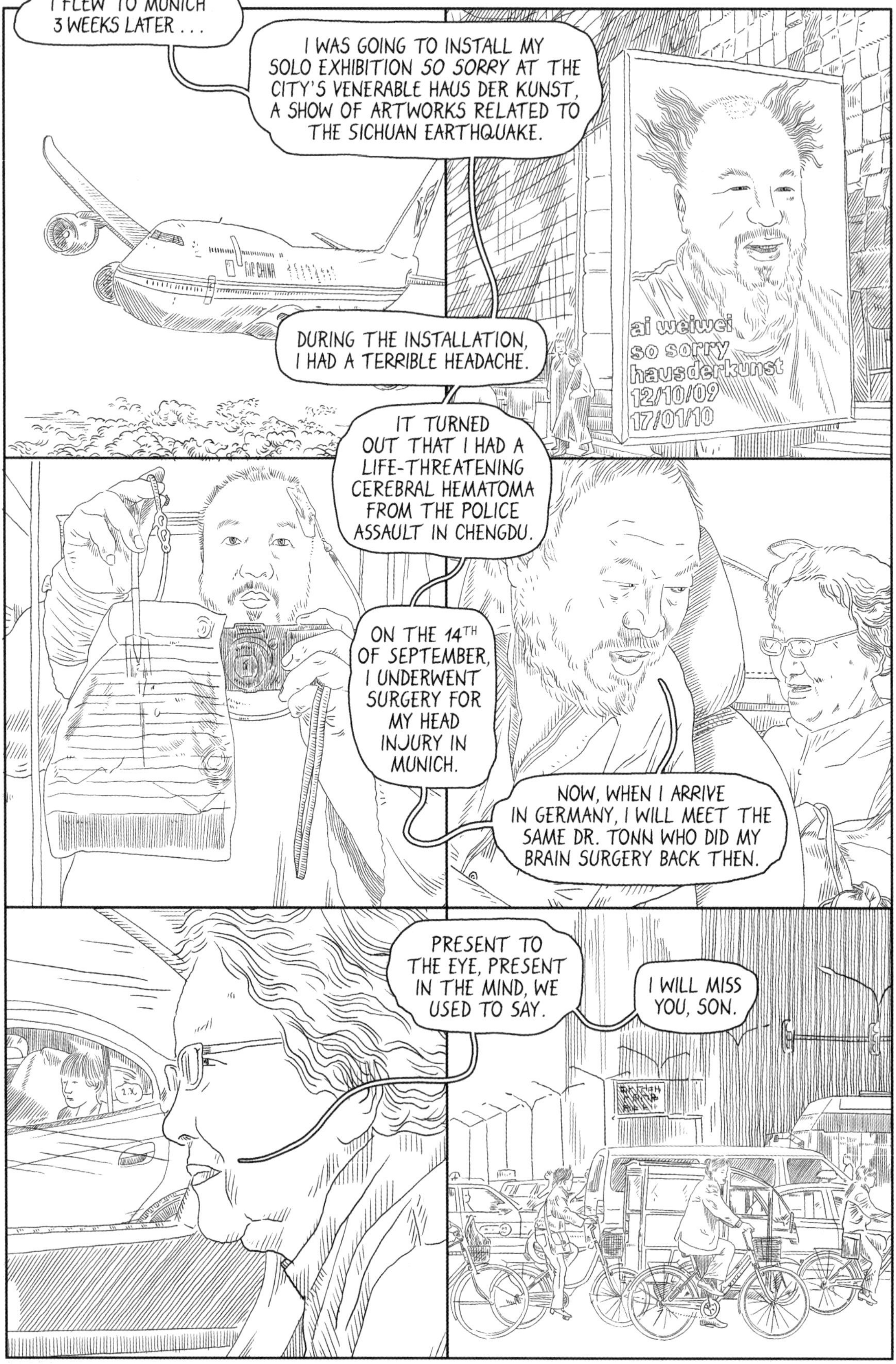
I FLEW TO MUNICH 3 WEEKS LATER . . .
I WAS GOING TO INSTALL MY SOLO EXHIBITION *SO SORRY* AT THE CITY'S VENERABLE HAUS DER KUNST, A SHOW OF ARTWORKS RELATED TO THE SICHUAN EARTHQUAKE.
ai weiwei
so sorry
hausderkunst
12/10/09
17/01/10
DURING THE INSTALLATION, I HAD A TERRIBLE HEADACHE.
IT TURNED OUT THAT I HAD A LIFE-THREATENING CEREBRAL HEMATOMA FROM THE POLICE ASSAULT IN CHENGDU.
ON THE 14TH OF SEPTEMBER, I UNDERWENT SURGERY FOR MY HEAD INJURY IN MUNICH.
NOW, WHEN I ARRIVE IN GERMANY, I WILL MEET THE SAME DR. TONN WHO DID MY BRAIN SURGERY BACK THEN.
PRESENT TO THE EYE, PRESENT IN THE MIND, WE USED TO SAY.
I WILL MISS YOU, SON.

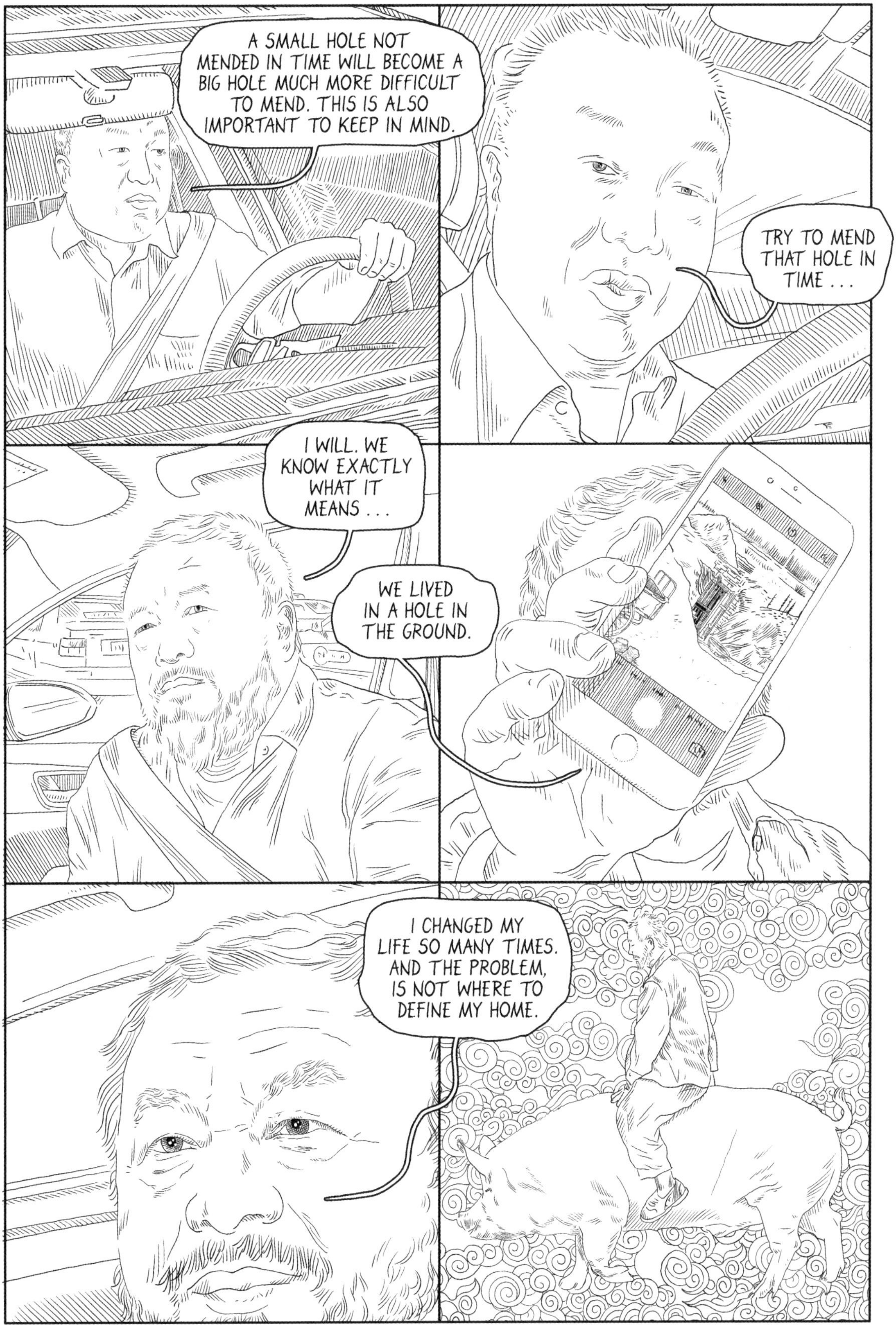
A SMALL HOLE NOT MENDED IN TIME WILL BECOME A BIG HOLE MUCH MORE DIFFICULT TO MEND. THIS IS ALSO IMPORTANT TO KEEP IN MIND.
TRY TO MEND THAT HOLE IN TIME . . .
I WILL. WE KNOW EXACTLY WHAT IT MEANS . . .
WE LIVED IN A HOLE IN THE GROUND.
I CHANGED MY LIFE SO MANY TIMES. AND THE PROBLEM, IS NOT WHERE TO DEFINE MY HOME.

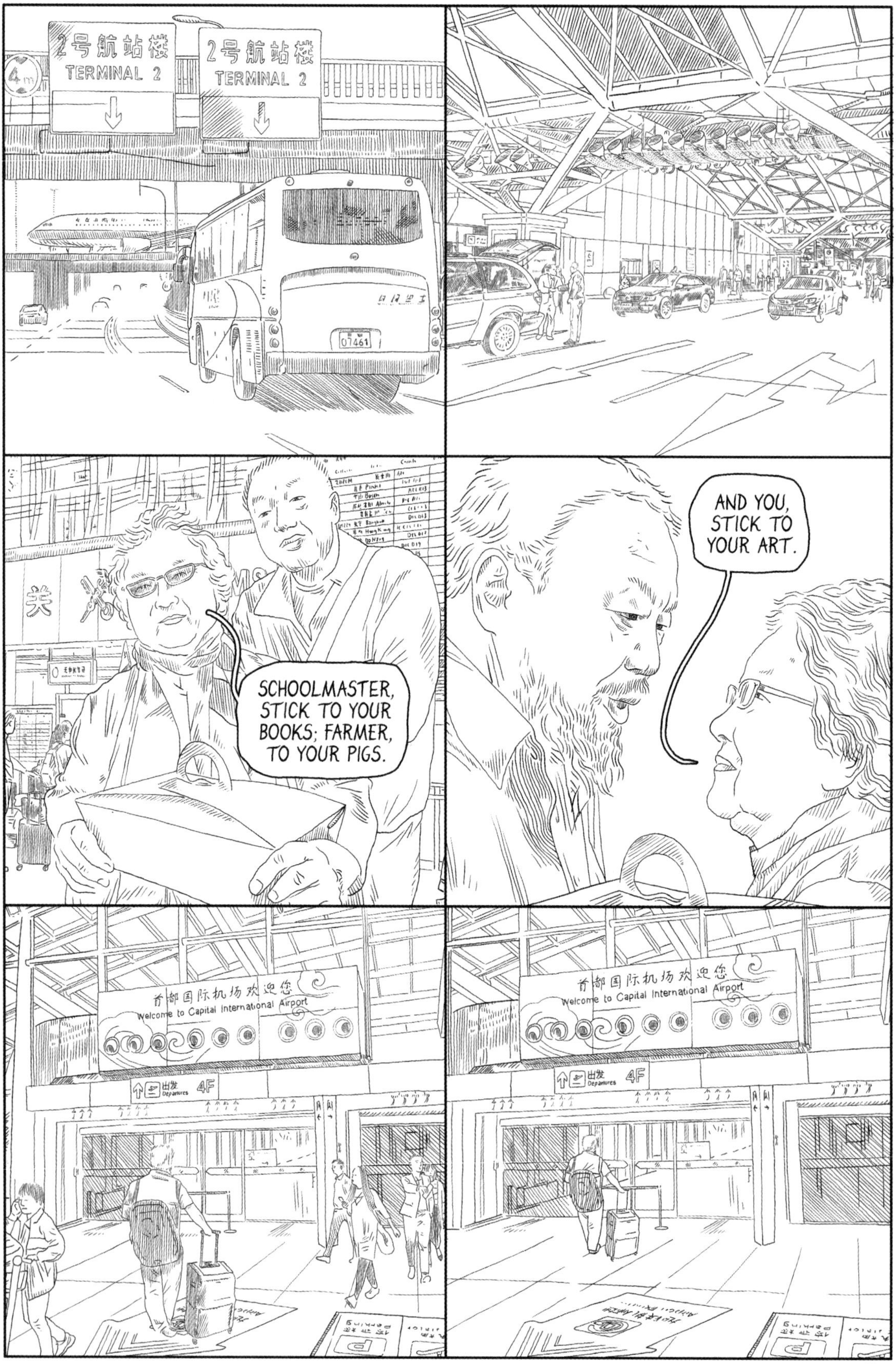

2号航站楼
TERMINAL 2
2号航站楼
TERMINAL 2
SCHOOLMASTER, STICK TO YOUR BOOKS; FARMER, TO YOUR PIGS.
AND YOU, STICK TO YOUR ART.
Welcome to Capital International Airport
出发 Departures 4F
Welcome to Capital International Airport
出发 Departures 4F

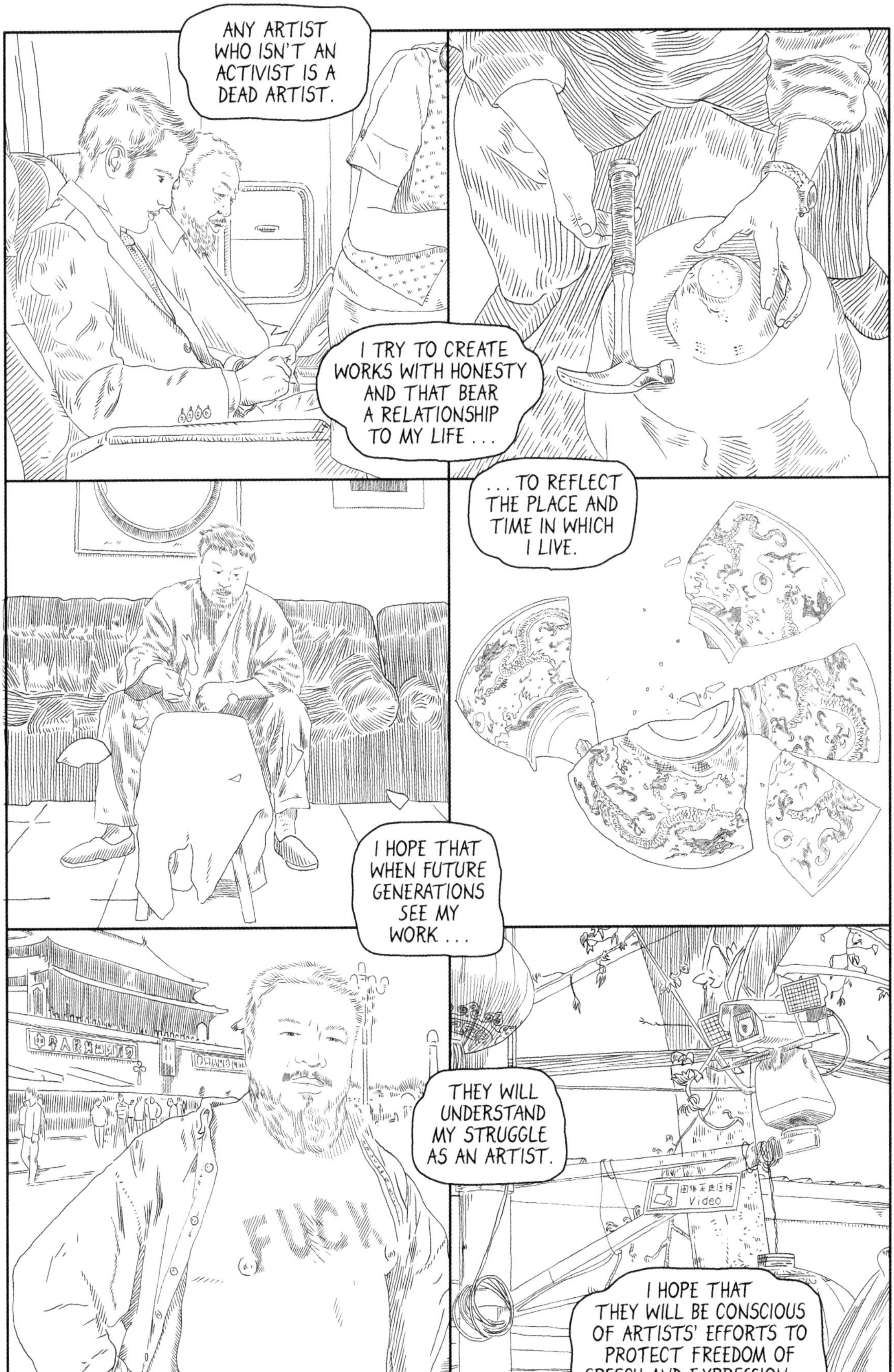
ANY ARTIST WHO ISN'T AN ACTIVIST IS A DEAD ARTIST.
I TRY TO CREATE WORKS WITH HONESTY AND THAT BEAR A RELATIONSHIP TO MY LIFE . . .
. . . TO REFLECT THE PLACE AND TIME IN WHICH I LIVE.
I HOPE THAT WHEN FUTURE GENERATIONS SEE MY WORK . . .
THEY WILL UNDERSTAND MY STRUGGLE AS AN ARTIST.
Video
I HOPE THAT THEY WILL BE CONSCIOUS OF ARTISTS' EFFORTS TO PROTECT FREEDOM OF SPEECH AND EXPRESSION . . .

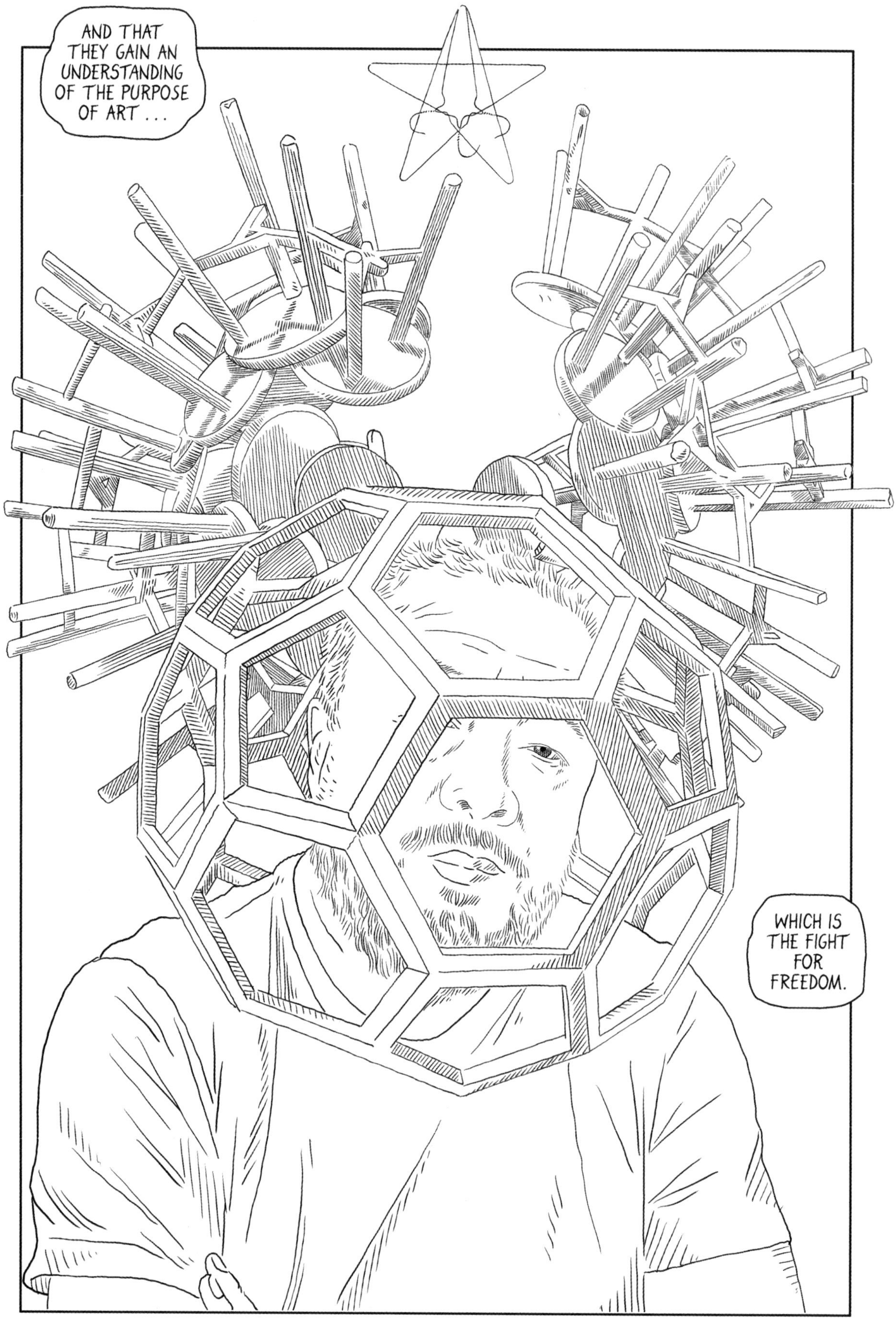
AND THAT THEY GAIN AN UNDERSTANDING OF THE PURPOSE OF ART . . .
WHICH IS THE FIGHT FOR FREEDOM.

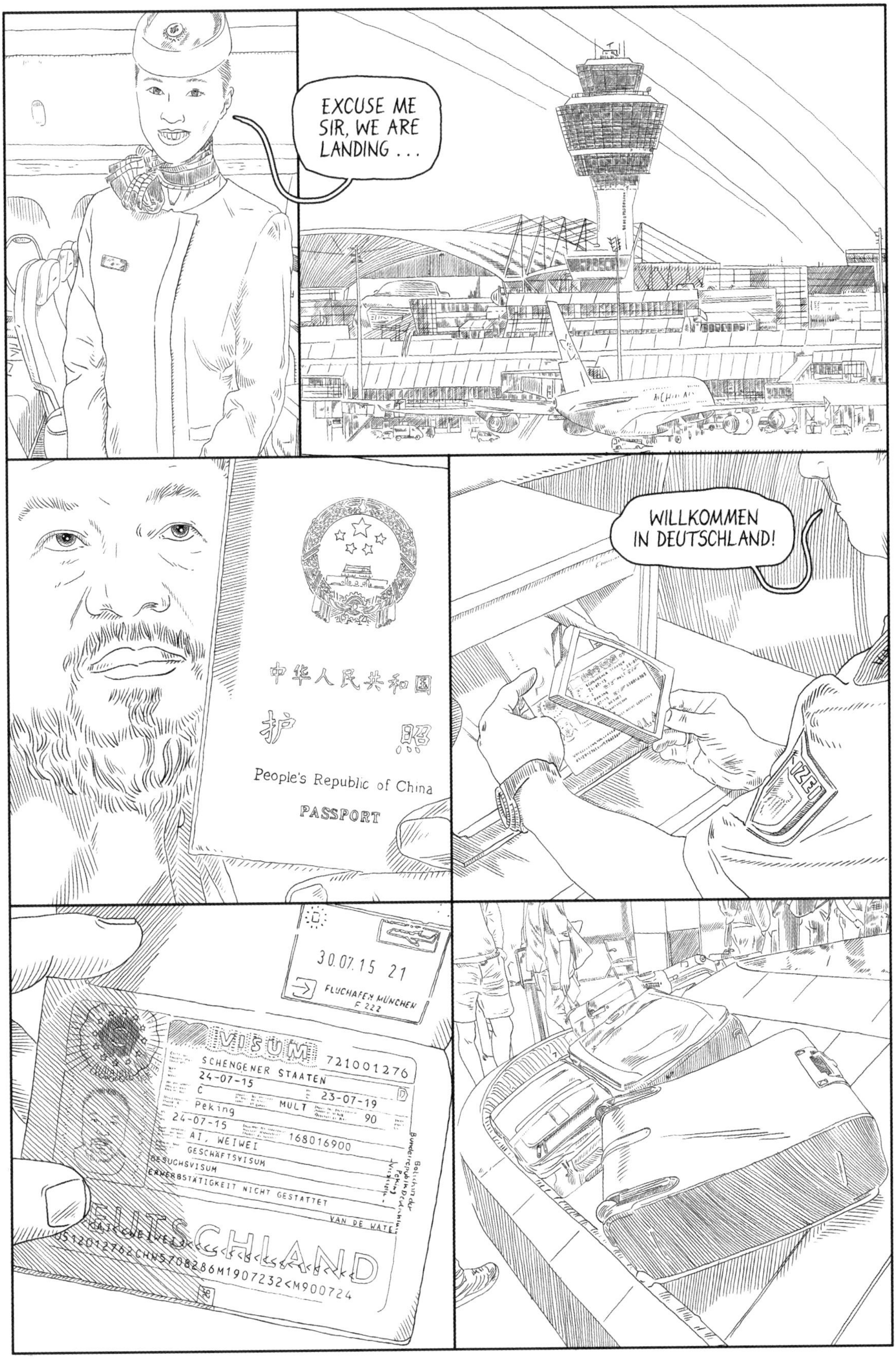
EXCUSE ME SIR, WE ARE LANDING . . .
中华人民共和国
护照
People's Republic of China
PASSPORT
WILLKOMMEN IN DEUTSCHLAND!
30.07.15 21
F 222
VISUM
721001276
SCHENGENER STAATEN
24-07-15
C
MULT
23-07-19
Peking
90
24-07-15
168016900
AI, WEIWEI
GESCHÄFTSVISUM
BESUCHSVISUM
ERWERBSTÄTIGKEIT NICHT GESTATTET
VAN DE WATE

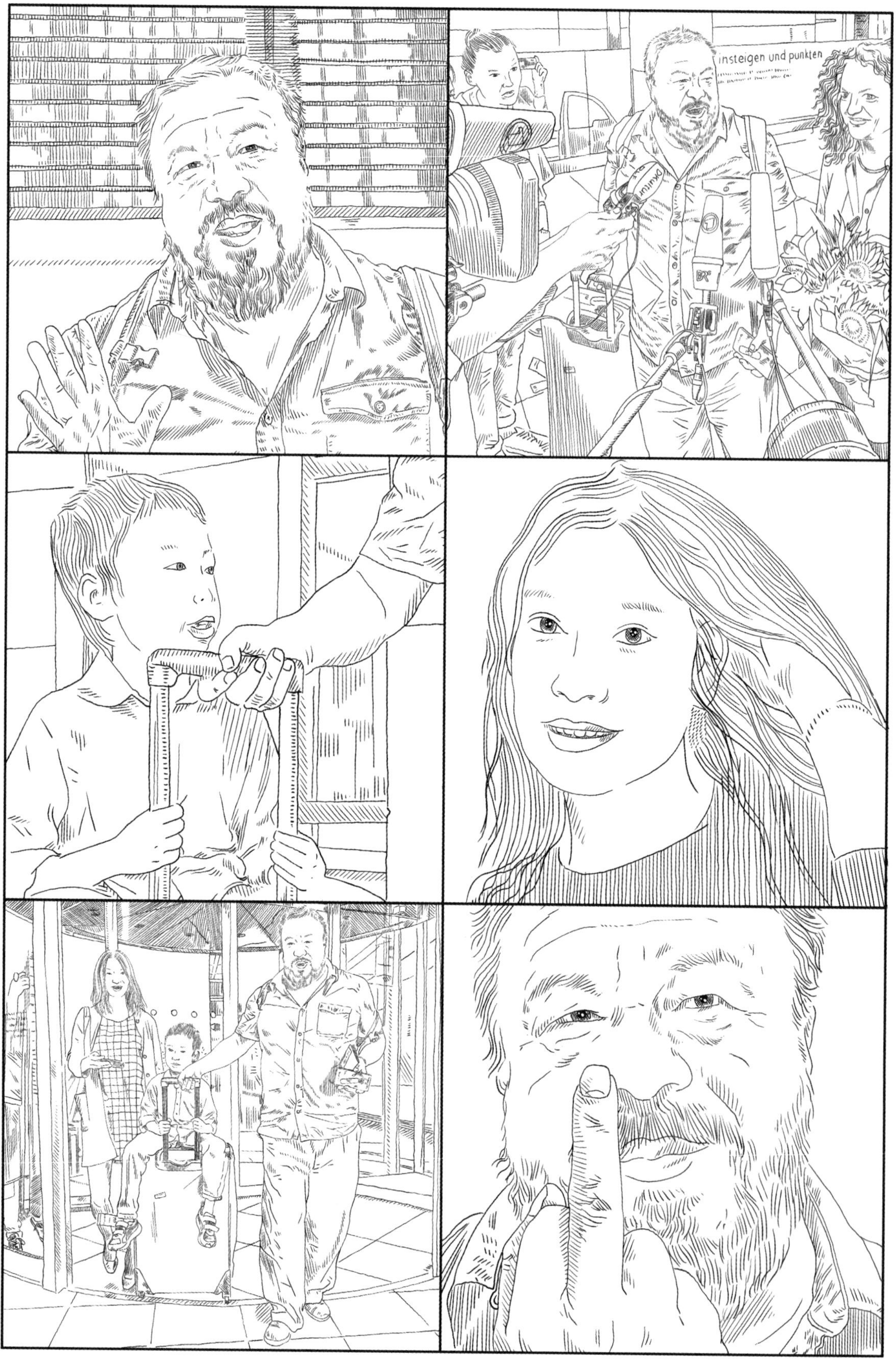
insteigen und punkten

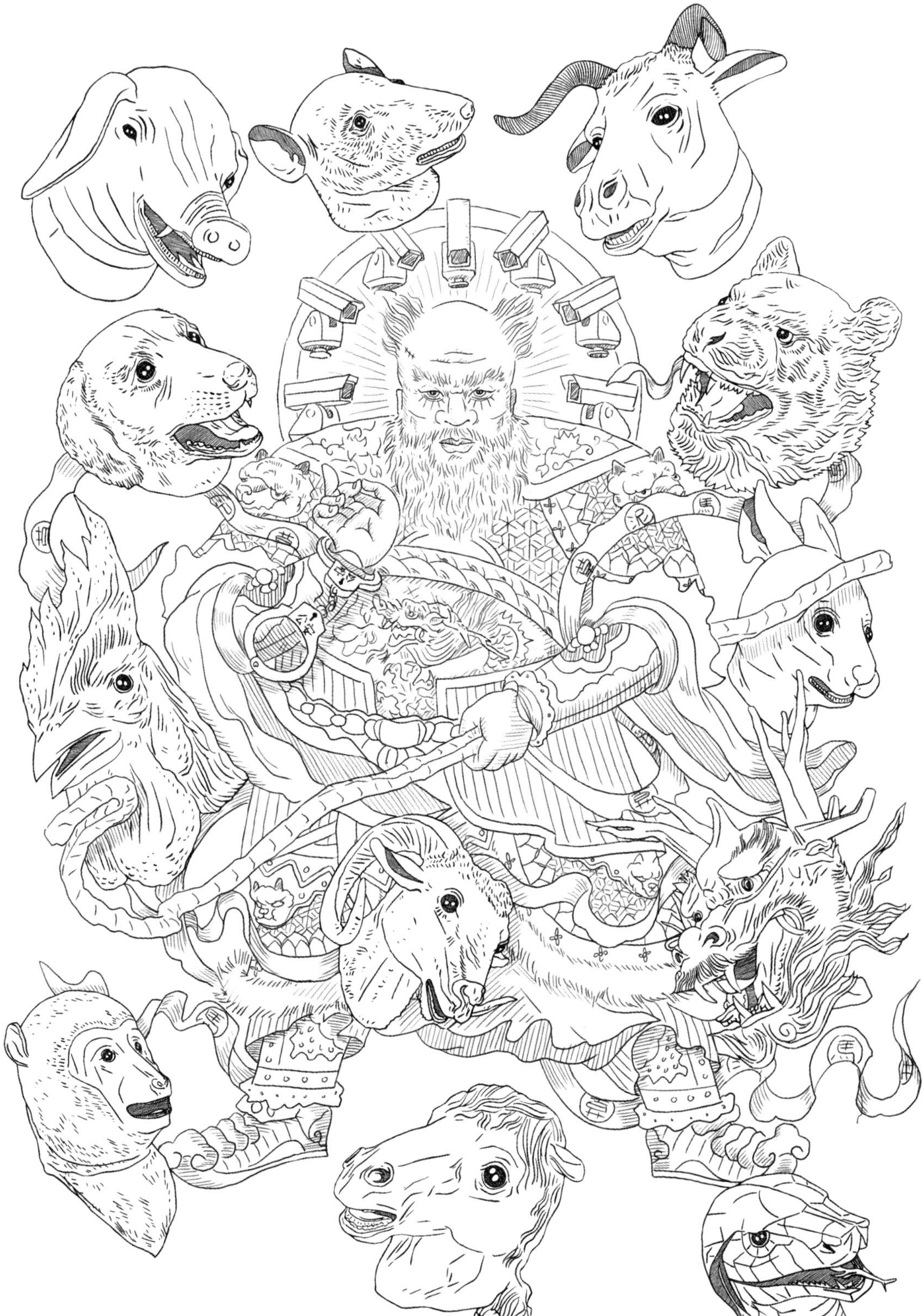

ABOUT THE AUTHOR

AI WEIWEI leads a diverse and prolific practice that encompasses sculptural installation, filmmaking, photography, ceramics, painting, writing, and social media. Born in 1957 in Beijing, China, he is a conceptual artist who fuses traditional craftsmanship and his Chinese heritage and moves freely between a variety of formal languages to reflect on contemporary geopolitical and sociopolitical conditions. Ai Weiwei's work and life regularly interact and inform one another, often extending to his activism and advocacy for international human rights.

Over the past two decades, Ai Weiwei has exhibited extensively at institutions and biennials worldwide, including the Design Museum, London; Albertina Modern, Vienna; Museu de Arte Contemporânea de Serralves, Porto; Kunstsammlung Nordrhein-Westfalen, Düsseldorf; Oca do Ibirapuera, São Paulo; Public Art Fund, New York; Israel Museum, Jerusalem; Fondazione Palazzo Strozzi, Florence; Andy Warhol Museum, Pittsburgh; National Gallery of Victoria, Melbourne; Royal Academy of Arts, London; Martin-Gropius-Bau, Berlin; Brooklyn Museum, New York; German Pavilion, 55th Venice Biennale, Venice; Hirshhorn Museum and Sculpture Garden, Washington, DC; Taipei Fine Arts Museum, Taipei; Turbine Hall, Tate Modern, London; Haus der Kunst, Munich; Mori Art Museum, Tokyo; documenta 12, Kassel; and Kunsthalle Bern, Bern. The artist's memoir *1000 Years of Joys and Sorrows* was published in 2021. Ai Weiwei lives and works in Beijing, China; Berlin, Germany; Cambridge, United Kingdom; and Lisbon, Portugal.

ABOUT THE CONTRIBUTORS

ELETTRA STAMBOULIS is a Greek Italian writer and art curator. She has written numerous graphic novels and comics articles that have been published in many languages around the world. She specializes in reality-based comics and has curated European exhibitions of the work of Joe Sacco and Marjane Satrapi. As a curator, her work is dedicated to the promotion of artists at risk, and she recently has curated exhibitions of work by Zehra Doğan, Badiucao, and Victoria Lomasko.

GIANLUCA COSTANTINI is an Italian cartoonist, journalist, and activist. He has contributed to numerous publications and is the author of several graphic novels. He is well known for his drawings related to human rights campaigns all over the world. He collaborates with organizations such as the Committee to Protect Journalists, ActionAid, and SOS Méditerranée. In 2019, he received the Art and Human Rights Award from Amnesty International.

Published in the United States by Ten Speed Graphic, an imprint of the Crown Publishing Group, a division of Penguin Random House LLC, New York.
TenSpeed.com

Ten Speed Graphic and colophon are trademarks of Penguin Random House LLC.

Grateful acknowledgment is made to the following for permission to reprint previously published material:

Graywolf Press and Jonathan Cape, a member of The Random House Group Ltd: Excerpts from *June Fourth Elegies* by Liu Xiaobo, translated by Jeffrey Yang, copyright © 2012 by Liu Xiaobo, translation copyright © 2012 by Jeffrey Yang. Reprinted with the permission of The Permissions Company, LLC, on behalf of Graywolf Press, Minneapolis, Minnesota, graywolfpress.org, and Jonathan Cape, a member of The Random House Group Ltd.

Host Publications: "Ode to the Dog" by Pablo Neruda, translated by George Schade from *Fifty Odes*, copyright © 1996 by Pablo Neruda. Reprinted by permission of Host Publications.

Paul Merchant: Poem 106 of the one-line poems from *Monochords* [Gk: Monochorda] by Yannis Ritsos, translated by Paul Merchant (Portland: Trask House Books, 2007). Original Greek version published in 1980 by Kedros Editions, Athens. Translation reprinted by permission of Paul Merchant.

Typeface: Costantini by Gianluca Costantini

Library of Congress Control Number: 2023941102

Hardcover ISBN: 978-1-9848-6299-0
Trade Paperback ISBN: 978-1-9848-6300-3
eBook ISBN: 978-1-9848-6301-0

Printed in Malaysia

Editor: Kaitlin Ketchum
Editorial assistant: Kausaur Fahimuddin
Designer: Chloe Rawlins | Co-designer: Meggie Ramm
Cover artist: Ai Weiwei | Interior artist: Gianluca Costantini
Letterer: Gianluca Costantini
Production manager: Dan Myers
Proofreader: Kate Bolen

Ai Weiwei Studio: Yun-hua Chen, Cui Xing, Jennifer Ng, Nadine Stenke, Kimberly Sung, Chin-chin Yap, Fart Foundation

10 9 8 7 6 5 4 3 2 1

First Edition